Miguel A. Aijón Oliva

Constructing Us

Beihefte zur Zeitschrift für romanische Philologie

Herausgegeben von
Claudia Polzin-Haumann und Wolfgang Schweickard

Band 435

Miguel A. Aijón Oliva

Constructing Us

The First and Second Persons in Spanish Media Discourse

DE GRUYTER

ISBN: 978-3-11-076602-8
e-ISBN (PDF): 978-3-11-064344-2
e-ISBN (EPUB): 978-3-11-064077-9

Library of Congress Control Number: 2019935309

Bibliographic information published by the Deutsche Nationalbibliothek
The Deutsche Nationalbibliothek lists this publication in the Deutsche Nationalbibliografie; detailed bibliographic data are available on the Internet at http://dnb.dnb.de.

This volume is text- and page-identical with the hardback published in 2019.
Typesetting: Integra Software Services Pvt. Ltd.
Printing and binding: CPI books GmbH, Leck

www.degruyter.com

Acknowledgments

Research for this book was aided by a grant from the Spanish Ministerio de Economía y Competitividad (reference number FFI2016-74825-P). It also received funding from the Cabildo Insular de Tenerife (Programa *María Rosa Alonso* de Ayudas a la Investigación en Humanidades y Ciencias Sociales).

I am especially indebted to Prof. Dr. María José Serrano (Universidad de La Laguna), without whose expertise and unfailing support the book would not have come into being. I am also grateful to the rest of the research team *Comunicación, Sociedad y Lenguajes* (CoSoLen) as well as to all other fellow researchers, at the Universidad de Salamanca and elsewhere, who have kindly offered advice and help at some point along the way, and who are too numerous to mention.

The editors of the BZrP series, Prof. Dr. Claudia Polzin-Haumann and Prof. Dr. Wolfgang Schweickard, together with Ms. Gabrielle Cornefert and Ms. Christina Lembrecht, provided invaluable guidance during the process of revision and publication.

Finally, very special thanks go to Encarna, Pepe, Pope and the rest of my family and friends, who make it all worthwhile.

https://doi.org/10.1515/9783110643442-201

Contents

Acknowledgments — V

Outline of this book — 1

1 Linguistic choice and the construction of meaning — 5
1.1 Meaning, choice and isomorphism — **5**
1.2 From linguistic variation to communicative choice — **9**
1.3 The cognitive construction of entities through formal choice — **17**
1.3.1 Salience — **18**
1.3.2 Informativeness — **31**
1.3.3 Salience and informativeness at play in the construction of referents across discourse — **35**
1.4 Summary — **39**

2 Variable grammar: the continuum of syntactic functions — 41
2.1 Functions as prototypes — **41**
2.1.1 Central vs. peripheral functions; the role of agreement — **43**
2.2 Subject agreement — **45**
2.3 Object agreement — **50**
2.3.1 The intermediate functional nature of clitics — **50**
2.3.2 Object and clitic co-occurrence — **55**
2.3.3 Salience and informativeness in object agreement — **61**
2.4 Variation and choice between the subject and object prototypes — **64**
2.5 Variation and choice between the object prototypes — **69**
2.6 Summary — **76**

3 The first and second persons: discourse in grammar — 79
3.1 The discursive-cognitive value of grammatical persons: From anaphora and deixis to reference — **79**
3.1.1 First- and second-person forms in Spanish — **82**
3.2 Salience and informativeness in the first and second persons — **85**
3.3 The non-prototypical features of first- and second-person objects — **90**
3.3.1 General distribution across object contexts — **95**

3.3.2 Distribution of the different grammatical persons across object contexts — **97**
3.3.3 Distribution according to the perceptibility of the clause subject — **100**
3.3.4 Variable formulation and placement of object pronouns — **104**
3.4 Discursive datives: The indexation of "unexpected" participants — **110**
3.5 Summary — **117**

4 The singular first person: *the speaker* — 119
4.1 The subparadigm and its meaning — **119**
4.2 The construction of reference — **121**
4.3 Variable expression and placement of pronouns — **126**
4.4 Functional encoding — **137**
4.5 Summary — **144**

5 The plural first person: *more than the speaker* — 147
5.1 The subparadigm and its meaning — **147**
5.2 The construction of reference — **151**
5.2.1 Speaker-blurring — **153**
5.2.2 Audience-exclusive — **155**
5.2.3 Audience-inclusive — **159**
5.2.4 Pragmaticalized — **164**
5.3 Variable expression and placement of pronouns — **168**
5.4 Functional encoding — **176**
5.5 Summary — **181**

6 The singular second person: *the addressee* — 183
6.1 The subparadigm and its meaning — **183**
6.2 The construction of reference — **187**
6.2.1 Specific — **187**
6.2.2 Nonspecific — **189**
6.2.3 Speaker-inclusive/objectivizing — **192**
6.2.4 Pragmaticalized — **197**
6.3 Variable expression and placement of pronouns — **202**
6.4 Functional encoding — **212**
6.5 Summary — **217**

7 **The plural second person: *the audience* — 221**
7.1 The subparadigm and its meaning — **221**
7.2 The construction of reference — **225**
7.2.1 Specific — **225**
7.2.2 Semispecific — **227**
7.2.3 Nonspecific — **231**
7.3 Variable expression and placement of pronouns — **233**
7.4 Functional encoding — **237**
7.5 Summary — **240**

8 **The displaced second persons: *addressees and audiences far away* — 243**
8.1 The subparadigms and their meaning — **243**
8.2 The construction of reference — **248**
8.2.1 *Usted* — **248**
8.2.2 *Ustedes* — **253**
8.3 Variable expression and placement of pronouns — **256**
8.4 Functional encoding — **267**
8.5 Summary — **272**

9 **The construction of style across textual genres — 275**
9.1 Linguistic choice and sociocommunicative style — **275**
9.1.1 Subjectivity, intersubjectivity and objectivity — **278**
9.1.2 Stylistic features considered — **280**
9.2 The study of variation and choice across textual genres — **282**
9.3 Participant indexation — **287**
9.4 Person choice — **294**
9.5 Variable expression and placement of pronouns — **302**
9.6 Functional encoding — **311**
9.7 Summary — **320**

10 **The construction of style across participant identities — 323**
10.1 Style and identity — **323**
10.2 Socioprofessional identities in media communication — **326**
10.3 Participant indexation — **329**
10.4 Person choice — **334**
10.5 Variable expression and placement of pronouns — **345**
10.6 Functional encoding — **350**
10.7 Summary — **356**

11 Conclusions — 359

12 References — 363

Appendices

Appendix I: Codes used for the identification of examples — **381**

Appendix II: Conventions used in the transcription of radio texts — **382**

Outline of this book

The purpose of the present study is to investigate what linguistic description has traditionally referred to as the first and second persons, which constitute a complex array of functional strategies for the development of cognitive representations of the speaker and other people and entities. The choice of some grammatical person entails a particular viewpoint of the participants involved in communication and of the events they take part in. For the same reason, it can also strongly condition the interpretations made by others.

In a language like Spanish, grammatical person is the most basic and pervasive linguistic resource for the configuration of reference and viewpoint. Speakers can explicitly associate the content of discourse with their own selves by way of singular first-person choices. They can just as well displace the viewpoint towards a broader human group where they are still included – through the plural first person – or else towards their interlocutor or audience – through the singular and plural second persons, which, as will be seen, are further divided into two different grammatical subparadigms in Spanish. Of course, one can also opt to avoid first- and second-person elements altogether and contemplate discourse as apparently unrelated to the participants. If language is the most important semiotic code by which social life is developed, the scientific interest of the ways people construct – or avoid to construct – themselves as well as others through linguistic choices becomes evident.

The basic starting point for this approach to the first and second persons is that they do not exist outside the forms chosen to make them present in discourse, that is, they are meanings constructed through linguistic choices. Certainly, such forms are most often used to index entities from the extralinguistic world. But the construction of certain communicative roles, such as *speaker, addressee* and so on, together with the sets of rights and duties they respectively involve, is only possible by way of linguistic choices. When people formulate first-person-marked elements – which in Spanish include deictic pronouns, verbal endings and clitics, and possessives, among others – what they do is turn themselves into *the speaker*, with all the consequences this may have on how they are perceived by others within the communicative context, as well as on their actual chances to achieve their goals. Even if the social value of language has (most) often been approached from the perspective of the evaluations attached to particular linguistic forms – with no clear explanation of how such attachment came into being in the first place – it will be hypothesized that, at least at levels beyond phonology and prosody, the social values of linguistic elements are not independent of their intrinsic meanings themselves. In other words, if

https://doi.org/10.1515/9783110643442-001

formal choices become associated with particular social values in the communities where they are used, this must have some connection with what they communicate at the semantic, discursive and cognitive levels.

In fact, this is particularly obvious with the sets of grammatical forms used to index the direct participants. The often-noted egocentric (but also listener-centered) nature of human language is manifested in a wide variety of traits that point to the special nature of the first and second persons as against third ones, and further justify the interest of studies of the sort proposed here. These participants tend to be highly individuated and contextually recognizable entities, most clearly when communication consists of just two people interacting with each other. In terms of the discursive-cognitive approach to be developed, they possess a high degree of *salience*. This interactional prototype can be extrapolated to a much wider variety of situations where the first and second persons can also be used. In turn, the third person is a rather heterogeneous category whose reference can in principle be any sort of reality, from human beings that are present in the context but are not encoded as direct participants, to any other animate or inanimate beings, as well as entire propositions, which in principle represent the lowest possible degree of salience and individuation. Third persons are most often scarcely salient; however, their association with the transmission of new information endows them with a different kind of discursive and cognitive relevance that will be termed *informativeness*. In spite of the apparent opposition, throughout this study it will be contended that all discursive referents are subject to the same underlying dimensions of salience and informativeness, which condition their ways of formal encoding and their functional possibilities.

The empirical analysis will first address each of the Spanish first and second persons separately, then combine them all in an investigation of grammatical choice as the construction of sociocommunicative styles. The study will be restricted to contexts where some participant is accorded a central clause function, i.e. those of subject and accusative/dative object, and to the specific syntactic features related to the configuration of such functions. Centrality is a syntactic dimension understood as the capacity – or necessity – of clause constituents to establish agreement with the verbal nucleus. This means that not only stressed subject and object pronouns will need to be considered, but also the deictic-anaphoric morphemes indexing their referents within the verb: verbal endings marked for person and number, in the case of subjects, and verbal clitics marked for person, number, and sometimes also case and gender, in that of objects. Agreement has been viewed as a grammatical reflection of the discursive and cognitive salience of referents; consequently, whenever speakers make the verb agree with some referent, they are enhancing the salience of the latter to some extent. This is evident in the case of the direct participants, which in fact establish verbal agreement in most if not all contexts where they are encoded as subjects or objects. In turn, their overt formulation as pronouns and their placement within the clause are rather variable.

Moreover, the allocation of a given syntactic function to a certain referent is itself a matter of variation and choice that should not be overlooked. Speakers, when according themselves a subject vs. object role, will be further constructing their particular status in the communicative context, just as they can do with their addressees and any other referents. Until quite recently, most studies of functional variation in Spanish have been exclusively devoted to subjects, usually dealing with their variable formulation and placement within the clause. Even if syntactic objects have not raised the same interest – with the exception of quite specific features such as the choice between accusative and dative clitics – it is possible and desirable to apply analogous theoretical and analytical models to their study. The discursive and cognitive repercussions of the functional encoding of the participants will thus be investigated, starting from the discussion of what syntactic functions themselves are. As will be exposed, the choice between functions is also parallel to variations in the salience and informativeness of referents.

The study will be based on contemporary Peninsular Spanish as reflected in a corpus of written and oral media discourse from Salamanca, a medium-sized town in the central-western region of Castile and León. Media communication is a multidimensional domain of human activity where a wide array of textual genres and speaker identities come together, making it possible to observe how linguistic choices are used for the construction of meanings at multiple levels. The *Corpus de Lenguaje de los Medios de Comunicación de Salamanca* (MEDIASA) contains slightly more than 300,000 words equally distributed between a written-press subcorpus and a radio one, both of which are further subdivided into several textual genres.[1] It will be subjected to quantitative and qualitative analysis in order to obtain an exhaustive picture of first- and second-person usage and its meaningful repercussions in media interactions. All examples from the corpus will be identified by means of specific codes (see Appendix I). We will also draw on made-up examples across the theoretical discussions and the formal descriptions of the grammatical subparadigms under study, as well as on occasional excerpts from sources

1 The text of the corpus was published as an apprendix to Aijón Oliva (2006a) and is available at: gredos.usal.es/jspui/handle/10366/138326.

external to the corpus – mainly nationwide mass-media and websites, always duly identified – in order to further illustrate potentially interesting points.

The book is organized as follows. Chapters 1 to 3 develop the theoretical and analytical frame to be adopted in this study. First, the basic concepts substantiating an approach to linguistic choice as the construction of meaning are introduced and discussed. These concepts are subsequently integrated into a model of grammatical functions as prototypes characterized by the co-occurrence of formal and semantic features, which is then applied to the first and second grammatical persons in Spanish. Chapters 4 to 8 are respectively devoted to the analysis of each of the first and second persons under analysis. The structure followed is always the same – formal description of the subparadigm and interpretation of its inherent meaning; description of the kinds of contextual references it can construct; analysis of the variable formulation and placement of personal pronouns; analysis of subject vs. object encoding. Starting from the findings made, Chapters 9 and 10 jointly investigate the distribution of all first and second persons and their discursive-cognitive meanings across the textual genres and participant groups featured in the corpus. This makes it possible to infer and explain several dimensions of sociocommunicative style in media discourse. Finally, the main conclusions of the study and some directions for further research are detailed.

1 Linguistic choice and the construction of meaning

1.1 Meaning, choice and isomorphism

Human language is at once the most important system structuring thought and the most versatile resource for the accomplishment of goals in social contexts. Due to this dual nature, it seems of little use to view any linguistic element as anything other than the conjunction of a form and a meaning. Language is quite accurately designed to organize the human experience of the world, and most often it is also quite accurately employed by people to satisfy their needs. According to Gee (2014), the three major functionalities of verbal languages are those of conveying information (*saying*), carrying out activities (*doing*) and taking up socially significant identities (*being*). Many other scholars, even if through different labels and classifications, have similarly contemplated the existence of what may be termed the *informational, transactional* and *insertional* functions of language (cf. also Rickford 2001, 224).[1] It is especially interesting to note that such functions are rarely difficult to detach from one another in actual instances of language use. In order to understand what people say in some situation, it is usually necessary to also understand what they mean to achieve by saying it, as well as the kind of identity they assume in doing so. The conjunction of these informations – respectively encoded and deciphered through the grammatical, pragmatic and sociolinguistic competences (Hymes 1972; Bachman/Palmer 1989) – is what makes a communicative act meaningful to its participants. Discourse will tend to adopt the most suitable form for the achievement of the goals pursued or, in other words, for the construction of the meanings intended.

This amounts to saying that what is usually termed *meaning* is a complex, multilayered and hardly objectifiable phenomenon, even if it is (or should be) the main goal of any scientific inquiry into language and communication. Semantics is the basic level of language and is undetachable from all other ones (Dirven 2005, 23), but it actually includes much more than *semantic* values in a

1 Of these functions, *saying* – the informational one – is probably the less relevant one in everyday communication. Quite ironically, it has also been the primary if not the only concern of most research on language until the emergence of the linguistics of communication – and perhaps even afterwards. Saying also appears to be the function that most speakers consider prototypical, probably as a result of the way we have been taught to think about language (Gee 2014, 238).

https://doi.org/10.1515/9783110643442-002

restricted sense: "Information [...] about the pragmatic / discoursal / textual / register characteristics associated with a particular form can be represented in the meaning pole of the corresponding construction alongside purely semantic information" (Nikiforidou 2009, 19). In other words, linguistic choices generate meaning at a wide variety of semiotic levels simultaneously. These levels are usually segregated by scholars for analytical convenience, but in actual communication they tend to be perceived by speakers as an internally coherent whole. Furthermore, meaning is hardly limited to verbal language, but is rather a multimodal phenomenon, most often stemming from the joint action of various communication systems (Coupland 2007; Kress 2010).

Meaning can thus be understood as the cognitive correlate of anything that is perceived through the senses. Things do not exactly have *meaning* in themselves; rather, they have the capacity to be granted some meaning by those who perceive them. Even if the cognitive effect of sensory stimuli may be largely idiosyncratic, there needs to be some interpersonal invariance in meaning for communication to be possible at all. This can derive from the sensory features of things themselves – i.e. *iconic* meaning – or from some kind of social agreement – *symbolic* meaning. However, meaning is also highly variable depending on the interaction of stimuli with different features of the context. Thus any particular linguistic element will have the potential to create particular meanings, but it will only do so when effectively used and interpreted in a communicative situation. The meanings will not be totally equivalent to the ones that would be generated through a different choice, even if we can think of many forms and constructions intuitively considered to be "synonymous" at some level – most often the descriptive semantic one. It should also follow that there is no consistent theoretical difference between *meaning* and *function* in language. All of its possible functions entail the creation of (informational, transactional, insertional) meanings in some context; the differences among functions stem from the types of meanings that become more prominent to users in each case.

The concept of *choice* is also a crucial one for the understanding of how meaning is constructed in human communication. Its usefulness – as against, perhaps, the inevitably more structural notion of *variation* – was already acknowledged by García (1983, 181–182) through these words:

> What is, after all, the object of linguistic analysis? The recent emphasis on formalization seems to have deflected attention from a fundamental fact: namely, that in a given context form *X*, rather than *Y* or *Z*, is used. [...] Even a purely distributional analysis must ultimately account for the fact that *X*, rather than *Y* or *Z*, appears in the given context.

It is obvious that communication would make little sense if people lacked the possibility of choosing what meanings to communicate – and, from the opposite perspective, what meanings to interpret. However, this naturally leads to the problem of *willingness*. Meaning being such an elusive and multilayered phenomenon, it will always be possible to question whether someone really *intended* to communicate what we interpret. This becomes evident if we assume that, in many cases, speakers are not really free to choose among two or more possibilities. Expressive freedom can be strongly conditioned by the communicative norms of specific situations, but also by speakers' own personal and social features, including their command of different linguistic forms and varieties.

Nevertheless, the extent to which these and other circumstances are relevant will largely depend on the analytical perspective adopted. An attitudinal study will be concerned with what speakers actually intend to communicate, just as a perceptual one will try to elucidate what listeners or readers actually interpret. For their part, sociolinguistic and educational inquiries will usually be more interested in what communicative choices reveal about the social affiliations or the educational attainment of people. These and many other approaches to language and communication are of course valid and scientifically interesting, but it must be borne in mind that each of them will necessarily cover just a partial area of a very broad realm. In turn, we can formulate a general concept of *choice* that is applicable to all such inquiries, irrespective of their specific goals: choice is the capacity people have to communicate some meaning in some context. It is not indispensable to elucidate whether they wanted to communicate precisely that, nor whether they could have communicated something else, or just nothing at all. In this sense, communication will emerge from (not necessarily willing and conscious) acts of simultaneously formal and meaningful choice.

The concepts of *meaning* and *choice* as outlined above lead to the consideration of a third one that is often termed *isomorphism*. For communicative choice to make any sense, the meaning – or, more accurately, the *meaning potential* – of each linguistic element must somehow be different from those of all other elements in the system, including allegedly synonymous ones. This is no doubt a particularly debatable point; however, research on linguistic choice – just as on linguistic variation, for approaches handling the latter notion – seems scarcely motivated if the existence of a regular association between the production of some sensory stimulus and the generation of some cognitive correlate is not accepted as a given.[2] The intuitive fact that some communicative contexts favor

2 It would probably be safe to restrict our claims on isomorphism to the domain of morphosyntax, as Croft (2010, 336) suggests after rejecting assumptions on strong form-function isomorphism: "The forms of individual linguistic expressions may be the same, but they occur in different constructions which have distinct functions". Also, García (2009) characterizes

the choice of certain elements over other ones – for example, due to their different degrees of "formality" or "politeness" – may be taken as sufficient indication that there is some difference in meaning between them. This begs again for a complex view of what *meaning* means, overcoming its mere identification with conceptual and propositional contents.

The notion that meanings are inherent to forms has been put forward in different ways, perhaps most concisely in Bolinger's (1977, x) axiom "one form for one meaning, and one meaning for one form". According to Haiman (1985, 19), "recurrent identity of form between different grammatical categories will always reflect some perceived similarity in communicative function" (see further discussion in García-Miguel 2015, 211). This is a basic tenet for functional and cognitive approaches to language, which are all inspired by the view that the relationships among linguistic elements cannot be understood without taking into account their semantic and pragmatic features (Kuznetsova 2015, 4–5). Most prominently among these approaches, construction grammar (Goldberg 1995; 2003; 2006; Tomasello 2003, among others) holds a view of syntactic constructions as "stored pairings of form and function" (Goldberg 2003, 219) that remain relatively stable over time, which is clearly coincident with the position adopted in the present study.

Another important point that follows is that every distinction within language needs to be gradual in nature. This favors a view of linguistic categories as prototypes that elements in actual discourse will match to different degrees. There is no systematic difference between prototypes and deviations from them, since both are produced by the same factors related to meaning construction (Bybee 2010, 2–6). Variationist linguistic studies have shown that the use of linguistic variants rarely follows an all-or-nothing pattern according to the context. Rather, speakers will generally use the different forms available to them with different frequencies. Diverse (e.g. geographical, social, emotional) features of speakers themselves, as well as of communicative situations, can be significantly correlated with those frequencies, thus make some choices more prototypical than others in each context. This is actually the very raison d'être of variationist research, which aims to uncover patterns of variable usage as reflections of social evaluation and of ongoing processes of linguistic change.

---

syntax as a motivated or non-arbitrary linguistic level, as against the lexicon. Even so, and given that every linguistic element can simultaneously construct meanings at a variety of semiotic levels, a more general view of isomorphism seems worth pursuing.

The sociolinguistic competence of speakers should in turn incorporate some knowledge about the quantitative patterning of choices across different kinds of situations. What is even more important for the present study, any meaning associated with a linguistic form will also be more frequent and expectable – that is, more prototypical – in some situations than others. To put it another way, "internal" linguistic meaning is hardly independent of language-external semiotic elements; rather, it interacts with the latter in often complex ways. One major goal of research on language use in social contexts should be to uncover and adequately explain the nature of such interaction.

In spite of all this, investigations in linguistic variation, rather than pursuing such a vision of facts that could make it possible to develop a theoretical model of linguistic choice, have usually preferred to deny isomorphism. Or, perhaps more accurately, to limit its validity to the so-called "extralinguistic" factors of variability, considering that the latter are unrelated to meaning proper (cf. Silva-Corvalán/Enrique-Arias 2017, 152–161). It is necessary to further discuss the problems posed by such a kind of approach and how they can be overcome.

1.2 From linguistic variation to communicative choice

In the classic, i.e. Labovian view of linguistic variation, any set of alleged linguistic alternatives that do not mean exactly *the same* – in the sense of being "different ways of saying the same thing" or proving identical as for their "descriptive content" or their "truth value" (Weiner/Labov 1983; Chambers 2003; Tagliamonte 2012, etc.) – cannot be approached as facts of variation. This is because speakers may intend to convey different things through each choice, with no real agency of external factors. Meaning invariance is thus necessary for correlations between linguistic and extralinguistic variables to be feasible at all (cf. Tagliamonte 2006, 86–94). However, from the early times of variationist research it became evident that such an approach could only be readily applied to different possibilities of formal realization at the phonetic and prosodic levels – precisely those whose elements lack descriptive content. Doubts about the possibility of synonymy in morphosyntax were first raised by Lavandera (1978; 1984) and further elaborated by Romaine (1981; 1984), García (1985) and Cheshire (1987), among others. Investigations carried out in different languages suggest that each grammatical construction is associated with the transmission of a particular meaning. This is also quite evident with lexical and discursive phenomena.

The discussion about the role of meaning in linguistic variation has been a long and not always productive one. This is partly because mainstream variationism, instead of considering the possibilities offered by isomorphism for the construction of a general theory of variation, has preferred to hold on to the methodological necessity for synonymy – a position that owes much to its origin in the structural and generative linguistic paradigms. The pioneering studies of morphosyntactic variation in English (e.g. Labov 1969; Sankoff 1973) set the official stance of the school up to this day, which is clearly summarized in Labov's (1978, 2) response to Lavandera's groundbreaking 1978 paper:

> How do we know that someone talks like a countryman unless we know that there are rural forms and urban forms with the same meaning? How do we know that someone has spoken politely to us, unless we know that he chose one of several ways of saying the same thing, in this case the more mitigating variant?

Through the preceding words, Labov appears to be asserting a merely commonsense fact – all speakers of a language are likely to have some notion that there are different linguistic alternatives to express the same content, each of them being typically associated with some non-linguistic feature, such as rural vs. urban origin of the speaker, or higher vs. lower politeness of the sociocommunicative situation. On the other hand, it must be acknowledged that isomorphism does not appear to be so intuitive for common speakers. This is arguably due to the fact that most people hold a notion of meaning similar to the one espoused by Labov, which is clearly dependent on cultural tradition and academic training. It is interesting to observe that, in the excerpt transcribed, the author avoids resorting to examples in the domain of phonology – where, as already noted, variationist methodology is apparently unproblematic – citing instead (lexical) synonyms as well as politeness formulae. However, in doing so he actually highlights the core problem with the traditional approach to linguistic variation. If speakers can perceive some linguistic choice as more or less "polite" than a different one, it is precisely because they do not say the same – not even at the level of descriptive meaning, because not all such meanings will be considered equally "polite" by a human community. We can further illustrate this crucial objection with some examples from Spanish.

In order to request something in this language, speakers can use a verb like *querer* 'to want' in the singular first person, followed by an object NP or embedded clause. However, the verb can be conjugated in several different tenses including the present simple (*quiero* 'I want'), the imperfective past (*quería*, lit. 'I used to want'), the conditional (*querría* 'I would want'), or the subjunctive (*quisiera*, roughly 'I might want'). Most speakers are likely to perceive differences among these choices as to their respective degrees of politeness, *quiero* being the most literal or assertive one – therefore running the risk of being interpreted as "imposing" – while *quisiera* is quite a hypothetical or non-assertive way to express a desire, thus easy to interpret as "mitigating", to employ Labov's own term. However, it should be evident that the expectable pragmatic interpretations of each choice stem from the very fact that they have different meanings even at the descriptive semantic level. The present simple is inherently associated with the description of factual, ongoing events – even if the particular context may make it clear that the events recounted do not fulfill these conditions in the real world, e.g. in historical or fictional narratives – just as each of the other tenses entails a different viewpoint of the event and its factuality.

Another good example is one that will be the subject of extended discussion later on (see Chapters 6 to 8). Spanish offers two basic grammatical subparadigms for the encoding of the addressee in discourse, namely *tú* or *vos* (example 1a), i.e. the second person proper, as against *usted* (1b), the latter representing the use of third-person morphemes to index audiences, which has traditionally been characterized as a more "polite" or "formal" way of address. As indicated by the glosses, the choice of grammatical person is manifested in both the inflection of the main verb *querer* and the reflexive clitic adjoined to the subordinate infinitive.

(1a) ¿Quier- es sentar- te?
want 2ND.SING.PRES sit 2ND.SING.REFL.CL
'Do you want to sit (yourself) down?'

(1b) ¿Quier- e sentar- se?
want 3RD.SING.PRES sit 3RD.SING.REFL.CL
'Do you [*polite*] want to sit (yourself) down?'

Again, it does not seem difficult to suspect that the respective sociocommunicative values of each choice will be connected with their very formal and semantic features. The inherent function of grammatical third persons is the discursive encoding of entities external to the direct participants. When they are used to encode addressees, this function will still be present, granting those addressees a particular cognitive status that is clearly different from that of second persons proper. In other words, the choice of a certain grammatical person entails a way of constructing its referent in discourse, which, in the proposed examples, is likely to result in the perception of the latter as being at either a shorter or a longer distance from the speaker. In (1b), it is only the context that will make it evident that the question is addressed to a conversational partner, since it might just as well denote a third-person referent ('Does he/she want to sit down?').

Finally, with regard to synonymy at the lexical level, it often seems difficult to demonstrate that the conceptual content of two lexical items is different.

However, it should also be noted that dictionaries rarely define two or more terms using exactly the same words and without attaching at least some indication of usage (e.g. geographical, social, situational) to any of them. Such indications, which usually deal with "extralinguistic" or "encyclopedic" matters – thus have often been seen as unworthy of consideration on the part of linguists – do form part of the meaning of words; otherwise lexicographers would not include them in dictionaries, i.e. *linguistic* repertoires, even in those not primarily concerned with contextual usage. Dictionaries are necessarily social and cultural (Wolf/Polzenhagen 2014), since any linguistic variety is deeply rooted in the community that speaks it. Speakers obviously need to be aware of conventionalized usage values, just as they need to know conceptual meanings proper, if they are to choose and interpret words adequately. The most usual Spanish word for 'dog' (*perro*) is used in the standard dictionary of the Real Academia (RAE 2018) to define apparent synonyms such as *chucho* and *tuso*, which however incorporate some relevant characterizations that are absent from the former: "despective" and "colloquial" in the first case, "colloquial" in the second one.

> "*chucho, cha*
> 1. m. y f. despect. coloq. *perro*."
>
> "*tuso, sa*
> 1. m. y f. coloq. *perro*."[3]

The situational labels provided by dictionaries are often clearly intuitive and lack descriptive accuracy, which suggests the difficulty of pinning down meaning and differentiating among its various possible layers, as well as the need for scientific linguistic and communicative research in order to accomplish this.

It is therefore difficult to see the usefulness of describing grammatical choices like *tú* and *usted* as "descriptively/referentially equivalent", or groups of lexical items such as the ones proposed as "synonymous" or "interchangeable". Each choice has the potential to communicate different things when used in a certain

---

3 Another alleged synonym, *can*, is also defined by this dictionary as *perro*, but with no usage indications, implying that both are synonyms proper. However, most speakers of Spanish, provided they know the word *can* at all, will probably characterize it as highly formal or obsolescent. One of several informally consulted speakers described it as a *palabra de crucigramas* 'crossword term', suggesting that in current usage it is difficult to find it outside this kind of context. It must be pointed out that the dictionary of the Real Academia rarely marks lexical items for high formality, and only sometimes does so for obsolescence, which suggests some bias as to what features of meaning should be made explicit in a repertoire of the supposedly standard lexicon.

context. The complexity of meaning – itself the most polysemous term – is actually what justifies the analysis of linguistic variation and makes it a compelling scientific enterprise (Aijón Oliva/Serrano 2010a; Serrano/Aijón Oliva 2011). Speakers choose forms in order to construct meanings, not to keep them unaltered across different choices. Even more crucially, examples like the ones discussed above show that it may be possible to jointly analyze and explain all the cognitive levels at which meaning is constructed. A choice indicating physical and interactional "distance" from the speaker, such as *usted* – correlating with third-person morphemes – will at the same time suggest social "distance" from him/her; much more so, of course, if the participants are aware that a choice indicating greater "closeness", i.e. the second person proper, might have been used as well. However, the existence of different options does not really affect the meaning of either choice by itself (Aijón Oliva/Serrano 2013, 61–62), even if structuralist and variationist approaches have assumed that the meaning of linguistic forms is derived from their oppositions to others within formal paradigms.

It must also be acknowledged that a number of reasons – not all of which are of a scientific nature – have probably made it advisable for many variationists to hold on to synonymy. As pointed out, research has shown that qualitative differences – situations where a linguistic variant is exclusive of some geographical zone, social group, etc., never appearing in others – are rather exceptional (Chambers 2003, 56–59). What we will usually have is differences in the frequency with which each group of speakers resorts to each variant. What is more, variants can alternate in the speech of a single individual within a single interaction, and even within a single speech turn. It would seem to follow that, if variants really had inherently different meanings, they should not be expected to alternate in such an apparently free and even hazardous fashion as they often do. Again, in order to explain this, it seems necessary to overcome both the traditional stance on synonymy and an excessively simplified concept of isomorphism. There needs to be some motivation for every communicative choice – even if the speaker is not aware of it or cannot explicitate it – and it will be the duty of the researcher to explain why forms associated with different meanings can co-appear in the same context.

Together with this, ideological concerns may also have hindered the development of variationist research as a quest for the meanings constructed by formal variants. Lavandera (1978, 179–181) envisaged a "dangerous hypothesis" that had already been put forward in Bernstein's (1971) controversial studies on *elaborated* vs. *restricted* codes, which reflected the unequal ability of schoolchildren to decontextualize discourse according to their respective familiar and social backgrounds. Students from a more privileged milieu tended to have a greater variety of expressive resources at their disposal when facing the task of constructing narrative texts. It really does not seem unreasonable to hypothesize that, due to a variety of reasons, different social groups should be inclined to choose certain linguistic elements – and the meanings they can construct – more often than others. This would in turn cause the development of different *communicative styles* (cf. also Lavandera 1984, 13–15). In fact, Hasan's (2009) studies on semantic variation empirically demonstrate many of Bernstein's earlier claims; significant differences are found in the kinds of meanings typically constructed by middle-class vs. working-class families in everyday interactions. The problem is that, as also predicted by Lavandera, "this evidence could be used incorrectly to attribute to some groups the inability of thinking certain meanings" (1978, 179–180). From a scientific viewpoint, what can actually be asserted is that different social groups and communicative situations will tend to correlate with different communicative preferences, which of course should not imply any qualitative judgments about them.

Finegan/Biber (1994; 2001) outline a sociolinguistic model that explicitly echoes the views of the preceding authors: communicative differences across social interactions and across the groups of speakers taking part in them are of a functional and not just formal kind. This would also mean that, contrary to the usual assumption, the situational axis of variation has precedence over the societal one (2001, 263–265). Many other authors have similarly suggested that grammatical forms are actually form-meaning (or form-function) compounds and, crucially, that such compounds vary across the social and situational continua (see e.g. García 1985; D. Sankoff 1988; Eckert 2008; Serrano 2011a, 155–162; Terkourafi 2011). Semantic variation appears to be fundamental for the development of a general theory of language use (Robinson 2010). Hypotheses on the existence of (mostly quantitative) semantic differences among social groups can be basically right as long as they are pursued from rigorously scientific and non-evaluative perspectives.

Even if all the apparent problems of a functional-cognitive approach to variation as simultaneously involving form and meaning can be refuted with relative ease, they seem to have been more influential than the abundant empirical facts suggesting that real synonymy, if it exists at all, is the exception rather than the rule in natural languages. Also, the rejection of possible differences in meaning spoils the chance to find a unitary explanation for all the observed correlations of particular linguistic variants. Factors of variation are still viewed as basically independent forces – as the term *independent variables* itself suggests – and interactions among them are seen as flaws in the analysis that need to be cleared away, when in fact they only reveal some meaningful connection between the factors that can be the key to explain the co-occurrence among them and with linguistic choices.

The supposed incorporation of cognitive insights into the variationist model in recent times seems to be hardly more than a nominal recognition that such insights might be useful. When Labov (2014, 23) states that "[c]ognition is not of course limited to the content of what is being said, but is sensitive to systematic variation in the way in which the message is delivered, yielding information on speakers' relations to the addressee or audience as well as on their own social characteristics", he is actually reasserting the traditional stance – there are unitary, invariable *messages* that can be delivered in different ways and whose meaningful correlations are just of a situational and social nature, thus do not affect *meaning* proper.

Even recent works that do consider semantic and pragmatic factors as relevant for the explanation of grammatical variation seem to be hampered by the traditional concerns. For example, Torres Cacoullos/Schwenter (2008) analyze the variable formulation of reflexive clitics with the Spanish movement verbs *subir* 'to go up' and *bajar* 'to go down' in examples like *(Me) bajé del autobús* 'I got (myself) off the bus'. They find significant correlations with aspectual factors – the clitic is more often formulated in uses related to telicity – as well as pragmatic – it is more frequent when the participants are perceived as being directly involved in the event – and situational ones – it is more frequent in oral than written discourse. Even if this all clearly begs for a general explanation that could give sense to the different quantitative results, the authors do not attempt at it, seemingly accepting that the constructions with and without the clitic are synonymous – and thus that their correlations at the different levels are unrelated to one another. However, it is possible to infer that their results are connected with the reduction of transitivity and the internalization of the event within a participant that are general features of reflexive constructions in Spanish (Gutiérrez Ordóñez 2002, 299; García-Miguel 2003, 74). In other words, the cases analyzed are most likely a grammatical manifestation of discourse subjectivization. Even the higher frequencies of reflexivity in oral discourse are amenable to such an explanation: as shown by a number of studies, grammatical choices related to self-indexation and subjectivity are generally more usual in conversation than in other kinds of discourse (Dahl 2000; Aijón Oliva/Serrano 2013, ch. 4).

Finally, there have also been attempts at compromise solutions between synonymy and isomorphism. It has been suggested that, even if it does not seem possible to guarantee identity of meaning among syntactic variants, it can at least be assumed that the latter can be contextually "neutralized", that is, they can be used to fulfill the same communicative function in a given situation, with virtual meaning nuances being mostly irrelevant to speakers (Sankoff/Thibault 1980; Sankoff 1988, 153–154; Poplack/Tagliamonte 2001, 88–91; Tagliamonte 2006, 76). Functional neutralization or *weak complementarity* would in fact be a prerequisite for the explanation of processes of linguistic change in non-phonological levels: if a given element can progressively replace other ones, it is because they are perceived as equivalent by speakers, who nonetheless will tend to prefer some of the alternatives due to factors of a social, stylistic or any other sort.

Such proposals based on functional neutralization merely entail the concession that variants *may not* be really synonymous, but can anyway appear in the same contexts. This can hardly remedy the shortcomings of an approach still relying on synonymy. For one thing, supposed functional equivalence would make it possible to analyze completely different and structurally unrelated forms as variants in the usual sense, provided they can be shown to fulfill an equivalent function in some context. All of the utterances in (2), as well as hundreds of others we may imagine, could be used to give a negative answer to the offering *Are you coming for a walk?* (cf. Silva-Corvalán/Enrique-Arias 2017, 155–156, from where the examples have been adapted). However, it seems scarcely feasible to describe them all as variants of the same variable, let alone to base an empirical variationist investigation on them.

(2a) I'm tired.

(2b) It's cold outside.

(2c) This book is really exciting.

(2d) Joe is coming in a while.

Therefore, views on neutralization are again inspired by a very limited conception of linguistic variation as the mere alternation of somehow equivalent options that are only distinguished by their typical associations with geographical zones, social groups and/or communicative situations. It seems preferable for studies on variation to keep focusing on linguistic forms such as the ones traditionally analyzed, i.e. different realizations of a phoneme, structurally related grammatical constructions, or lexical units with an analogous conceptual content. Such sets of forms are in fact those where variation can be most interesting to analyze, partly due to the often subtle nature of the differences among them. If the linguistic system tolerates the co-existence of formally and semantically similar elements, often over very long periods, it must be because each of them has its own communicative usefulness. Isomorphism is not incompatible with a view of language as inherently variable, but rather offers the key to the theoretical explanation of variability. Variation and choice are constitutive of the linguistic system itself and, given the social nature of language, must be part of its description: "If a usage-based model of the language implies a social conception of linguistic facts, then a social conception of linguistic facts also implies a variationist model of the language" (Geeraerts 2010, 240). Language is a system of options shared by the minds of the individual members of a community; each individual needs to internalize this system in his/her mind in order to become a member of the community (Harder 2010), but at the same time will contribute to its constant re-shaping. Any fact of linguistic variation and change necessarily involves both the level of individual use and that of collective norms.

In sum, and going back to the basic notions presented in Section 1.1, the traditional view of variation as *alternation* should be replaced with its consideration as *choice*. A speaker who chooses to formulate a linguistic element will at the same time be choosing a particular way to construct meaning according to the context. Communication is a multi-faceted phenomenon, and meanings can be constructed simultaneously at a wide variety of levels, from the syntactic-semantic to the pragmatic-discursive and social-situational ones. Such construction is what the term *style* encapsulates (Auer 2007; Coupland 2007; Erickson 2011; Aijón Oliva/Serrano 2013) and is in no way limited to linguistic elements – it affects gesture and movement, personal aesthetics and dressing, place of residence, work, everyday habits and any other aspect of social life. The main goal of research on language usage should be to seek general explanations for stylistic choices, that is, to describe the cognitive meanings they are aimed at constructing, as well as how they tend to be interpreted by others (see further Chapters 9 and 10).

1.3 The cognitive construction of entities through formal choice

As stated at the beginning of this chapter, language is the most important resource for the cognitive organization of human experience. The present study starts from the principle that entities of any sort – e.g. animate or inanimate, concrete or abstract, individual or collective ones – as well as the events they come to be involved in – actions, processes, states – are constructed, i.e. given some cognitive representation, mainly by means of linguistic expression. The construction of such entities, which will be called *referents* here, is usually carried out through lexical and grammatical elements such as NPs, pronouns and deictic-anaphoric morphemes. In turn, events are constructed through *clauses* prototypically organized around a verbal nucleus and whose functional structuring is tightly connected with the cognitive status accorded to each of the referents taking part in them. Finally, *discourse* is any internally coherent succession of clauses across which referents can progressively appear, disappear or undergo changes in their cognitive representation.

All this amounts to saying that reality – a certain kind of reality, no more or less "real" than any other possible ones – is constructed in the minds of speakers through language. This study will be concerned with a number of ways in which entities, and especially the direct participants of communicative acts, are constructed through grammatical means. The formal variants offered by a language allow for different conceptualizations of entities and events; the choice of some possibility may be related to a wide variety of factors, according to which that choice will be interpretable. This is evident in the resources used by speakers to refer to themselves as well as those they are addressing, i.e., those subsumed under the categories of first and second person, which will constitute our main interest.

The way referents are cognitively represented by speakers, regarding both their inherent features and the roles they are accorded in specific events, seems to be at the core of clause configuration and discourse construction; as so, it can explain many aspects of linguistic choice in context. In this section we will discuss two theoretical notions that have previously been put forward as the discursive-cognitive bases of referent construction, namely *salience* and *informativeness* (Aijón Oliva/Serrano 2013, 28–31; Serrano 2013a), showing how they can be subdivided into more specific facets.[4]

1.3.1 Salience

This notion is associated with referents that are cognitively important for speakers (Croft/Cruse 2004, 49–50). Such importance can be due to different reasons related to both their intrinsic features and the status they acquire within a given context, and makes them apt for becoming a sort of stepping stones for the production and interpretation of discourse. Salient referents are at the *center of attention* of the participants (Lambrecht 1994, 94; Grosz/Joshi/Weinstein 1995), that is, there is high awareness of their presence in the context, to the point that they are often crucial for the global comprehension of the latter. They tend to

4 The characterization of salience and informativeness as *discursive-cognitive* notions will be used throughout this book in order to capture the fact that the cognitive construction of reality is undetachable from the linguistic elements used to express – to embody – it, as well as from elements in any other semiotic domains that may prove relevant in a given communicative context. Such a vision would seem to follow quite naturally from a functional-cognitive approach to linguistic variation and choice as outlined in the preceding sections.

dominate discourse progression and become the primary viewpoint from which it is regarded. This explains why they should have been described as *known, predictable* or *recoverable* entities, among many other terms that most often capture just particular contextual facets of a rather abstract notion.

Salience can have quite varied linguistic correlates, most evidently concerning the way referents are formally configured. Grosz/Joshi/Weinstein (1995, 208) note that such configuration is indicative of the degree of inference load placed upon the hearer, that is, the resources the latter will need to extract the information from discourse. In this respect, the association between referent salience and formal omission seems to be widespread across languages. According to Givón (2010, 169), zero anaphora reflects a universal pregrammatical principle that can be articulated as "Leave predictable information unexpressed". In turn, less predictable, i.e. more informational referents (see §1.3.2 below) will tend to be explicitly formulated. It has been suggested that the degree of salience of a referent – often understood as the distance between its previous explicit mention and the present clause – will tend to be inversely proportional to the amount of linguistic material employed for its discursive encoding (Givón 1983, 18; Ariel 1988, 69–70). However, many possible motivations can override this general tendency in particular contexts (Dumont 2016, 163–164). We will also see that, at least in the case of Spanish, a distinction needs to be established between zero anaphora proper – which would in principle lead to the progressive oblivion of the referent – and anaphora using deictic-anaphoric elements coindexical with the unexpressed referent, the latter situation being the one that actually reveals high salience.

Most discussions of salience and similar notions appear to mix different considerations related to either the cognitive construction of referents themselves or that of events, which is a consequence of the fact that in real language usage they are difficult to detach – an entity that is itself cognitively salient will be more likely to be granted salient status within the clause and across discourse. Even so, it is possible to theoretically demarcate the different concepts that fall within the general domain of salience, in order to better understand its relevance for linguistic choice. To this end we will propose a further distinction between the more specific facets of *perceptibility, autonomy* and *accessibility*, the first notion involving features of the referent itself, the second one its role in a particular clause-event, and the third one its status within a wider discursive context. This threefold taxonomy contemplating the phrasal, clausal and textual levels of referent construction goes somewhat farther than dichotomic classifications contemplating *prominence* and *topicality* (Dumitrescu 1998), as well as our own distinction between *inherent* and *discursive* topicality in previous approaches to the subject (Aijón Oliva 2006a, 186–192). As will also be exposed, each of the three levels comprises a variety of even more specific features.

a) *Perceptibility*. This first level of salience concerns features of the referent itself. It is intended to capture the fact that not all entities are equally distinct in human cognition, and thus that not all of them are equally eligible for becoming the center of attention. It can be hypothesized that the primary object of cognitive representation is the self; that is, the most perceptible entity for any person will in principle be him/herself. This seems coherent with the fact that most if not all languages have particular grammatical devices for self-expression and/or self-indexation, whose reference is generally unequivocal (see further Chapter 4).[5] The second most perceptible entity should consequently be the one the speaker is addressing, particularly when it is a specific and identifiable person, e.g. in face-to-face conversation. Both of the direct participants are more perceptible than any entities external to the communicative exchange; this is precisely what the grammatical category of *person* reflects (Siewierska 2004, 5–8). First and second persons are the main resources offered by most languages for the discursive-cognitive construction of the entities with the highest perceptibility, their very ordinal characterizations being hardly random. However, and more crucially, they are at the same time possibilities of communicative choice. Speakers can choose to construct themselves as a second or third person instead of a first one – or even as no person at all, e.g. through an impersonal clause – thus renounce some of their own inherent perceptibility in order to construct a less prototypical meaning in a given context. An important part of our analysis will in fact be devoted to elucidating the cognitive motivations and communicative repercussions of the choice of grammatical persons and their variable referential scopes.

Together with person, other features involved in perceptibility, and where formal and semantic-referential considerations are intermingled, are *animacy* and *definiteness*. They primarily concern referents external to the direct participants, the latter being of course generally animate and definite. Animacy has been shown to be a fundamental factor in referent construction (e.g. Branigan/Pickering/Tanaka 2008; Malchukov 2008), with many linguistic facts suggesting the higher salience of animate third persons as against inanimate ones. In many languages, grammatical phenomena such as those related to (subject or object) verbal agreement are variably or categorically conditioned by the (in)animacy of referents (see e.g. Halpern 1998; Ormazabal/Romero 2007).

As regards definiteness, it is a complex notion involving syntactic, semantic and referential factors (Lyons 1999; Abbott 2005). In many instances of

5 In turn, the plural first person will be described as reducing the perceptibility of the speaker (Chapter 5). Naturally, the same happens with the plural second person in contrast with the singular variant denoting the specific addressee.

grammatical choice it is difficult to ascertain whether it is determinacy – i.e. the presence of a determiner beside a noun – individuation – the perception of the referent as a particular individual rather than a class – or specificity – the fact that the referent is an existing and identifiable entity – that is actually at play. Given the peculiarities of the first and second persons, our analyses will be primarily concerned with specificity, i.e. whether the referent is a person or group of people that can be identified by the speaker, or rather is unknown to the latter, as is generally the case with press and radio audiences.

A good illustration of the linguistic relevance of person, animacy and definiteness as particular features of perceptibility – but also of the difficulty to demarcate their respective areas of influence in actual usage – is offered by the variable marking of accusative objects with the particle *a* in Spanish (Laca 2006; Fábregas 2013; Aijón Oliva 2015). Descriptive grammars have often viewed the formulation of the particle as prompted by the human or animate nature of the object referent. However, the following made-up examples suggest that there is actually a continuum of possibilities, from categorical marking with personal pronouns (3a) – which, by the way, also trigger verb-object agreement through clitics like *te* – as well as lexical objects with animate specific referents (3b) to practically categorical absence of the particle with inanimate referents (3e). The combination of animacy with nonspecificity (3c) and indeterminacy (3d) yields variably acceptable solutions. This shows that, while (in)animacy can indeed be the most relevant feature, other ones related to definiteness also interact with the choice.

(3a) Te buscaba *(a) ti
'I was seeking you.'

(3b) Buscaba *(a) Pablo/*(a) mi hermano
'I was seeking Pablo/my brother.'

(3c) Buscaba (a) un voluntario
'I was seeking a volunteer.'

(3d) Buscaba (?a) voluntarios
'I was seeking volunteers.'

(3e) Buscaba (*a) mi chaqueta
'I was seeking my jacket.'

Given the relevance of perceptibility in grammatical structure and usage, some researchers have attempted to arrange different discursive elements along scales based on their intrinsic salience, trying to elucidate which particular features of perceptibility have primacy over the rest, sometimes even with alleged crosslinguistic validity. One of the earliest proposals is Silverstein's (1976, 122), who outlines the following hierarchy from highest to lowest salience, based on the relative animacy and referentiality of different types of NPs (cf. also Dixon 1979, 85):

(4) *Silverstein's perceptibility scale*
Second person > first person > third-person pronoun > human proper noun > human noun > animate noun > inanimate noun

The most eye-catching detail in (4) may be the placement of the second person above the first one, which clearly contradicts our previous assumption that the speaker should enjoy the highest perceptibility among entities. It must now be recognized that the cognitive primacy of either person over the other is not free from controversy. In the specific case of Spanish, it it interesting to observe that a number of verbal tenses do not have different morphemes for the first and third persons (e.g. imperfective past: *vivía* 'I/he used to live'; conditional: *iría* 'I/he would go', as well as subjunctive forms), while the second person is almost invariably distinguished through its specific verbal ending *-s*. Also, it has been pointed out that interactional politeness is a factor that usually prompts speakers to metaphorically place their audience above themselves through grammatical choices associated with higher salience (e.g. Myhill 1989, 241–242). However, in our view the fact that the second person is often constructed through choices associated with higher salience in order to facilitate the accomplishment of communicative goals does not imply for it to be inherently more salient than the first one. Rather, it stresses the need to approach linguistic variants as inseparable from meanings, in this case those related to interactional factors (see further Sections 6.3 to 6.5).

Aissen (2003, 437), in a study of variable object marking across different languages, breaks Silverstein's scale into two different ones by separating the dimensions of animacy and definiteness. In her view, these are actually the only relevant factors as regards the formulation of the object-marking particle (*a*, in the case of Spanish):

(5) *Aissen's perceptibility scales*
a) Animacy scale: human > animate > inanimate
b) Definiteness scale: personal pronoun > proper noun > definite NP > specific indefinite NP > nonspecific NP

Of course, perceptibility scales are not theories of any sort in themselves, but just taxonomies aimed at clarifying which kinds of entities are more likely to attract the attention of speakers, and thus to become salient in communicative contexts. However, as already pointed out, salience is not only dependent on the features of referents themselves; their role within the event constructed through a clause also needs to be taken into account.

b) *Autonomy*. This second level of salience is intended to subsume the cognitive features related to the syntactic functions and semantic roles accorded to referents within the clause, the latter being understood as the linguistic construction of an event. The prototypical clause, as formalized in Langacker's (1991, 285–286; 2008, 357) canonical event model, describes a transaction of energy from a subject-agent to an object-patient, whose prototypical grammatical expression is the active declarative clause. In turn, the degree or intensity of this transaction is usually encapsulated in the gradual notion of *transitivity* (Hopper/Thompson 1980; Thompson/Hopper 2001), which is a property of the event as a whole rather than of the referents taking part in it. However, the canonical event cannot be understood irrespective of the very contrast of perceptibility between its two central participants, as noted by Comrie (1989, 128): "the most natural kind of transitive construction is one where the A is high in animacy and definiteness, and the P is lower in animacy and definiteness" (cf. also Næss 2007, 22–24). Aijón Oliva/Serrano (2013, 31–32) and García-Miguel (2015, 219) build on assessments like this in order to describe the prototypical features of the central participants of the event that are summed up in Figure 1.1, including several features that are not restricted to this second level of salience. In particular, the feature *accessible* is obviously more connected with the discursive facet of salience we term *accessibility* (see §1.3.3 below).

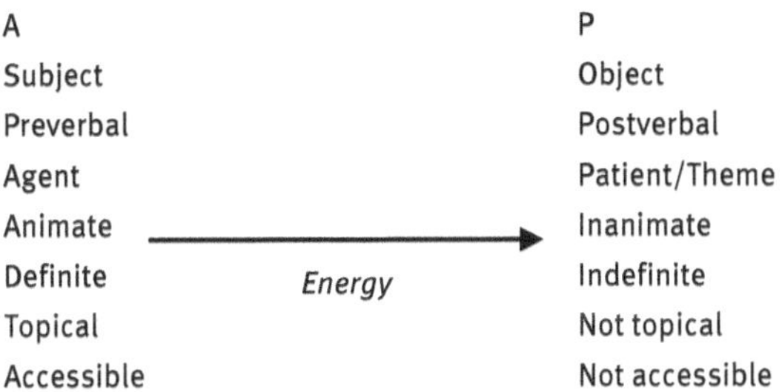

Figure 1.1: Syntactic, semantic and discursive features of the central participants in the prototypical clause-event.

Objections might be raised as regards the features of (in)definiteness and (in) animacy. In Hopper and Thompson's standard model of transitivity, both A and P are prototypically highly definite, which results in the latter being strongly affected by the event (see also Taylor 1995, 206). This is obviously well suited to highly transitive verbs such as *kill* – where the patient, as a matter of fact, should also be animate. In turn, our main focus on the discursive-cognitive contrast between referents makes it sensible to assume that such contrast should be stronger between an animate, definite referent and an inanimate, indefinite one. Thus a clause with the verb *break* involving an animate agent vs. an inanimate patient need not be less transitive than one with *kill* and two animate participants; rather, the higher perceptibility of the patient in the latter context should make it be interpreted as comparably more autonomous.

A third type of participant that is frequently labelled as S, and prototypically encoded as the subject of an intransitive clause, has intermediate values regarding the different features considered in Figure 1.1. It is usually neither an agent nor a patient, but the experiencer of a process or state (e.g. *The child is growing; The willow died*). Even when the verb denotes an action proper, the energy is not transferred to a different entity, but rather results in some benefit or harm to the subject (*She runs very fast*). The intermediate nature of S as regards autonomy justifies the fact that some languages, including most European ones, should opt for accusative alignment – i.e. A and S have the same case marking – while others have ergative alignment – it is S and P that are marked in the same way (García-Miguel 2015, 219–220). This depends on whether S is cognitively represented as analogous to an agent, thus as more autonomous, or rather as a patient, thus as more affected.

As for ditransitive clauses, R – a participant who receives the result of the energy transaction despite not being directly involved in it, as A and P are – has prototypically analogous features to those of A in monotransitive contexts, with the main exception of syntactic placement, which is most often postverbal. However, in languages like Spanish, it is necessarily marked with an object particle (see Section 2.5). On the other hand, T – the entity transferred in ditransitives – is similar to P in monotransitives, but with an even higher preference for inanimacy and postverbal placement. All this makes it possible to propose scales of syntactic functions according to semantic autonomy, in line with those based on referent perceptibility:

(6) *Autonomy scales of clause participants*
a) A > S > P
b) R > P > T

Therefore, syntactic functions are directly related to salience continua. The scale in (6a) represents the continuum between subject and object encoding, while the one in (6b) encapsulates that between accusative and dative object encoding (see respectively Sections 2.4 and 2.5). In Spanish, dative encoding, which is mainly associated with R – but is also often used to encode S, as well as nonprototypical instances of P – entails higher autonomy than the accusative (or *direct object*), which prototypically encodes both P and T (García 1975, 274–277; García Salido 2013, 69). The referent of a dative object is most often human and is not conceived as being directly affected – hence the usual label *indirect object* – by the transaction of energy. Its higher salience is primarily reflected in its stronger tendency to trigger verbal agreement in comparison with the accusative (Aijón Oliva 2006a, 276, 279).

However, this apparent cognitive primacy of the dative is typologically infrequent and seems to contradict the hierarchy of grammatical relations, according to which argument indexing in the verb should primarily occur with more salient participants (Siewierska 2004, 43; García-Miguel 2015, 239). This should make the following scale more expectable:

(7) *Hierarchy of syntactic functions according to the expectability of verbal agreement*
Subject > object 1 (direct/primary) > object 2 (indirect/secondary) > oblique

Whereas the hierarchy clearly applies to Spanish as regards its extreme points – subjects categorically agree with the verb, while obliques never do – it seems to fail at the intermediate steps, given that indirect objects show greater easiness for verbal agreement. The fact that in this language R appears to have cognitive primacy over both P and T (Comrie 2012, 20) seems to assimilate it to languages distinguishing between a primary and a secondary object, rather than a direct and an indirect one. This stance has been most significantly maintained by Company Company (2001). In ditransitive constructions, the attention of speakers appears to be oriented to the interaction between two referents with similar degrees of perceptibility – encoded as the subject and the dative object – rather than to the manipulation of a patient by an agent.

In early salience scales of syntactic functions based primarily on English (e.g. Givón 1983, 22), the cognitive primacy of the direct object over the indirect one was usually accepted. It must be borne in mind that English syntax makes it possible to encode a receiver or beneficiary as an accusative, as shown by the acceptability of R-passivization in some ditransitive constructions, e.g. *I was given some instructions*. In turn, semantic roles of this sort in Spanish are generally restricted to dative encoding and cannot function as the subject of a passive (**Yo fui dado unas instrucciones* 'I was given some instructions').[6]

In fact, in later revisions (e.g. 2001, 426) Givón would specify that the hierarchy of grammatical functions need not be coincident with that of semantic roles, where the receiver would clearly rank above the patient. This, added to the prototypically high perceptibility of R, as well as to its usual discursive accessibility (see below), usually makes it a better candidate for morphematic indexation in the verb. What most languages do is mark R with a functional index – the particle *a* in Spanish, or *to* in English – thus assimilate it to obliques; however, it is not so usual to have it agree with the verb, as is often the case in Spanish (García-Miguel 2015, 240).

In our view, the assumption that accusative objects should have a stronger preference for verbal agreement stems from a confusion between salience – or its clause-level manifestations that we have subsumed within the notion of *autonomy* – and a different criterion for participant hierarchization, namely *centrality*. The latter is best illustrated by functional models of argument structure as *valency* (e.g. Gutiérrez Ordóñez 2002, 295–299), where the verb is compared to the nucleus of an atom, its arguments occupying increasingly peripheral layers of the shell. In Spanish, the subject and the accusative object, respectively being the prototypical ways of syntactic encoding for A and P, can be considered the most central participants; they are in fact the ones required for the canonical event to make sense. Their usual syntactic obligatoriness parallels their strong semantic involvement in the event. In turn, the dative generally denotes a participant that is not so strongly involved – it is neither the origin nor the destination of the energy transaction, but rather an entity that somehow benefits or suffers from it, that is, a receiver, beneficiary or owner.[7] The encoding of participants as

6 Perhaps due to the influence of English, in contemporary mass-media discourse it is not rare to find scarcely standard constructions where a receiver is passivized (Moure 1996, 94), usually with communication verbs like *preguntar* 'to ask': "El técnico del Atlético *fue preguntado* por la posibilidad de entrenar al Inter en un futuro" 'The Atlético coach *was asked* about his chances to train Inter in the future' (https://as.com/futbol/2016/11/12/primera/1478962210_410310.html; accessed 4/7/2018).

7 Spanish has a tendency to the verbal indexation of dative objects that are not contemplated in the argument structure and do not seem to play a clearly defined role in the event. These so-called *ethical datives* are pragmatic devices suggesting some personal interest or involvement on the part of a referent, most often the speaker (see Section 3.4). Also, given that the argument structure of verbs simultaneously specifies expected syntactic functions and expected semantic roles, in this book we will usually replace the term *argument structure* with the more cognitively-oriented one *eventive structure*.

oblique objects or adjuncts denotes even lower degrees of involvement. Therefore, centrality can be connected with salience in the sense that the subject, the accusative and the dative are the functions that agree or can agree with the verb in Spanish. In fact, we will often refer to them as *central functions* across this study. But higher centrality is not necessarily parallel to higher salience, as shown by the particular case of accusative objects, which are prototypically less salient than both subjects and datives. It is not by chance that prototypical accusatives lack particle marking in Spanish, just as subjects do (Ø *María compró* Ø *un coche* 'María bought a car'). In turn, it is non-prototypical accusatives as well as datives, endowed with higher perceptibility and autonomy, that often need to be marked in order not to be confused with the subject (Ø *María vio* a *Pedro* 'María saw [to] Pedro') (Aijón Oliva 2015, 20–21).

To sum up, the autonomy of referents is mainly connected with their *syntactic function* – particularly manifested in verbal agreement, which in Spanish is categorical with subjects and variable with accusative and dative objects (see further Chapter 2) – and their *semantic role* – with agents being prototypically autonomous and other roles, such as those of beneficiary or owner, also correlating with relatively high degrees of autonomy, while patients and themes are scarcely autonomous. Autonomy makes it possible to explain why dative objects are more salient than accusative ones, and thus tend to display higher rates of verbal agreement in variable contexts.[8]

c) *Accessibility*. This third notion – a well-known one in discourse studies – will be used here to characterize salience at the discursive level, i.e. beyond the borders of the clause. The accessibility approach has been famously developed in Ariel's works (e.g. 1990; 2001; 2009). More accessible referents are those that the speaker considers easier to identify by the audience at a given point in discourse, taking into account the previous shared context. A typically accessible referent would be the main character in a narrative text. This character will act as a reference point for the concatenation of successive events, namely the actions he/she carries out or the things that happen to him/her. Other referents can also appear at any particular clause and establish a contrast of salience with that main participant.

8 Actually, the dative appears as a particularly complex function that will merit special attention throughout this study. Whereas they are less central to events than accusatives, the referents of dative objects tend to show many of the perceptibility features prototypically associated with subjects.

Accessibility affects the very organization of individual clauses, conditioning e.g. the variable expression and placement of referents within them. It is therefore not independent of autonomy – in Figure 1.1 above we did cite preverbal vs. postverbal placement as one of the features distinguishing between the prototypes of A and P. In fact, all features related to perceptibility and autonomy are projected onto discursive contexts in order to fully realize the cognitive construction of referents. For this reason, this third level encompasses the preceding ones, and it is usual to have the term *accessibility* stand for *salience* itself. Clause-initial or, in any case, preverbal positions are prototypically associated with referents already known or that serve as departure points for a subsequent clause describing an event; their way of formulation will condition how the latter is interpreted (Virtanen 2004, 84–95). This is the property often termed *topicality*, and it is also often equated with accessibility and salience.

There is general consensus that, in the absence of some special communicative intention, speakers are likely to structure discourse from what is already known towards what is yet unknown, i.e. from old to new information (Fried 2009, 293). The main difficulty lies, of course, in clearly defining what is meant by terms like "known" or "old" as against "unknown" or "new". For a referent to be known, thus accessible, it does not always need to have been formulated in the preceding context; however, it should somehow be inferable from it. A given frame or schema, understood as a conceptual context of variable specificity that can include the physical and cultural environment as well as the text-internal world itself (Lambrecht 1994, 90), will establish a set of presuppositions and thus condition the extent to which some referent can be perceived as already known. Notions like these have been put forward to explain, for example, the use of the definite article in examples like *I attended a wedding last week where* the *priest gave a strange sermon*. Even if no priest had been previously mentioned, the presence of such a referent is inferable from the moment the frame "wedding" – and the cultural presuppositions attached to it in Western societies – is established; compare ?*I attended a wedding where* the astronaut *gave a strange sermon* (see further Prince 1981; Silva-Corvalán 1984).

In turn, "new" or "unknown" referents, rather than being necessarily absent from the preceding context, should be understood as not directly inferable from it, e.g. because they counter the presuppositions and expectations derived from a given frame, or simply because they are unexpected. We will associate such cases with the notion of *informativeness* (see §1.3.2 below).

As regards discourse construction proper, accessibility can be conceptualized as the *activation* of a referent across a given stretch (Chafe 1987; 1994). Together with the basic categories of *active* and *inactive* referents, Chafe (1987, 28–31) distinguishes that of *semi-active* or *accessible* ones, being those that can be recalled when some frame is evoked across discourse, even if they have not been explicitly mentioned, as the priest in our preceding example. However, just like all other notions reviewed across the present discussion, activation should be viewed as gradual rather than scalar. It is the formal variation of referents across discourse that makes it possible to evaluate the extent to which they are activated – which takes us back to matters of perceptibility. Higher activation of a referent is usually manifested in its tendency to adopt simpler formal configurations, to the point of dispensing with explicit formulation and maintaining its presence across clauses through mere deictic-anaphoric morphemes. As observed by Croft (1988, 175):

> [B]oth pronouns and agreement markers are used to identify and maintain the identity of their referents across discourse [...] [T]he speaker must make a choice as to which entities will continue to be cross-referenced and which ones will not. Naturally, the most important or salient entities will continue to be cross-referenced, and those tend to be the most animate ones, the most definite ones, and the ones most central to the events being reported.

Choices like continued cross-reference indicate that speakers view a referent as highly activated and thus as not requiring repeated expression in order to be identified by the audience. Omission and, to a lesser extent, preverbal placement are associated with high contextual salience (Hinterhölzl/Petrova 2011, 180–182). Croft's quote above also makes it clear that those referents higher in perceptibility and autonomy – although he uses the term *centrality* – are better candidates for achieving accessibility. Activated referents should in principle remain activated until they move away from the center of attention, most often due to their displacement by others – and from then on it will usually be necessary to explicitly formulate them again in order to bring them back – or to a change in frames that renders them not presupposed or inferable.

Together with this, Givón (2010, 195) notes that accessibility, although usually understood as a property of discursive referents, also concerns predicates, as shown by the fact that verbless clauses – meaning those elements with prosodic independence from the tonal group of a verb in oral discourse – almost always appear in adjacency to another clause whose verbal nucleus governs the former as a zero anaphora:

> [T]he almost absolute requirement of adjacency in zero anaphora can be interpreted to mean continued mental activation of the persisting topical referent in focal attention or working-memory. One could likewise suggest that the equally near-absolute adjacency requirement on verbal zero-anaphora means the very same thing: continuing mental activation of the persisting governing predicate in focal attention or working-memory.

Even so, discourse construction is to a great extent dependent on the relative salience of referents, which, as reviewed across the preceding discussion, is undetachable from their inherent features such as animacy and definiteness, their syntactic encoding and semantic role within the clause, as well as their topicality and activation across discourse. An analysis of the discursive-cognitive construction of referents will need to take this range of features and their specific linguistic correlates into account.

d) *Summary: partial salience scales.* The three levels of salience proposed here – perceptibility, autonomy, accessibility – as well as their linguistic manifestations are intricately connected in real usage, to the point that it will often prove hard to elucidate which ones are at play in a particular linguistic choice. The inherent features of a referent, such as person, animacy and definiteness, will condition its likeliness to be accorded certain syntactic functions and semantic roles within the clause, as well as to achieve topicality and remain activated across a discourse stretch. In this book it will be repeatedly observed that the first and second persons, whose referents are necessarily constructed as animate and definite, strongly tend to be encoded as clause subjects; when they appear as objects, they most often show the syntactic and semantic features prototypically associated with dative rather than accusative ones. At the discursive level, these persons are clearly inclined to indexation through deictic morphemes rather than to explicit formulation; in the latter case, they will be formulated by means of personal pronouns rather than lexical NPs.

It should have become clear that the linguistic features connected with referent salience are numerous and establish complex interactions with one another. Most studies proposing salience (topicality, accesibility, etc.) scales (Silverstein 1976; Dixon 1979; Givón 1983; 2001; Ariel 1990; Aissen 2003, etc.) have tried to accommodate features related to more than one of our levels. However, they have faced the problem of specifying their relative hierarchization. This seems feasible only if the scale is based on a particular linguistic phenomenon (e.g. ergativity in Silverstein and Dixon's studies, object marking in Aissen's). As pointed out above, definiteness seems to be subordinate to animacy in Spanish, at least as regards object marking with the particle *a*, but the outcome of their interaction in particular contexts is not totally predictable, let alone if a wider range of linguistic phenomena should be considered. No doubt we are a long way from the formulation of a general discursive-cognitive scale combining all relevant facets of salience and proving crosslinguistically valid. It seems safer to propose specific scales based on just one particular factor, like the ones in (8) below, which are meant to summarize the main points of the discussion. As also noted, not all of them are uncontroversial even if restricted to Spanish – for example, the primacy of either the first or the second person remains a matter of debate – but the present study will offer some evidence in support of the proposed arrangements.

(8) *Some partial scales of referent salience*
a) *Features of perceptibility*
Person: first > second > third
Animacy: human > non-human animate > inanimate
Definiteness: determinate specific > determinate nonspecific > indeterminate
b) *Features of autonomy*
Syntactic function and preference for verbal agreement: subject > dative> accusative > oblique/adjunct
Semantic role: agent > beneficiary/experiencer/owner > patient/theme > locative others
c) *Features of accessibility*
Topicality: preverbal > postverbal
Activation: omission with indexation (verbal endings > clitics > other morphemes) > pronoun > lexical NP

Going back to the theoretical frame outlined in Sections 1.1 and 1.2, it is also important to highlight the logical inseparability between linguistic choice and cognitive construction. It is not just that referents tend to be formulated as pronouns or altogether omitted *because* they are salient; at the same time, the choice of a certain way of formulation is what grants them a certain degree of salience, since speakers use choices in order to establish what is more or less important for the understanding of discourse, continuously providing their audience with clues about it.

The progression of discourse also requires the existence of referents that cannot be described as salient, but rather are constructed upon the bases laid by already salient referents. Their discursive-cognitive features will be subsumed here under the notion of *informativeness*, which is to be considered as the opposite pole of salience in a continuum with a wide range of intermediate possibilities.

1.3.2 Informativeness

This notion could be described – just like salience – as a sort of importance in speakers' cognitive representation of reality, although it actually constitutes the flip side of the coin. While salient elements are those strongly anchored in the context shared by speakers, informative ones are those introduced *ex novo* amidst that context and thus put forward as candidates for acquiring salience in subsequent clauses. If salient referents are placed at the center of attention, informativeness can be connected with the *focus of attention*, understood as the set of discursive resources used to call others' attention upon some entity (cf. Brennan 1995; Sanford et al. 2006).

In this sense, informativeness is parallel to the degree of newness a referent is attributed at some point of discourse, considering the easiness with which it can be retrieved or inferred from the preceding context (cf. Beaugrande/Dressler 1981, 141–160 on the textual notion of *informativity*). As exposed, newness is not restricted to entities previously "unknown" to the audience in a literal sense (such as e.g. the postverbal subject in *To the village came a book seller*), but to any referent whose presence in discourse and/or role in the event are not viewed as directly inferable from the context. This can result in different contextual interpretations, such as emphasis, contrast or counter-expectation. Chafe's notion of *activation cost* (1994, 71–81) is a proposal in the same direction, aimed at capturing the variable straightforwardness of reference retrieval. Activation is a concept we have already connected with salience at the discursive level; less salient referents are more difficult to (re)activate, thus more informative.

The distinction between salience and informativeness is also roughly similar to that between *accessibility* and *importance* as exposed by Givón (2001, 277): "[a]ccessibility is an *anaphoric* property of referents, having to do with their availability in some pre-existing *memory* representation. Importance is a *cataphoric* property of referents, having to do with the requisite *attention* assigned to them for building up new memory representation". In other words, salience could be characterized as backward-looking – both in discourse and in time – whereas informativeness would be forward-looking (see also Grosz/Joshi/Weinstein 1995 on backward- and forward-looking centers).

In a Spanish utterance with an informationally focalized first-person subject such as *El pastel lo compré yo* 'The cake was bought by me', lit. 'The cake bought I', it would be inaccurate to describe the speaker as a new or unpredictable entity, given the inherently presupposed nature of the direct participants (see further Section 3.2). Rather, what is seen as new to the audience is the speaker's relationship to the rest of the utterance, specifically the role he/she is to be accorded within the event – this is actually what the audience is expected not to know, and justifies the explicit formulation of the first-person pronoun, as well as its clause-final placement and its likely prosodic prominence. In fact, Lambrecht (1994, 49) states that "The conveying of information is in principle independent of the previous mention or non-mention of the designatae of the different constituents in a sentence". New information can be considered as such only to the extent that it appears amidst a partially given proposition. Anyway, in practice it is often not easy to detach the informativeness of a referent *per se* and that which results from its relationship with the context – just as happens with salience.

Salience and informativeness can thus be viewed as the poles of a continuum that characterizes the discursive-cognitive construction of referents (Serrano 2013a). Drawing on an array of functional and cognitive investigations, García Salido (2013, 300) proposes a similar distinction between *referential accessibility* and *informational newness* as different facets of attentional relevance. The main reason why it seems preferable to formalize these two opposed notions rather than simply talking of higher vs. lower salience is that the latter perspective might suggest that informative referents are not cognitively "important" in their own right. In fact, when speakers introduce such referents in discourse, they tend to choose linguistic features that will make the audience direct their attention towards them. The mere choice between a definite article and an indefinite one is usually parallel to a noticeable variation in the degree of salience vs. informativeness of the referent:

(9a) Ana llevaba en la mano el libro

(9b) Ana llevaba en la mano un libro
'Ana was carrying in her hand the/a book.'

Even if in both cases *the book* is the more informative referent – as suggested by its clause-final placement – it is clearly less so in (9a), where the definite article *el* serves as indication that it is retrievable from the preceding context or, in any case, is readily identifiable by the audience. In turn, *Ana* is salient in both cases, although the discursive accessibility of this referent could be considered higher if it had been formulated as a pronoun (*ella* 'she'). The referents of pronouns are either inferable from the preceding context or identifiable in the physical situation; it is hardly by chance that the first and second persons can only be formulated pronominally. Even higher salience would correlate with the omission of the referent and its indexation through deictic-anaphoric morphemes, in this case the third-person verbal ending.

According to Givón (1983, 18), the accessibility of a referent in a context is inversely proportional to the amount of linguistic material used to encode it: "The more disruptive, surprising or hard to process a topic is, the more coding material must be assigned to it". Actually, terms such as *disruptive, surprising* and *hard to process* are descriptive of some of the contextual values typically associated with informativeness. Following the salience scales proposed by some authors, the most salient referents will tend to be encoded as a zero anaphora; the least salient and more informative ones will be formulated as lexical NPs. In Chafe's (1994, 73) terms, explicit formulation suggests that the referent was previously not activated (i.e. out of the center of attention and not inferable from the discourse frame), therefore entails a higher activation cost than that of already activated or semi-activated ones. Pronouns can be placed at an intermediate point along the continuum; they are unbound grammatical elements used to construct referents that are already activated in discourse – which makes it possible for the audience to identify them – but are not (yet) situated at the center of attention – which makes some kind of mention still necessary.

It is also interesting to observe a third referent that is also present in (9a, b) above, namely *la mano* 'her hand', which it is not clearly associated with either salience or informativeness. In a discursive context it would probably be a newly mentioned element, but would hardly be viewed as important – also, the definite article *la* in the Spanish version and the possessive *her* in the English one suggest its relative accessibility, being easily inferable from the frame "human body". More importantly, it is unlikely to achieve continuity along the subsequent discourse. Its placement in the middle of the clause iconically suggests the ambiguity of its discursive-cognitive status. We will show that a similar situation holds with first- and second-person referents when they are formulated at postverbal but not clause-final positions (see e.g. Sections 4.3 and 6.3).

Therefore, the preverbal position is the prototypical one for topical, scarcely informative referents that are taken as the starting point for the utterance (Halliday 2004, 64). Conversely, it is postverbal and especially clause-final positions that are associated with informativeness (Gutiérrez Bravo 2008, 378–381; Serrano 2012, 112), which is consistent with the usual progression from older to newer information. While referent expression itself entails some degree of informativeness as against omission-indexation, this can be further nuanced by placing the referent at a given point of the clause. It must be borne in mind that the association between syntactic position and informativeness is also dependent on utterance modality. *Wh-* questions entail an inversion of the prototypical declarative clause, placing the informationally relevant elements at the beginning. In turn, responses to such questions, in order to be pragmatically adequate, usually need to place the required information at the end. In the following example, (10b) only seems acceptable with prosodic emphasis on the initial prepositional phrase. This kind of inversion can take place for particular communicative reasons related to the different contextual values of informativeness we have alluded to.

(10) ¿Dónde vive tu hermana?
'Where does your sister live?'

(10a) Mi hermana vive en Madrid.
'My sister lives in Madrid.'

(10b) ?En Madrid vive mi hermana.
'In Madrid lives my sister.'

In sum, linguistic choices for the encoding of referents are formal correlates of the continuum between salience and informativeness. These notions are thus associated with opposite features as regards a) the perceptibility of referents – third-person ones, and especially those lacking animacy and definiteness, will tend to be higher in informativeness; b) their autonomy in the clause – accusative objects with the semantic role of patient or theme, as well as referents in non-central syntactic functions, will usually be more informative; and c) their accessibility in the discursive context – as illustrated in this section, explicit formulation and particularly postverbal placement are generally associated with informativeness. In fact, the latter features, specifically pertaining to the level of discourse, appear to be among the most significant formal indications of the degree of salience vs. informativeness of referents, and will merit detailed attention across our analyses. In the last subsection of this discussion we will further specify the main formal manifestations of the discursive-cognitive status of referents across Spanish discourse.

1.3.3 Salience and informativeness at play in the construction of referents across discourse

Figure 1.2 builds on some of the scales in (8) above in order to schematize the semantic, syntactic and discursive features prototypically associated with either salience or informativeness, or else indexing intermediate values in the continuum. It must be stressed that the description is based on Spanish and is not intended to be straightforwardly applicable to any other language, even if a major goal of functional-cognitive research should be to unveil the general principles underlying referent construction by means of linguistic choice. The features are disposed in several rows according to the phenomena involved – animacy, semantic role and so on, with the last two rows specifying subsets within expressed referents – and in three columns conventionally representing points along the salience-informativeness continuum. Most combinations of features are in principle possible, yielding a wide variety of possible outcomes as regards cognitive construction.

As already stressed, subject vs. object agreement is a particularly complex and relevant phenomenon in Spanish grammar that will be more extensively discussed in Chapter 2. As for referent omission, it can only be considered an index

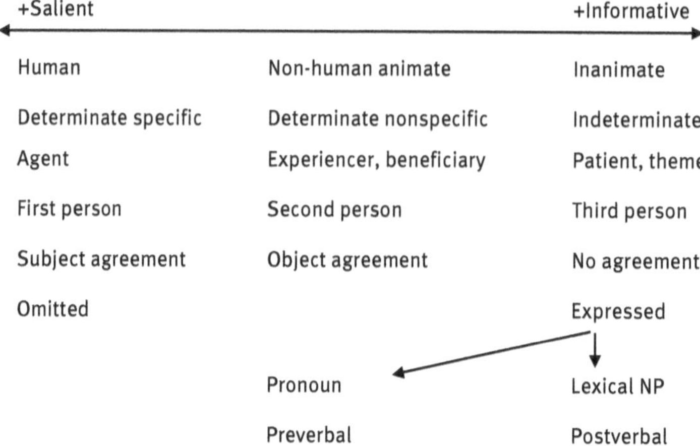

Figure 1.2: Semantic, syntactic and discursive features of referent encoding in Spanish and their correlation with salience vs. informativeness.

of high salience if the reference is maintained across successive clauses by way of verbal agreement morphemes or other deictic-anaphoric elements. Therefore, the grammatical choice we will conventionally term *omission* would be more accurately described as *morphematic indexation without explicit formulation.* A referent that is neither formulated nor morphematically indexed across discourse can only be thought to be out of the speaker's attention, lacking both salience and informativeness. In our view, this is why verbal zero anaphora in the sense of Givón (2010; see §1.3.1 above) generally requires strict adjacency to the clause where the verb was formulated. A conjugated verb does not construct a referent proper, but rather an event; thus it cannot be repeated through pronouns or bound morphemes unless the entire event is re-constructed as a referent, e.g. *it* in *We opened the windows, but it didn't help much.*

Besides, many of the features considered in the figure can be further specified, e.g. object agreement in Spanish can be subdivided into accusative and dative agreement (although with significant caveats; see Section 2.5). Linguistic choice in connection with the cognitive construction of referents is exactly what the present study aims at delving into, as far as the direct participants of communicative acts are concerned.

Although the discussion has so far been mostly illustrated with made-up examples, it should always be borne in mind that the notions of salience and informativeness only make sense within some discursive context, and that the formal features of a referent in a particular clause cannot be fully explained without taking that context into account. Travis (2007, 107) observes that the most decisive factor for subject expression in Spanish is a change in the reference of the subject from the immediately preceding clause. This is a result of the informativeness associated with explicit formulation, which is often contextually interpreted as contrastivity with other referents present. Discourse construction is undetachable from the evolution of referents along the continuum, which will most often follow the direction from higher informativeness to higher salience. This seems quite natural considering that newly introduced referents will first be placed under the focus of attention and later – provided they achieve continuity across discourse – will tend to settle at the center of attention. The opposite progression, even if contextually possible, is less prototypical.

This is also one of several conclusions drawn in Aijón Oliva's (2017) study of the discursive-cognitive construction of third-person referents in a quite specific textual genre, namely radio broadcastings of football (soccer) games. This kind of discourse proved to be particularly useful for observing variations in salience and informativeness, due to the constant introduction and replacement of referents – mainly the players, sometimes also the referee, the team coaches or the crowd – as the game progresses. If a player manages to keep the ball for some time – that is, for some consecutive clauses in the narrative – his/her grammatical encoding will usually undergo quick and notorious changes: from postverbal to preverbal placement and then to omission-indexation, as well as from zero verbal agreement to object agreement and then to subject agreement. All this can be illustrated with the following example, containing a series of shifts among three different players (*Azkoitia, Otero* and *Rubén*). Italics are used to indicate explicit mentions whereby each of them are brought back to the focus of attention.

(11) e:l balón en juego ya: / en poder del Elche es *Azkoitia* Azkoitia el que envía hacia la banda derecha / para la llegada por aquel lado de *Otero:* / Otero / que: recula: amaga: / tra:ta de: buscar ayuda la encuentra: / de nuevo en *Rubén* / aguanta Rubén / la pone para *Otero* / Otero que quiere centra:r / juega con *Azkoitia* en la fronta:l <Dep-Pu-191204-18:00>[9]
'The ball is now in the possession of the Elche club. It's *Azkoitia* who sends it to the right lane, upon the arrival of *Otero*. Otero, who backs down, pretends to give a pass, looks for help and finds it again in *Rubén*.

9 All examples taken from the MEDIASA corpus, which will be the basis for our quantitative and qualitative analyses, are followed by an identifying code between angle brackets. The meanings of the elements forming the codes can be consulted in Appendix I. In turn, Appendix II details the main conventions used in the transcription of spoken discourse.

Rubén resists, sends it back to *Otero*. Otero wants to center it, plays with *Azkoitia* on the front line...'

Below is a more detailed, clause-by-clause analysis of the evolution of two of the referents, *Rubén* (11a) and *Otero* (11b), across the stretch. Interestingly, in both cases the player is first introduced as a non-agreeing prepositional adjunct, denoting the direction followed by someone else or the destination of the ball (*para la llegada de Otero; la encuentra de nuevo en Rubén*). Then, when the player has taken control of the ball, his grammatical encoding shifts to that of subject, either postverbal (*aguanta Rubén*) or preverbal (*Otero que quiere centrar*). If he still holds the ball in the following clause, he will usually become omitted (Ø *la pone*; Ø *juega*). The excerpt thus offers an easy illustration of how notorious variations in salience and informativeness can take place across very short discourse stretches.

(11a)	1. la encuentra: / de nuevo *en Rubén* /	[Prepositional adjunct]
	2. aguanta *Rubén* /	[Postverbal subject]
	3. Ø la pone para Otero /	[Omitted subject]

(11b)	1. la pone *para Otero* /	[Prepositional adjunct]
	2. *Otero* que quiere centra:r /	[Preverbal subject]
	3. Ø juega con Azkoitia en la fronta:l	[Omitted subject]

This is of course not meant to suggest that a third-person referent cannot be firstly introduced in discourse as, for example, a preverbal subject – omitted subjects being understandably much rarer as a way of first mention, unless the situational context should offer unequivocal cues for their identification. Likewise, a highly activated referent that appeared as an omitted subject in the immediately preceding context can suddenly be explicitly formulated again and/or be accorded a different syntactic function, just because the eventive structure of the new clause begs for a redistribution of semantic roles, thus for some alteration in salience and informativeness. Actually, the abovementioned study of football broadcasting shows that syntactic encoding does not appear to follow such a regular pattern as expression and placement do. For now, what the model in Figure 1.2 above is aimed at describing is just the prototypical association of each linguistic feature with some point in the continuum between salience and informativeness, not the largely unpredictable – but undoubtedly very interesting – outcomes of referent construction in particular contexts such as the ones examined in the cited study.

1.4 Summary

In this chapter we have presented and discussed a set of basic notions for the development of a functional and cognitive approach to linguistic choice. Meaning, which constitutes the basis for both human cognition and communication, should be the fundamental goal of any sort of inquiry into language usage. In fact, no linguistic element can be scientifically analyzed without taking into account the meanings it is able to construct at all possible semiotic levels, as well as its interaction with other meaningful elements in the context. The placement of meaning at the center of research naturally promotes a shift from the traditional, structural notion of *linguistic variation* to the more dynamic one of *communicative choice*. Also, the merging between variationist and functional-cognitive approaches to language makes it possible to adopt an isomorphic perspective whereby linguistic elements are viewed as undetachable from particular cognitive representations, superseding more traditional stances on synonymy that can hardly capture the complexity of meaning construction.

The investigation to be developed in this book is concerned with the ways entities and the events they take part in are constructed in discourse and cognition. Following some previous studies, we have proposed *salience* and *informativeness* as the basic discursive-cognitive notions underlying the linguistic encoding of referents; both of them can be further subdivided into at least three different levels, respectively related to the perceptibility of the referent, its autonomy within the clause and its accessibility across discourse. Each of these in turn correlates with a variety of semantic, syntactic and discursive traits, of which some preliminary instantiations in Spanish have been presented across the discussion. We have also considered *transitivity* as a magnitude whereby events are cognitively interpreted, but that is itself hardly detachable from the participants themselves and the degree to which they contrast in salience. The most important conclusion to be drawn is that there is no consistent difference between linguistic choice and cognitive construction – all choices are aimed at constructing some meaning for the people communicating in a certain context.

In the following chapter we will go deeper into the syntactic side proper of referent encoding and clause organization, proposing an approach to Spanish syntactic functions as prototypes among which broad zones of variability can be observed in real usage. We will especially discuss the role played by verbal agreement as well as some related syntactic and semantic features in the construction of referents and of discourse altogether.

2 Variable grammar: the continuum of syntactic functions

2.1 Functions as prototypes

The conjunction between functional-cognitive and variationist approaches to human language becomes easy as soon as linguistic categories and functions are viewed as prototypes, i.e. as ideal sets of features that actual choices will match to different degrees. This, in turn, makes grammatical variants amenable to quantitative description according to co-occurring contextual features, communicative purposes and/or cognitive representations (Delbecque 2002; 2005; Geeraerts 2010; Serrano/Aijón Oliva 2011) in order to discover how the interaction between them creates meaning. The present study will adopt a view of syntactic functions as sets of choices at different linguistic levels, all of them contributing to the construction of referents and events in discourse.

Functions such as *subject, accusative object, oblique* or *adjunct*, as usually defined in grammatical descriptions of Spanish and other languages, entail the co-occurrence of various formal, semantic and discursive features related to the continuum between salience and informativeness as discussed in Chapter 1. If an element within a clause matches a sufficient amount of the features associated with a functional prototype, it can be ascribed to the latter. However, perfect identification is likely to be the exception rather than the rule; there are wide diffuse areas among the different syntactic functions, just as among other linguistic categories (Keenan 1976).

It is common for syntacticians to find elements that do not give a straightforward response to some functional test, or that match some features of a prototype but not others. While subjects in Spanish are basically characterized by their agreement in person and number with the ending of the verbal nucleus, some subjects are more prototypical or canonical than others (Helasvuo/Huumo 2015). A prototypical subject will rank high as regards features like animacy, definiteness, autonomy, agentivity, topicality and contextual activation – that is, all those we have connected with higher cognitive salience. Any changes in those features will result in some detachment from that prototype, thus will alter the cognitive construction of the referent. If such detachment is strong enough, agreement with the verb can even fail and the characterization of the referent as subject may become problematic (see further Section 2.4).

A prototypical accusative object can in turn be described with features opposite to those of the subject: inanimacy, indefiniteness, lack of agentivity,

https://doi.org/10.1515/9783110643442-003

topicality and activation, etc. It is interesting to observe that many Spanish syntactic objects that would be described as *accusative/direct* actually match just one of the two main functional features usually accorded to this function (Alarcos Llorach 1994, §333; Moure 1996, 84, 92–102):

a) They can be indexed by means of accusative clitics adjacent to the verbal nucleus: *Ella tiene un barco* > *Lo tiene* 'She has a boat/She (acc cl) has'.
b) However, they can hardly be formulated as the subject of a passive paraphrasis: *Ella tiene un barco* > ?*Un barco es tenido por ella* 'She has a boat/A boat is had by her'.

This reflects the lack of patienthood of the object in this context – it is a T participant rather than a P one (see §1.3.1b above) – as well as the low transitivity of the clause as a whole, in connection with the meaning of the verbal nucleus. Of course, functional possibilities will multiply as more features related to salience and informativeness are taken into account. For example, an animate object will be somewhat farther from the accusative prototype, which should condition the outcome of functional tests – e.g. increasing the acceptability of dative clitics instead of accusative ones (Section 2.5).

As pointed out in the previous chapter, the canonical clause is characterized by the contrast of salience between its two central participants. The clause in example (1) can be seen as fairly close to the prototype, the subject being highly salient and the object informative. In turn, (2) is a scarcely prototypical clause with a verb describing a psychological process and selecting the experiencer as a (dative) object, whereas the function of subject is accorded to the origin or cause of the process (*los jarrones* 'vases'). In these cases the object will most often be animate, definite and preverbal, while the subject will tend to display the opposite features. Actually, the only feature they retain from their respective alleged syntactic functions is the type of agreement – subject vs. object – they establish with the verb (see Sections 2.2, 2.3). Precisely due to its atypical functional-cognitive nature, (2) is a type of construction that will receive special attention across our analyses of the first and second persons.

(1) Juan romp- -i- -ó un jarrón
Juan break THEME.V 3RD.SING.PAST a vase
'Juan broke a vase.'

(2) A Juan le gust- -a- -n los jarrones
To Juan 3RD.SING.DAT.CL please THEME.V 3RD.PL vases
'Juan likes vases', lit. 'To Juan vases are pleasing.'

More generally, objects show wide syntactic and semantic variability in Spanish monotransitive clauses (García-Miguel 2015, 243–245). They can approach the accusative prototype, as the object in example (1), or else the dative one, as that in (2); but there are also many instances where ascription to either prototype is hardly straightforward. This problem is in turn largely absent from ditransitive constructions, due to the very contrast in salience between two objects that are respectively associated with each of the prototypes (cf. Hentschel 2013; Aijón Oliva 2018a). However, in an approach to grammar as undetachable from semantic and discursive choices, we can even assume that any functional allocation, being a significant facet of the construction of a referent, is placed along the continuum between salience and informativeness; in other words, that the functional and cognitive frontier between subjects and objects is also a diffuse one. Some evidence of this will be offered below.

Besides, syntactic functions or relations need to be considered not only language-specific, but also construction-specific (Bickel 2010, 400; Croft 2010, 341–345), which makes it difficult to envisage a general theory of functions. However, languages usually offer a limited set of morphosyntactic options for case marking, each of which can subsume different semantic roles (Croft 1991, 158–159). Actually, from the isomorphic perspective adopted in this study, all elements that can be described as e.g. *subject* must have something in common – something that can only be elucidated by specifying the *prototypical* features associated with this function – in spite of their possible interpretations in particular contexts.

2.1.1 Central vs. peripheral functions; the role of agreement

In many languages, highly salient elements are more often indexed in the verbal nuclei of clauses and impose their grammatical features on the elements complementing them (Company Company 2001, 7; Siewierska 2004, 43; Ortmann 2011, 240–241). The existence in Spanish of both subject and object agreement systems justifies a functional and cognitive demarcation between *central* and *peripheral* syntactic functions (Vázquez Rozas 1995, 62–65; García-Miguel 1999, 101–102; 2015, 207). The notion of centrality was approached in §1.3.1b, where we saw that each type of event specifies some participants as central, i.e. as necessary for the event to make sense. At the syntactic level, this is mainly reflected on the possibility – often requirement – of agreement between them and the verb. Central functions in Spanish are those traditionally termed *subject, accusative/direct object* and *dative/indirect object*. On the other hand, what we will generally refer to as *obliques* and *adjuncts* constitute an array of partially different functions whose unifying grammatical feature is their impossibility to be indexed in the verbal nucleus. They correlate with referents having lower salience and whose roles in the event are constructed as cognitively less important than those of central participants.

In Spanish, agreement is a matter of variation and choice with complex cognitive implications that will be extensively addressed. It happens at the phrasal, syntactic and discursive levels. In an NP such as *los niños educados* 'the polite children', all three words are inflected with the masculine gender morpheme *-o* as well as the plural number morpheme *-s*. If the NP is encoded as the subject of a clause, the verb will be inflected with a third-person plural morpheme *-n: Los niños educados llama-n a la puerta* 'Polite children knock on the door'. At a broader discursive level, agreement is also the main grammatical device used to keep a referent activated across successive clauses, as was already observed in §1.3.3. Obviously, it is deictic-anaphoric elements that will make it possible for the audience to identify discursive referents when they are not constantly formulated across clauses. In example (3), the specific human referent cited at the beginning re-appears in all subsequent clauses, thanks to either verbal endings realizing subject agreement or verbal clitics realizing object agreement; there is even a case of reflexivity where both the verbal ending and the clitic index the same referent (observe the indications between square brackets in each case). Nominal and adjectival elements such as *asesor* 'advisor' and *tirado* 'stranded' also establish masculine and singular agreement with the initial referent and help it stay at the center of attention.[1]

(3) A *Félix Colsa lo* [3rd sing cl] dejaron fuera de la lista del Senado y las urnas *le* [3rd sing cl] dejaron compuesto y sin acta de diputado, pero al final no *le* [3rd sing cl] va a ir tan mal como asesor en la Diputación. Asesorar ya veremos qué *asesora* [3rd sing infl], pero no *se va* [3rd sing cl & infl] a quedar tirado. <Art-Ga-070404-3b>

'F. C., they left (*him*) out of the list for the Senate, and the ballots left (*him*) out of the Congress as well, but in the end things won't be so bad (*for him*) as an advisor at the Provincial Council. We still have to find out what (*he*) can advise on, but at least (*he*) won't get stranded.'

1 It is important to stress that neither verbal endings nor clitics can be considered equivalent to expressed subjects or objects in Spanish (or English). For this reason, in our English translations all cases of indexation without explicit formulation of a referent will be indicated with parentheses.

Verbal agreement will be understood as the morphosyntactic process whereby the nucleus of the clause incorporates deictic-anaphoric morphemes indexing any of the participants that are conceived as central to the event. Such indexation is a functional manifestation of salience. Centrality does not necessarily correlate with salience, as shown by accusative objects, which are usually more central to events than dative ones, but at the same time are less inclined to agreement than them. However, only central functions provide discursive referents with the possibility to achieve the high degree of salience associated with verbal agreement.

In Section 2.2 we will further discuss subject agreement in Spanish and specify its most significant theoretical and analytical aspects. In turn, Section 2.3 will deal with object agreement, this being a more complex phenomenon since it is mandatory in some contexts and variable – or even dispreferred – in others. In any case, all variants of subject and object agreement will be explained as correlating with the degree of salience achieved by referents in particular discursive-cognitive contexts. Building on this, Sections 2.4 and 2.5 will further develop our approach to Spanish syntactic functions as a continuum by respectively investigating contexts of variability between the subject and the objects, and between both of the object prototypes.

2.2 Subject agreement

The variable expression and placement of subjects has for decades been a major topic of studies in Spanish syntactic variation and choice (Enríquez 1984; Bentivoglio 1987; Cameron 1993; 1995; Miyajima 2000; Silva-Corvalán 2003; Matos Amaral/Schwenter 2005; Travis 2007; Ortiz López 2009; Brown/Rivas 2011; Travis/Torres Cacoullos 2012, among many others). Aijón Oliva/Serrano (2013), in a book-length study that constitutes a major precedent of the present one, developed an approach to subject variation and choice as the creation of communicative styles in interaction. Depending on which participant is chosen as the clause subject, as well as on further formal choices such as the omission vs. formulation of referents and their placement within the clause when formulated, different interpretations of the utterance will be favored against other possible ones. It must however be pointed out that the choice and formal encoding of subjects is only a part – probably a small one – of the manifold formal and meaningful strategies that can be used for the creation of communicative styles (see further Chapters 9 and 10). Also, it is necessary to more thoroughly discuss what makes a referent become the subject of a clause and what cognitive status it acquires this way.

Person and number agreement between subject NPs and verbal endings is in principle categorical in Spanish, whose conjugational paradigm offers different forms for most grammatical persons and tenses: (*yo*) *como* 'I eat', (*tú*) *comiste* 'you (sing.) ate', (*ellos*) *comerán* 'they will eat', etc. This, in turn, often makes the formulation of the NP optional. Its omission would seem most expectable with first- and second-person referents, whose identification is usually straightforward, but can also happen with any third-person entity that is considered by the speaker to be unequivocally identifiable across a given stretch; in other words, any one that is activated.

However, some circularity can be perceived in the characterization of subject agreement as categorical. If agreement fails, the clause will be described as lacking a subject, i. e. as impersonal; in other words, what makes something a *subject* in syntactic terms is precisely its coreference with the verbal ending. There are usage contexts where oscillation between agreement and non-agreement can be observed. Impersonal presentative constructions with the verb *haber* 'there be' should canonically lack agreement between this verb and the referent it introduces, e.g. the plural NP *problemas* 'problems' in (4a). Nevertheless, there is also a nonstandard variant where the referent is reanalyzed as the subject and thus agrees in person and number with the verb (4b) (see further Section 2.4).[2]

(4a) Si el Gobierno no cede, habrá [3rd sing] problemas

(4b) Si el Gobierno no cede, habrán [3rd pl] problemas
'If the Government doesn't give in, there will be problems.'

In standard Spanish grammar, only non-prepositional lexical or pronominal NPs can establish subject agreement with the verb. A clause can of course contain more than an element that qualifies for this function. In (5) we have two non-prepositional third-person singular NPs (*la tormenta* 'the storm' and *la cosecha* 'the harvest') as well as a verb conjugated in the third-person singular. In cases like this, the allocation of syntactic functions and the interpretation of the event will be carried out mainly on world-knowledge grounds – it is difficult to imagine a harvest ruining a storm – but also partly on collocational and prosodic ones – in a declarative transitive clause with unmarked intonation, the subject is prototypically placed at the left.

2 Interestingly, the corresponding presentative constructions in English show a similar vacillation regarding agreement between the verb and the NP it introduces (e.g. *There are four bottles left* vs. *There's four bottles left*); however, in this case it is the variant with agreement that is considered more standard and formal (Leech/Svartvik 2013, §548).

(5) La tormenta [3rd sing] arruinó [3rd sing] la cosecha [3rd sing]
'The storm ruined the harvest.'

In other words, while coreferentiality with the verbal ending is the primary feature associated with the prototype of subject, there are many other non-categorical features also taking part in its characterization: animacy and definiteness, semantic agentivity, preverbal placement or omission within the clause, all of which correlate with high cognitive salience (Aijón Oliva/Serrano 2013, 73). They all help shape a certain functional prototype that actual referents in discourse will approach to different degrees according to their linguistic configuration.

The phenomenon of subject agreement poses a number of further problems. For one thing, it is not clear whether agreement is indeed the basic function of those elements that are usually characterized as agreement morphemes, given that they actually share many of the discursive properties of pronouns. The most evident case in this sense is that of object clitics (see the following section), but the problem also concerns more grammaticalized elements such as the subject-agreeing verbal endings we are dealing with. Whereas it seems easy to assume that the morpheme *-mos* in (6a) is realizing subject agreement with first-person plural *nosotros* 'we', it is not so evident that the same morpheme be establishing agreement with third-person NP *los españoles* 'Spaniards' in (6b) – even if most common speakers, if requested to identify the subject of the clause, would most likely select this element.

(6a) Nosotros [1st pl] vivimos [1st pl] relativamente bien
'We live relatively well.'

(6b) Los españoles [3rd pl] vivimos [1st pl] relativamente bien
'Spaniards (we) live relatively well.'

(6b) is actually a rather peculiar construction of Spanish where a verb conjugated in the first- or second-person plural appears to establish subject agreement with a clause-integrated third-person lexical NP. In contexts of this sort it is arguably the verbal ending that makes the subject identifiable – which means it is hardly a mere agreement marker – while the lexical NP would have been formulated with the goal of further specifying its referential scope. Such an analysis is supported by the fact that the construction is not attested with singular first- or second-person verbal endings (**El profesor viv-o relativamente bien* 'The teacher (I) live relatively well'), but only with plural ones indexing human groups whose reference might not prove transparent to the audience and thus require specification (De Cock 2014, 156–157). Functional approaches tend to assume that elements like verbal inflections can act as agreement markers in some contexts – when they co-occur with a coreferential NP in the clause – and as deictic-anaphoric elements in others – when they help keep track of a referent that has been previously mentioned in the context or is identifiable in the situation (García Salido 2013, 101–102).

However, the latter solution is still not fully satisfactory. It suggests some dependency on the traditional description of verbal endings, clitics or pronouns as basically substitutive of other discursive elements (Mühlhäusler/Harré 1990, 49–50). A broader notion of reference and deixis such as is adopted here, based on discursive-cognitive construction, makes it possible to state that the function of agreement markers is not to repeat elements – or, more precisely, to relieve speakers of the need to repeat them – but rather to signal the continued presence across discourse of those that are considered more relevant for its understanding, i.e. more salient. If the subject is categorically indexed by verbal inflection in Spanish, it is because of its construction as the main participant in the event described. The long controversies on whether it is bound verbal morphemes or their coreferential free NPs that have the "primary" status or that "actually" carry out syntactic functions (cf. Radatz 2008, 191) can also be solved through this sort of approach. As exposed across the previous chapter, referents will be constructed in different ways according to the degree of salience vs. informativeness they are accorded in each context. Explicit formulation will itself entail the suggestion that the referent is not salient enough to be tracked through mere indexical morphemes.

In general, what has come to be encoded as subject will tend to retain this status, at least until some other referent enters into competition with it (see also §1.3.3 above). In example (7) we can observe how a specific human referent – a local mendicant – is first introduced through his first name, then indexed through a possessive and an accusative clitic, and for the rest of the stretch is kept activated through singular third-person verbal endings. All other occasional referents (*un teniente coronel, ciudades portuguesas, un andamio*, etc.) require explicit formulation, in coherence with their lack of contextual salience, and rapidly go out of attention.

(7) *Andrés dejó* Angola con seis años, después de perder a *sus* padres "en la guerra". Un teniente coronel *lo* llevó a Portugal y allí *estudió* en distintos internados hasta los 18 años. Hoy *tiene* 48 y también un amplio currículum y experiencia en la calle. Durante algún tiempo *trabajó* <sic>en distintas en la construcción ciudades portuguesas</sic> hasta que *se cayó* de un andamio y *se quedó* cojo. Entonces, *cambió* la paleta

y el cemento por la guitarra y *tocó* de verbena en verbena y de fiesta en fiesta < Rep-Ga-221203-17>

'*Andrés* left Angola at 6, after losing *his* parents "in the war". A lieutenant colonel took (*him*) to Portugal, where (*he*) studied at several institutions until turning 18. Today (*he*) is 48 and has an extensive curriculum and experience in street life. For some time (*he*) worked as a builder in different Portuguese towns until (*he*) fell from a scaffold and (*he*) became lame. Then (*he*) left the trowel and the cement for the guitar and (*he*) started playing from one local festival or party to another.'

In turn, when a subject is expressed, it is usually because the speaker does not conceive it as salient enough to be identified through mere morphematic indexation. This results in variable contextual interpretations related to informativeness, such as emphasis, contrast, disambiguation, etc. (see §1.3.2 above). Figure 2.1 sums up the association between the omitted subject and salience, as well as that between the expressed subject and informativeness (see also Aijón Oliva/Serrano 2013, 119). However, the fact that indexation through verbal endings is necessary in both cases shows that subject agreement always entails a certain degree of salience. Also, as pointed out, many other formal and semantic features related to referent perceptibility, autonomy and accessibility need to be taken into account in order to ascertain the degree of salience vs. informativeness of the referent.

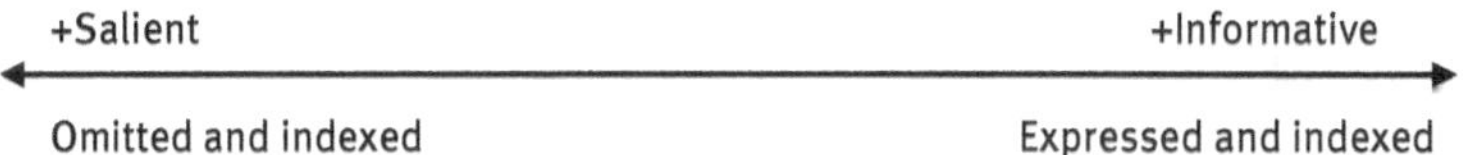

Figure 2.1: Agreement and variable expression of subjects in the continuum between salience and informativeness.

The categoricity of subject agreement is also related to its being a necessary participant for the great majority of linguistically encoded events. Most verbal lexemes select a subject in their eventive structure, and even supposedly impersonal verbs such as those indicating weather phenomena (example 8a) can be forced to agree with a referent in e.g. metaphorical contexts such as that of (8b).[3] We should also recall the tendency to reanalyze alleged accusative

3 The need for a subject is of course more evident in other languages where non-referential pronouns are required by the corresponding constructions: French *Il pleut*, English *It's raining*, German *Es regnet*, etc.

objects as subjects in one-participant presentative constructions with *haber* 'there be', as illustrated in (4a, b) above.

(8a) Está [3rd sing] lloviendo
'It's raining.'

(8b) Están [3rd pl] lloviendo piedras [3rd pl]
'Stones are raining.'

It is easy to understand why most if not all clauses should require the presence of at least one participant – the cognitive construction of events would make little sense if no entities were involved in them. The referent placed at the center of attention will most often be encoded as the clause subject, that is, it will match the grammatical information of the morphemes at the right of the verbal root, even if such morphematic coincidence can sometimes appear to fail (see further Section 2.4 on variation between subject and object encoding in one-participant contexts). In turn, the appearance of accusative and dative objects generally depends on how the particular event is constructed, namely as an intransitive, monotransitive or ditransitive one.[4]

As noted by De Cock (2014, 35), even if clause objects have not nearly received as much attention as subjects in research on syntactic variation and choice, they should be studied from the same theoretical and analytical perspective. For this reason, the following section will correspondingly discuss object agreement and its implications for referent construction.

2.3 Object agreement

2.3.1 The intermediate functional nature of clitics

The diachronic emergence in Spanish of a system of object agreement, together with its variability at different synchronic stages, has been approached from formal, functional and sociopragmatic perspectives (Llorente/Mondéjar 1974; Suñer 1988; García-Miguel 1991; Enrique-Arias 1993; 1997; Franco 1993; 2000; Aijón Oliva 2006a; 2006b; 2010; García 2009, 79–81; Aijón Oliva/Borrego 2013;

4 Importantly, eventive structure is not necessarily predefined by the verbal lexeme, or at least depends to some extent on speakers' contextual choices – as already exemplified in (8b) – which means that unexpected central objects may be constructed (see especially Section 3.4).

Belloro 2015; Serrano 2017a, 137, among others). Accusative and dative objects can be indexed in the verbal nucleus through a set of coreferential object clitics which are variably marked for person, number, gender and case. Table 2.1 displays the different units and their grammatical characterizations in standard European Spanish.

Table 2.1: European Spanish verbal clitics and their grammatical features.

		Singular			Plural		
1st person		*me*			*nos*		
2nd person		*te*			*os*		
3rd pers	Object agreement	Dative	Accusative		Dative	Accusative	
			Masc./ Neuter	Fem.		Masc.	Fem.
		le	*lo*	*la*	*les*	*los*	*las*
	Subj agr	*se*					

As can be observed, there are considerable differences as to the grammatical features each unit is marked for. This is easy to connect with the perceptibility of referents and the easiness of their contextual identification. Whereas first- and second-person clitics only indicate person and number, third-person ones further distinguish between dative and accusative case, with the latter units also incorporating gender marking. Finally, the distinction between *object* and *subject agreement* has been added to the table in order to capture the fact that third-person clitic *se* is only found in contexts of reflexivity, i.e. when indexing the subject itself: *Pedro* se *vistió* 'Pedro dressed (himself)' vs. *Pedro lo vistió* 'Pedro dressed (him/it)'. Of course, even in reflexive constructions the clitic indicates that the referent of the subject is also constructed as an object. First- and second-person clitics are used for both transitive and reflexive contexts, e.g. *Pedro me vistió* 'Pedro dressed (me)' vs. *Yo me vestí* 'I dressed (myself).' Reflexivity in Spanish is a rather complex phenomenon that can only be superficially addressed within the limits of this book. Reflexive uses of the first and second persons will generally be viewed as just particular cases of subject encoding where the event is internalized within the subject. In turn, the present discussion on object agreement will be restricted to transitive contexts proper.

Clitics evolved from Latin accusative and dative object pronouns, which in that language were stressed units with considerable positional freedom (Rivero 1986). In Spanish, they have reached a degree of grammaticalization with no parallel in most other Romance languages, which has been put in connection with the assiduous contact between Castilian and the Basque language at very early stages. The latter language has a complex conjugation system whereby both the subject and dative and accusative objects are regularly indexed by verbal morphemes (López García 2009, 57). The grammatical status of Latin object pronouns has thus undergone radical changes and, in spite of the enduring descriptive tradition whereby clitics are still labelled as "unstressed pronouns" (e.g. Barcia López 2015; Paredes García 2015), in current functional approaches it is generally accepted that they are rather more similar to agreement markers. Conversely, their relationship with coreferential stressed objects is quite similar to that between overt subjects and verbal endings (Fernández Soriano 1999a, 1226). Even so, a number of formal and functional peculiarities still point to their intermediate status between pronouns and bound morphemes in present-day Spanish, which makes them a particularly interesting area of grammatical variation and change (Pena Seijas 1999, 4324; Aijón Oliva/Borrego 2013, 93–97; Belloro 2015, 71–83).

First, clitics are unstressed units appearing in strict adjacency to the verb. In (9a), the negative particle *no* cannot be inserted between first-person *me* and the verbal root. Quite to the contrary, the coreferential first-person stressed object *a mí* can easily be separated from the verb and be formulated at different points in the clause (9b), which certifies that its relationship with the nucleus belongs to the syntactic domain rather than to the morphological one. Actually, the only linguistic element that can appear between a clitic and the verb it depends on is another clitic. In (10), if the third-person NP *los documentos* is indexed through the accusative clitic *los*, the latter needs to be inserted between *me* and the root, following a general ordering rule whereby first-person morphemes need to precede third-person ones (Perlmutter 1971, 44–45).

(9a) No me enseñó los documentos
*Me no enseñó los documentos
'He didn't (1st sing cl = *me*) show the documents.'

(9b) A mí no me enseñó los documentos
No me enseñó los documentos a mí
'He didn't (1st sing cl = *me*) show the documents to me.'

(10) No me los enseñó
'He didn't (1st sing cl = *me*) (3rd pl masc acc cl = *them*) show.'

As shown by the examples, orthographical norms still treat preverbal clitics as independent words. However, when they are formulated to the right of the verb – which in contemporary standard Spanish happens only when the verb is conjugated in an impersonal form (11) or in the imperative (12) – they must appear attached to it, even if for now we will separate them with hyphens in order to facilitate their identification. With imperative forms, at least in most European varieties, they also tend to receive a secondary stress, this being another likely remnant of their pronominal origin. Thus, in (12) *encuéntralas* would roughly be articulated as [en'kwentra'las].

(11) No es bueno remover-lo tanto
'It's no good to stir (3rd sing masc acc cl = *him/it*) so much.'

(12) Encuéntra-las
'Find (3rd pl fem acc cl = *them*).'

More importantly, not even all the units forming the paradigm of clitics seem to be equally grammaticalized, with first- and second-person forms, as well as third-person dative ones, showing further progress towards their total conversion into agreement morphemes, as suggested by their progressive loss of grammatical informations (see again Table 2.1). This probably reflects the salience prototypically associated with the direct participants, as well as with the referents of dative objects. A significant fact in this respect is the tendency of dative forms to lose number inflection and generalize singular *le* with all third-person referents, either singular or plural (Company Company 2001, 23–25; Huerta Flores 2005). This (nonstandard) solution is actually more the rule than the exception in conversation and other kinds of spoken discourse such as radio programs, as in example (13) from the corpus. The phenomenon is also hardly alien to written-press discourse (14). However, it usually happens in contexts of co-occurrence with the coreferential object (see further §2.3.2) such as these; in other words, it seems to require for referent identification to be unequivocal.

(13) ya iba siendo hora que se *le* dedicara una canción *a los chicos buenos* / que alguno tiene que quedar entre tanto maleante < Mus-Ci-230903-17:10 >
'It was high time that someone (3rd sing dat cl = *to him/her*) dedicated a song *to good boys* – I guess there must be some left amidst so many thugs.'

(14) Aunque se quede si(n) cabalgata, el barrio *le* pide *a los Reyes* una guardería, un centro para los mayores y paz para todos. <Rep-Ad-031204-21>

'Although there will be no Epiphany parade, the district (3rd sing dat cl = *to him/her*) asks *the Three Wisemen* for a kindergarten, a center for the elderly, and peace for everyone.'

In turn, singular agreement is far less usual when the plural object is at the preverbal position (*A los niños le di caramelos* 'To the children (3rd sing dat cl = *to him/her*) I gave some sweets') and when it is not formulated within the clause, having appeared in previous ones. Although number marking should in principle be less necessary with these more topical or activated referents, it can be argued that it is their higher perceptibility that forces standard plural agreement. In fact, no less than 28 (85%) of the 33 plural referents of *le* found across the corpus are nonspecific, such as the one in (13) above. As for (14), the clitic has probably become part of the culturally lexicalized construction *pedirle* [*algo*] *a los Reyes* 'to ask the Three Wisemen [for something]'. The same reasoning helps explain the lower frequency of singular agreement when *le* is used to index an audience constructed as third-person *ustedes* (see further §8.1.1).

Actually, there is synchronic evidence that the whole system of third-person clitics is undergoing a process of simplification whereby a few portmanteau forms, such as *le* and masculine accusative *lo*, are becoming able to index any referent as long as it is easy to identify in the context. This is common usage in some varieties of Spanish in contact with non-Indoeuropean languages (Fernández-Ordóñez 1999, 1343–1347). The following examples from our radio subcorpus show that *lo* can be coreferential with a grammatically feminine singular referent such as *una mezcla progresiva* 'a progressive blending' (15) and even with a feminine plural one such as *todas las asociaciones* 'all associations' (16). The solutions are of course nonstandard, but they do not appear to sound unnatural in relatively spontaneous discourse.

(15) una integración / una mezcla / progresiva pues como *lo* ha habido: y:- y lo ha:- y *lo* habrá siempre en:- / en:- / en América Latina < Var-Pu-281204-12:30 >
'An integration, a progressive blending such as there (3rd sing masc acc cl = *him/it*) has been and will always be in Latin America.'

(16) y: después: lógicamente todas las asociaciones *lo* integran personas / cada persona: / m:arca: / su línea: de acció:n <Var-On-080104-12:55>
'And then, obviously all associations (3rd sing masc acc cl = *him/it*) it is people that form. Each person will draw their own line of action.'

Moreover, Belloro's (2012; 2015) studies show that clitics can be closer to either free pronouns or bound morphemes depending on the geographical variety considered. In general, Peninsular varieties are more conservative than Canarian and American ones as regards the persistence of pronominal features inherited from Latin. To this we can add that, given the existence of diachronic and dialectal variability, it seems only natural to also expect functional differences associated with the particular syntactic and discursive context. In other words, within the same variety we may find more "pronominal" and more "affixal" uses of clitics – as already suggested by the preceding examples.

An approach to grammatical structure and usage as inherently variable makes it possible to account for all the facts reviewed so far, and provides a satisfactory answer to the question whether clitics belong in the domain of syntax or rather in that of morphology. While they still resemble independent words in a number of respects, they tend to behave like deictic-anaphoric bound morphemes. They can thus be described as *agreement markers* whereby relatively salient elements are indexed in the verbal nucleus. This is particularly evident when they co-occur with their coreferential stressed object within the clause, the latter kind of context deserving further discussion.

2.3.2 Object and clitic co-occurrence

When clitics index referents that are not formulated within the clause, they might still be described as *pronouns* filling a slot in the eventive structure. However, when both elements co-appear in the same clause (as in examples 13 and 14 above), such a view is more difficult to sustain. There has been a good deal of research on the phenomenon termed *clitic doubling* (e.g. De Kock 1998, 79–96; Correa 2003; Anagnostopoulou 2006; Belloro 2012; Hentschel 2013), which is of paramount importance to understand the functional and cognitive nature of clitics. However, in the present study this term, together with the frequent characterizations of co-occurring clitics as "pleonastic" or "redundant", will be avoided – they imply that a syntactic object can be "duplicated" with a clitic, both of them having an analogous grammatical status. Such a stance is scarcely motivated in light of the formal and functional features of these morphemes in present-day Spanish. We should rather view co-occurrence as explicit formulation together with morphematic indexation, just as happens with clause subjects whenever they are endowed with some informativeness (see again Section 2.2). It would seem scarcely intuitive to attribute clitics the capacity of filling a slot that is already occupied by a pronoun or a lexical NP. In Spanish, the formulation of two or more elements with the same function in the clause is in principle not allowed unless they appear in coordination.

Cases of co-occurrence between stressed objects and clitics are not attested in most Romance languages – with the exception of Romanian and some dialects of Italian and French (Belloro 2015, 87) – unless the object is a dislocated topic. Compare e.g. standard French (17) with Spanish (18). In the second case, there is no apparent need for a pause in speech nor a comma in writing. The respective approximate translations into English are slightly different as well; there actually seems to be no way to express the semantic nuance conveyed by the Spanish clitic. It is not fulfilling a syntactic function by itself, but just indexing its referent in the verbal nucleus, thus signalling the relatively high degree of salience it is granted in the context.

(17) La table, je vais *la* nettoyer
'The table, I'm going to clean *it*.'

(18) La mesa *la* voy a limpiar
'The table (3rd sing fem acc cl = *it*) I'm going to clean.'

Let us now review the main contexts where verbal agreement with expressed objects is mandatory, those where it rarely happens, and those where variability is observed. First, object agreement is practically categorical when the object is a personal pronoun, which obviously includes first- and second-person referents. In (19), the pronominal first-person object *a mí* needs to be indexed through the coreferential clitic *me*. In fact, all clauses where any of the direct participants is constructed as an object require clitic agreement, whether the stressed pronoun is formulated or not.

(19) <A> ¿y en qué estás trabajando? /
<B> en un taller de coches /
<A> ah mu boN:Ito: / ¿y cuándo *me* vas a arreglar *a mí* el coche? <Mus-Di-251104-13:20>
'A: So where do you work? – B: At a car repair shop. – A: Oh, cool. So, when (1st sing cl = *me*) are you going to repair my car *to me*?'

As noted by Siewierska (2004, 150), "[p]erson agreement with just the first and second persons is much more common" in languages across the world. In Spanish, the obligatoriness of clitic agreement with first and second persons when constructed as central objects is undoubtedly connected with their grammatical and discursive-cognitive status – their existence is presupposed in acts of communication, they are animate and definite entities, and they are always formulated as pronouns (see further Chapter 3). Therefore, while both the omission of the object (20a) and its expression (20b) are usually correct, the omission of the clitic (20c) is not.

(20a) Me regalaron Ø una chaqueta
(20b) Me regalaron a mí una chaqueta
(20c) *Ø regalaron a mí una chaqueta
'They (1st sing cl = *me*) gave a jacket (to me).'

Third-person pronouns also require the formulation of a coreferential clitic (Fernández Soriano 1999a, 1248), as in (21) below. This can be viewed as yet another manifestation of the grammatical relevance of animacy, given that it is rather uncommon for inanimate entities to be encoded as personal pronouns such as *él* 'he, him' or *ella* 'she, her' unless headed by prepositions indexing peripheral functions. Hence the scarce naturalness of (22a), where *a ella* stands for *la mesa* 'the table' and is constructed as a dative object with a coreferential *le*. In turn, in (22b), where *a ella* functions as an oblique and cannot be indexed with a clitic, the personal pronoun is totally acceptable. Anyhow, this also points to the influence of definiteness and of perceptibility altogether, insofar as pronouns generally denote entities that are readily identifiable in the discursive context.

(21) María es muy simpática. A ella le daremos una invitación
'María is very nice. To her (3rd sing dat cl = *to him/her*) we will give an invitation.'

(22a) La mesa está vacía. (??A ella) le pondremos un mantel
'The table is empty. On it (lit. To her) (3rd sing dat cl = *to him/her*) we will put a tablecloth.'

(22b) La mesa está vacía. Acércate a ella
'The table is empty. Get close to it (lit. to her).'

The categoricity of clitic agreement with object pronouns in dative or accusative functions has sometimes favored the perception that the stressed object is redundant with respect to the clitic, which would be the "real" object (Barrenechea/Orecchia 1970; Moure 1996, 95). However, it seems risky to attribute a redundant nature either to the object or to its coreferential clitic if it is our intention to develop a general explanation of object agreement. Moreover, it would be scarcely coherent to assume that the clitic is the basic element with pronominal objects while in other contexts to be reviewed below it is fact the verbal morpheme that is optional, and sometimes even dispreferred.

As for preverbal third-person lexical objects, clitic formulation is also the usual solution with them (example 23a); therefore, they align with first- and second-person referents and pronominal ones in general, which no doubt has much to do with the topicality associated with the initial position. Agreement can fail to occur if the preverbal object is prosodically stressed and an emphatic or contrastive interpretation is favored (Fernández Soriano 1999a, 1247), which clearly connects clitic omission with informativeness (23b). The solution, however, seems to be infrequent in actual usage; no similar instances were found across the MEDIASA corpus.

(23a) El llavero lo guardé en el bolso
'The keyring I (3rd sing masc acc cl = *him/it*) put into the handbag.'

(23b) EL LLAVERO, no el móvil, Ø guardé en el bolso
'The keyring, not the cell phone, I put into the handbag.'

Also, the clitic can be absent with indeterminate preverbal objects, as suggested by the comparison between (24a) and (24b).

(24a) El café no lo he traído
'The coffee I (3rd sing masc acc cl = *him/it*) didn't bring.'

(24b) Café no (?lo) he traído
'Coffee I didn't bring.'

Finally, the contexts imposing the strongest restrictions to object agreement are those with postverbal third-person lexical objects. It is important to note that these will in principle be the less salient, most informational referents within the domain of central syntactic functions (see §1.3.3 above). In such cases, the formulation of the coreferential morpheme is generally easier with dative objects (Weissenrieder 1995; Aijón Oliva 2006a, 264), which will be indexed through *le* or *les*, than with accusative ones. The following examples, both of which have been taken from the same opinion piece of our written-press subcorpus, illustrate how postverbal objects can be accorded different degrees of salience in connection with agreement vs. non-agreement. In (25), the clitic is formulated to index a human referent with the semantic role of beneficiary, i.e. quite close to the dative prototype – note, in passing, the use of singular *le* instead of the more standard *les*. On the other hand, in (26) agreement fails with two successive inanimate referents constructed as accusatives. Alternatives with the clitic, i.e. *El tiempo no* (?*las*) *cura las heridas abiertas* and *El tiempo* (?*lo*) *mitiga el dolor*, are clearly dispreferred, and hardly any instances of the sort were found across the corpus.

(25) Se pasan la vida –generalmente demasiado corta– enfrascados en su trabajo y en dar*le a sus hijos* lo mejor <Art-Ad-290704-4>
'They spend their lives – usually too short ones – absorbed by their jobs and trying to give (3rd sing dat cl = *to him/her*) *their children* all the best.'

(26) El tiempo, a pesar de lo que digan, no Ø cura *las heridas abiertas*, pero afortunadamente Ø mitiga *el dolor*. <Art-Ad-290704-4>
'No matter what they say, time does not heal *the open wounds*, but fortunately it does mitigate *the pain*.'

The stronger preference for agreement with dative objects appears to be shared by most varieties of Spanish (Melis/Flores 2005). However, American dialects seem to be more innovative than European ones as for the generalization of accusative agreement. It is sort of a stereotype of varieties like Argentinian Spanish to have particularly high rates of clitic agreement with postverbal, non-pronominal accusative objects such as those in (26). However, Barrenechea/Orecchia (1970) already found that the differences with other varieties were scarcely significant. More importantly, the choice is generally restricted to referents that, even if formulated after the verb, are contextually salient to some extent. Belloro (2015, 51) cites the example *Lo llamaron enseguida a un médico* 'They (3rd sing masc acc cl = *him/it*) called a doctor right away'. Even though the referent had not been previously mentioned, the discursive context – a conversational narrative about a man suffering a heart attack – had activated a particular discourse frame that probably made the appearance of a doctor expectable.[5]

All in all, the hypothesis that stressed objects are grammatically redundant might be coherent with contexts of mandatory agreement – such as first- and second-person ones – but it is obviously harder to accomodate with others where the clitic is most often omitted. It is thus the latter that would seem to be pleonastic; actually, its presence does not seem to correlate with any differences in descriptive meaning. This is what has made it possible to talk of *clitic*

5 Neuter pronouns such as *eso* 'it, that' and especially *todo* 'everything' also favor the expression of a coreferential *lo* even when postposed to the verb: *Ya lo he revisado todo* 'I have already (3rd sing neut acc cl = *it*) revised everything'. The very meaning of the latter pronoun seems to make it intrinsically salient or presupposed.

doubling and approach it as a grammatical variable in a traditional sense, i.e. as an abstract construction comprised of a set of synonymous formal realizations (see examples in Silva-Corvalán 1994, 124–148; Urrutia/Fernández 1995; Weissenrieder 1995; Moreno Fernández 2001).

Whether it is the object or the clitic that is described as pleonastic, this reveals a rather traditional view of linguistic usage whereby some elements are considered to be the "real" ones, while others merely repeat them (García-Miguel 1991, 378–379). Of course, from our theoretical approach there will always be some difference in meaning between agreeing and non-agreeing objects. To consider expressed and indexed objects as "doubled" or "repeated" is not different from applying such characterizations to expressed subjects, which would be doubled by verbal endings.[6]

It is interesting to note – and this will be a significant point for our analyses of the first and second persons – that the communicative repercussions of the choice between pronoun omission and expression also seem to be analogous for subjects and objects. Davidson (1996) observed that overt subject pronouns in Spanish add "pragmatic weight" to the utterance; when the pronoun is a first-person one, it helps underline the personal commitment of the speaker towards the content expressed, quite particularly with *verba cogitandi* and when the speaker is encoded as the clause subject (see also Aijón Oliva/Serrano 2010b; Posio 2011). Stewart (2000, §5) views expressed first-person pronouns as reducing the illocutionary force of the utterance – since they help stress its personal nature – while suggesting a stronger commitment of the speaker to its content. Aijón Oliva/ Serrano (2013, 116–117) conclude that subject expression connects the content of the utterance with the personal circumstances of the referent – thus deprives it of general validity – and helps convey higher pragmatic assertiveness. In turn, subject omission is related to the epistemic modalization of the content as shared knowledge (see further Section 4.3).

It has been pointed out that the notion of pragmatic weight as an explanation of the communicative values of subject expression in Spanish is equally applicable to object expression (De Cock 2014, 148–149). Also, Luján (1999) jointly analyzes subjects and objects when approaching the choice between referent expression and omission-indexation, led by the conviction that the conditioning factors are basically the same in both cases. The discussion so far should have

6 The latter stance can however make sense from a diachronic point of view, if we consider Givón's (1976) well-known hypothesis that expressed subjects result from the evolution of discourse topics, while verbal morphemes marking subject agreement are the outcome of subject pronouns adjacent to the verb that have become grammaticalized.

made it clear that object agreement is a significant feature of referent construction, thus can be analyzed in terms of cognitive salience and informativeness.

2.3.3 Salience and informativeness in object agreement

The indexation of dative and accusative objects through verbal clitics is undetachable from discursive-cognitive construction, as suggested by the contexts of categoricity and variation reviewed above, where grammatical person, animacy, definiteness, syntactic function and placement within the clause all appear to play some role (cf. Aijón Oliva 2006a, 313–337 and references therein). Even in constructions where an object is informationally focalized, such as *wh-* questions, the formulation of the clitic, being an atypical choice in itself, is facilitated to some extent by the presence of e.g. an animate referent. Thus clitic agreement would be acceptable in a context like (27a) if the speaker intended to suggest that he/she already knows the person in question – maybe because his interlocutor has mentioned that person before – but is not able to clearly identify them. In turn, agreement is clearly ungrammatical with inanimate referents in the same context (27b).

(27a) ¿A quién (?lo) llevaste a la casa del campo?
'Whom (3rd sing masc acc cl = *him*) did you take to the country house?'

(27b) ¿Qué (*lo) llevaste a la casa del campo?
'What did you take to the country house?'

Again, clitic formulation will be much easier when the object displays features clearly associated with the dative prototype – most clearly in co-occurrence with an accusative object, as in (28) – which points to the higher salience of this prototype, whose agreement morphemes are comparably more grammaticalized (see §2.3.1).

(28) ¿A quién le diste tu número?
'Whom (3rd sing dat cl = *him/her*) did you give your number?'

As already exposed with regard to subjects, the association of verbal agreement with salience makes it a relevant resource for discourse construction. Agreeing referents, even if they are always endowed with some salience, are more informative when explicitly formulated than when just morphematically indexed. A referent that is at the center of attention across successive clauses will usually remain activated through agreement morphemes, whether they are of a subjective or objective kind. The short excerpt in (29) shows instances of both types of morphemes, all of them denoting a previously formulated referent, namely a retired local sportsman. As shown in the translation, all indexations of the referent would need to be carried out through stressed pronouns in English.

(29) Su peor momento deportivo fue quizá aquellas olimpiadas en las que *era* favorito pero *le* pudieron los nervios. Pero lo que realmente peor *llevó* durante su carrera fueron las lesiones. Su operación de estómago y las afecciones de rodilla *le* mantuvieron lejos de la bicicleta durante largas temporadas. <Rep-Ga-290104-18>
'The lowest point in his sport career was perhaps those Olympic Games where (*he*) started as a favorite, but anxiety overwhelmed (*him*). However, what (*he*) really suffered from was injuries. His stomach operation and knee injuries kept (*him*) away from cycling for extended periods.'

In turn, the contexts with simultaneous object expression and clitic indexation discussed in §2.3.2 can be described as correlating with intermediate degrees of salience, as already noted by Belloro (2007, 131): "clitic doubling can be interpreted as the formal correlate of an intermediate level of referent accessibility, along a continuum which has weak pronouns (i.e. clitics) and lexical NPs at either end". These objects are salient enough to agree with the verb, but at the same time they are informative enough to require explicit formulation. Therefore, the three variants obtained from the combination of variable agreement and variable object expression can be placed along the salience-informativeness continuum as in Figure 2.2.

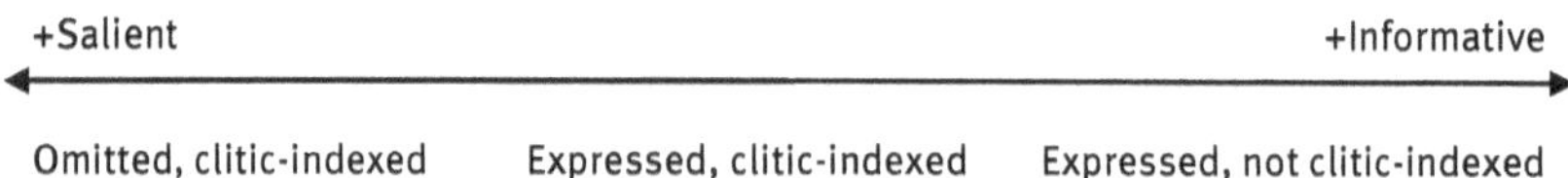

Figure 2.2: Variable agreement and expression of objects in the continuum between salience and informativeness.

The variant of expression without indexation did not appear in Figure 2.1 above since, as pointed out, agreement with subjects is categorical – or, in more precise terms, an element that does not agree with the verbal ending will not be ascribed to the subject prototype (see also Section 2.4). Expressed, non-indexed objects entail the lowest salience and highest informativeness within central syntactic functions, actually being close to the realm of peripheral ones. As exposed, this variant is mostly restricted to non-pronominal third-person objects formulated after the verb, and it becomes more frequent the more they match the prototypical features of accusatives.

Still, some objections might be posed against the systematic association between clitic agreement and referent salience, which in any case show that the outcome of particular contextual configurations is not always totally predictable, given the amount and variety of factors that need to be taken into account. Fernández Ramírez (1987, §115.4) and Fernández Soriano (1999a, 1249) note the atypical preference for clitic formulation in certain contexts where the object is a postverbal subordinate clause, thus has a very low degree of salience – it is even questionable whether or to what extent clauses are conceived as entities, although the possibility of indexing them through clitics *lo* and *le*, as well as by neuter pronouns like *esto, eso* 'it, that' confirms that they can be constructed as discursive referents. Examples (30–32), adapted from the aforementioned authors, illustrate contexts where it would be usual for the accusative clitic *lo* to appear, particularly in spontaneous conversation.

(30) ¡Ya lo creo que vas a ir!
'I sure (3rd sing neut acc cl = *it*) believe that you will go!'

(31) Te lo juro que no he hablado con ella
'I (3rd sing neut acc cl = *it*) swear to you that I didn't talk to her.'

(32) Ya se lo he dicho que vendrás
'I already (3rd sing neut acc cl = *it*) told her that you'll be coming.'

The possibility should not be discarded that, in actual usage, some of such solutions be due to the topicalization of the embedded clause to the right, or to its unpremeditated addition along the way. Also, it must be noted that most instances appear with a limited number of communication or cognition verbs, as also observed by the authors. Constructions like *Ya lo creo* 'I sure believe it' and *Te lo juro* 'I swear it to you' are highly lexicalized and apparently unanalyzable; clitic omission is even unnatural with this interpretation in (30): ?*Ya Ø creo que vas a ir*. There are actually a good number of Spanish constructions where clitics have become part of lexical items and seem to have lost their indexical capacity, e.g. *pasarlo bien* – or *pasarla bien*, in American varieties – 'to have a good time', lit. 'to go through it well'; or *Me las pagarás* 'I'll get my revenge', lit. 'You'll pay them to me'. Finally, the formulation of clitics in contexts such as those of (31) and (32) might also be prompted by the fact that the content of the utterance is in some way accessible to the speaker (see also Belloro 2015, 50–54). In fact, it would seem atypical to utter *Te lo juro que...* followed by some completely new content; rather, the construction is useful to stress something already said. This points yet again to the general association between agreement and referent salience.

2.4 Variation and choice between the subject and object prototypes

At the beginning of the present chapter it was stated that syntactic functions are prototypes that appear as a continuum of possibilities in actual usage, and that this continuum is parallel to the discursive-cognitive one between salience and informativeness. From the discussion we can conclude that the function of subject represents the grammatical expression of the most salient participant – even if a variety of contextual features can modulate its salience as against that of other participants. Obliques, adjuncts and peripheral elements are in turn associated with the pole of informativeness. For their part, dative and accusative objects occupy intermediate zones of the continuum, the dative being in principle closer to the pole of salience, given its association with animate referents and relatively autonomous semantic roles.

From the variable nature of functions it also follows that there need not be a sharp distinction between what is a subject and what is not; rather, we may well find contexts of functional oscillation. It is true that agreement through the verbal ending would appear to set up a barrier between the subject and the rest of functions – either a referent agrees with the ending, and thus it is a subject, or it does not, and thus it is an object. However, we have already alluded to some syntactic contexts where an element that would seem to qualify as subject fails to establish agreement, just as there are others where some element can unexpectedly impose its morphological features on the verbal ending, thus assume the basic functional feature of the subject and the cognitive salience associated with it.

This happens, first, in Spanish existential constructions with *haber* 'there be' (see also examples 4a, b above). In standard grammatical description they are viewed as impersonal constructions (RAE 2009, §41.6) where the verb must be conjugated in the singular third person, irrespective of the number features of the postverbal NP. However, the variant with plural subject agreement is not infrequent in media discourse, as well as in some Eastern Peninsular and American varieties (see e.g. Gómez Molina 2013; Claes 2016). Compare (33a) with nonstandard (33b). The most interesting fact to be noted is that, in a merely taxonomical analysis, the NP *grandes avances* 'great advances' would respectively be labelled as accusative object and as subject, based on verbal agreement itself.

(33a) Ha habido [3rd sing] grandes avances [acc] en cirugía ocular

(33b) Han habido [3rd pl] grandes avances [subj] en cirugía ocular
'There have been great advances in eye surgery.'

As already noted by descriptive grammarians such as Fernández Ramírez (1986, 132–133), the atypical grammatical nature of impersonal *haber* constructions can easily lead speakers to reinterpret the supposed accusative object as a syntactic subject. As pointed out, the great majority of verbs prefigure a subject in their eventive structure; in clauses where there is generally only one referent qualifying for a central syntactic function, it is understandable that speakers should tend to accord it the default one.

Passive and impersonal constructions with the verbal clitic *se* (Mendikoetxea 1999; Pedersen 2005; Aijón Oliva 2010) also show a wide range of variability as regards agreement. In the passive construction, the verb should agree with a non-prepositional NP alluding to the (usually inanimate or indefinite) patient or theme, as in (34a), where *venden* 'sell' matches third-person plural *pisos* 'apartments'. However, it is not uncommon to have the NP reanalyzed as an accusative object, with the verb conjugated in the singular third person and lacking a recoverable subject, that is, as an impersonal form (34b). In this case it would be possible to index the referent through an accusative clitic if it were placed at the preverbal position of the clause or had been mentioned in a previous one, that is, if it had some salience: *Se los vende*, which can be taken as confirmation that it has been constructed as an object.

(34a) Se venden [3rd pl] pisos [subj]

(34b) Se vende [3rd sing] pisos [acc]
'Apartments are sold/[One] is selling apartments.'

Conversely, in the standard impersonal construction with *se*, the verbal nucleus governs a (generally animate) object headed by the particle *a*. The latter should block the possibility of agreement, since subjects in Spanish must in principle be non-prepositional (35a). Although the solution in (35b) might appear to violate a basic rule of grammatical agreement, it is relatively frequent in contemporary

Spanish, including media discourse (Azofra Sierra 2010, 153). No examples were found in the corpus, but (36) shows one from an external written-press source.

(35a) Se castigó [3rd sing] a todos los culpables [acc]

(35b) Se castigaron [3rd pl] a todos los culpables [subj]
'All the culprits were punished', lit. '[One] punished all the culprits.'

(36) Además, afirmó que el país se centraría en la mejora de la atención de los centros hospitalarios en los que *se atienden a los recién nacidos y sus madres*. [www.actuall.com; accessed 4/14/2018]
'Besides, she stated that the country would focus on improving medical care at the hospitals where newborns and their mothers are looked after (lit. [one] looks after newborns and their mothers).'

In these cases, the capacity of the particle *a* to block subject agreement seems to be overcome by the animacy of the referent and, perhaps more importantly, by the fact that the latter is the only central participant in the clause, which is the most significant contextual condition shared by all the constructions reviewed so far. Even when the referent can be characterized as an accusative object, as in (35a), it is hardly a prototypical one, rather approaching the formal and semantic features associated with datives. Besides, in constructions with *se* it has been common for agreement to be carried out through the dative forms *le/les* from early stages of the language (*Se les castigó*) rather than the a priori more coherent accusative ones (*Se los castigó*) (Santiago 1975, 95–98). Still, many geographical varieties tend to interpret these contexts as of accusative proper (Fernández-Ordóñez 1999, 1338).

Therefore, the presence of only one participant that can be accorded a central function appears to be the main contextual condition for subject-object encoding variability. If the punisher(s) in (35a, b) were constructed into the event instead of being concealed through the impersonal variant, they would prototypically appear as the subject, while the punished ones would be the accusative object, e.g. *El director castigó a los culpables* 'The headmaster punished the culprits'. Likewise, even if *advances* in (33b) hardly matches any of the features prototypically associated with subjects, being an indefinite, inanimate, postverbal NP that in the more standard variant (33a) is encoded as an accusative, it may still qualify for establishing subject agreement in the absence of any other element with higher salience within the event. The existence of only one central participant will often trigger an attraction of the verbal inflection, which will come to match its person and number features, even in cases where the solution is rejected by grammatical norms.

The variability between passivization and impersonality in constructions with *se* is actually a complex issue, showing the tensions between the general rules of grammar and the cognitive interpretation of events and their participants, and is of great usefulness for the study of the continuum between salience and informativeness. However, even the most prototypical impersonal verbs, i.e. those constructing weather phenomena (*llover* 'to rain', *amanecer* 'to dawn'), can come to agree with an NP in metaphorical uses (see example 8b above). Also, they often co-appear with locative elements that seem to occupy the functional slot of the subject: *Aquí llueve mucho* 'Here (it) rains a lot' (Fernández Soriano 1999b; Fábregas 2014).

As has also been observed, the fluctuation between subject and object encoding may occur in either direction and is connected with semantic features of the referent such as animacy and definiteness. Inanimate subjects in passive constructions can be reinterpreted as the objects of impersonal ones, just as animate objects in impersonals can be reinterpreted as the subjects of passives. Depending on a range of variable features at the syntactic, semantic and discursive levels, the referent agreeing with the verb will approach the prototype of subject to a higher or lower degree. In fact, traditional descriptive grammars used to describe the subject as "the one who carries out the action indicated by the verb" or "what is being talked about", thus taking either the prototypical semantic role of the subject – *agent* – or its most usual discursive status – *topic* – as its defining feature (Bosque/Gutiérrez-Rexach 2009, 272; Pruñonosa/Serra 2011, 214–215). Such definitions, just as the functional consideration of the subject as "the element that agrees with the verbal ending in person and number", are all incomplete in the sense that they fail to recognize that it is only the *prototype* of subject that can be defined, and that this needs to be done by considering a variety of features at different levels.

In spite of the realization that the frontier between subjects and verbal objects is not as clearcut as it might seem, in the case of the first and second persons it must also be noted that the existence of different pronouns and agreement morphemes for either function would seem to widen the gap between them. That is, while a non-prepositional third-person NP such as *el libro* 'the book' can function either as subject (37) or as accusative object (38) with no formal alterations, this is apparently not possible with the singular first person, as can be observed in the examples. A first-person subject will be formulated as *yo* and an object as (*a*) *mí*. These units will respectively correlate with a subject-agreeing verbal ending such as *-í* and with the object-agreeing verbal clitic *me*.

(37) Yo le- í el libro
I read 1ST.SING.PAST the book
'I read the book.'

(38) A mí el libro me sorprend- ió
To me the book 1ST.SING.CL surprise 3RD.SING.PAST
'The book surprised me.'

There are quite numerous and recurrent syntactic constructions like (38) in Spanish where a human cognizer or experiencer, most often the speaker or the addressee, is not encoded as a subject – as would seem expectable from the perspective of perceptibility – but as a central object. This happens with epistemic verbs (*parecer* 'to seem') and others indicating psychological assessments (*gustar* 'to please', *interesar* 'to interest') or processes (*asustar* 'to scare', *preocupar* 'to worry', *sorprender* 'to surprise', etc.). What the example shows is that there is also some fuzziness between subject and object encoding in monotransitive constructions of this sort, which again reveal the aforementioned tension between grammatical rules, which make the referent be encoded as an object, and cognitive salience, which makes it approach many of the features associated with subjects. In spite of its syntactic function, the referent tends to become the main viewpoint for discourse construction and interpretation, as also suggested by its strong tendency to preverbal placement (see further Sections 4.3, 4.4). Actually, there are nonstandard solutions in spoken discourse where the experiencer is formulated as a subject pronoun but establishes object rather than subject agreement. This happens most often with the singular first person. In (39), taken from the radio subcorpus, we find *yo me parece* 'I (1st sing cl) it seems' instead of the standard *a mí me parece* 'to me (1st sing cl) it seems'.

(39) *yo me parece* que- ¡hombre! / que es muy:- sobre todo es muy / m:uy pobre muy pobre decir / e: a todos durante quince días de campaña: / que tu único objetivo en: la vida como grupo político como (org)anización política es / desbancar a La(n)zarote <Var-Co-230503-12:40>
'*I* (1st sing cl = *to me*) it seems that, well, it's sad, it's very sad that anyone should spend fifteen days of the campaign telling everyone that their only goal in life as a political group, as a political organization, is to oust L. from his seat.'

Other variable features such as the preference for preverbal placement within the clause suggest that first- and second-person objects, due to the inherent salience of their referents, are cognitively quite closer to subjects than to third-person objects. Note that in (38) above the first-person pronoun *a mí* is clearly topicalized, appearing even before the subject *el libro*. Also, the distinction between two kinds of central objects (accusative and dative) in these persons is scarcely motivated on merely formal grounds – the same tonic pronouns and clitics are used for either function. The implications of the sincretism between objects will be discussed in Chapter 3. Let us now review the formal and semantic variability between the accusative and dative prototypes by paying attention to third-person contexts.

2.5 Variation and choice between the object prototypes

Even in such contexts, it is often difficult to elucidate whether an element should be described as an accusative/direct object or as a dative/indirect one. While subject-object variability is generally observed in clauses with only one participant whose salience is amenable to modulation through grammatical choice, accusative-dative variability is basically found in monotransitive clauses with a subject and another central participant whose syntactic and semantic features do not clearly match those of either the accusative or the dative prototype. In turn, in ditransitive contexts the distribution of functions, together with the contrast in salience it entails, is usually much more evident. The latter case is illustrated in (40), where *mi madre* 'my mother' has an animate, definite referent; plays the semantic role of beneficiary, i.e. a relatively autonomous one; is preceded by the object particle *a*; and establishes verbal agreement through the clitic *le*. In turn, the accusative *unos libros* 'some books' has basically the opposite features: inanimacy and indefiniteness, the non-autonomous semantic role of theme, lack of object marking, and lack of verbal agreement. The contrast between both objects could have been made even stronger, for example, had the dative object been formulated at the preverbal position and thus made topical (*A mi madre le regalé unos libros*).

(40)	Le	regal-	é	a mi madre	unos libros
	3RD.SING.DAT.CL	give	1ST.SING.PAST	to my mother	some books

'I gave some books to my mother.'

However, in other ditransitive contexts the objects, and particularly the dative, can approach different functional prototypes, including peripheral ones, as will be discussed below. Once again it is important to be aware of the danger of circularity whenever matters of functional encoding are addressed. The decision on what kind of object a referent is constructed as – provided such a decision needs to be made in the first place – can only be based on the particular features associated with each functional prototype, starting with verb agreement. It may well be argued that the truly relevant task is not to label elements according to some functional taxonomy, but to discover what their formal, semantic and discursive features can tell us about their cognitive interpretation, based on salience and informativeness.

As for monotransitive clauses, García-Miguel (2015, 235–236) notes that many Spanish verbs contemplating only one central object in their eventive structure oscillate between the construction of the latter as an accusative and as a dative, depending on a wide range of contextual factors including object marking, agency vs. patienthood, or preverbal vs. postverbal placement. The only feature that could in principle be put forward as a systematic criterion for functional differentiation is again agreement. As shown in Table 2.1 above, the paradigm of Spanish clitics has inherited case distinctions from Latin, resulting in the existence of *lo*/*los* (masculine, neuter) and *la*/*las* (feminine) for the accusative vs. *le*/*les* for the dative. However, this system is subject to wide variability in many geographical varieties, dative clitics appearing with verbs a priori selecting an accusative object and vice versa. The detailed analysis of the phenomena usually termed *leísmo*, *laísmo* and *loísmo* (Fernández-Ordóñez 1999; Klein-Andreu 2000; DeMello 2002; Flores Cervantes 2006) is outside the scope of the present investigation.[7] But if, as we have seen, the frontier between subjects and objects is sometimes fuzzy, no less should be expected from that between the object prototypes, both of which use the same morphological procedure for verbal agreement, only with supposedly different forms. Other relevant formal and semantic differences between them have been instantiated in (40) or previous examples across this chapter:

a) Datives tend to have animate referents, while accusatives tend to have inanimate ones.
b) Datives are associated with more autonomous semantic roles, such as beneficiary, experiencer and owner, while accusatives are associated with less autonomous ones, such as patient and theme.
c) Expressed dative objects are marked with the particle *a*, while accusatives are usually unmarked unless they are animate and definite.

7 It will however be necessary to consider them in relation to displaced second persons, which match the formal features of third ones (see Chapter 8).

d) When formulated as postverbal lexical NPs, it is more frequent and acceptable for datives than accusatives to establish clitic agreement with the verbal nucleus.
e) The possibility of being constructed as the subject of a passive paraphrasis is restricted to accusatives, but even among the latter it is subject to severe restrictions, being natural only with highly transitive clauses: *El coche fue robado* 'The car was stolen' vs. ??*El coche fue tenido* 'The car was had'.

Of course, an apparently accusative object can display some features associated with datives and thus approach the latter prototype to a certain extent. Referents formulated as personal pronouns will necessarily be marked with the particle *a*, just as datives are: *La eligieron* *(*a*) *ella* 'They elected [to] her'. In turn, indeterminate lexical NPs are usually unmarked: *Eligieron* (?*a*) *representantes* 'They elected representatives'. Also note the different solutions as regards the formulation of agreement clitics. Variable features such as the ones cited are parallel to gradations in salience and informativeness.

If the existence of case distinctions in third-person clitics has been used to justify the distinction of two types of central objects in Spanish, it is interesting to observe that many verbal lexemes can take either case in similar contexts, the choice again being undetachable from semantic and discursive factors (Roegiest 2005). Compare accusative *la* with dative *le* with the verb *asustar* 'to scare' in the following examples:

(41) A María la asustó Pedro acercándose por detrás
'María (3rd sing fem acc cl = *her*) Pedro scared by approaching from behind.'

(42) A María le asusta pensar en el futuro
'María (3rd sing dat cl = *to him/her*) it scares to think of the future.'

Whitley (1998, 119) notes that speakers tend to choose "accusative when they perceive a relatively forceful or active impact, and dative for a weaker effect". In (41) there is a human and agentive subject, *Pedro*, that carries out a clearly delimited action, in a perfective tense, on an object that is interpreted as being directly affected by the event. All this coherently correlates with the choice of an accusative clitic that underlines the patienthood and, more generally, the lack of autonomy attributed to its referent. On the other hand, in (42) *María* is constructed not as patient but as the experiencer of a feeling provoked by an inanimate subject – actually a complement clause, thus scarcely salient. Besides, the present simple suggests that the event is seen as an ongoing process rather than a delimited action. In this second context, the (dative) object is cognitively not far from what in a different eventive structure would have been constructed as the subject. Interestingly, the clitics we have taken to be the most expectable ones in either example can hardly be considered necessary choices, particularly in (42), where it would seem quite possible for a speaker to opt for accusative *la*, with the intention to e.g. suggest that thinking of the future causes the referent some suffering, as a more transitive event would do.

The dative as a functional prototype shares some features with the subject and others with the accusative, which situates it halfway between them in the continuum from salience to informativeness. García (1975, 99, 134) already described the dative in Spanish as the participant having an intermediate degree of *activity*, this concept being similar to ours of autonomy. There is some tendency to formulate it before the accusative in ditransitive constructions, particularly when the referent is animate and specific (Company Company 2001, 28–29); also, it is more often omitted from the clause, in accordance with its higher rates of verbal agreement (Comrie 2012, 20). Finally, the possibility of being encoded as the subject of a passive paraphrasis is restricted to accusatives. All these formal and functional features, summed up in Figure 2.3, suggest that the dative correlates with more salient – perceptible, autonomous and accessible – referents than the accusative does.[8]

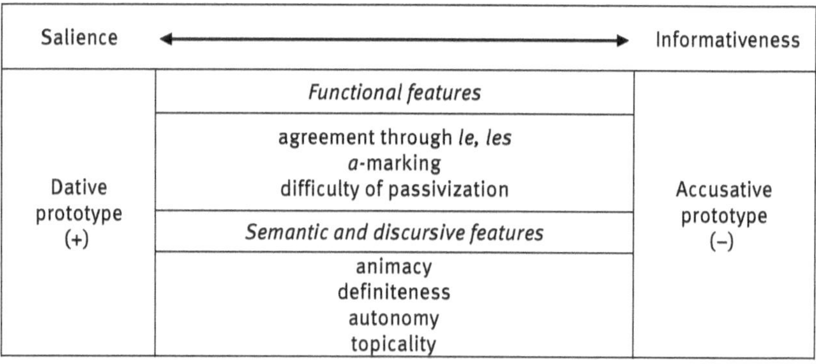

Figure 2.3: Linguistic features in the continuum between the central object prototypes.

8 The cognitive primacy of the dative over the accusative appears to be based on general cognitive principles related to human experience. For example, Vitale (1981, 44–47) notes that in Swahili two-object clauses the verb is typically made to agree with the dative (*indirect*) object; however, in monotransitive constructions with animate direct objects, agreement with the latter also happens.

There is still some controversy on whether the accusative/dative distinction is valid or in any case useful for the grammatical analysis of Spanish. Company Company (2001) contends that this language has evolved from the differential case marking of Latin towards a typological alignment with languages where the relevant distinction is that between a *primary* and a *secondary* object. Such an evolution would be tied to the usually higher cognitive salience of dative object referents, and would be evidenced by a number of variable features across dialects and historical stages. For instance, when a dative object with a plural human referent is cliticized through the number-invariable form *se* – as always happens in contiguity with an accusative clitic (e.g. *Se* [dat] *lo* [acc] *di a ellos* 'I gave it to them') – many American varieties of Spanish will transfer the plural morpheme *-s* to the latter clitic, even if the solution might seem constructionally illogical (*Se los di a ellos*, with the plural form *los* actually having a singular referent). For the author, this is evidence that the primary object tends to impose its grammatical features on the verbal nucleus: since *se* cannot be pluralized, number agreement is transferred to the clitic denoting the secondary object. However, some other points in Company's argumentation are disputable (cf. García-Miguel 2015, 214–216). The main conclusion to be drawn is that, no matter how we may label and describe the object prototypes, the role played by salience in their differentiation is difficult to overstate.

The distinction between salience and centrality (§1.3.1b) is also necessary to fully understand the cognitive nature of datives. While the participant encoded as dative is usually more salient than the accusative and less salient than the subject, at the same time it is less central to the event than both of them. As we know, their semantic role can be that of beneficiary, owner or experiencer, among other possibilities depending on the context, but in any case they are not conceived as patients or themes of actions. In other words, their participation in the transaction of energy is not a direct one, which seems to justify their usual characterization as *indirect objects*.[9] Their presence is also

9 However, datives can also be thought to have different degrees of patienthood, thus of semantic closeness to the accusative prototype, depending on the event. In *Juan le rompió un brazo a Pedro*, lit. 'Juan (3rd sing dat cl = *to him/her*) broke an arm to Pedro', it would seem equally possible to argue that *Pedro* is interpreted as the owner of the arm – this being the supposed semantic role of the dative in this context – or as a patient of the whole action. Also significant is the case of the verb *pegar* 'to hit', lit. 'to paste', taking a dative object that denotes the patient of a physical aggression. In this construction an accusative object denoting what is "pasted" has come to be regularly elided, e.g. *Luis le pegó* [*un puñetazo*] *a su hermano* 'Luis (3rd sing dat cl = *to him/her*) pasted [a punch] to his brother'. In fact, the verb shows some tendency to select accusative clitics, even in varieties adjusting to etymological distinctions: *Denunció a su marido porque la pegó* 'She denounced her husband because he (3rd sing

often less indispensable for the clause to be well-formed and for the event to be readily interpretable. In Spanish, dative clitics are in fact recurrently used to introduce participants that are not even contemplated in the eventive structure, suggesting they nonetheless have some kind of involvement (see Section 3.4).

The lesser centrality of datives also explains the fact that they can approach either the formal and semantic features associated with subjects or, on the other side of the centrality-peripherality continuum, those of prepositional obliques, and even those of adjuncts (cf. Cifuentes/Llopis 1996, 49–61; Aijón Oliva 2006a, 216–234). These are non-central functions in the sense that they cannot establish verbal agreement through clitics. There are many postverbal third-person NPs headed by the particle *a* whose functional characterization is ambiguous between the dative and the oblique, which translates into variable acceptability of clitic agreement. Such acceptability is often related to the animate vs. inanimate character of the object referent, which in turn correlates with slightly different interpretations of the event itself and the role played by the referent within it. A verb like *pertenecer* 'to belong' will help illustrate this point.

(43a) Este coche pertenece a la alcaldesa/Le pertenece
'This car belongs to the mayor.'

(43b) Este coche pertenece a una serie limitada/??Le pertenece/Ø Pertenece a ella
'This car belongs to a limited series.'

In (43a), the object headed by the particle *a*, whose referent is a definite human being, easily admits verbal agreement through the dative form *le*. On the other hand, in (43b) the formulation of the morpheme is scarcely natural. The inanimate object only seems to be commutable for a stressed pronoun (*Pertenece a ella*), which supports its functional characterization as an oblique. The difference between both examples is parallel to divergent interpretations of the event; whereas in the first one the verb retains its literal meaning of possession, in the second one it merely indicates inclusion within a certain group. The semantic role played by the object is accordingly quite different in each case.

Similarly, the following pair with *afectar* 'to affect' shows how different functional descriptions (dative vs. oblique) are favored depending on the

fem acc cl = *her*) hit', which means that the dative is reinterpreted as an accusative in the absence of another referent.

animacy of the referent and the transitivity of the clause. It is easy to perceive that only in (44a) is the referent affected in a relatively literal sense.

(44a) Este problema afecta a muchas personas/Les afecta
'This problem affects many people.'

(44b) Este problema afecta a la propia estructura social/?Le afecta/Ø Afecta a ella
'This problem affects social structure itself.'

Interestingly, the co-occurrence of objects and verbal clitics seems to be dispreferred even in contexts like (44a): *Este problema* (?*les*) *afecta a muchas personas.* This can be interpreted as a further suggestion that these datives are placed right on the border between central and peripheral clause grammar. The clitic would be much easier to formulate with preverbal objects: *A muchas personas les afecta ese problema*, in connection with the higher salience entailed by this position.

In the case of the first and second persons, the obligatoriness of agreement whenever they are constructed as *a*-marked central objects problematizes the accusative vs. dative distinction (see further Section 3.3). In turn, it draws a relatively neat distinction between central objects and those that do not readily accept object agreement. For example, with *referirse* 'to refer' it does not seem possible to index the first-person oblique *a mí* through a clitic (45a, b). Also, (46) is an example taken from the corpus of a construction where clitic formulation seems impossible (*por lo que* (**me*) *respecta a mí*) and the object matches the functional prototype of oblique. In fact, the construction itself is a clearly grammaticalized one, used for the explicit topicalization of a referent and with little functional variation.

(45a) En su discurso se refirió a mí

(45b) *En su discurso se me refirió
'In his speech he referred to me.'

(46) pues no lo sé / mira • hasta cierto punto / por lo que Ø respezta *a mí* maja yo ni m(e) había enterao que (la campaña) era: / a tal efezto <Var-On-281204-13:35>
'Well, I don't know. To some point, and as regards *me*, dear, I hadn't realized that [the campaign] was pursuing such a goal.'

In the case of verbs of motion like *acercarse* 'to approach', both the oblique (47a) and dative (47b) constructions are possible with first- and second-person referents. The semantic interpretation of either construction will of course not be identical. In the first case, the participant is viewed as the destination proper of the displacement; in the second one, it is understood as more of a beneficiary. Also, in (47b) the pronominal object can be contextually omitted, given that it is already indexed through the clitic.

(47a) El perro se Ø acercó a mí

(47b) El perro se me acercó (a mí)
'The dog (1st sing cl = *me*) approached me.'

However, with an inanimate third-person object such as *la casa* 'the house', clitic agreement is again dispreferred in these contexts (47c). If formulated (47d), it will result in the metaphorical humanization of the house. This shows yet again the association between verbal agreement and more salient referents.

(47c) El perro se Ø acercó a la casa

(47d) ??El perro se le acercó (a la casa)
'The dog approached the house.'

Even though the main goal of the present section was to discuss variation between accusative and dative objects, the preceding examples have helped us show that syntactic objects can also approach other functional descriptions according to the context. We can conclude that the functional-cognitive continuum between the accusative and dative prototypes correlates with wide variability in actual usage. This even affects the basic functional features supposedly distinguishing between them, i.e. dative vs. accusative clitic agreement, as well as object marking vs. non-marking with the particle *a*. The perceptibility of the referent, including its degree of animacy and definiteness, can be decisive as regards the assimilation of the object to a certain syntactic prototype. Besides, other variable features connected with autonomy and accesibility, including explicit formulation vs. omission-indexation, as well as placement within the clause, can also condition the functional description and cognitive interpretation of any discursive referent.

2.6 Summary

An approach to grammar as inherently variable and designed to serve communicative needs implies for grammatical categories and functions to be viewed as prototypes that choices in actual discourse will approach to different extents. In Spanish, verbal agreement, consisting of the indexation of referents in the clause nucleus through verbal endings and verbal clitics marked for person and number, is the basic feature characterizing central clause functions. Together with other formal, semantic and discursive features related to salience and informativeness – animacy, definiteness, agentivity, topicality, etc. – agreement makes it possible to describe three prototypes of central functions in this language, which have been respectively labelled *subject, accusative object* and *dative object*. The accusative is associated with the lowest salience among them, while the dative is associated with the lowest centrality, usually denoting participants that are only indirectly involved in the event.

The observation of actual usage reveals wide areas of variability among these prototypes, where manifold combinations of the features associated with each of them are possible. In clauses with only one central participant, the latter can variably agree with the verbal ending, and consequently be described as either a subject or an object. In two-participant clauses, there is usually an evident contrast between the subject and the object; however, with psychological and other verbs selecting the cognizer or experiencer as an object, the distribution of salience vs. informativeness is often far from that of the prototypical clause. Also, in monotransitive contexts the object will often oscillate between the accusative and dative functional characterizations, as shown by the variability in clitic choice and marking of the object with *a*. Again, the degree of perceptibility, autonomy and accessibility of the referent will strongly condition its functional description; this includes, among other things, the extent to which it is viewed as affected by the action of the subject. Finally, there is also variation between dative and oblique objects, as manifested in their variable easiness for clitic agreement. All this reflects the inseparability between grammatical choice and discursive-cognitive construction.

The first two chapters of this book have developed the basic principles of a functional-cognitive approach to grammatical choice as the construction of meaning. In Chapter 3 we will turn to the general linguistic features of the Spanish first and second persons, which are the main interest of the empirical investigation to be developed. In real discourse, these persons show a strong tendency to assume the formal and semantic features associated with the prototype of subject, as a consequence of the inherent salience of the direct participants. Their construction as syntactic objects will therefore be seen as a more marked choice with the capacity to generate particular communicative effects in context. We will subsequently conduct a preliminary quantitative and qualitative analysis of the first- and second-person objects found across the corpus. This will make it possible to test a hypothesis thas has already been hinted at across the present chapter, namely that there is just one prototype of central object with these persons. It will be shown that first- and second-person objects tend to compete with the clause subject for the position of highest salience. This is also evidenced by the occasional use of first- and second-person clitics that do not correlate with objects prefigured in the eventive structure, but have the power to make their referents present in discourse.

3 The first and second persons: discourse in grammar

3.1 The discursive-cognitive value of grammatical persons: From anaphora and deixis to reference

The category of person – a particularly relevant one in the majority of human languages – results from the grammaticalization of the expressions used by speakers to refer to themselves (first person), their interlocutors (second person) or other entities not directly involved in the communicative exchange (third person). In languages like Spanish, person marking is found in a variety of morphemes, including stressed pronouns (e.g. *yo* 'I', *ti* 'to you (sing.)'), verbal endings (*leía-mos* 'we used to read', *leía-n* 'they used to read'), verbal clitics (*te vi* 'I saw you (sing.)', *los vi* 'I saw them') or possessives (*tu* 'your', *nuestro* 'ours'). As has often been noted, there are significant functional and cognitive differences between the first and second persons on one side and the third one on the other, to the point that their traditional inclusion within a unitary category is far from uncontroversial. Benveniste (1966, 255) concluded that the third person does not really belong to the category and should be labelled the *non-person*. Bhat (2004, 4) points out that "we need to differentiate between (i) personal pronouns (especially of first and second persons) on the one hand and (ii) the remaining pronouns on the other", the latter being more accurately termed *proforms*. This is mainly because "[t]he function of first and second person pronouns is primarily to indicate the two principal speech roles, namely that of 'being the speaker' and 'being the addressee' respectively" (2004, 6). Even so, the consideration of some non-Western languages shows that two-person morphological systems are hardly a linguistic universal (2004, 134). Siewierska (2010, 42), while assuming the existence of three different persons, underlines the higher cognitive accessibility of the first and second ones. Third-person referents are more often expressed in discourse, in accordance with their usually higher informativeness, and can adopt a wider variety of formulations.

According to López García (1998, 502), first- and second-person pronouns should actually be described as nouns, given that they readily designate a particular extradiscursive entity, not some referent *within* discourse. This would be supported by the fact that no NP can usually be formulated in the grammatical slot of one of these forms: *Yo soy mexicano/*Miguel soy mexicano* ('I am Mexican/Miguel am Mexican'). However, cases of apparent agreement between third-person NPs and plural first- or second-person verbal endings in Spanish, e.g. *Los profesores somos muy exigentes* 'Teachers (we) are very demanding'

https://doi.org/10.1515/9783110643442-004

(see Section 2.2 above) could be viewed as counterexamples. They at least suggest the convenience of distinguishing between singular and plural persons, the latter having a much wider referential capacity that can include entities external to the communicative exchange. In any case, it is most often assumed that first- and second-person grammatical forms are always deictic (Fernández Soriano 1999a, 1213).

In turn, third-person forms do have pronominal features proper, since they act as substitutives for nouns that can be recovered from the discursive or situational context (see also Bosque/Moreno Cabrera 1990, 45). In a similar vein, a distinction was proposed in Aijón Oliva (2006a, 183–185) between *primary* and *secondary deixis*, based on the assumption that the primary or direct referents of third-person morphemes are actually not entities, but rather the NPs designating the latter. In other words, they do not establish a direct but mediated relationship with entities, unlike what (apparently) happens with forms indexing the direct participants. The latest grammar by the Real Academia (RAE 2009, §16.1a) groups together proper nouns and first- and second-person pronouns under the label of *unique designative resources* – they cannot be thought to substitute any coreferential elements in the discursive context, but rather to designate particular extradiscursive entities.

Neither are such proposals free from controversy. For one thing, demonstrative pronouns can point to a referent for which no NP is clearly retrievable from the discursive context, but whose identification is still unequivocal in the communicative situation, e.g. *¿Qué es eso?* 'What is that?' The label *unique designative resources* would thus seem to be applicable to these pronouns in such contexts. In fact, and contrary to the more traditional intuition, anaphoric reference does not appear to be the essential function of third-person morphemes. They are not necessarily substitutes nor do they repeat previously mentioned nouns or NPs, as was already inferred from our discussion of object agreement (Section 2.3; see also García Salido 2013, 56–58 on anaphora). It would seem more appropriate to state that, just as first-and second person forms, they are mainly *deictic*, i.e. their reference can be retrieved from the non-linguistic context. However, the kind of deixis they establish is not a directly extradiscursive one; they can more accurately be viewed as pointing to elements of the cognitive scene that is constructed through discourse (Cornish 1999, 25–26). The discursive continuity of a referent through deictic-anaphoric elements such as agreement morphemes is, according to the same author, a signal of "referential and attentional continuity" (1999, 63), i.e. of accessibility in our terms.

In fact, the usual view of first- and second-person forms as inherently deictic is also troublesome. It can hardly explain, for instance, why there are frequent uses of the second person that do not index a particular interlocutor, but rather are applicable to anyone in certain circumstances, and often most evidently to the speaker him/herself: *Cuando eres joven, no te preocupas por la vejez* 'When you are young, you don't worry about growing old' (see further §6.2.3). As regards the plural persons, deixis is often just partial, since their reference can include external people who need not be present, and may even be nonspecific or unknown to the speaker (*Todos buscamos la felicidad* 'We all seek happiness'). As in other cases, assuming the inseparability between linguistic choice and cognitive construction makes it possible to solve apparent contradictions that have been the source of much unfruitful debate to this day.

The distinction between deixis and anaphora is often not straightforward in the actual uses of indexical units (cf. Fossard/Garnham/Cowles 2012), nor is it really motivated from a cognitive point of view, as already noted by Ariel (1990, 5–7). The general phenomenon of *reference* operates with respect to the mental representation of entities – what is termed *cognitive construction* in this book – and not to the entities themselves. Also, most languages use the same forms for deictic and anaphoric functions indistinctly, as is the case with demonstratives (Dixon 2003; see, however, Jauncey 2011, 93 for an apparent exception in an Austronesian language). For these reasons, the term *reference* seems more adequate to describe the function of discursively indexing – by grammatical and/or lexical means – an entity that may be present in the discursive, the extradiscursive and/or the cognitive domains. The second of these, corresponding to the so-called "real world", is clearly amenable to invention or deception, for example when imaginary characters and events are introduced in narrative discourse. However, the extradiscursive (non-)existence of what is talked about does not necessarily condition the form of discourse nor its cognitive interpretation. Similarly, an event constructed by linguistic means cannot be considered to be discursively and cognitively less "real" just because it did not take place in the empirical world. Language use is the choice of certain forms aimed at constructing certain meanings in the minds of people, i.e. creating a particular cognitive reality that is not equatable to reality in the empirical sense, but need not be less relevant to people than the latter.[1]

1 In short, deixis does not depend on whether the referents are or not "real" or whether they are or not present in the communicative context, but rather on their cognitive representation. The referential function is inherent to the first- and second-person forms to be studied and justifies their very existence within the linguistic system. Also, reference is largely subjective; it concerns the way a speaker conceptualizes some scene and its participants (De Cock 2014, 27).

This view of facts also has quite significant repercussions for the understanding of Spanish first- and second-person forms. Contrary to what common sense might suggest, as well as to what most grammatical descriptions have assumed, first-person elements do not necessarily denote the actual person speaking or writing, but rather *the speaker* as a communicative role (Siewierska 2004, 1–2; Gardelle/Sorlin 2015, 2–3) and, from the approach adopted here, *the speaker* as a discursive-cognitive construction that can only be realized by means of language. In other words, the primary function of a pronoun like *yo* 'I' is not to refer to the actual person who is speaking or writing, but rather to construct *the speaker* into an event and a discursive context, which in turn will condition how the latter are interpreted. Being *the speaker* entails a set of communicative rights and duties, together with a particular cognitive status (see also Section 4.1). The same can be said of the singular second person, used to construct *the addressee* (Section 6.1), as well as of their respective plural variants, which pose further difficulties for referential interpretation (Sections 5.1–5.2; 7.1–7.2).

Therefore, rejecting the usual distinction between deixis and anaphora and replacing it with the more integrative, discursive-cognitive notion of *reference* appears to be an advantageous choice for the kind of investigation proposed here. It is still true that the extradiscursive side of reference can prove crucial for the understanding of how these persons are used in actual discourse, which will make it necessary to extensively discuss their respective referential possibilities across the following chapters. But, as pointed out, the cognitive implications of reference go far beyond the mere connection between linguistic elements and extralinguistic entities.

3.1.1 First- and second-person forms in Spanish

Together with the singular first and second persons constructing the speaker and the addressee, as well as their plural variants, it must be noted that in Spanish, much like in other Romance languages, there is an additional singular and plural second-person subparadigm that has usually been described as "formal" or "respectful". It is represented by the stressed pronouns *usted* and *ustedes*, respectively coming from the third-person NP *vuestra merced* 'your mercy' and its plural (Lapesa 2000). In grammatical terms, they should actually be described as third persons rather than second ones. When they are encoded as subjects, they correlate with third-person verb inflections; in object contexts, they are indexed through third-person clitics, e.g. *La*$_i$ *llamé a usted*$_i$ 'I (3rd sing acc fem cl = *her*) called you'. In turn, a functional-cognitive approach to grammar makes it preferable to consider them a peculiar kind of second persons (see also García 2009,

49; Aijón Oliva/Serrano 2013, 112–113). Here we will use the label *displaced second persons* to refer to this non-prototypical way of indexing interactional partners through third-person forms (see further Section 8.1).

Table 3.1 presents an overview of the referential elements available in standard European Spanish for the encoding of the first and second persons in central syntactic functions, namely subjects and accusative/dative objects. The table includes four types of grammatical forms – subject pronouns, subject verbal endings, object pronouns and object verbal clitics. As already exposed, there are no formal distinctions between the accusative and dative cases in these persons. An exception would be the displaced second persons, which, being formally third-person subparadigms, are further marked for gender in the accusative case (*lo/los* vs. *la/las*). However, it will be shown that in the corpus analyzed they correlate with dative, gender-unmarked *le/les* in all syntactic contexts, thus resembling the behavior of first and second persons proper. Apart from this, the only instances of gender marking across the paradigm are those of stressed plural pronouns *nosotros/nosotras* and *vosotros/vosotras*, the feminine variants also being mostly absent from the corpus.

Table 3.1: First- and second-person referential morphemes in European Spanish.

Person	**Subject pronouns**	**Subject verbal endings**	**Object pronouns**	**Object verbal clitics**
Singular first	Yo	-o, -oy, -é, -í, Ø	(*a*) mí	me
Plural first	nosotros, -as	-mos	(*a*) nosotros, -as	nos
Singular second	Tú	-s, -ste, Ø	(*a*) ti	te
Plural second	vosotros, -as	-is, -d	(*a*) vosotros, -as	os
Displaced singular second	usted	-a, -e, -o, Ø	(*a*) usted	le [dat], la/lo [acc]
Displaced plural second	ustedes	-n, -ron	(*a*) ustedes	les [dat], las/los [acc]

It must be noted that what in grammatical terms is labelled *first and second persons* constitutes a limited set of elements – mainly those represented in the table – used for the discursive-cognitive construction of the direct participants of communication, whose actual number and contextual identities can be unpredictably diverse. In this sense, we can mention just a few facts of referential variability that will be prove relevant for our analyses of particular persons:

a) The singular second person (*tú*), besides its prototypical use for the indexation of a specific addressee, is often employed with a nonspecific interpretation – being supposedly addressed to any individual who may be listening, as in radio broadcasting. The same happens with the rest of second-person subparadigms. *Tú* can also have a speaker-inclusive reference whereby it becomes allusive to any person that can be concerned by some state of things, and often primordially the speaker him/herself. This capacity is shared – even if in less evident ways and with lower frequencies – by the rest of singular persons (*yo* and *usted*).
b) The plural first person (*nosotros*), whose basic discursive feature is reference to the speaker together with others, can actually denote any group of people, from the smallest possible ones – e.g. the speaker and the addressee – to all of mankind and even non-human entities. Interestingly, it can also be used to index just the person speaking, who for some reason would opt to construct his/her own reference as that of a plurality.
c) Similarly, plural second persons (*vosotros* and *ustedes*) can be subject to quite varied referential interpretations from which only the speaker appears to be systematically excluded, and which will be easy to observe in a corpus of media discourse where very different human groups are addressed.

This might lead to conclude that any grammatical person can be used to construct any possible reference in a given context. Not to mention the fact that speakers can also opt for constructing themselves as third persons – as famously done by Julius Caesar in his autobiographical writings (Billows 2009, 198) – or just to conceal their own presence in the discursive-cognitive scene through agentless passive or impersonal constructions. What this all suggests is that extralinguistic reference may be relevant for the discursive-pragmatic interpretation of particular instances of person choice, but is hardly a part of the intrinsic meaning of persons themselves, which is only explainable in cognitive terms. It is thus necessary to assume that each grammatical person has an inherent meaning that is at the basis of its possibilities to acquire particular referential interpretations under particular contextual conditions. The isolation of the meaning of each person will in fact be a fundamental task for the type of investigation to be developed here. It will help understand their quantitative patterns of variation as well as their discursive-pragmatic motivations in usage contexts, thus elucidate how referents are cognitively constructed through their choice.

3.2 Salience and informativeness in the first and second persons

The given or presupposed nature of the first and second persons has often been noted: "first and second person referents acquire the given status naturally from the conversational context itself" (Chafe 1987, 26; see also Ariel 2001, 31; Posio 2012, 340). Notions like *communication* or *interaction* make little sense without at least someone who speaks/writes and someone who listens/reads. It can even be argued that everything is incidental except for those two basic participants that, as pointed out, need to be understood as discursive-cognitive constructions rather than extralinguistic entities. This is why, on a salience scale, the first and second persons should be placed above the third one (see §1.3.1d). Still, it is true that salience, just as informativeness, can only be properly assessed when referents are constructed within a specific discursive context.

The linguistic forms prototypically used to refer to the direct participants can thus be considered to accord their referents a high degree of salience just by being chosen for their construction. In accordance with this, the reference of these forms will usually be unequivocal in the context. The identifiability of referents is inversely proportional to the complexity of their linguistic formulation, including the richness of grammatical informations. In most languages, first- and second-person pronouns and morphemes are not marked for gender, and sometimes neither for number, which can easily be put in connection with the high accessibility of their referents (Ariel 1990, 73): the more accessible an entity is in some context, the smaller amount of explicitly encoded information will be required for its identification. Differences in this respect can even be observed between the singular and plural persons. As shown in Table 3.1 above, whereas *yo* and *tú* are gender-unmarked, the corresponding plural forms *nosotros* and *vosotros* do have masculine and feminine variants. This, together with their greater phonological complexity – three syllables – situates them closer to the prototype of pronouns, i.e. elements used to encode referents that are recoverable from the discursive or situational context, but whose identification is not considered straightforward (see also Figure 1.2 above). As will be observed, these pronouns have very low rates of expression in our data – lower, in any case, than those of the singular ones, which might seem surprising from the point of view of inherent salience. However, it is also true that speakers often disambiguate their reference through appositional lexical NPs whose discursive status is similar to that of overt pronouns.

All this seems to naturally explain many of the formal and functional peculiarities of the first and second persons. The direct participants have a narrow array of encoding possibilities – the closed list of personal pronouns, verbal endings and clitics we have displayed in the table. It should be kept in mind that the description is restricted to central syntactic functions; with peripheral ones, the range of elements is somewhat expanded (e.g. possessives, vocatives). In turn, third persons, together with the same possibilities (example 1a), can also use other kinds of pronouns such as demonstrative and indefinite ones (1b, c), as well as lexical NPs of any degree of complexity (1d). Again, the choice of some way of encoding will closely parallel the extent to which the referent is viewed as accessible. As for the relative richness of grammatical information, third-person forms are regularly marked for gender: *él* 'he'/*ella* 'she'; *este* 'this one (m.)'/*esta* 'this one (f.)' and, as we know, even accusative third-person clitics have masculine/neuter and feminine forms.

(1a) Él volvi-ó al trabajo
'He went [3rd.sing] back to work.'

(1b) Ese volvió al trabajo
'That one went back to work.'

(1c) Alguien volvió al trabajo
'Someone went back to work.'

(1d) El obrero que había sufrido el accidente volvió al trabajo
'The worker who had suffered the accident went back to work.'

All this supports the view that first- and second-person encoding is inherently associated with higher salience and lower informativeness than third-person encoding. Even so, it seems necessary to further specify how these notions – and especially informativeness – can be applied to the analysis of discursive referents whose existence, as pointed out, needs to be presupposed for communication itself to make sense, quite unlike external referents that seem to fit in much better with the approach developed. According to Halliday (2004, 91), deictic and anaphoric elements are necessarily *given* and thus cannot be *informative*, unless they are endowed with contrastive value in the context:

> There are a number of elements in language that are inherently 'given' in the sense that they are not interpretable except by reference to some previous mention or some feature of the situation: anaphoric elements (those that refer to things mentioned before) and deictic elements (those that are interpreted by reference to the 'here-and-now' of the discourse). Typically these items do not carry information focus; if they do, they are contrastive.

It has also been pointed out that informative factors, at least as they are most often understood, are probably not the most relevant ones for the explanation of the expression and placement of elements in discourse (Gundel/Fretheim 2009, 153–157). Undoubtedly, the analysis of the linguistic forms used to encode the direct participants begs for a different conception of *given* and *new information*, and of salience and informativeness altogether, from those that have been most usual in discourse studies. The recurrence of first- and second-person agreement morphemes across a stretch of discourse should not be viewed as a mere strategy to keep their referents activated and identifiable. The direct participants may have diverse extradiscursive references, but *the speaker* and *the addressee* as discursive-cognitive constructions are in principle not subject to ambiguity. Rather, repeated morphemes will constitute an indication that the referent is so salient that it is basic to the interpretation of discourse. This is often evident in first-person narrative stretches, such as (2), taken from a written opinion piece with obvious literary elaboration. The absence of any referent qualifying as a potential competitor to the narrator – the text is nominally devoted to storks, but the viewpoint adopted is a clearly personal one – makes pronoun expression unnecessary whether he encodes himself as a subject or as an object.

(2) *Terminé* mi periplo en el Patio de Escuelas, sentado en el umbral de una puerta en la penumbra que proyectaba la estatua del maestro Fray Luis.

Contemplé largo rato a las cuatro <cigüeñas> que remataban otros tantos pináculos a ambos lados de la plateresca fachada universitaria. *Me* recordaron –por su actitud expectante– a cuatro estudiantes que ocuparan los asientos más altos del anfiteatro, en el solemne momento que pronunciaba el maestro: "Decíamos ayer".

Que es numerosa la colonia de zancudas, salta a la vista; *llegué* a contar la otra noche casi un centenar, y no *exagero*. <Art-Ga-200804-5>
'(*I*) finished my journey at the Patio de Escuelas, sitting on the threshold of a door, under the shadow cast by the statue of the master Fray Luis. For a long while (*I*) watched the four [storks], each of them crowning a pinnacle at either side of the plateresque university façade. They made (*me*) think – due to their expectant attitude – of four students occupying the highest seats of the amphitheater at that solemn moment when the master uttered, "As we were saying yesterday...". The colony of wading birds is evidently a numerous one; the other evening (*I*) counted up to nearly one hundred, and (*I*)'m not exaggerating.'

For the same reasons, with the direct participants the role of informativeness goes beyond the mere identification of supposedly non-activated referents. Starting from the general correlation between higher accessibility and greater formal simplicity, a relatively higher degree of informativeness will be manifested whenever speakers use more linguistic material than is necessary for referential identification. In the case of the first and second persons, this will happen whenever they formulate not just subject/object agreement morphemes, but also coreferential personal pronouns – sometimes also lexical NPs, in the case of the plural persons. The expression across discourse of stressed elements denoting some direct participant reveals an intention to place the focus of attention on the latter, which can hardly be done through verbal endings or clitics alone. This of course does not mean for them to be "new" or unrecoverable from the preceding context, but rather that there is some need to make their presence in the discursive-cognitive scene explicit beyond mere morphematical indexation. In example (3), the repeated use of both subject and object first-person pronouns (*yo, a mí*) as well as others encoding peripheral functions (*para mí* 'for me') appears to highlight the personal nature of the argumentation under development.

(3) pero cuando *a mí* me preguntas *yo* te lo digo / *yo* sigo diciendo que *a mí* me parece que Jose / e:n:- en: casa: fundamentalmente:: / bueno / pues e: m m: / *para mí* es:- es muy discutible tan discutible / que no admite discusión por otro lado <Dep-Co-221104-14:35>
'But when it's *me* that you ask, *I* tell you. *I* will keep on saying that *to me* it seems that Jose, especially when playing at home, is *for me* a highly questionable player. So questionable that he is actually beyond question.'

Interestingly, all instances of expressed pronouns in the preceding stretch, whether subject- or object-encoding, appear at the preverbal position in their respective clauses. As will be repeatedly observed, this is by far the more frequent solution with first- and second-person pronouns. Preverbal placement is an intermediate solution with regard to salience and informativeness: while expression reduces salience as against omission-indexation, the placement of the pronoun at the position associated with the subject-agent in the canonical clause makes the referent move away from the pole of informativeness. This results in quite profitable communicative effects for argumentative discourse with an explicitly subjective orientation (see especially Section 4.3 on the placement of singular first-person pronouns, as well as Section 9.5 on the stylistic interpretation of pronoun placement).

In turn, the formulation of these pronouns at the prototypically informative clause-final position, rather than entailing newness in a conventional sense, is a resource of focalization used to create a variety of possible contextual effects, such as contrast or counterexpectation, e.g. *El cristal lo rompiste tú* 'The glass, it is you who broke', lit. 'The glass (3rd sing acc masc cl = *him/it*) broke [2nd sing] you'. As pointed out in §1.3.2, it is not really the referent that is seen as new or unrecoverable, but rather its relationship to the rest of the utterance; in this case, the fact that it was the addressee and not anyone else who broke the glass. Conversely, the clause-initial object *el cristal* establishes verbal agreement through a clitic, indicating its higher contextual salience.

Postverbal expression often underlines the existence of a contrast with other referents that may or not be expressed, as can also be observed in (4). The focalization of the subject pronoun *nosotros* 'we', whose referent is viewed as the one capable of performing the action, is reinforced by the addition of *mismos* 'same, selves'.

(4) si quieres en estos momentos que nos estás escuchando pues coges / marcas (el número de la empresa) / y te / AUTOrregalas un ramo de rosas / porque hoy es hoy / qué le vamos a hacer / ¿no? / ¿para qué vamos a esperar a que vengan y nos lo regalen? / pu(es) ya está: / nos lo regalamos *nosotros mismos* <Mus-Di-200503-12:25>
'If you feel like it, right now and as you listen to us, you can dial [the number of the company] and treat yourself with a bouquet of roses. I mean, you only live once, right? Why should we wait for someone else to come and give it to us? That's it – *we ourselves* [postv.] can give it to us.'

The power of pronoun formulation altogether to highlight the relationship between a referent and the whole event makes it a useful resource for the management of interpersonal relationships, as has been noted from sociopragmatic approaches such as the one based on interactional (im)politeness. Brown/Levinson (1987, 67) cite the explicit mention of a semantic agent as a face-threatening act, which is understandably most evident when objectionable facts are attributed to that agent. Therefore, when a conversational partner is criticized or attacked by the speaker, second-person pronoun expression can be a strategy to stress the responsibility of the former. Guerra Bernal (2007) reaches similar conclusions in a study of the pragmatic values of subject expression in a particular contentious context, namely that of debates amidst a TV reality show (see also Serrano 2012; 2017b). Consider example (5) from the corpus; even if the speaker opts for the displaced second person, usually described as a "respectful" way of address, his intention is clearly of attacking his political rival. This interpretation is favored by two almost consecutive cases of subject pronoun expression.[2]

(5) estamos hablando de unas cantidades / que parece que no es nada pero es que es muchísimo *usté ha puesto* / prácticamente el doble de lo que *tenía* previsto en ese programa / porque *usté* no *organizó* bien la gestión del:- / del programa <Inf-On-080104-13:50>
'We're speaking about amounts of money that may look like no big deal, but they are in fact massive. *You+* have spent practically twice as much as (*you+*) had planned to spend on that program, just because *you+* didn't manage the program appropriately.'

As can be inferred, the contextual manifestations of salience and informativeness with first- and second-person referents often concern not so much the structuring of information across discourse as the management of personal identities and interpersonal relationships. The underlying cognitive factors are always the same; the contextual repercussions can in turn be quite varied. This will be discussed in detail across our qualitative analyses of the different grammatical persons and the syntactic choices involved in their construction across discourse.

3.3 The non-prototypical features of first- and second-person objects

An important correlate of the inherent salience of the direct participants is their strong tendency to be functionally encoded as subjects, as well as to play agentive or, in any case, relatively autonomous semantic roles. As shown in Table 3.2, across the MEDIASA corpus only some 20% of first- and second-person referents encoded in central clause functions are indexed in the verbal nucleus through a clitic. The rest of them establish subject agreement.

This makes it possible to assume that subject encoding is the prototypical syntactic choice with first- and second-person referents. Subjects of this kind and their discursive-cognitive foundations were devoted a monographic study in Aijón Oliva/Serrano (2013). For the same reason, it seems interesting to apply

2 In the English translations, given the lack of an equivalent address system in this language, we will conventionally add the symbol + to both *you* and *you guys* in order to indicate that it is a displaced second-person form that has been used.

Table 3.2: General distribution of the central functions with the first and second persons.

Syntactic function	#	%
Subject	6,735	79.9
(Acc/Dat) Object	1,691	20.1
Total	8,426	100

an analogous analysis to the rather less usual choice of object encoding, following a preliminary inquiry in Aijón Oliva (2018a). If, as discussed in the previous chapter, grammatical functions are disposed along a discursive-cognitive continuum that correlates with many other formal and semantic continua – including animacy, definiteness, agentivity and so on – these objects should not be expected to usually match the features of the most prototypical object, i.e. the accusative – associated with low salience and high informativeness – but rather to approach the less prototypical features of the dative (see also Moure 1996, 53–54). What is proposed in this section is an investigation of the likely tension between grammatical choice and cognitive construction when the referents of syntactic objects are not of the most prototypical sort.

However, as has already been noted, there are no formal differences between accusative and dative encoding with these persons. There is just one object pronoun for each person and number and, with the exception of the displaced second ones, just one clitic form as well. Clitic agreement can be considered categorical with first- and second-person objects whether they are omitted or expressed, and in all clausal positions. With regard to object marking with the particle *a*, it is also generalized with first- and second-person objects: *Nos llaman* *(*a*) *nosotros* 'They're calling [to] us'. Thus, what we actually need to investigate is the syntactic contexts where these objects appear – distinguishing between verbal lexemes that generally select accusative vs. dative objects – as well as some variable features of their syntactic formulation – pronoun expression and placement within the clause. This way it should be possible to elucidate the extent to which object encoding is sensitive to the particularly high salience of these referents. More specifically, the following four questions will be addressed:

a) Whether first- and second-person objects appear more often with verbs selecting an accusative or else a dative object. The functional criteria used to classify verbs in this regard will be specified below. We start from the hypothesis that these objects will appear more often in contexts identifying with the dative prototype. As regards ditransitive contexts, usually characterized by a strong functional and cognitive contrast between objects, we should also expect first- and second-person referents to be preferably accorded the dative role, while the referent of the accusative object should most often be a third-person inanimate one.

b) Whether the different grammatical persons under study have different degrees of association with either object type. If first persons are considered to be the most salient ones for the speaker, they should also have the highest rates of occurrence in dative contexts. The preference for this function should be weaker with prototypical second persons, and more so with displaced second ones, which in fact are formally third persons. However, as has been exposed (§1.3.1), there is no general consensus on whether it is the first or the second person that has higher inherent salience in Spanish, which makes the results less predictable. Also, differences can be expected to show up between singular and plural persons.
c) Whether the function accorded to the referent correlates with the features of the clause subject. The hypothesis put forward in this case is that first- and second-person referents will appear more frequently in dative contexts with subjects less salient than them. In order to test it, clauses with a third-person subject will be analyzed, this person entailing lower salience than the first and second ones. We will further distinguish between animate and inanimate third-person subjects, and also consider impersonal clauses.
d) Whether and to what extent the variable expression and placement of first- and second-person object pronouns within the clause correlate with accusative vs. dative contexts. Even if several hypotheses might be ventured in this last case – given that two partly different albeit related functional features are simultaneously considered – it seems sensible to expect some preference of datives for the combinations entailing high and intermediate salience – respectively object omission and preverbal expression – while accusatives should more often correlate with postverbal expression, associated with low salience.

More generally, this preliminary investigation of first- and second-person objects will make it possible to test many of the claims made in Chapters 1 and 2 about salience and informativeness, as well as their formal and semantic correlates. By supporting the view that there is only one prototype of central object that is functionally and cognitively opposed to that of the subject, it will also lay the bases for the subsequent specific analyses of each grammatical person in Chapters 4 to 8.

The classification of monotransitive verbs according to the functional type of object they select was based on a number of functional tests (Porto Dapena 1997, 20–21; Campos 1999, 1529–1530). These take into account the usual behavior of third-person objects, which are the ones allowing for the observation of case differences. The most obvious one is the preference for accusative clitics (*lo, la, los, las*) vs. dative ones (*le, les*). Another matter of object variation already discussed, namely marking with *a*, is also significant given that the particle usually precedes object referents that can compete in salience with the subject, i.e. those approaching the dative prototype. There are actually verbs that will select an object with *a* even if the referent is inanimate or indefinite. When there is an apparent contradiction between the outcomes of either basic test, i.e. when a verb tends to agree through accusative clitics but at the same time marks objects with *a* – the opposite combination being unusual – it is difficult to make a decision, as will be illustrated just below.

An additional test is the possibility of passivizing the clause by turning the central object into a subject-patient, which in Spanish – in contrast to e.g. English – is restricted to more-or-less prototypical accusative objects in events with relatively high transitivity. Compare (6b) and (7b), the latter showing a psychological verb that does not easily admit passivization. In fact, the construction is altogether a relatively infrequent one in Spanish and tends to be associated with written, formal discourse such as that of academia or the press (see e.g. Seco 1996, 162–163; Aijón Oliva 2013b).

(6a) Los diputados insultaron al presidente

(6b) El presidente fue insultado por los diputados
'The congressmen insulted the president/The president was insulted by the congressmen.'

(7a) Los diputados inquietaron al presidente

(7b) ?El presidente fue inquietado por los diputados
'The congressmen unsettled the president/The president was unsettled by the congressmen.'

Of the 1,691 clauses with first- and second-person objects in our database, 137 (8.1%) turned out to have monotransitive verbs whose object is difficult to ascribe to either the accusative or dative prototype. We will refer to these as *intermediate-object* verbs. Rather than constituting a grammatical oddity, these are the contexts where the non-discrete nature of syntactic functions becomes most evident.

The most numerous group within this subset is that of verbs denoting psychological processes as in (7a, b) above, e.g. *asustar* 'to scare', *fastidiar* 'to annoy', *preocupar* 'to worry', etc., whose variability between accusative and dative encoding was already briefly reviewed in Section 2.5. The most prototypical lexeme in the group is *gustar* 'to like', lit. 'to please', some authors in fact talking of *gustar*-type verbs (Vázquez Rozas 2006; Rivas 2016), as will also be done here. Their subject is most often inanimate and rather less salient than the (human) referent acting as the experiencer of the process; such imbalance in salience promotes a strong dominance of the OVS order when both participants are formulated.[3]

Also functionally intermediate is the object of *hacer* 'to make' and *dejar* 'to let' in their causative constructions, i.e. when that object is at the same time the logical subject of an embedded clause indicating what the referent is made or allowed to do (Enghels 2012). In these cases, the choice between accusative and dative clitics partly depends on whether the embedded clause is a transitive or intransitive one. If the subordinate verb has an accusative object itself, the object in the main clause will show dative features, usually agreeing through *le, les* (8b); otherwise it will approach the accusative prototype, preferring accusative clitics (9b). Generative grammar has usually viewed case assignment in these contexts as depending on verbal (in)transitivity (Franco 1993, 221); however, the solutions are far from categorical. DeMello (2001, 148) shows that there is significant vacillation in clitic choice with causatives, and in fact the alternative options in our examples would also be possible. As for passivization, it is hardly acceptable in either case.

(8a) A las siete dejaron a la niña ver la tele
'At seven o'clock they let the girl watch TV.'

(8b) A las siete (le/?la) dejaron ver la tele
'At seven o'clock they let her watch TV.'

(9a) A las siete dejaron a la niña salir
'At seven o'clock they let the girl go out.'

(9b) A las siete (la/?le) dejaron salir
'At seven o'clock they let her go out.'

---

3 However, not all psychological verbs take functionally intermediate objects. In cases like *doler* 'to hurt', *encantar* 'to delight', *importar* 'to matter', *interesar* 'to interest', *parecer* 'to seem' or *gustar* itself, the object has clearly dative features. The clitics used for agreement are generally *le/les*, except in some varieties that tend to mark gender instead of case (i.e. with *laísmo* or *loísmo*; see again Section 2.5, as well as Alarcos Llorach 1994, §265). Passivization is generally ungrammatical.

Similar to causatives are other verbs whose object is at the same time the subject of a clause headed by *a: ayudar* 'to help', *enseñar* 'to teach', *invitar* 'to invite' or *obligar* 'to force, to oblige'. In some cases, their object had a more-or-less fixed case marking in Latin that has undergone alteration over time. While ADIUTARE 'to help' regularly selected a dative (Lapesa 2000, 284), in present-day Spanish the object of *ayudar* seems to be functionally closer to the accusative, as suggested by the possibility of passivization (*Fue ayudado* 'He was helped'), although wide variability is again observed as regards clitic choice. Finally, other verbs with a functionally ambiguous object are *advertir* 'to warn', *avisar* 'to warn, to alert' and *informar* 'to inform' in contexts where they select, together with the (human) object, another one headed by *de* that indicates the content of the warning or information (10a-c).

(10a) Informaron a Ana de que estaba admitida
'They informed Ana that she had been admitted.'

(10b) (La/?Le) informaron de que estaba admitida
'They informed her that she had been admitted.'

(10c) Fue informada de que estaba admitida
'She was informed that she had been admitted.'

In (10b) the accusative clitic is probably more frequent in most varieties of Spanish, and the passivization in (10c) is also relatively natural. However, the existence of parallel constructions with the same verbs where the object is clearly encoded as a dative – due to the elision of the particle *de* before the embedded clause and the reanalysis of the latter as an accusative object – results in wide functional variability, and makes it safer to include these contexts among functionally intermediate ones.

After this exposition of the difficulties encountered for the functional classification of verbal objects, the following subsections will respectively address research questions (a) to (d) as posed above.

3.3.1 General distribution across object contexts

Table 3.3 shows that, according to our first hypothesis, first- and second-person referents are much more frequently encoded as the objects of verbs regularly taking third-person dative objects rather than accusative ones. Almost three

Table 3.3: General distribution of the first and second persons across syntactic object contexts.

Syntactic context	#	%
Accusative	303	17.9
Dative	1,251	74
Intermediate object	137	8.1
Total	1,691	100

quarters (74%) of the total items appear in contexts assimilable to this prototype, with an additional 8.1% in functionally intermediate ones.

Therefore, leaving aside cases of subject encoding, dative contexts are by far the most frequent ones for the discursive encoding of the direct participants. The latter will much more often play the semantic roles of beneficiary, experiencer or owner than those associated with accusatives, i.e. patient or theme. Still, the latter can be observed when a participant is constructed as the patient of the actions carried out by an animate subject, such as *llevar* 'to take, to carry' (11, 12) or as the theme of a psychological process or state, such as *conocer* 'to know' (13).

(11) los países cuyos gobiernos, contra la opinión mayoritaria de la población, *nos* llevaron por el peor de los caminos imaginables. <Art-Ga-070404-5a>
'The countries whose governments, ignoring the prevailing view among the population, took (*us*) along the worst conceivable path.'

(12) cómo rec- / m: reclamar / cuando vas a los hoteles: / que no has cont- que has contratado y no *te* llevan a los hoteles: / que tú has contratado <Var-SE-230903-12:45>
'How to submit a complaint when you want to go to the hotels you've booked and they don't take (*you*) to the hotels you've booked.'

(13) los que *me* conocéis y: yo creo que en Salamanca *me* conoce: bastante gente / sabéis cómo soy <Dep-Co-080104-14:35>
'Those of you who know (*me*) – and I think there are many people in Salamanca who know (*me*) – you know how I am.'

In many cases, the construction of a first- or second-person object in an accusative context seems to correlate with a metaphorical and scarcely transitive interpretation of the event, as can be perceived in (11) above. The same happens in the following excerpts with *separar* 'to separate' (14) and *devolver* 'to take back' (15). This suggests the intrinsic difficulty for referents of these persons to match the accusative prototype, even with verbs a priori selecting this kind of object.

(14) temas inédito:s / como esa *Última estación* que acabas de escuchar: / exactamente cuando *nos* separan doce minuto:s / de las doce del mediodía: <Mus-Di-251104-11:50>
'Unreleased tracks such as this *Última estación* you've just listened to, when exactly twelve minutes separate (*us*) from twelve o'clock.'

(15) El reportaje publicado por este diario en el último suplemento dominical *me* ha devuelto a aquella tarde del 6 enero de 1997 <Art-Tr-241104-4>
'The story published in the latest Sunday supplement of this journal has taken (*me*) back to that evening of January 6, 1997.'

Besides, there are practically no ditransitive contexts in the corpus where the accusative object has a first- or second-person referent. Direct participants in such contexts will be invariably accorded the dative slot, most often with the semantic role of beneficiary or receiver, as in (16).

(16) Yo sé que hace meses no estaba en condiciones de pedir nada y asumía que tendría que ir al filial o lo que *me* diera el club, pero *me* dieron una oportunidad y no puedo por más que estar agradecido <Not-Ga-200804-36b>
'I know that some months ago I wasn't in a position to demand anything, and I assumed I'd have to go down to the side team or take whatever the club might want to give (*me*), but they offered (*me*) a chance and I can only be grateful.'

3.3.2 Distribution of the different grammatical persons across object contexts

As for question (b), the hypothesis put forward was that there would be quantitative differences among the grammatical persons considered – including their singular and plural variants – regarding the preference for accusative vs. dative contexts. Their respective token numbers and percentages are displayed in Table 3.4.

Table 3.4: Distribution of the different grammatical persons across object contexts.

Person	Accusative		Dative		Intermediate		Total	
	#	%	#	%	#	%	#	%
1st sing (*me*)	66	12.3	426	79.6	43	8	535	31.6
1st pl (*nos*)	149	26.8	364	65.5	43	7.7	556	32.9
2nd sing (*te*)	42	14.4	223	76.4	27	9.2	292	17.3
2nd pl (*os*)	9	16.1	42	75	5	8.9	56	3.3
2nd+ sing (*le*)	19	13.9	108	78.8	10	7.3	137	8.1
2nd+ pl (*les*)	19	16.5	88	76.5	8	7	115	6.8
Total	303	17.9	1,251	74	137	8.1	1,691	100

Even though the percentages are similar in most cases, and do not sharply differ from the general ones displayed in Table 3.3 above – showing a clear dominance of dative contexts in all cases – some data are worth highlighting. The singular variant always has higher rates of dative encoding than the plural, most evidently in the case of the first persons, with a 14-point advantage for the singular (79.6 vs. 65.5%). The percentage of dative encoding with the singular first person is actually the highest one in the table and exceeds the general one of 74 in 5.6 points. This is easy to put in connection with the naturally high salience of the speaker. Accusative contexts with this person correspondingly show the lowest frequency (12.3%). First-person dative encoding is thus a particularly recurrent choice that will need to be further discussed taking its contexts of occurrence and discursive-pragmatic motivations into account (see Section 4.4).

In turn, the plural first person is the one most often constructed in accusative contexts (26.8%) and the only one that diverges from the general tendencies to some extent. It is also worth noting that its token number is the highest one in the table (556), which probably reflects its discursive versatility (see Section 5.2). It seems only natural that singular referents should prove more perceptible and altogether salient than plural ones. This is particularly true of the plural first person, which always includes the speaker but extends his/her reference towards a wider group whose actual limits are often difficult to pin down. In this sense, observe the repeated use of the clitic *nos* 'us' with a scarcely delimited reference across (17). The stretch includes both accusative contexts (*llamar* 'to call', *hacer* 'to make') and dative ones (*hablar* 'to talk', *ofrecer* 'to offer').

(17) Ahora también se vende de casa en casa, pero es otra cosa. *Nos* llaman por teléfono (¡quién demonios le ha dado nuestro número!), y *nos* hablan de un seguro. Llaman al timbre de la puerta, y *nos* ofrecen una biblia al tiempo que la ocasión de hacer*nos* hijos o testigos, según los casos. <Art-Ad-221104-6>
'Today there's still door-to-door selling, but it's a different story. Someone calls (*us*) on the phone – who on earth gave them our number? – and starts talking (*to us*) about some insurance. Someone rings our bell and offers a Bible (*to us*), together with the opportunity to make (*us*) children or witnesses, as the case may be.'

The author intends for the readership to share his views when discussing supposedly everyday situations that anyone is likely to associate with their own personal experience. The referential fuzziness of the plural first person, a priori correlating with lower salience, may be partially accountable for its comparatively high rates of accusative encoding – in the example reviewed, two of the four tokens were classified as corresponding to this prototype. All the same, dative contexts are clearly preferred even with this person, accounting for nearly two thirds of the total cases.

As for the prototypical and displaced second persons, they all show a similar patterning, 75% to 79% of their object tokens occurring in dative contexts. As pointed out, the singular variants always have somewhat higher rates of dative encoding, although the differences are smaller than those observed with the first persons.

We should however not limit ourselves to drawing the conclusion that all first and second persons are much more often constructed in dative contexts than accusative ones. It can be just as revealing to formulate the statement the other way around – it is the contexts where first and second persons typically appear that are more suitable for the encoding of any referent according to the features of the dative prototype. In such contexts, the referent is accorded a relatively autonomous semantic role that could also result in its encoding as a subject; still, the dative is sometimes chosen due to the particular eventive structure of the verb and other concurrent factors. Among the latter we should primarily cite the cognitive status of the clause subject. Going back to (17), all four clauses with the clitic *nos* have plural third-person verbs that can be considered impersonal – the audience is not expected to recover a subject, be it *ellos* 'they' or *alguien* 'someone', as used in the translation. This leaves the objectual plural first person as the only central participant in all of these clauses but the third one, where the accusative *una biblia* 'a Bible' is anyway scarcely salient. The repercussions of the contrast in salience between the object and the subject will now be further addressed.

3.3.3 Distribution according to the perceptibility of the clause subject

In order to rank subjects according to perceptibility, we will take into account the features of grammatical person and (in)animacy, the latter only within third persons. These features will of course condition the range of verbal lexemes the subject can be combined with, as well as the distribution of syntactic functions and semantic roles among the remaining participants. We have also distinguished impersonal clauses in order to observe how first- and second-person objects tend to behave when there is no syntactic subject. The hypothesis is that the frequency of first- and second-person dative encoding should be inversely proportional to the salience of the subject. Table 3.5 shows the results obtained.

Table 3.5: Distribution according to the perceptibility of the clause subject.

Subject	**Accusative**		**Dative**		**Intermediate**		**Total**	
	#	%	#	%	#	%	#	%
1st	53	15.8	259	77.1	24	7.1	336	19.9
2nd	29	31.5	58	63	5	5.5	92	5.4
2nd+	16	26.7	42	70	2	3.3	60	3.5
3rd, animate	130	25.8	336	66.8	37	7.4	503	29.7
3rd, inanimate	57	9.2	497	80.6	63	10.2	617	36.5
Impersonal	18	21.7	59	71.1	6	7.2	83	4.9
Total	303	17.9	1,251	74	137	8.1	1,691	100

Among other interesting facts, the contexts where first- and second-person dative objects have the highest proportion (80.6%) are clauses with inanimate third-person subjects. These in turn show the lowest percentage of accusatives (9.2%). In these cases the object often behaves as a logical subject, as shown by its tendency to be placed before the verb or just omitted, whereas the syntactic subject – often an embedded clause, thus having a very low degree of perceptibility – tends to occupy the more informative postverbal position. Most of the tokens correspond to *gustar*-type verbs (example 18) and similar ones such as *quedar* 'to remain, to be left' (19).

(18) *a mí me* gustaría que partiésemos de la base / de:- / ya no de una escasez / de contenidos infantiles / en los medios / sino casi de una ausencia TOTAL / de los mismos <Var-Pu-211204-12:25>
'I would like (lit. *To me* it would be pleasing) for us to start from the basis that children's contents are not just scarce in the media – they are almost totally absent from them.'

(19) Sin embargo, todavía *nos* queda el don de la palabra y la escritura, que es lo que estoy haciendo en estos momentos <Car-Ga-051104-6>
'However, we still have (lit. [*to us*] there still remains) the gift of speech and writing, which is what I am doing right now.'

Clauses with inanimate subjects also have the highest number of functionally intermediate objects (63 tokens). Again, these are mostly constructions with monotransitive psychological verbs such as *preocupar* 'to worry' (example 20), whose object oscillates between the accusative and the dative prototypes depending on contextual features such as the salience of the subject and the transitivity of the event (see Section 2.5 above).

(20) *Me* preocupa bastante que en numerosas zonas de la ciudad existan tantos solares abandonados. <Car-Ga-200804-6b>
'It worries (*me*) quite much that there should be so many abandoned sites in numerous areas of the town.'

As pointed out, these are the contexts where the tension between syntactic encoding and cognitive salience becomes most evident. First- and second-person objects tend to adopt features associated with the subject, most clearly the omission or preverbal placement of pronouns. In turn, expressed inanimate subjects are relegated to the position of higher informativeness. It is scarcely expectable to have an inanimate subject – much less so if it is an embedded clause – select some direct participant as an accusative object, this function being prototypically associated with patienthood in transitive events. Still, the corpus contains up to 57 instances of such a configuration. In a few of them, the speaker presents him/herself or another direct participant as a sort of (psychological or even physical) victim of a situation or event (example 21). However, most are clearly metaphorical, as in the cited use of *separar* 'to separate' by a radio broadcaster indicating the time remaining until the turn of the hour (see 14 above). There are also cases like (22), where an inanimate subject metonymically stands for a human agent, which easily explains the construction of the first-person patient in an accusative context. As can be inferred from the example, even in such cases the subject tends to be postposed to the verb, while the object is preposed or just indexed through clitics.

(21) (de adolescente) yo vi / películas violentas y eso no *me* ha convertido / en un ser violento / hay ot- / hay otros- son otros los factores / que: *nos* llevan a aquello <Var-Pu-211204-12:40>
'[As a teenager] I used to see violent movies and that did not make (*me*) a violent creature. There are other factors involved that can take (*us*) to such a situation.'

(22) Se paró a socorrer*nos* un coche con matrícula de Castellón (CS) en el que viajaban dos chicos jóvenes. <Car-Ga-221203-6a>
'There stopped to assist (*us*) a car with a Castellón – CS – plate, in which two young men were travelling.'

Impersonal clauses, with 21.7% accusatives, seem to align with animate-subject rather than inanimate-subject ones. This is probably due to the fact that in most impersonal constructions a human agent is assumed even if not functionally realized, as in (23), with a third-person plural verb lacking a recoverable subject.

(23) –Siempre ha estado muy vinculado al asociacionismo empresarial.
–Siempre que *me* llamaron estuve. <Ent-Ga-201204-11>
'A: You+'ve always had close ties with entrepreneurial associationism. – B: Whenever I was required (lit. they called [*me*]), there I was.'

As for the remaining contexts, they do not seem to adjust to the expected progression, i.e. the more salient the subject, the higher the rates of accusative objects. Actually, clauses with a singular first-person subject achieve the second-highest percentage of dative encoding (77.1%), even surpassing animate third-person subjects as well as impersonal clauses. This is partly due to the very features of our token database. Since we are not considering third-person objects, whenever there is a first-person subject the object will be a second-person one.[4] Aside from the

4 Note that reflexive clauses where the subject and a central object are coreferential (*Me lavé las manos*, lit. 'I washed (me) the hands') are not considered. These objects do not seem to be assimilable to the rest, their basic meaning being the internalization of the event within the subject. As for the possibility of partial coreference, i.e. for the subject and the object to coincide in person but differ in number, it is an infrequent and often ungrammatical construction in Spanish: ?*Nos apunté al concurso* 'I inscribed (us) into the contest'; **Me disfrazamos de astronauta* 'We disguised (me) as an astronaut'.

fact that there is not a clear difference in salience between both persons, some tendency can be detected in media discourse not to encode the addressee or audience as an accusative object, perhaps in connection with matters of interactional politeness. The speaker will tend to avoid the suggestion that the people addressed are perceived as patients or that they lack autonomy (see further Section 6.4).

Conversely, the highest frequency of accusatives is obtained in contexts with a second-person subject and a first-person object. In line with the preceding observations, we could hypothesize a strategy on the part of speakers to assume a subordinate position as against their addressees by according them the most salient syntactic function, prototypically associated with agentivity and autonomy. In (24), just after A utters *Me ha pillado* 'You+'ve caught (me)', B accepts the move by constructing himself as the subject: *Le he pillado* 'I've caught (you+)', causing a clearly humorous effect. While the context is an accusative one, the clitic chosen is dative *le*, as is customary with the displaced second persons (see 26 below as well as Section 8.1), which again promotes a metaphorical interpretation of the event.

(24) <A> yo no *le* nie:go / e: doctor que *a mí:* desde luego el (tema) que más: *me* ha llamado la atención es lo del vino en la vejez ¿e:h? /
<B> <risas> /
<A> también *le* digo que:- / que ahí *me* ha pillado ¿eh? /
<JAG> ahí *le* he pillado <Var-SE-230903-13:40>
'A: I won't deny it (*to you+*), doctor, that the [topic] that struck (*me*) the most was the one about wine in old age. – B: [*Laughs.*] – A: I must also tell (*you+*) that you+'ve caught (*me*) with that one. – B: With that one I've caught (*you+*).'

However, first-person accusatives are frequent in the corpus with a plural object referring to the company responsible of a commercial (25) or the radio station a broadcaster speaks on behalf of (26). In the second example, the functions are rapidly reversed from *les acompañamos* 'we'll keep you guys+ company' to *si nos han elegido* 'if you guys+ have chosen us'. Object self-encoding reveals a similar intention to adopt a subordinate position and thus secure the approval of the audience.

(25) librerías y dormitorios a medida / con la mejor calidaz / y: a precios de fábrica: / no lo piense más: / y venga a visitar*nos* <Anu-Co-230503-13:10>
'Custom-made bookcases and bedrooms of the highest quality and at cost price. Don't think twice and come to visit (*us*).'

(26) comenzamos: / y ya saben *les* acompañamos: / si *nos* han elegido / hasta las dos menos cuarto: / de la tarde <Var-On-080104-12:45>
'We're starting now. And as you guys+ know, we'll keep (*you guys+*) company – if you guys have chosen (*us*) – until 1:45 p.m.'

3.3.4 Variable formulation and placement of object pronouns

Besides requiring indexation in the verbal nucleus through a clitic, first- and second-person objects can be formulated in the clause as stressed object pronouns preceded by the particle *a* (e.g. *a mí, a ti*). When this happens, they can be placed either before or after the verb. Such patterns of variation closely mirror those of clause subjects, which can be just indexed through the verbal endings or also explicitly formulated as pronouns, usually endowed with analogous mobility within the clause. In this last subsection we will investigate whether there are different tendencies in the formulation and placement of such objects according to the functional context where they appear. Since we have associated the accusative prototype with higher informativeness, objects in this kind of syntactic context should be expected to have higher frequencies of expression as well as of postverbal placement. First, Table 3.6 shows the results for expression vs. omission.

Table 3.6: Variable formulation of pronouns across object contexts.

Formulation	Accusative		Dative		Intermediate		Total	
	#	%	#	%	#	%	#	%
Expression	16	5.3	127	10.2	13	9.5	156	9.2
Omission	287	94.7	1,124	89.8	124	90.5	1,535	90.8
Total	303	17.9	1,251	74	137	8.1	1,691	100

Pronoun omission, associated with highly accessible referents, is overwhelmingly preferred in all functional contexts, which is coherent with the intrinsic salience of first- and second-person referents and the easiness of their identification through agreement morphemes. However, the results for the different syntactic contexts seem to contradict the hypothesis posed: accusatives have just 5.3% of expression, while datives almost double that figure with 10.2%. In fact, the 127 overt pronouns in dative contexts represent 81.4% of the total tokens of expression. As for intermediate-object contexts, their rate of this variant falls in between those of the others, but is quite closer to that of datives. It seems necessary to clarify why both types of syntactic contexts achieve higher percentages of pronoun formulation than accusative ones.

First, it must be pointed out that, of 140 expressed pronouns in dative and intermediate contexts, 90 (64.3%) appear in similar contextual circumstances: they are mostly singular first-person pronouns selected by *gustar*-type monotransitive verbs. The corpus contains abundant instances of expressed pronouns in constructions such as *a mí me parece* 'to me it seems', *a mí me gustaría* 'to me it would be pleasing', etc. They appear within argumentative discourse where the speaker tends to emphasize his/her own involvement in the content, usually establishing a contrast with the positions held by others (27, 28).[5]

(27) Curiosamente Rovira ha abierto una sucursal en cada provincia para vender sus ideas separatistas, independentistas y de expolio del patrimonio, y monta agencias en cada provincia y tiene empleados. *A mí* eso no *me* preocupa, porque la sociedad salmantina sigue estando y pensando con los mismos que estuvo y pensó en 1995. <Ent-Ga-020604-27>
'Curiously, Rovira has opened an office in each province in order to sell his views in favor of secession, independence and despoilment of the cultural heritage; so he's setting up agencies and hiring employees in every province. *To me* that is not really disturbing, since the Salamanca society keeps thinking the same and standing by the same ones as in 1995.'

(28) todos sabemos / cómo: está el: / patrimonio: / de:- / perdón / e:l presupuesto: del Ayuntamiento / *a mí me* gustaría tener el: dinero que fuera necesario para comprar (el teatro) <Var-On-080104-13:00>
'We all know about the situation of the Town Council's estate – I mean, its budget. *I* would like (lit. *To me* it would please) to have the money needed to buy [the theater].'

In the first example, taken from a journal interview to a politician, *a mí* is clearly topicalized and preposed even to the clause subject *eso* 'that'. After exposing the deeds and goals of an opponent, the speaker alters the viewpoint of

5 The situation is quite similar with some verbs encoding the experiencer as a subject, such as *creer* 'to think, to believe'. In *(yo) creo* '(I) think', pronoun expression by far surpasses omission (see Sections 4.3–4.5 below as well as Aijón Oliva/Serrano 2010b). The argumentative contexts where these constructions usually appear promote strategies of self-expression.

discourse through first-person pronoun expression, resembling strategies of turn-taking in conversation (see further Section 4.3). In (28), another politician, presenting the poor financial situation of the administration as common knowledge (*todos sabemos* 'we all know'), expresses a personal desire through overt *a mí*. Constructions of this sort, as against subject self-encoding ones, contribute to the downplaying of personal responsibility (Section 4.4).

In sum, the higher rates of expression in dative and intermediate contexts as against accusative ones are mainly due to the preference for first-person (subject and object) pronoun formulation with psychological verbs in argumentative discourse. An important point to be made across our analyses is that quantitative patterns are seldom sufficient for the explanation of language choice; the observation of individual examples makes it possible to unveil the discursive-pragmatic motivations of variants that would appear to contradict the expectable patterns from the perspective of referent salience.

As regards the preverbal vs. postverbal placement of the 156 expressed pronouns, Table 3.7 shows the dominance of preverbal objects in dative contexts (75.6%), while the choice would be dispreferred in accusative ones (37.5%). Intermediate-object contexts have an even lower percentage of preposition than accusative ones; however, the token numbers for both of them are rather low, which makes it difficult to draw firm conclusions.

Table 3.7: Variable placement of pronouns across object contexts.

Placement	Accusative		Dative		Intermediate		Total	
	#	%	#	%	#	%	#	%
Preverbal	6	37.5	96	75.6	4	30.8	106	67.9
Postverbal	10	62.5	31	24.4	9	69.2	50	32.1
Total	16	10.3	127	81.4	13	8.3	156	100

The difference between dative and accusative contexts is coherent with the preceding remarks on pronoun expression. In the course of argumentation, speakers often emphasize their own involvement in discourse through stressed first-person pronouns placed in the topical clause-initial position. Preverbal dative objects, their 96 tokens representing 61.5% of the total expressed pronouns, tend to adopt the prototypical formal and semantic features of subjects. As already pointed out, most examples appear with verbal lexemes describing psychological processes and used for the expression of opinions and judgments. The referent of the object is usually the speaker him/herself (example 29) or, in some cases, a certain human group he/she speaks for (30). 82 of the 96 tokens are first-person ones. The expressed pronoun at the beginning of the utterance enhances the subjectivity of the latter, as against the subtler presence of the speaker associated with mere clitic indexation (see further Section 9.5).

(29) bueno lo de segundas partes como hablábamos antes del *Padrino a mí* / siempre me parece mejor la s:egunda parte del *Padrino* que la primera <Var-SE-300503-19:50>
'Well, regarding second parts, as we were saying before about *The Godfather, to me* the second part of *The Godfather* always seems better than the first one.'

(30) *a los: salmantinos* se *nos* hace esTRAño / e: / recibir a veces esplicaciones de este tipo / de: decir "no esto no es de:- / este es de mi área esto no: esto es de la otra concejalía" <Var-On-080104-12:45>
'*To us, the Salamanca people*, it is sometimes kind of strange to receive explanations of the sort, like "Oh no, this matter just doesn't concern my area, it's in another department." '

Besides, preverbal pronoun expression is endowed with a potential for contrastiveness that makes it useful as a resource for turn-taking in conversation, particularly whenever the speaker intends to distance him/herself from anyone else's stance – even if subject pronouns are much more frequent for the same pragmatic function.

(31) – ¿Por quése ha tardado tanto tiempo en aprobar la Constitución europea?
– *A mí* no *me* parece que haya pasado tanto. La magnitud tiempo en relación con Europa es distinta a la de un país concreto. <Ent-Ad-071204-7>
'A: Why did it take so long to approve the European Constitution? – B: *To me* it does not seem to have taken so long. Time as a magnitude is different at the European level than at that of particular countries.'

Postverbal pronouns, if altogether infrequent, are more expectable in accusative and functionally intermediate contexts. As we know, postposition is typical of referents scarcely activated in the discursive-cognitive context, which through this choice are brought under the attention focus. Given that the postverbal position is also the prototypical one for the object-patient in the canonical clause, it can be hypothesized that in at least some of these contexts first- and second-person referents will be interpreted as scarcely autonomous.

This is manifest in (32), where the writer blames his explicit addressee for what he sees as betrayal against the local community, constructed through the plural first person. Its patienthood helps stress the responsibility of the agent.

(32) Lo que me extraña es que usted sea profesor de Historia y proponga el desmantelar el Archivo <de la Guerra Civil>. Pero comprendo que los favores en política se deben pagar sin mirar lo que conlleve dicho pago, como por ejemplo el vender*nos a todos los salmantinos*. <Art-Ad-290704-5>
'What puzzles me is that you+, a History professor, should propose the dismantling of the [Civil War] Archives. But I understand that political favors need to be paid without quarrelling about the price; even if it means betraying *us, all the Salamanca people*.'

As regards *gustar*-type verbs, postposition is unusual and often results in VOS rather than SVO or VSO constructions, which suggests that the object is still perceived as more salient than the subject. The choice, even if sharing the general discursive-pragmatic meanings of pronoun expression, is more of a strategy of speaker self-effacement than of informative focalization. Whereas (29) above showed the argumentative use of *a mí me parece* 'to me it seems', postverbal constructions like *se me ocurre a mí* 'it occurs to me' in (33) or *me da a mí* ('I have the impression', lit. 'it gives me [the impression]') in (34) suggest that the content is presented as more of a hypothesis than a personal stance. The placement of the pronoun right after the verb and not in the clause-final position correlates with relatively lower informativeness.

(33) nos decían / ayer y esta mañana / "no / es que date cuenta / que lo importante es que Pepe desaparezca definitivamente de la Unión Deportiva Salamanca <. . .> de una vez por todas" / y se me ocurre a mí / y digo / "ah pues sí / pues a lo mejor es verdaz / es cierto" < Dep-Co-080104-14:35>
'They were saying to us, yesterday and this morning, like "No, but look – what really matters is for P. to just disappear from the U. D. S. team [. . .] once and for all." And it occurs *to me*, and I say, "Oh well, yes, that might be true." '

(34) mientras tanto Tomás espera: / en la banda para entrar *me* da *a mí* que ni siquiera va a poder entrar <Dep-Pu-191204-18:50>
'Meanwhile, Tomás is at the side, waiting to come onto the pitch. I have the impression (lit. it gives *to me*) that he won't even have time to come on.'

In the rare cases adjusting to the SVO pattern, it is possible to interpret the first- or second-person referent as (metaphorically) affected by the agency of the subject, whose referent need not be animate, as in the following example where *la jugada individual* 'the individual move' is coreferential with a relative head acting as the subject of *sorprender* 'to surprise', while the plural first person is encoded as the postverbal object-patient.

(35) la: jugada individual / que *nos* ha sorprendido *a todos* / del delantero unionista: <Dep-Pu-191204-18:10>
'The individual move that has surprised *us all* from the Unión striker.'

Finally, some cases of postposition with displaced second-person pronouns may be aimed at avoiding the possible referential ambiguity of dative clitics *le* and *les*, which could be interpreted as indexing some third-person referent instead of the addressee or audience. This sort of compensation strategy would be justified by the scarcity of grammatical information of these morphemes, which on the one hand may prove advantageous when there is some intention to pragmatically efface a referent, but at the same time can make identification difficult without an overt pronoun (see further Section 8.3 on the issue of ambiguity with these persons).

(36) y en el Ayuntamiento / como *les* decía *a ustedes* / tambié:n esta mañana se ha hablado de obras <Var-Co-230503-13:40>
'And at the Town Council, as I was telling *you guys+*, there's also been talk about public works this morning.'

(37) y: / por supuesto esa riqueza es la que queremos *ofrecerles a ustedes* en esta sección de *Con mucho jus-* / m *gusto:* / cada::- / cada jueves <Var-On-080104-13:45>
'And of course such richness is what we want to offer *you guys+* every Thursday, in this section entitled *With pleasure*.'

The main conclusion to be drawn from the general quantitative and qualitative analysis of first- and second-person objects carried out above is that they clearly deviate from the prototype of accusatives. This is shown by their overwhelming preference for verbs selecting dative objects. Furthermore, their very low rates of pronoun formulation and of postverbal placement suggest that in most contexts their referents are highly accessible and topical (see also Aijón Oliva 2018a), which makes them approach the cognitive status of subjects. This is only natural given the inherent salience of the direct participants. The results also point to the non-discrete nature of syntactic functions discussed in Chapter 2 and to the close connection between salience and functional encoding. The neat distinction between a dative and an accusative object in Spanish, being controversial with third-person objects, is even more questionable in the case of first- and second-person ones – the lack of formal differences makes it possible to argue that there is only one object prototype, which, given its functional and semantic features, should in any case be described as dative rather than accusative. In turn, the relevant choice for the syntactic encoding of the direct participants is that between subject and object, which of course is also a gradual one and correlates with an array of variable features. Many other issues related to syntactic configuration and discursive-pragmatic meaning have also been advanced and will need to be more thoroughly discussed in the following chapters.

For now, the findings obtained in this section will be expanded in the following one by examining a significant phenomenon, namely the formulation of first- and second-person object clitics when their referents are not a priori accorded any role in the eventive structure of the clause.

3.4 Discursive datives: The indexation of "unexpected" participants

What we will term *discursive datives* can be thought to belong in the discursive domain rather than the syntactic one, even if they are not formally different from any other cases of verbal agreement through object clitics. The salience of the direct participants makes it possible for them to assume some formal features of central objects even when they do not play a defined semantic role within the event. However, as will be observed, functional tests show that they are not syntactic constituents proper. Descriptive and functional grammars have variably referred to these uses as *ethical, interest, sympathetic, non-agreeing, superfluous* or *commodi-incommodi* datives (see e.g. Porto Dapena 1997, 31–33; Gutiérrez Ordóñez 1999, 1915–1917; RAE 2009, §35.7).[6] Their formal and functional classification is a complex task, terminological variety reflecting notable differences among the categories proposed and the criteria on which they are based.

6 In grammatical description, the term *interest dative* (*dativo de interés*) often alludes to a different construction where the reflexive clitic is coreferential with the verbal ending, i.e. with the clause subject, and helps reinforce the involvement of the latter in the event: *Juan (se) leyó el libro entero en un rato* 'Juan read [himself] the whole book in just a while' (Barra Jover 1996). The indexation of a participant with no syntactic function or semantic role in the event described is clearly a different phenomenon.

However, the basic motivation for these constructions is the intention to discursively index a participant that is a priori not contemplated in an event, and can in that sense be considered "unexpected", which endows the choice with a particular discursive-pragmatic meaning.

Examples (38a) and (39a) are proposed as preliminary illustrations of the phenomenon. The clitics highlighted in italics respectively index the speaker and the addressee as apparent dative objects. However, neither *estudiar* 'to study' nor *salir* 'to come out' require the formulation of a dative object for the cognitive construction of the event. As in other cases, the English translations are just attempts at approximately capturing the discursive-pragmatic values conveyed by the Spanish clitics.

(38a) Este niño no me estudia nada
'This kid doesn't study at all (on me).'

(39a) Mañana te sale la nueva película de Batman
'The new Batman movie is coming out (on you) tomorrow.'

The fact that these clitics apparently index dative – not accusative – objects is supported, first, by their possibility to co-occur with non-coreferential accusative objects, as is the case of *la nueva película de Batman* in (39a). Also, even if the phenomenon is rare with third-person referents – probably in connection with its pragmatic meaning (Romero Morales 2008, 42–43) – the clitics used should in any case be *le* and *les*, at least in dialects conforming to the standard etymological system:

(38b) Inés se queja de que el niño no le estudia nada
'Inés complains that the kid doesn't study at all (on her).'

(39b) Jaime está contento porque mañana le sale la nueva película de Batman
'Jaime is happy because the new Batman movie is going out (on him) tomorrow.'

The non-syntactic nature of these apparent dative objects becomes patent in the difficulty to formulate a coreferential stressed pronoun within the clause – unlike what happens with dative and accusative objects proper, as analyzed in §3.3.4 above. The following alternatives to (38a) and (39a) are scarcely acceptable; the same would happen with the third-person variants in (38b), (39b).

(38c) ?Este niño *a mí* no me estudia nada

(39c) ?Mañana te sale *a ti* la nueva película de Batman

More significantly, the clitic can co-appear with another dative morpheme that does index a syntactic object, as in (40), where *le* is coreferential with *al niño* 'to the kid', while *un cero* 'an F' is the accusative object, and *me* realizes the discursive indexation of the speaker.

(40) Al niño me le pusieron un cero en Matemáticas
'To the kid (on me) (to him) they gave an F in Maths.'

We might wonder why the indexation of participants not prefigured in the eventive structure is carried out through dative-agreement morphemes and not subject or accusative ones. This is likely related to the fact that the dative correlates with less central participants than either of those functions. The subject is associated with the highest centrality, usually corresponding to the entity responsible for an action or experiencing a psychological process or state. Subjects are necessary in most Spanish clauses, which explains why this function cannot be accorded to a participant that is not conceived as playing any clear role. The same explanation should apply with accusative objects. Introducing either function as a discursive strategy would entail a higher cognitive cost. Going back to (38b), the use of an accusative clitic (*la estudia*) would radically change the interpretation of the event, turning *Inés* into a semantic theme, rather than a participant who is just attributed some involvement – most probably of an emotional kind. As for (39b), the formulation of an accusative clitic (*lo sale*) is just not possible, the verb being a priori intransitive.

Relatively low centrality is itself a characterizing trait of the objects traditionally labelled *indirect* (cf. Vázquez Rozas 1995, 88 as well as Section 2.5 above). They are prefigured by prototypical ditransitive verbs (*dar* 'to give', *decir* 'to tell', *preguntar* 'to ask') as well as by many intransitive ones encoding a human experiencer as a dative, such as *gustar*-type ones and others whose subject is the less perceptible referent, often a part or possession of the other one, e.g. *faltar* 'to lack', lit. 'to fail', *doler* 'to hurt'. With many other verbs, datives will only appear when speakers resort to grammatical means to indicate a particular relationship with the subject or the accusative, e.g. natural or acquired possession: *Le rompieron las ventanas a Pedro* 'They (to him) broke the windows to Pedro') (cf. Gutiérrez Ordóñez 1999, 1883–1915). In the following excerpt from the corpus, the formulation of *me* constructs the speaker as the owner of the hamster in question, but at the same time suggests her involvement in an event that emotionally affected her.

(41) <La gata> Me la regalaron mis compañeras de clase cuando estudiaba séptimo de EGB. Se *me* acababa de morir un hámster y ellas sabían que me gustaban mucho los animales. <Ent-Ga-150604-18>
'[The cat] was a gift from my classmates when I was in the 7th grade. A hamster had just died (*on me*) and they knew I was very fond of animals.'

Involvement as a pragmatic factor is also basic for the understanding of discursive datives. However, in these cases it will not be possible to accord the referent the syntactic function of dative object nor a semantic role such as *owner*; for example, if the speaker were talking about something or someone that could not be understood as a possession of theirs: *Se me murió Michael Jackson* 'M. J. died (on me)', uttered by a fan of the artist. The formulation of the pronoun becomes difficult just by altering the relationship between the referents. This shows that discursive dative clitics are used by speakers to construct someone – most often themselves – into an event where they would in principle not be expected. Besides, the fact that the clitics cannot co-appear with coreferential pronouns or lexical NPs indicates that their referents are attributed high salience. It is thus no wonder that the phenomenon should usually be attested with first- and second-person referents, and at most with topical third-person ones, as might be the case in (38b) and (39b) above.

Therefore, discursive datives, rather than agreement morphemes correlating with syntactic constituents as such, are indexical elements used to suggest the involvement of their referents in the discursive-cognitive context. They offer a clear instantiation of how discourse construction can resort to lower-level grammatical elements and exploit the meanings intrinsically attached to them – in the case of clitics, their systematic association with relatively salient referents.

In the corpus, most instances of the phenomenon are found in radio texts, particularly those from music programs, where a clearly conversational style is most often displayed (see Chapter 9). They can be put in connection with pragmatic strategies of broadcasters to suggest personal rapport with their audience. This is all the more notorious with verbs whose eventive structure makes the formulation of a dative object hardly expectable. Here are examples with *estrenar* 'to use or try something for the first time' and *asustarse* 'to get scared'. The indexation of participants – the nonspecific addressee in (42), the speaker in (43) – suggests analogous motivations in both examples. In the first one, the broadcaster implies that the songs in his station are not just played – they are played with the anonymous listener in mind and offered to him/her. In (43), the speaker manages to convey his own interest in the third-person referent's not getting scared by adjoining a first-person singular clitic to the verb, which has an obvious expressive effect in this written context.

(42) la canción que os vamos a poner / también inédita se llama / *Lo noto:* // recuerda <. . .> dos temas nuevos: / en esta mañana que *te* estrenamo:s:: <Mus-40-220803-11:45>
'The song we're going to play, also unreleased so far, is called *Lo noto.* Remember, there's two new singles we're playing (*on you*) for the first time this morning.'

(43) Bienvenido al Día Nacional de la Salud. No se *me* asuste Ricardo García Juan ni ninguno de los miembros de su organigrama sanitario <Art-Ga-221203-4b>
'Welcome to the National Health Day. Let R. G. J. and all the members of his medical staff not get scared (*on me*).'

Another intransitive verb with some number of cases is *irse* 'to leave', being the reflexive variant of *ir* 'to go'. Through the discursive dative, the speaker suggests the repercussion of someone's departure on him/herself (44) or a wider group where he/she is included (45). The reflexive construction of the verb results in the coalescence of two clitics, of which the one indexing the subject will always precede the discursive dative (*te-me; se-nos*), in accordance with general rules of clitic ordering (Perlmutter 1971, 44–45; Fernández Soriano 1999a, 1264).

(44) antes de escuchar uno de los destacaz- / a: de los destacados: / hacemos una / m:ínima parada / no te *me* vaya:s:: <Mus-40-220803-10:25>
'Just before listening to one of our top entries, we are making a very short stop. Don't leave (*on me*).'

(45) un álbum que Manuel Carrasco: se *nos* fue a grabar / ha:sta Italia y el resultado: / lo tienes ya en tus mano:s <Mus-Di-251104-10:25>
'M. C. left (*on us*) for Italy in order to record this album, and the result is now in your hands.'

The choice can even result in atypical solutions from the perspective of standard grammar, but which are again explainable on discursive-pragmatic grounds. In both of the following excerpts, the intuition of grammatical discordance appears to have led speakers to reformulation.

(46) también / *les:* mencionaremos- *les* contaremos / e:se: homenaje que se va a desarrollar hoy / a:l músico Dámaso Ledesma <Var-SE-300503-19:20>
'We will also mention (*to you guys+*) – we will tell (*you guys+*) about the tribute to be paid today to musician D. L.'

(47) esto es un intercambio de cromos / Antonio *nos* ha compartido- *nos* ha dao este: recuerdo / de este dato que desconocíamos de la Plaza Mayor <Var-SE-011204-13:25>
'This is like trading cards at school. Antonio has shared (*to us*) – he's given (*us*) this memory of his, a fact we didn't know about the Major Square.'

In (46) the clitic could actually be interpreted as indexing a dative object proper: *mencionar* 'to mention', despite being rarely constructed with a dative, is a *verbum dicendi* that might well follow the basic ditransitive pattern of many others like *decir* 'to say, to tell'. However, just after formulating the construction, the speaker quickly rewords it as *les contaremos* 'we will tell (you guys+)', replacing the verb with another one that is felt to be more suitable to that scheme. The case of (47) is a similar one. The eventive structure of *compartir* 'to share' contemplates an accusative object together with an oblique, i.e. *to share sth with sb*. The speaker turns the latter into a dative through clitic indexation: *nos ha compartido* 'has shared (to us)', enhancing the salience of the plural first-person referent. However, the grammatical anomaly of the result again seems to trigger reformulation through ditransitive *dar* 'to give'.

Besides, apparent discursive datives may become lexicalized as part of specific constructions, such as *si te soy sincero* 'to be honest', lit. 'if I'm honest (to you)', as in (48). While *ser* 'to be' does not prefigure a dative object, the modalizing value of the construction favors its interpretation as a communication verb with a receiver or beneficiary in its eventive structure.

(48) <A> ¿estará: Zé Tó:: en condiciones para el domingo? / ¿qué le pasa a Zé Tó? / <B> pues: yo / si *te* soy sincero / le veo m:uy muy poco optimista <Dep-Co-080104-14:45>
'A: Will Zé Tó be ready to play on Sunday? What's the matter with Zé Tó? – B: Well, to be honest (*to you*), I don't see him optimistic at all.'

As can be inferred, fluctuations in the eventive structure of verbal lexemes are frequent and tightly connected with discursive-cognitive construction. All this is reflected on the functional continuum of datives themselves, from objects proper in ditransitive constructions to merely discursive indexations (Gutiérrez Ordóñez 1999). Just as there are non-syntactic dative clitics, in other contexts the dative is actually prefigured, but its omission has become so lexicalized that, when the clitic does appear, it is possible to perceive the enhancement of referent salience that is common to all the examples reviewed so far. In (49), instead of the argumentative reinforcer *por no decir* 'not to say', the speaker opts for the less automatized *por no decirte* 'not to say (to you)', exploiting the discursive-pragmatic effects of addressee indexation.

(49) y también nos llegaba una noticia: / que nosotros / *te* hemo:s e / venido / dando a lo largo: de las últimas semanas por no decir*te* mese:s <Mus-Di-251104-10:40>
'We have also received some news that we have been advancing (*to you*) over the past weeks, not to say (*to you*) months.'

In turn, when a construction with agreement has come to be lexicalized, the involvement of the referent can be further stressed through the formulation of the object pronoun. Explicit formulation correlates with lower salience, but in turn highlights the personal scope of the content and its argumentative orientation, particularly with singular first-person indexations (see Section 3.3 above). This is what happens in (50), where, instead of the usual discursive tag *no me digas que no* 'don't tell (me) it's not so', we find *no me digas a mí que no*, with an overt first-person object pronoun.[7]

(50) <A> pues yo no los he p- / no los he probado pero es que me parece una mezcla rarísima Santiago //
<B> ¡pero es estupenda: / no *me* digas *a mí* que no! / precisamente / en eso consiste la cocina <Var-SE-300503-19:40>
'A: Well, I've never tried it, but it seems to me like a really weird mixture, Santiago. – B: But it's a great one! Don't tell *me* it's not so! That's what cooking is really about.'

The preceding exposition on discursive datives has made it possible to further observe how first- and second-person object clitics enhance the contextual salience of the direct participants in contexts where they do not play a clear semantic role. Their morphematic indexation in the verbal nucleus helps suggest

7 There is also a variant with elision of both the clitic and the pronoun, i.e. *No digas que no* 'Don't say it's not so'. It should entail the lowest degree of speaker involvement, dispensing with indexation altogether.

personal involvement in the event and thus contributes to the achievement of specific pragmatic goals.

3.5 Summary

First- and second-person forms are the main linguistic means used to construct the direct participants of communicative acts. These participants are presupposed by communication itself and need to be viewed as discursive-cognitive constructions rather than as "real" extralinguistic beings, even if they usually coincide with straightforwardly identifiable human entities. Their high perceptibility is reflected in the relative simplicity of first- and second-person subparadigms and their scarcity of grammatical informations, especially in comparison with the wide array of possibilities available for the construction of external entities.

When encoded in central clause functions, the first and second persons need to be indexed in the verbal nucleus, either through subject-agreeing verbal endings or object-agreeing clitics. However, there is variation as regards the formulation of coreferential stressed pronouns – sometimes lexical NPs with the plural persons – as well as their placement within the clause, most significantly the position they adopt with respect to the verb. The preliminary empirical analyses carried out in this chapter show that the syntactic encoding of first- and second-person referents is an area of linguistic variation and choice that cannot be understood irrespective of the construction of cognitive meanings at various levels, including the semantic, discursive-pragmatic and social ones. While we have paid special attention to first- and second-person objects, given their less prototypical features and the scarce attention they have received in comparison with subjects, it is true that the latter function is overwhelmingly more frequent and constitutes the prototypical choice with them. Both types of functional encoding need to be integrated within a general view of syntactic configuration as a basic resource for the discursive-cognitive construction of entities and events.

The following five chapters form the main body of the investigation and are respectively devoted to each of the grammatical persons under analysis, with Chapter 8 simultaneously dealing with the singular and plural displaced second persons. The first section of each chapter will present the formal-functional description and succint diachronic discussion of the grammatical subparadigm in question, trying to paraphrase and explain its inherent meaning – e.g. *the speaker* for the singular first person – as well as its implications for discursive-cognitive construction. In the second section, we will analyze the referential possibilities of each person – i.e. the different entities or groups it can be interpreted to refer to – in actual communicative situations. Participant (non)specificity as well as inclusion vs. exclusion will prove to be fundamental notions for the analysis of person reference in Spanish. In the third section, patterns of quantitative variation and contextual usage regarding the variable expression and placement of pronouns will be discussed, following the lines of the preliminary analysis presented in this chapter. We will take into account the inherent relationship of syntactic variants with salience and informativeness, as well as the discursive-pragmatic repercussions of their choice in interactional contexts. A similar kind of analysis will be applied in the fourth section to the choice between subject and object functional encoding, the latter variant usually being rather less frequent and favoring a particular cognitive construction of participants. In a final section, the main findings of the chapter will be summed up and contrasted with those of other grammatical persons.

4 The singular first person: *the speaker*

4.1 The subparadigm and its meaning

The subject pronoun *yo* (< Lat. EGO) and its associated subparadigm of referential morphemes are the grammatical means whereby the person speaking or writing is prototypically constructed in Spanish. The verbal endings indicating subject agreement with this person are different vowels and diphthongs at the end of the nucleus: *-o* or *-oy* in the simple present (*digo* 'I say', *soy* 'I am'), *-é*, *-í* or *-e* (with irregular stressed roots) in the perfective simple past (*hablé* 'I spoke', *comí* 'I ate', *vine* 'I came'), and so on. Many forms are homonymous with those of the singular third person, e.g. the imperfective simple past (*cantaba* 'I/he used to sing'), the conditional (*saldría* 'I/he would go out') and all subjunctive tenses. This homonymy could be taken to support the hypothesis that the second person is actually the most salient one in Spanish, given that its referential morphemes are rarely if ever ambiguous (see §1.3.1a above on the relative salience of the first and second persons). However, lack of grammatical specification is also a typical feature of highly salient elements, as has also been observed across the preceding chapters.

The stressed object pronoun is *mí* – always preceded by *a* or a preposition marking a peripheral function – coming from the Latin dative pronoun MIHI, while the corresponding clitic form is *me*, from the accusative pronoun ME. Formal case distinctions being long lost, *mí* and *me* are now correlative forms used to index any first-person central object. When the first-person object pronoun is to be preceded by the preposition *con* 'with', the amalgamated form *conmigo* (< CUM ME-CUM) needs to be used instead of **con mí*. Finally, first-person possessive determiners and pronouns (*mi, mis, mío, mía*, etc.) are variably marked for gender and number. As pointed out, the present investigation will focus on the functions of subject and central object. The following made-up examples and their glosses make it possible to observe how the singular first person is morphematically indexed and variably formulated in both subject (1, 2) and object (3) contexts.

(1) (yo) escuch- -o
I listen 1ST.SING.PRES
'I listen.'

(2) (yo) los escuch- -a- -r- -é
I 3RD.PL.MASC.ACC.CL listen THEME-V FUT 1ST.SING
'I will listen to them.'

https://doi.org/10.1515/9783110643442-005

(3) (a mí) no me escuch- -a- -r- -án
to me not 1ST.SING.CL listen THEME-V FUT 3RD.PL
'They won't listen to me.'

The basic discursive-cognitive meaning of the grammatical singular first person will be paraphrased as *the speaker*. The use of this person for the construction of a referent places the responsibility on the latter to carry out a communicative act through language. At the same time, it claims for this participant the right to be acknowledged the capacity of speaking by others. It is actually the use of self-referential first-person forms that makes someone qualify as the speaker or writer in a given context – when anyone takes the turn from someone else in conversational interactions, he/she will most often start with either a subject first-person pronoun or an object one (see 4.3 below). According to Mühlhäusler/Harré (1990, 91–94), the first person has a double indexical power – it indexes the spatio-temporal coordinates of the utterance in connection with those of the speaker, but also the responsibility of the speaker for the illocutionary force and perlocutionary effects of the utterance, e.g. its trustworthiness. We could suggest that there are two basic ways of speaking and writing, namely an *implicit* one – whereby discourse is produced with no formal indexations of the person who is producing it – and an *explicit* one – whereby a participant asserts his/her status of speaker; such an assertion is carried out, first and foremost, through first-person grammatical forms (Aijón Oliva/Serrano 2010b, 15). The distinction is tightly connected with that between discursive-cognitive subjectivity and objectivity, which are the main factors underlying the continuum of socio-communicative styles (see especially Section 9.1).

The speaker is, however, always basic to discourse production and interpretation. Wherever there is discourse, there needs to be someone producing it, who can in turn be formally manifested or not. To this we can add that, if referent salience is understood as the cognitive status of referents that results from their perceptibility, autonomy and accessibility, it seems only natural to assume that the most salient referent for someone speaking or writing should a priori be him/herself. If the speaker is made explicit in discourse, a variety of linguistic choices – pronoun formulation vs. mere morphematical indexation, preverbal vs. postverbal placement of the pronoun, subject vs. object encoding – can be resorted to in order to modulate the construction of this participant. Actually, across the subsequent analysis it will be observed that the patterns of grammatical choice are not always the most expectable ones if only inherent salience were taken into account.

In sum, the very act of self-identifying as a speaker or writer through the use of grammatical first-person forms will invest anyone with a particular discursive-cognitive status – they will be accorded the capacity, as well as the responsibility, to produce discourse and thus promote a certain cognitive construction of everything that is within it. The first and most relevant decision for a speaker to make is, naturally, who the addressee or audience is, since the latter will also be cognitively singled out from all other possible entities (see Sections 6.1 and 7.1 on the notions of *addressee* and *audience*). However, the use of second-person forms to construct others is also a way of self-affirmation – precisely because it is the speaker that has the power to identify someone else as "the other" – thus constitutes a more subjective choice in itself that the absence of first- and second-person indexations altogether. Speaker status depends on the features of the communicative situation itself, but also, whenever interactional roles are not clearly predefined, on the negotiation of communicative roles by the participants, which is often carried out through discourse markers and constructions containing personal indexations (see e.g. Fuller 2003).

The singular first person can thus be viewed as the set of grammatical resources used to construct the speaker, i.e. the participant who is explicitly producing discourse in some context, as well as assuming the power to accord different communicative roles to others. We will now turn to the analysis of the referential possibilities of this person, in order to ascertain which kinds of extradiscursive entities can be constructed into discourse and cognition through its choice.

4.2 The construction of reference

As should be inferred from the preceding discussion, *the speaker* is not necessarily equivalent to "the individual speaking or writing". However, it is true that, among grammatical persons, the singular first one appears to correlate with the lowest degree of referential variability – the great majority of tokens in the corpus appear to have the specific person speaking or writing as their referent. *Yo* is thus not so clearly amenable to the referential shifts and ambiguities that are often found with other persons, such as the plural first one or the singular second one (see Sections 5.2 and 6.2 below). However, the degree to which the forms in this subparadigm are really intended to denote a specific human being depends on the context – not to mention the fact that the extradiscursive existence of such a human being need not be taken as a given, since also fictional characters can be speakers. In the domain of media communication, the self appears to be a particularly complex construct. People often do not talk solely on their own behalf, but rather on that of the associations or corporations they represent in the context (Xiang 2003); different references thus tend to overlap within the same participant. Of course, there is also the possibility for speakers to assume false, imaginary or nonspecific identities depending on the context.

The latter happens, for example, in radio commercials featuring voice actors who play anonymous, archetypal characters expressing necessities, desires or opinions the targeted audience is expected to identify with. Examples (4) and (5) are taken from two such texts where voices intended to represent different social groups – respectively a young woman and two middle-aged friends – convey stances that should expectably be shared by people approaching those sociodemographic archetypes. The speakers are thus constructing a particular reality where they do not speak for themselves, but actually for those expected to be listening.

(4) si *volviera a casarme:* / *cambiaría* de traje: / de iglesia / ha:sta de novio: / pero N:UNca de restaurante: <Anu-To-080803-11:40>
'If (*I*) were to get married again, (*I*)'d change wedding dresses, churches – even grooms. But never restaurants.'

(5) <A> *he quedado* con Eva en Biblos y *llego* tarde / ya *me* ha llamado / dos veces /
<B> tranqui:lo / se estará tomando algo / en Biblos / tienen unas raciones / es: / -quisitas / espera / *me voy* contigo < Anu-SE-281204-13:55>
'A: (*I*) was to meet Eva at B. and (*I*)'m late. She's already called (*me*) twice. – B: Don't worry. She must be having a drink at B. They have delicious dishes. Wait! (*I*)'m going with you.'

Such uses are referentially similar to the *nonspecific* second persons that are more often found in the discourse of advertising and in media broadcasting in general (see §6.2.2) – they are intended to be assumed by (some or all) listeners as referring to themselves. In fact, it is the audience rather than the speaker that actually realizes extradiscursive reference by assigning the most relevant contextual interpretation to the person chosen; this is also true of the rest of grammatical persons (Posio 2012, 343). The possibility of nonspecific interpretation with the singular first person is clear whenever a fictional character acts out recurrent attitudes in everyday situations (example 6). Also involved here is the question of polyphony that proves so relevant for the analysis of literary discourse (Reyes 1984).

(6) Unos cachorros caninos comparten el protagonismo con conejitos de pelo largo tras el cristal. El niño dice "mamá, *yo quiero* uno, se lo *pido* a los Reyes". Hay que saber decir que no. <Rep-Ad-071204-12>

'Some puppies share the spotlight with long-haired little rabbits behind the shopping window. The child says, "Mom, *I* want one of those, (*I*)'m gonna ask the Three Wisemen for it." One needs to know how to say no.'

The use of the singular first person intending for addressees to interpret it as denoting themselves appears as a subtle discursive-pragmatic choice, more so than that of e.g. second persons with the goal of persuading others. This is because the speaker in these contexts is actually a fictional character talking just for him/herself, thus cannot be held accountable for the attribution of his/her personal stance to others. It is in any case the audience that will be responsible of self-identifying with it. We can thus conclude that this particular sort of non-specific singular first person, even if not very frequent outside spoken commercials, is a significant resource for argumentation and persuasion.

There are other contexts where the forms of the subparadigm do not entail the assumption of a fictional or archetypal identity but still seem to refer not just to the speaker, but to anyone who might find him/herself in an analogous situation. These uses can be considered referentially similar to those of speaker-inclusive or objectivizing second persons (§6.2.3) and can appear even when the stance or experience at stake is a clearly personal one – we could actually speak of *audience-inclusive* uses of the singular first person. However, their apparently scarce conventionalization, together with the intuitive tendency to interpret *yo* as referring to just the individual who is speaking, makes many examples doubtful as to their intended reference. The following ones can be taken as illustration.

(7) ¿ves? este es uno de esos temas que podemos cantar sin problema de: / "*llego:* no *cojo* el tono: / qué al:to / qué agudo" / ¿eh? / tan normal <Mus-Di-251104-13:35>
'You see? This is one of those songs we can sing with no need to go like "(*I*) can't reach, (*I*) can't get the pitch, it's so high, so sharp." No problem here, right?'

(8) El principal objetivo del voluntario de Aspace es conseguir que las personas con algún tipo de parálisis cerebral, "disfruten de la vida como *yo mismo* lo hago", apuntó. <Rep-Ga-260804-15>
'The main goal of a volunteer at Aspace is to make people with any type of cerebral palsy "enjoy life as *I* do myself", she pointed out.'

In (7), the broadcaster is mimicking a typical attitude of people trying to perform a high-pitched song. The actual reference of the singular first person in this context may be difficult to delimit – it could be interpreted as yet another case of character performance – but in any case it is clearly not restricted to the one speaking. In (8), the interpretation of *yo* as having an extended reference is favored by an interesting detail – the person quoted, a female volunteer, adjoins to the pronoun the intensifying adjective *mismo* 'myself' in its masculine form, instead of the expectable feminine one *misma*. Masculine forms are used as gender-unmarked in Spanish, which suggests that this speaker is not specifically thinking of herself but also of any of his colleagues at the association; after all, she is being interviewed as a spokesperson for the latter. The same unmarked use is found in (9) below with *ciudadano* 'citizen (masc.)'; the singular first person is again used to construct a participant whose extradiscursive reference goes beyond the person speaking and is meant to be applicable to any citizen in the situation described. However, there is a final transition to a more clearly individual reference with *yo creo* 'I think', whereby the particular stance of the speaker is summed up.

(9) hay / informes del Consejo de Estado / donde / una reclamación como la que *yo* ciudadano *me* están rechazando / *me* la debe / de pagar el Ayuntamiento / y luego el Ayuntamiento debe negociar con la empresa: / concesionaria / eso es lo que *yo creo* que deben de hacer los ciudadanos reclamar / la vía administrativa / ante el Ayuntamiento <Inf-SE-301104-14:25>
'There are reports by the Council of State saying that if *I*, as a citizen, have a claim rejected (*to me*), it is the Town Council that must pay (*me*) the costs. And then it is the Council that will have to negotiate with the concession holder. That's what *I* think citizens need to do – to request the administrative procedure before the Town Council.'

We can also point out that, in all of the preceding examples, the use of a speaker-inclusive or objectivizing second person would have been possible as well, i.e. *no coges el tono* 'you can't get the pitch' in (7); *como tú mismo lo haces* 'as you yourself do' in (8), etc. This is of course not meant to say that both choices should be "synonymous" or "equivalent" in any sense. Both grammatical persons appear to fulfill similar pragmatic functions in the contexts reviewed, but the basic meanings entailed by either of them will still be present and somehow condition the interpretation of utterances.

Finally, the referential analysis of grammatical persons needs to take into account constructions that show a tendency to pragmaticalization in parallel to a progressive blurring of personal reference. They behave much like fixed forms not resulting from syntactic operations concerning the establishment of agreement between the verb and a linguistically encoded referent, rather approaching the features of discourse markers. In the case of the singular first person, there is often ambiguity as to the extent to which the individual speaking is actually referring to him/herself, or rather using a conventionalized modality marker in order to indicate degrees of certainty and/or personal involvement regarding the content. This is the case with forms like (*yo*) *creo* 'I think, I believe', (*yo*) *digo* 'I say' and (*a mí*) *me parece* 'it seems to me'. In oral discourse they show high frequencies of occurrence, as well as notable positional freedom within utterances (cf. Aijón Oliva/Serrano 2010b and Posio 2013 on *creo*). The verbs in the three following examples have not been formulated before the embedded clause they should govern from a syntactic viewpoint, which suggests they are being used as more of discursive resources.

(10) al final la lesión se queda en una rotura: de fibras en los isquiotibiales / muslo / izquierdo *creo* ¿no? <Dep-On-141204-15:15>
'The injury finally comes down to harmstring fiber breakage in your left thigh, *I think*, right?'

(11) ya se habla / ya ven ustedes ya escuchan ustedes de la / r:ecolección de setas / claro que para eso tendrá que llover algo *digo yo:* <Var-SE-230903-12:30>
'There's already talk, as you guys+ can see and hear, about mushroom picking. But well, it will have to rain a little before that, *I guess* (lit. I say).'

(12) hay un: par de temas / que además / *me parece* hoy aparecen publicados en la prensa en función de lo que argumentan otras formaciones políticas <Var-Co-230503-12:45>
'There are a couple of issues that also, *it seems to me*, have come up in today's newspapers, in relation to what other political groups are arguing.'

As is the case with the discursive datives reviewed in Section 3.4, the communicative power of these first-person inflected verbs lies in their capacity to index the speaker – not necessarily the individual speaking – and thus indicate some sort of relationship between the latter and the content of utterances, instead of constructing it as detached from personal viewpoints. In spite of the pragmaticalization process undergone by constructions of this sort, it is important to note that they are all subject to variation in the formulation and placement of the first-person pronoun (e.g. *creo*/*yo creo*/*creo yo*), which, from a constructional perspective, suggests that there are in fact three different constructions, thus three different meanings involved in each case. Variation according to pronoun expression and placement entails significant discursive-pragmatic differences that will be further discussed below.

While it is still true that most uses of the singular first person in the corpus are specific ones, that is, they are not seemingly intended to discursively construct any entity other than the actual individual speaking or writing, the different cases reviewed show that intended extralinguistic reference is a complex matter and often proves difficult to operationalize. Zobel (2016), in a study of "impersonal" readings of the singular first person in German, also notes the frequent difficulty in detecting such uses, given their lack of specific grammatical encoding. However, this should hardly represent a problem for an approach assuming the existence of invariable intrinsic meanings that can have varied contextual repercussions. The speaker as a discursive-cognitive construction is always the same, but the interpretation of who the speaker is, and of the relationship between the speaker and the content of discourse, will be rather variable according to the context, often with subtle semantic and pragmatic nuances in connection with particular formal choices. In subsequent chapters it will be shown that the different referential variants alluded to here – such as the nonspecific, audience-inclusive and pragmaticalized ones – are often more recurrent and conventionalized with other grammatical persons, thus easier to identify in usage contexts.

4.3 Variable expression and placement of pronouns

The quantitative analyses will be based on all the singular first-person tokens found across the corpus, that is, all cases of subject or object first-person verbal indexations, even in constructions that appear to be partly pragmaticalized, for the reasons exposed above. Other grammatical persons will require different methodological decisions (see especially Section 5.2 on the plural first one), since there are clearly fixed constructions not allowing for any formal variation, and with such a diffuse referential value that they are probably not even interpreted as participant indexations in contemporary usage.

The corpus contains a total 2,698 clauses with singular first-person subject or object indexations.[1] In this section we will start by analyzing the variable formulation of stressed pronouns in those clauses. Table 4.1 shows the respective percentages of expression and omission of singular first-person *yo* and (*a*) *mí*.

1 Cases of reflexivity, where the referent is simultaneously indexed through subject and object agreement morphemes, are counted as subject tokens, based on the consideration of reflexivity as a discursive-cognitive reinforcement of the subject (see also §2.3.1 above).

Table 4.1: Expression vs. omission of singular first-person pronouns.

	Subject (*yo*)		**Object (*a mí*)**		**Total**	
	#	%	#	%	#	%
Expression	569	26.3	84	15.7	653	24.2
Omission	1,594	73.7	451	84.3	2,045	75.8
Total	2,163	80.2	535	19.8	2,698	100

As exposed in the preceding chapter, omission-indexation is the dominant choice with first- and second-person referents, which is easy to put in connection with the high discursive-cognitive salience of the direct participants, and especially with their perceptibility. Even so, the scores of expression with singular first-person pronouns (24.2% altogether) are by no means negligible in comparison with those of others to be reviewed below. Also, this person, just like most others, achieves higher percentages of pronoun formulation when encoded as a subject (26.3 against 15.7%). This will need some explanation, since according to our general hypothesis on the relationship between salience and syntactic functions, the subject is prototypically associated with the most salient participant, which in turn should make it expectable for objects to be more often formulated.

Omission of *yo* and *a mí*, accounting for three quarters of the total singular first-person tokens in the corpus, can be considered to be the unmarked choice in most discursive contexts. In fact, when discourse is constructed from the viewpoint of the speaker – as usually evidenced by first-person indexations across consecutive clauses – and no other referent in the context can compete for the position of highest salience, it will be possible to find extensive discourse stretches with no instances of pronoun formulation (see example 13, as well as Chapter 3, example 2). In turn, the contextual competition among referents is one of the most evident triggers of pronoun expression, as shown by the contrast established between *yo* and *tú* as possible subject-agents of the event in (14).

(13) es cierto *corrí* con: mucha cabeza y: / con una: sangre muy fría / cosa que:: *hago* muy pocas veces / porque: *tuve* el valor de: ir allí alante y: / y- / no / tu- / no *di* la cara / en muchas ocasiones porque: / *fui:* / siempre resguardada segunda y tercera / y:: / la verdá que cuando: / *podía:* haber / tirado un poquillo en mitad de la carrera / no *me* convenía y: / *hice* lo que *pude* <Dep-On-141204-15:25>

'It's true, (*I*) ran wisely and with a cool head, which is something (*I*) seldom do. (*I*) had the courage to move forward, but (*I*) didn't really show my intentions; rather, (*I*) stayed hidden in the second and third positions, and truly, when halfway along the race (*I*) could have sprinted a little, this didn't suit (*me*) fine. And well, (*I*) did what (*I*) could.'

(14) <A> a lo mejor luchando / a contracorriente // tengo: / que abrirme por dentro y gritar: / lo que hoy tenemos que contar // ¿lo cuentas *tú* o lo digo *yo*? / <B> casi mejor que lo dices *tú* <Dep-Co-080104-14:30>
'A: Perhaps fighting against the tide, I need to tear myself open and shout what we need to say today. Shall *you* say it, or shall *I*? – B: *You* may as well say it.'

However, to explain pronoun formulation as motivated by the competition between discursive referents or the supposed difficulty to identify them may prove oversimplifying and dependent on particular contexts. It must be kept in mind that most first-person verbal endings and clitics are grammatically non-ambiguous. While it is true that the endings for the first and third persons are homonymous in several tenses, such as the conditional and subjunctive ones, there is never isomorphism with the singular second person, which means that a second-person agreeing verb can hardly be misinterpreted as to its reference. Hypotheses on "functional compensation", relating the expression of pronouns to reference disambiguation in contexts of morphematic homonymy, have been put forward for Spanish (e.g. Hochberg 1986) but are not convincingly supported by the data (Cameron 1993; Silva-Corvalán/Enrique-Arias 2017, 176–178). In fact, even when the referents in contrast are the specific individual speaking and another specific one listening, pronoun expression seems practically inescapable, as happens in example (14) above. Also, in (15), the speaker exposes the request made by an external institution and the response he has given. The formulation of *yo* in the latter clause is coherent with the explicit contrast established between both of the referents and their respective stances.

(15) siempre y cuando: / noh pongamoh de acuerdo en las condicione y todo eso / porque la Fe(de)ración Ehpañola *nos* decía de que: había que pagar un: / canon: de: / quinientos euro / y: *yo* le he dicho: que no <Dep-Co-080104-15:00>
'As long as we can reach an agreement on the conditions and such, because the Spanish Federation was telling (*us*) that we needed to pay a 500-euro fee, and *I* said to them no way.'

This begs for a broader view of the contextual motivations and repercussions of pronoun expression, particularly in the case of first and second persons. We have shown that informativeness cannot be merely understood as the discursive status of new, unexpected or non-inferable third-person referents, but rather must also be applicable to first- and second-person ones (see Section 3.2). Expressed pronouns, being most often unnecessary for the identification of these referents, must be aimed at constructing meanings that can hardly be accomplished through omission-indexation alone. The person speaking feels the need to make his/her own presence more notorious to the audience, i.e. to explicitly make him/herself *the speaker* by coming under the focus of attention through a stressed referential form. Therefore, our distinction in the previous section between *implicit* and *explicit* ways of speaking, depending on whether the speaker is discursively encoded, becomes more complex by taking into account features of constructional choice such as pronoun expression and placement.

The formulation of a pronoun is intended to make the audience direct their attention towards its referent. In the case of the singular first person, the choice between expression and omission is of paramount importance, since the interpretation of utterances will be conditioned by the degree to which the speaker appears to be involved in them. The excerpt transcribed in (13) above was clearly constructed from the viewpoint of the speaker, but it lacked overt personal pronouns. In other cases, such pronouns are recurrent and help construct a more subjective kind of discourse. The potential has often been noted of expressed subject pronouns to enhance the assertiveness of utterances and underline personal responsibility for the content (Bentivoglio 1987, 61; Davidson 1996; Stewart 2003). The choice is typical of argumentative discourse where people are expected to talk for themselves and expose their own subjective stances. Excerpt (16) is taken from the same interview in (13) and was uttered just a few seconds later; in turn, (17) is from a phone call to a program by an anonymous listener. In both of them we can observe the formulation of *yo* with psychological verbs (*creo, pienso* 'I think') with a largely pragmaticalized modalizing function.

(16) *yo creo* que: / todo lo hace la esperiencia y: los años / porque: / siempre: poco a poco y: / competición co- / tras competición se nota y:- // y oye *yo creo* que: s:í / que todo esto te lleva a lo que: requiere: una carrera atlética <Dep-On-141204-15:25>
'*I* think it's all a matter of experience and age, because you always notice some progression, little by little and race after race, and well, *I* do think so – all this makes you acquire what is needed for an athletic career.'

(17) *yo pienso:* / que: bueno: en:- en parte tiene: / culpa pues- / pues eso la:- / la gente que tiene allí su:- / su puesto / pero en parte / también tiene culpa el Ayuntamiento <...> porque: / *yo* he:- / he estado: en: un: mogollón de sitios <Var-SE-230903-13:55>
'*I* think that, well, this is partly the fault of the people who have their stalls there, but it's also partly the Town Council's fault. [...] Because *I*'ve been to a whole lot of places.'

Therefore, the choice between omission and expression of the pronoun correlates with different degrees of discursive-pragmatic emphasis on the speaker's involvement in the content discussed. Whereas an interviewee in a non-contentious context will often opt for pronoun omission, in an interview or debate where personal stances are discussed it will be easier to find instances of expression. (18) and (19) respectively illustrate both situations with the verb *gustar* 'to like', lit. 'to please', which as we know selects the human experiencer as a dative object. In cases of formulation, the pronoun is most often placed at the beginning of the utterance, suggesting the topicality of the referent and paralleling the usual behavior of subjects (see further below on placement).

(18) *Me* gustan los temas sencillos, temas que *me* preocupan. Observo la realidad, el paso del tiempo. También *me* gusta hacer críticas al amor o girar en torno a los sueños. <Ent-Ga-030604-18>
'(*I*) like (lit. they please [*me*]) simple subjects, subjects (*I*)'m concerned about (lit. that worry [*me*]). (*I*) also like criticizing love or dealing with dreams.'

(19) *a mí* lo que más *me* gusta / de este:- / de este jugador / m: de Cristian Lupidio / es esa capacidaz / guerrera que tiene <Dep-Co-080104-14:50>
'What *I* like (lit. What pleases *me*) most about this player, about C. L., is the fighting capacity he has.'

This amounts to saying that the choice between pronoun omission and expression is related to the features of the interaction and the communicative goals of speakers, strongly conditioning the interpretation of the content of discourse. Aijón Oliva/Serrano (2010b; 2013, 82–84) observe notorious correlations between the SV construction *yo creo* 'I think' and argumentative contexts (see again example 16). In turn, Ø *creo* is more often found with an epistemic value whereby the content is put forward as a hypothesis rather than as an opinion. Interestingly, this makes it possible for speakers to present clearly personal stances as more of hypothetical, seemingly objective facts through pronoun omission. In

(20), the speaker expresses his own judgment about the assessments previously made by an interlocutor. The omission of *yo*, while entailing lesser personal involvement than expression, helps present the content as somehow presupposed.

(20) la verdaz es que: / *creo* que le qui- / *creo* que tiene algo de razón nos hemos acostumbrado en general / a que como todos los días se pierden: puestos de trabajo por una cosa o por la otra / pues ya / m / como que no le prestamos: e / e: atención <Var-SE-211204-13:50>
'The truth is (*I*) think, (*I*) think you+ are partly right – in general we've grown used to jobs being destroyed everyday for one reason or another, so it seems that this no longer draws our attention.'

Now, the same analysis can be applied to modalizing constructions encoding the speaker as a syntactic object. The most frequent ones are those with the verb *parecer* 'to seem'. While its attributive construction is normally used to express a personal evaluation (*El resultado me parece bien* 'The outcome (to me) seems OK'), there is also a non-attributive one where it modalizes a content encoded as an embedded clause (*Me parece que lloverá* 'It seems (to me) that it will rain'). However, and quite in line with the previously reviewed *creer*, it can often be found at different syntactic positions, resembling the behavior of a discourse marker and having no formal connection with the clause it supposedly governs. The very formulation of the clitic *me* is variable, in accordance with the lesser centrality of datives as against subjects – it would be impossible to elide the subject-agreeing verbal ending in *creo*. According to Cornillie (2007, 20–22), variation in this context is related to the commitment and reliability of the speaker. The clitic helps present the statement as subjective, while its absence entails a displacement towards intersubjectivity (Ø *Parece que lloverá* 'It seems it will rain'). If there is clitic indexation, pragmatic meanings can be further modulated through the variable formulation and placement of *a mí*. The following examples illustrate the three possibilities. Of course, sequences with no pronoun and no clitic like (21) have not been included in our analysis, since they are not examples of participant construction through linguistic means. They avoid any indication that the viewpoint adopted is that of the speaker. Clitic indexation with pronoun omission as in (22) (*me parece*) is typically associated with expository rather than argumentative discourse and can, for example, reduce commitment on the part of the person speaking when he/she is not sure about some fact he/she is putting forward. Finally, as already noted, the variant with the overt pronoun (23), usually placed before the verb (*a mí me parece*), highlights the personal nature of an opinion in the course of explicit argumentation.

(21) la ley del 2002 se redactó, en teoría, para proteger al menor y alejarlo de la tentación de la borrachera. Y ahora *parece* que de lo que se trata es de alejarlo de donde molesta y protegernos los demás. <Art-Ga-221104-3>
'The 2002 law was drawn up, in theory, to protect minors and keep them away from the temptation of drinking. And now *it seems* that it's all about protecting the rest of us by keeping them away from where they can disturb.'

(22) a lo mejo:r ha acudido en alguna ocasión / pero *me* parece que era la primera vez / que iba a acudi:r e: Tato Goya / a un: consejo de administración <Dep-Co-080104-14:40>
'He may have been there some other time, but it seems (*to me*) this was the first time T. G. was going to attend a meeting of the management board.'

(23) una idea que *a mí me* parece bastante / insólita / original ya para la novela / y vamos a ver qué tal / se ha trahladado a la gran pantalla y es que / se des / -GAja la Península Ibérica: de Europa y empieza a navegar po:r loh mares <Var-Co-230503-13:55>
'It's an idea that *to me* seems quite unusual and original already in the novel, and we'll see how well it's been translated to the big screen. It's about the Iberian Peninsula breaking apart from Europe and sailing off to the seas.'

First-person pronominal expression in conversational discourse often functions as a turn-taking device, which also helps explain its high frequency across dialogic sequences (cf. also Davidson 1996, 562; De Cock 2014, 135, 149). This function is generally carried out through the subject form *yo* plus a psychological verb. In (24) we can again observe a succession of *yo creo* 'I think' constructions as both speakers alternatively try to regain the conversational turn. Interestingly, in the first turn participant A did not formulate the subject pronoun with the verb, probably because he was already in possession of the ground.

(24) <A> y: luego posteriormente pues es cuando (el árbitro) ha: señalado / penalti *creo* que ha sido sobre: / no sé si Jaime ¿no? /
<B> *yo creo* que sobre Jaime / e: la verdá es que era:-
<A> *yo creo* que es el- / de: los dos jugadores que caen / el: primero es en el que se produce el penalti / (el árbitro) deja seguir / y luego ya es cuando:- / cuando pita /
<B> *yo creo* que a Jaime le cazan antes / un poquito antes <Dep-Pu-191204-18:30>
'A: And it is only then that [the referee] has called a penalty; (*I*) think it's been on Jaime. – B: *I* think it's been on Jaime; it really was. . . – A: *I* think

it was on the first of the two players that fell down, but anyway [the referee] let the play continue, and it was only later that he whistled. – B: *I* think Jaime was hit before, shortly before.'

It is usually the preverbal subject form, with its prototypical association with agentivity and topicality, that has the power to earn the speaker the conversational turn while establishing his/her viewpoint as the one from which discourse is to be interpreted. The pragmaticalization of constructions like *yo creo* or *yo pienso*, together with their contextual versatility, is largely responsible for the higher percentage of subject- rather than object-pronoun formulation observed in Table 4.1. In fact, the first-person object *a mí* can also be part of a turn-taking construction, but it is less usual in such contexts. In example (25), taken from the same broadcast as the preceding excerpt, it is the speaker himself that voluntarily yields the turn to an interactional partner. Participant B, after encoding himself as *a mí* in the construction *dar la sensación* 'to sense', lit. 'to give the feeling', turns to subject self-encoding and pronoun omission with *creer* in the subsequent clause, thus constructing himself as quite more salient.

(25) <A> parece que sin: cambios o: / por el: momento / a:l: menos en la:s: e: filas: / unionistas José Ángel: /
<B> *a mí me* da esa sensación / en las unionistas: y / *creo* que también // en las filas del Elche <Dep-Pu-191204-18:00>
'A: It seems there are no player changes for the moment, at least among the ranks of the Unión team, J. A.? – B: *To me* it gives just that feeling. And (*I*) think it's the same with the ranks of the Elche team.'

Many of the preceding examples should have suggested the relevance of pronoun placement within the clause as a feature of variation establishing further differences among cases of formulation. Table 4.2 shows the positional patterns followed by overt subject and object singular first-person pronouns with regard to verbal nuclei.

Table 4.2: Preverbal vs. postverbal placement of singular first-person pronouns.

	Subject (*yo*)		Object (*a mí*)		Total	
	#	%	#	%	#	%
Preverbal	519	91.2	76	90.5	595	91.1
Postverbal	50	8.8	8	9.5	58	8.9
Total	569	87.1	84	12.9	653	100

The frequencies of either variant are quite similar with both syntactic functions; only about 9% of the expressed pronouns are placed after the verbal nucleus. This might suggest that there is not a significant gap in cognitive salience between first-person subjects and objects – *the speaker* as a cognitive construction is salient enough to overwhelmingly prefer the preverbal position even when not encoded as a subject. Most of the examples used so far to illustrate expression are indeed of preverbal pronouns. Speakers will place the forms referring to themselves at the beginning of the utterance in order to indicate that the subsequent content is to be interpreted from their personal viewpoint. This is especially evident with constructions such as *yo creo* and *a mí me parece*, which behave much like modalizing discourse markers.

In turn, postverbal *yo* and *a mí* are the choices deserving special attention now. It seems advisable to distinguish between cases of clause-final placement, which are usually easy to interpret according to informativeness – the choice is intended to bring the speaker under the focus of attention – and those where the first-person pronoun is located in some intermediate position after the verbal nucleus, most often right after it. In the latter case, the interaction between syntactic ordering and discursive-cognitive factors involves greater complexity. We will see that variants such as *creo yo* and *me parece a mí* have developed specific meanings in connection with the peculiarities of a syntactic position that is not associated with either high salience or high informativeness.

In clause-final contexts, there is usually an evident intention to attract attention upon the speaker with the goal of underlining his/her own involvement, and often implying that such involvement might be unknown to the audience or put into question by them. In (26), *yo* is first formulated before the nucleus; its subsequent postverbal reformulation with the same verb suggests that the referent is deprived of the relative presuppositionality associated with the initial position, in order to explicitly assert his participation in the event. Another frequent value of clause-final placement is the establishment of a contrast with some other referent in the context, as in (27), where A's postverbal *yo* is part of the unfavorable comparison drawn between herself and B – also note that the sequence had started with a preverbal instance of *tú* amidst an invitation for the addressee to take the initiative. Both examples illustrate particular contextual manifestations of the general discursive-cognitive value of postposition, namely the enhancement of referent informativeness.

(26) uno va siempre muy peinao muy engominao / el otro es muy jovencito bueno pues a mí me recuerda a los tebeos que *yo* leí: es que lo leí *yo* <VarCo-230503-13:15>

'One of them is always very well-groomed, slick-haired; the other is very young; well, they remind me of the comics *I* used to read – *I* [postv.] indeed read them!'

(27) <A> *¿tú* te atreve:s / con un: tema para llevarte: esa entrada totalmente grati:s? /
<B> sí pero *canto* muy ma:l ¿eh? /
<A> nada / pero si peor canto *yo:* <Mus-Di-251104-13:10>
'A: Do *you* dare sing a song in order to get that ticket absolutely for free? – B: Yes, but (*I*) sing really bad, you know. – A: But come on, *I* [postv.] sing even worse.'

Postverbal pronouns in non-final positions are clearly different from the perspective of discursive-pragmatic meaning. We will pay special attention to the most frequent VS constructions, namely *creo yo* and *me parece a mí*. In cases like these, the informative focusing associated with the final position is largely absent and the pronouns even seem to undergo a certain assimilation to verbal endings, that is, the meaning they add as against omission-indexation is quite more subtle than with either preverbal or clause-final postverbal pronouns.[2] Pragmatically, the choice results in some self-effacing of the speaker, who somehow eludes the involvement or responsibility associated with preverbal placement (Padilla García 2001, 249–251). In this sense, compare (28) and (29). The first excerpt shows the use of *yo creo* amidst a radio debate where the individual explicitly assumes the role of speaker and takes responsibility for the views expressed. The second one is produced across a non-contentious dialogue where *creo yo* helps the speaker hypothesize about the possibilities for some soccer players to be picked by the coach for an upcoming game. Besides, he subsequently makes it clear that the statement is a mere supposition.

(28) *yo creo* que s:í / hay una necesidad / de que el sector público / entre abiertamente en la oferta de contenidos infantiles / y además ya no segmentaos en un solo:- / en un s- en un solo:- en una sola franja horaria <Var-Pu-211204-12:35>
'*I* do think there's a need for the public administration to openly intervene the contents that are offered to children. Also, these should not be confined to a single time slot.'

2 This is also evident with the singular and plural displaced second persons, which have especially high rates of formulation right after the verb (see Section 8.3).

(29) pero Zé Tó: / tiene menoh papeletah que Juan PAblo por ejemplo / *creo yo* / pero yo es- pero es suponer ¿eh? es un suponer <Dep-SE-210504-15:40>
'But Zé Tó has fewer chances than Juan Pablo, for example, *I* [postv.] think. But I'm just guessing, you know? Just guessing.'

Object pronoun placement with *parecer* appears to follow similar patterns. In (30) the speaker utters *a mí me parece* when dealing with the controversial subject of Civil War mass graves being researched. This contrasts with *me parece a mí* in (31), where the tongue-in-cheek comparison between local alcohol laws and the American Prohibition is parallel to the formulation of the pronoun in a position suggesting lesser involvement of the speaker, namely right after the verb (see also §3.3.4).

(30) la memoria histórica: *a mí me* parece que: ahora está viviendo / un buen momento / m: / quizá / con: e: / e- e- estas situaciones que: han ocurrido de: / e: abrir las fosas comunes / y: demás de la Guerra Civil <Var-SE-300503-19:25>
'Regarding [the recovery of] historical memory, *to me* it seems it is going through good times now, thanks to these things that have happened, such as the opening of mass graves from the Civil War.'

(31) así solo se va a conseguir / que la gente: beba más / y: / es como la Ley Seca / *me* parece *a mí* / que: / cuanto más se prohíba más se va a hacer <Var-Pu-021204-19:15>
'This way they will only get people to drink even more. It's like the Prohibition: it seems *to me* that, the more it is forbidden, the more it will be done.'

From the examples it might be inferred that the meanings constructed through clause-intermediate postverbal placement are not quite different from those of pronoun omission (see also Aijón Oliva/Serrano 2010b, 25–26, 29). However, the presence of the pronoun must itself entail some degree of self-involvement. According to our model, intermediate clause positions should correlate with intermediate points along the salience-informativeness continuum. This means that referents in such contexts will possess scarce cognitive importance of any sort, which explains why constructions like *creo yo* and *me parece a mí* appear to generate pragmatic meanings such as self-effacement. The same conclusion can be drawn from observing the behavior of *digo yo* 'I [postv.] say' (example 32; see also

11 above). As against the more assertive *yo digo*, it is used as a modalizing discourse marker roughly meaning 'I guess' or 'at least that's my opinion' (Santos Río 2003, 340). Yet again the placement of the pronoun after the nucleus entails a reduction of personal involvement as against preposition, making the utterance more hypothetical than contentious.

(32) pues a ver si te recuperas te pones bueno enseguida: / porque tenemos el fin de semana: / a:hí y tieneh que salir a jugar al parque / ¡*digo yo:*! <MusDi-251104-12:15>
'Well, let's hope you'll recover and get well in no time, since we have the weekend ahead and you should go out to the park and play, *I guess*!'

Therefore, while omission-indexation of the singular first person suggests that the viewpoint of the speaker dominates discourse and there is no competition from other participants, the different variants of expression show the need to put some informational focusing on the speaker, thus highlight his/her involvement in the content. Preverbal expression correlates with the highest degree of involvement and is suitable for argumentative discourse where participants are expected to expose personal stances. Clause-final postverbal placement, while infrequent, appears when there is an intention to make the speaker contextually informative, due to e.g. a contrast between referents. As for clause-intermediate postverbal placement, it is a particularly complex solution that, in epistemic constructions such as *creo yo* and *me parece a mí*, indicates a downplaying of involvement as against preposition to the verb while still suggesting that the content is a personal contribution. It seems necessary to also analyze the differences in meaning associated with variation in syntactic function, which will make it possible to explain the choice among constructions such as the ones just cited.

4.4 Functional encoding

Some data on subject vs. object encoding for the singular first person have already been presented in the tables dealing with variable expression and placement. Table 4.3 resumes those data by taking syntactic function as a starting point and showing the distribution of the three formal variants considered – pronoun omission, preverbal expression and postverbal expression – across subject and object contexts.

Table 4.3: Functional encoding of singular first persons.

	Omitted		Expressed preverbal		Expressed postverbal		Total	
	#	%	#	%	#	%	#	%
Subject	1,594	73.7	519	24	50	2.3	2,163	80.2
Object	451	84.3	76	14.2	8	1.5	535	19.8
Total	2,045	75.8	595	22	58	2.2	2,698	100

In 80.2% of the cases where speakers encode themselves in a central syntactic function, they choose subject agreement. As exposed, in the majority of communicative contexts allowing for self-indexation, the person speaking or writing tends to encode him/herself as the main participant of events – whose prototypical way of linguistic expression is the subject-agent – usually also becoming the most accessible referent across discourse and establishing the viewpoint from which discourse is to be interpreted.

Repeated subject self-encoding across a discourse stretch will highlight the agency of the speaker in narrative contexts and/or their responsibility for the conceptual content in argumentative ones. In (33), the speaker dominates the progression of discourse through several cases of this syntactic choice when recounting a joke he played on some relatives. The first-person pronoun is only formulated in *yo llamé* 'I called', in parallel to the change in viewpoint from the individual previously mentioned.

(33) le *quiero* contar también una dec- / una anécdota / sobre:- *he: oído* a un:- / a un señor que: hablaba desde Andorra / pues *yo* desde Salamanca *llamé* / a unos tíos que ten:- / que: *tengo* / en:- / en Alicante / e: y- / y: <sic>difur / -cando</sic> mucho la voz le *pregunté:* / e: / "oiga mire le *llamo* de Radio Alicante es un concurso de:- / e: a ve:r si ve- / me aciertan el- / un premio de no sé qué" y le *dije* / "¿cuál es la plaza más bonita de Es- / de:- / de España?" <Var-SE-011204-13:30>
'(*I*) also want to tell you an anecdote about – (*I*) was just listening to this man who was calling from Andorra. Well, being in Salamanca *I* called some uncles (*I*) have in Alicante and, disguising my own voice, (*I*) asked them, "Hey, listen, (*I*)'m calling from Radio Alicante, this is a contest and you have the chance to win a prize of whatever". And (*I*) said, "What is the most beautiful square in Spain?" '

Object self-encoding, even if much less usual, shows a wider variety of contexts and pragmatic effects. In prototypical accusative contexts, it should be expected to attribute patienthood to the speaker. This choice is however not frequent across the corpus, basically occurring in narrative sequences dealing with facts that entailed some harm to the individual speaking (example 34). The excerpt includes verbs selecting an accusative (*insultar* 'to insult') just as others where the human object would be a dative (*hacer* 'to do', *decir* 'to tell'). The formal coincidence between objectual functions with the first and second persons seems to promote a levelling of semantic roles, since in all cases the speaker constructs herself as clearly affected by the behavior of someone else. Also note that the discursive-cognitive dominance of the speaker results in the invariable omission of object pronouns.

(34) n:ada: / que: / *me* llamó: / empezó insultándo*me:* y: después que *me* iba a hacer lo mismo que a mi amiga: / entonces le dije / que:- / que qué amiga • *me* dijo que la que: / habían: encontrao (muerta) en el porta:l <Inf-SE-180603-14:20>
'So, well, he called (*me*), he began by insulting (*me*), and then said he was going to do the same (*to me*) as he had done to my friend. So I asked him what friend, and he said (*to me*) it was the one they had found [dead] at the gateway.'

As observed in Section 3.3, the semantic roles of patient and theme, i.e. those prototypically associated with accusative objects, are not usual with first- and second-person objects. In particular, the speaker is much more often encoded as a cognizer or experiencer with verbs indicating psychological states and processes. However, the situation is complicated by the fact that some of these verbs – *gustar*-type ones – encode the human participant as a syntactic object, which makes this an especially interesting area for the analysis of functional encoding as a communicative choice.

Among the psychological verbs encoding the speaker as subject, the most frequent ones are *creer* 'to believe, to think', *pensar* 'to think', *querer* 'to want' and *esperar* 'to hope', some of which appeared in examples across the preceding section. We have discussed the pragmaticalization of some of them, most evidently *creer*, as discourse markers used for the modalization of discourse. As for (*yo*) *espero* 'I hope', it conveys a desire that will often be deontically interpreted as a request (35). As usual, the preverbal pronoun highlights personal involvement as against pronoun omission. In (36), *espero* has been formulated in the middle of the clause it should syntactically govern, showing the positional freedom of a discourse marker.

(35) y *yo espero* / que esa / solidaridaz / e sea / am:plia / que sea generosa / y no por las fiestas que vivimos sino por el desastre / que sufren otros pueblos <Var-On-281204-13:25>
'And *I* hope solidarity will be broad and generous, not just because of the ongoing holidays, but also of the disasters suffered by other people.'

(36) entramo:s: en el tiempo / como / todos los jueves también en este nuevo año: *espero:* / e:n el espacio: / en el que: / <. . .> Mar Nieto nos pone: / al tanto pues por ejemplo / de: / algo en lo que: / están las mentes de:- de c- / casi todos <Var-On-080104-13:35>
'Now comes the time, just like each Thursday and during all this new year – so (*I*) hope – for us to move on to the section where M. N. will give us an update on, for example, an issue that is in the minds of almost everyone.'

As for verbs encoding the experiencer as an object, i.e. *gustar*-type ones, the very difficulty to adequately translate them into English and other languages suggests the somehow counterintuitive nature of their eventive structure.[3] *Gustar* conjugated in the simple present (*me gusta*) and other factual tenses is used to expose the opinion or feeling the speaker has about someone or something (37), while in the conditional (*me gustaría*) it is used for the conjectural expression of a desire (38).

(37) porque ahora *me* gusta más Salamanca / el día veinticinco de mayo / voy a votar <Anu-Co-230503-13:00>
'Since (*I*) like Salamanca (lit. Salamanca pleases [*me*]) more now, on May 25th I'll be casting my vote.'

(38) "quizás he cambiado en que me siento más tranquilo en el campo, pero *me gustaría* mejorar aún más en el juego con la cabeza y ver las situaciones del partido con más calma" <Rep-Ga-260804-47>
'I may have changed in that I feel more at ease on the pitch, but *I* would like (lit. it would please [*me*]) to get even more skilled in using my head and to consider situations more calmly.'

---

3 Even in a language so close as Portuguese, the verb *gostar* encodes the human experiencer as subject, e.g. *Eu gosto deste lugar* 'I like (of) this place'. In turn, the referent causing the process is not encoded as an accusative or dative object, but as an oblique (*deste* 'of this'), thus as syntactically and semantically more peripheral.

The objects of these verbs are cognitively not quite different from what Givón (2001) calls *dative subjects* in English, i.e. syntactic subjects characterized by consciousness or volition, but not understood as initiating events. This is the case with verbs meaning physical or psychological perception such as *see, hear, feel, know* or *want.* According to the author, the human experiencer has a dative semantic role; however, subject encoding "makes it appear as if it is somehow more active, more involved or more responsible. In other words, it is made to metaphorically resemble an agent" (2001, 129). In turn, the object – what is seen, heard, wanted, etc. – is accorded the functional features associated with patients, even if it is usually not physically affected and does not undergo any perceivable changes. In fact, the corresponding Spanish verbs (*ver* 'to see', *sentir* 'to feel', etc.) follow an analogous syntactic-semantic pattern. The problem is that, with *gustar*-type verbs, such processes are actually contemplated from the opposite viewpoint. While the salience of human participants with cognizer or experiencer roles should favor their encoding as subjects, these verbs prefigure them as objects, thus reducing their autonomy in the event. They are constructed as a sort of patients of psychological processes, while the referents encoded as subjects would be the agents initiating such processes. This is the basic cognitive difference between human-subject constructions with *creer* or *esperar* on one hand and human-object ones with *gustar* or *parecer* on the other.

Most significantly, in *gustar*-type constructions the patterns of variable choice – mainly those concerning the placement of elements within the clause – show a strong tendency to replicate the prototypical syntactic order according to inherent salience and informativeness (see also Section 3.3). These contexts have atypically high rates of OVS ordering, in accordance with the fact that the main viewpoint of discourse is that of the human experiencers, while the entities or facts experienced by them are usually more informative and less salient. Thus, of the 65 tokens of *gustar*-type verbs where the first-person object *a mí* is formulated, 60 (92.3%) show this collocational pattern. Consider the following examples with *importar* 'to matter' (39) and *sorprender* 'to surprise' (40). The fact that in both cases the subject is an embedded clause makes its placement after the verb much more expectable.

(39) *a mí* no *me* importaría para nada irme a la zona del Caribe pero vamoh / como que:- / que no tengo tiempo <Mus-Di-251104-11:30>
'*I* wouldn't mind (lit. It wouldn't matter *to me*) going to the Caribbean, but well, I just don't have the time to.'

(40) si a las campañas electorales no se le da: / ese mati:z y t- e: aparece la ironía: / pues el buen humo:r / el chascarrillo pues e:nto(nc)es no sé: qué hacemos

aquí todos ¿no? / y *a mí* también *me* sorprende que además / e: / eso se vea como negativo / en un país como España <Var-Co-230503-13:10>
'If election campaigns can't be spiced up with some irony, good humor or joking, well, I just can't see what we're all up to, right? And also, *I* find it shocking (lit. it surprises *me*) that this should be regarded negatively in a country like Spain.'

The cognitive similarity between first-person objects with the semantic roles of cognizer or experiencer and syntactic subjects is evident in occasional instances of grammatical discordance, which due to their nonstandard character are generally found in oral spontaneous discourse (Alcaide Lara 1997). In such cases, it is the subject form *yo* rather than *a mí* that appears in correlation with the object clitic *me*. Thus, in (41) the speaker utters *yo me ha gustado* instead of the canonical *a mí me ha gustado*. High perceptibility and discourse topicality make the referent approach non just the functional but also the formal features of subjects. The pronoun *yo* appears to be more apt to signal the fact that the subsequent discourse will be constructed from the viewpoint of the speaker. In (42), grammatical reflection seems to have led this participant to reformulate the pronoun in order to produce the standard object-clitic correlation.

(41) *yo: m:e* ha gustado lo que he oído / con Rafa Sierra / y *espero:* que esta tarde:- m: esta tarde noche / m tengas voz y voto: con esa coherencia que / generalmente te caracteriza <Dep-Co-080104-14:35>
'*I* have liked (lit. *I* it has pleased [*me*]) what I've just heard from R. S., and (*I*) hope this afternoon, this evening you'll have a voice and a vote, with the coherence that generally distinguishes you.'

(42) bueno / *yo- a mí:* esta mañana *me* han preguntado: en otros sitios también <Var-Co-230503-12:55>
'Well, *I* – *to me* the same has also been asked elsewhere this morning.'

This also comes to underscore the non-discrete nature of syntactic functions discussed in Chapter 2. There is a range of possibilities between the prototypes of subject and object for the encoding of the speaker. Reprehensible as it may be from the perspective of grammatical norms, the correlation between *yo* and *me* is easily explainable if grammatical variation is seen as the simultaneous choice of linguistic forms and the meanings associated with them. *Gustar*-type constructions show some functional unstability due to the discrepancy between syntactic configuration and semantic autonomy, which is most often solved in favor of the latter – the unmarked ordering is (O)VS and, when expressed, the object pronoun is sometimes replaced with a subject one.

All in all, the discursive-pragmatic repercussions of the choice between subject and object encoding are best illustrated by the two great types of modalizing constructions we have distinguished, namely the subject-encoding type – (*yo*) *creo*, (*yo*) *pienso*, etc. – and the object-encoding one – (*a mí*) *me parece*, (*a mí*) *me gusta*, etc. While both are quite frequent in expository and argumentative discourse, the latter type attributes lesser responsibility to the speaker, presenting him/her as someone who experiences a thought or feeling rather than producing it. In such cases, the content of the utterance is to be interpreted as more of a hypothesis than a personal stance. As exposed in Section 4.3, such meanings can be further modulated through the variable expression and placement of the pronouns; both *yo* and *a mí* at a preverbal position will help enhance self-involvement. With epistemic verbs like *parecer*, there is even the possibility to elide the clitic (see 21 above), which entails a further step towards desubjectivization.

Different functional choices can even co-appear within a short stretch, helping steer the argumentation in a particular direction. In (43), while the speaker assumes responsibility for his supposition – that neither team has replaced any players for the second half of the game – through subject self-encoding, he also accepts the possibility that he be contradicted by another participant, in this case encoding the latter as a subject and himself as an object. As usual, the initial omission of the pronoun in *veo* '(I) see' turns into expression as soon as a contextual contrast between referents is envisaged.

(43) en las filas del Elche n:o *veo* cambios *yo* no *sé* si Jorge / *me* va a contradecir o no / pero *yo* en principio no *veo:*- no *veo:* cambios en:- en ninguna de las formaciones <Dep-Pu-191204-18:00>
'(*I*) can't see any changes among the ranks of the Elche club. *I* don't know if J. will contradict (*me*), but in principle *I* don't see any changes in either of the teams.'

The alternation between the two basic ways of functional self-encoding across different speech turns is also quite indicative of the construction of contextual identities by the participants. It is typical of radio broadcasters to prefer object self-encoding when talking to interviewees or to anonymous callers. In the latter case, the participation of the addressee is often encouraged through imperative forms such as *dime* and *dígame* 'tell me', which due to their pragmaticalization will hardly be interpreted as commands, but rather as phatic resources used to yield the floor. In (44), a contrast can be observed between the function adopted by the phone caller and the one assumed by the broadcaster – the former is expected to expose his/her own stance (as a subject), the latter to receive and accept it (as a dative object). A similar situation is reproduced in the fictional dialogue in (45), from a radio commercial, which suggests that the configuration can also be taken advantage of in other kinds of situations.

(44) <A> e: / *yo: quería* hacer un comentario sobre lo del rastro //
<B> ¡ah! / bien / *dígame* <Var-SE-230903-13:45>
'A: *I* just wanted to make some remarks about the flea market. – B: Oh, good. Tell *me*.'

(45) <A> te *voy* a dar / varias razones: / para que en esta primavera te acerques a comprar / tus zapatos: / a Eurocalzado:s /
<B> ¡*dime*! / ¡*dime:*! <Anu-40-130603-13:20>
'A: (*I*)'m going to give you several reasons to come and buy your shoes at E. this spring. – B: Tell (*me*)! Tell (*me*)!'

It would of course be interesting to analyze the pragmatic motivations and repercussions of subject vs. object self-encoding in different communicative situations and with different types of speaker identity (see also Sections 9.6, 10.6). As for the interplay between the syntactic encoding of speakers and that of addressees, it will be further discussed when approaching the singular second person in Section 6.4.

4.5 Summary

The speaker is primarily realized as a discursive-cognitive construction through singular first-person grammatical forms, including subject verbal endings, object clitics and stressed subject and object pronouns. While the extradiscursive reference of this person is most often the specific individual speaking or writing, contextual observation suggests a variety of possible referential shifts – nonspecific, audience-inclusive, pragmaticalized ones – that are also recurrent with other grammatical persons, and confirm the notion that discourse participants need to be understood as cognitive constructs – as well as socio-interactional conventions – rather than human entities in a physical sense. However, the latter are still important insofar as their actual identity and social status may condition the syntactic choices made for their discursive encoding. Assuming the role of speaker through first-person forms entails the right to produce discourse as well as the liability for its form and content, which will tend to be interpreted from the viewpoint of the participant in question.

The degree of speaker involvement, which is tightly connected with the modalization of the discursive content, can be further modulated through formal choices concerning pronoun expression and placement. In turn, subject vs. object encoding will correlate with the responsibility accorded to the speaker, in connection with the different degrees of autonomy respectively associated with these functions. Preverbal subject pronouns are associated with the highest self-involvement and responsibility – the speaker is made relatively informative in comparison with pronoun omission, but at the same time is placed in the position prototypically associated with semantic agency and autonomy. This makes the choice a recurrent one in argumentative discourse, and also explains its frequent use as a turn-taking device in conversation. Other constructional variants will result in some decrease of self-involvement and a parallel tendency to present the content of the utterance as hypothetical or as general knowledge rather than a personal stance. However, the inherent salience of the speaker is manifest in the strong preference for the omission or preverbal placement of first-person pronouns even in contexts of object encoding. Also, non-standard cases of correlation between subject pronouns and object clitics show that functional encoding is actually a continuum of possibilities in close connection with that between salience and informativeness.

5 The plural first person: *more than the speaker*

5.1 The subparadigm and its meaning

Nosotros (masculine) and *nosotras* (feminine) are the plural first-person personal pronouns used for both subject and object functions. As usual, in the latter case they need to be headed by *a* or some other preposition indexing a peripheral function. Also, as is common practice with Spanish gender-inflected forms, the masculine variant is often interpreted as unmarked, referring to extradiscursive groups where both male and female entities are included; it can even denote all-female groups, particularly in American varieties (Kany 1951, 99; Villars 2008).[1] The verbal ending *-mos* performs plural first-person subject agreement, while *nos* is the clitic used for object agreement. Examples (1–3) illustrate the basic possibilities.

(1) (nosotros) com- -e- -mos mucho
we (masc.) eat THEME-V 1ST.PL a lot
'We eat a lot.'

(2) (nosotras) í- -ba- -mos a trabajar
we (fem.) go IMP.PAST 1ST.PL to work
'We were going to work.'

(3) (a nosotros) no nos pag- -a- -ron
to us (masc.) not 1ST.PL.CL pay THEME-V 3RD.PL.PAST
'They didn't pay us.'

Nosotros and *nosotras* are the result of a diachronic process of agglutination. NOS was the Latin pronoun used for both the nominative and accusative cases; in the former contexts it started to be followed by indefinite *otros, otras* 'others', usually indicating the demarcation of a specific group within the first person,

1 However, a current line of sociopolitical thought advocates for the interpretation of masculine forms as only referring to male referents, thus for the need to make both grammatical genders explicit: *nosotros y nosotras* 'us (masc.) and us (fem.)', or else to use gender-opaque collective terms, e.g. *la ciudadanía* 'the population', *el alumnado* 'the student body', in order to avoid the cognitive "concealment" of women. While the interplay between grammatical and biological/social gender is a complex matter, it has been pointed out that such initiatives are hardly justified from both the perspective of common usage and that of grammatical norms (Bosque 2012).

https://doi.org/10.1515/9783110643442-006

from the late Middle Ages (Gili Gaya 1946). The compound later became of general use as the subject and object pronoun. *Nous autres* is also attested in French, where it is used to indicate the exclusion of the audience from the first-person reference (Booth 2009, 445). For its part, the original NOS evolved into the unstressed object clitic in both accusative and dative contexts. Some grammars and prescriptive handbooks still mention the use of *nos* as a stressed subject pronoun (e.g. Gili Gaya 2000, §173; RAE 2009, §16.2n), but this is extremely rare in contemporary Spanish and would in any case be restricted to so-called "majestic" uses (see §5.2.1 below).

As with the rest of first and second persons, whereas the formulation of agreement morphemes is mandatory with central syntactic functions, the correlative subject and object pronouns are variably expressed. Besides, not just *nosotros*, but also a singular first-person pronoun (*yo/a mí*) in coordination with any other pronoun or lexical NP should establish plural first-person agreement with the verb, as illustrated by *tú y yo* 'you and I' in (4). This is a preliminary indication that the plural first person entails an extension of the speaker's viewpoint towards a wider one.

(4) ya está ahí, a la vuelta de la esquina, en todos esos que *tú y yo llevamos* en el corazón, y en aquellos que no *conocemos* también, ya es Navidad. <Art-Ga-221203-5b>
'It's there, just around the corner, in all those people that *you and I* (*we*) carry in our hearts, as well as in all those (*we*) don't know – it's Christmas time.'

Moreover, plural first-person agreement morphemes often do not appear in coreference with pronouns, but rather with lexical NPs that are functionally and pragmatically similar to expressed subjects or objects. This peculiar construction was already commented on in Section 2.2 (see also Martínez 1999, 2764–2765; De Cock 2010; 2014, 155–164). Consider examples (5) and (6). In the first one, *los españoles* 'Spaniards' is followed by *carecíamos* '(we) didn't have'; the verbs in the subsequent clauses also have (subject or object) plural first-person agreement. In object-encoding contexts such as (6), the phrase in coreference with the clitic, as long as it is syntactically integrated in the clause, needs to be preceded by the particle *a*, mirroring the behavior of first- and second-person object pronouns.

(5) No hace tanto que *los españoles carecíamos* de vacaciones reales, *ignorábamos* lo que era el placer de viajar, de aquí que los extranjeros que *nos* visitaban eran mirados con una mezcla de curiosidad y envidia <Art-Ga-121203-5a>
'It's not been so long since *Spaniards* (*we*) didn't have holidays as such and

(*we*) had never experienced the pleasure of travelling; hence any foreigners who came to visit (*us*) were watched with a mixture of curiosity and envy.'

(6) He tenido pájaros, perros, peces y hámsters. *A toda la familia nos* gustan los animales. <Ent-Ga-150604-18>
'I've had birds, dogs, fish and hamsters. *All in the family* (*we*) like pets (lit. *To all in the family* [*to us*] pets are pleasing).'

These constructions make it possible to index a plural first-person participant through the agreement morpheme while specifying its contextual reference through the NP. Whereas it could be argued that the latter is actually an apposition to an omitted first-person pronoun, it must be noted that in the case of first and second persons such appositions should in principle be non-restrictive, i.e. *Nosotros, los españoles, carecíamos*... 'We, Spaniards, didn't have...' However, in most of the instances found across the corpus there is no comma or pause between the NP and the rest of the clause, which suggests that they are syntactically integrated. They will thus be analyzed as cases of subject or object expression, just like with overt *nosotros*. The same holds for the plural persons to be reviewed in later chapters (see Sections 7.1, 8.1).

Furthermore, plural first-person morphemes can be coreferential with relatives heading embedded clauses, such as *quienes* or *los que* 'those who'. This can give rise to rather complex constructions. In (7), the head *los que* fills the subject slot of the subordinate verb, precluding pronoun formulation (**los que nosotros dirigimos*). In turn, the whole embedded clause *los que dirigimos las empresas* 'those who (we) manage companies' functions as the subject of the main verb *somos* '(we) are'. The subsequent verb *hacemos* '(we) do' has the relative *que* 'that' as its subject.

(7) Los que *dirigimos* las empresas *somos* meros empleados que *hacemos* que funcione la máquina, pero sin los que están alrededor sería imposible. <Ent-Ga-201204-11>
'Those who (*we*) manage companies (*we*) are mere employees that (*we*) keep the machine working, but this would be impossible without all the others around.'

Finally, prepositional phrases and adverbs, in principle unable to establish agreement with the verb, can also help specify the reference of the subject or object. De Cock (2014, 180–182), following Fauconnier (1984), characterizes these elements as *space-builders* with a deictic potential. According to Fernández Soriano (1999b), they can be included within a special category she terms *locative subjects*. In (8), the topicalized phrase *en el Bar Cafetería Leonardo* refers not so much to the place itself as to the people working there, who would be the actual subject of *queremos* '(we) want'.

(8) *en el Bar Cafetería Leonardo: / queremos* que se sienta como en casa / y disfrute de nuestra cocina / s:iempre esquisita: <Anu-Co-260803-14:35>
'*At B. C. L.* (*we*) want you+ to feel at home and enjoy our always delicious cuisine.'

Such cases always entail the demarcation of some physical or temporal setting that stands for the people associated with it, e.g. *En España vivimos relativamente bien* 'In Spain (we) live relatively well'. The similarity between them and clause subjects proper – i.e. elements coreferential with the verbal ending – is underscored by the fact that, in contexts of contrast between referents, their occurrence makes an overt subject unnecessary or even impossible (see also Matos Amaral/Schwenter 2005, 119). In fact, the formulation of a pronoun (*En España nosotros vivimos relativamente bien*) begs for a different interpretation whereby *en España* has a merely locative value and it is not all inhabitants, but a rather more specific human group, that lives relatively well. The construction also occurs with plural second- and third-person conjugated verbs: *Aquí no tenéis esos problemas* 'Here (you guys) don't have such problems'; *En la Edad Media no usaban electricidad* 'In the Middle Ages (they) didn't use electricity'.

Nevertheless, space-builders in coreference with plural person morphemes are rarer in the corpus than either third-person NPs or relative heads in the same context. Also, given their more complex discursive-pragmatic status – there are often no clear indications whether they are intended to delimitate a human reference together with the physical or temporal setting – they will not considered among cases of subject or object expression in the statistical analyses.

The basic cognitive meaning of the plural first person will be paraphrased as *more than the speaker*. It entails a broadening of the singular viewpoint, suggesting that what is said concerns the speaker, but *not just* him/her. Serrano (2011b, 96–98) formulates this meaning as "other people and I", showing that its use entails a cognitive unfolding of the singular first person towards a broader sphere. The extradiscursive referent can be the whole of mankind and even non-human entities, just as it can be the speaker alone – but even in this case there will be an implication that the reference somehow goes beyond the individual. Mühlhäusler/Harré (1990, 170) find that the common denominator of all uses of the plural first person is "*I as speaker, but not necessarily indexical referent, plus someone else*". Referential interpretation needs to be contextually made, and in many contexts it will not be indispensable for the achievement of communicative purposes (Posio 2012, 343). In fact, the plural first person is the richest and most complex one among the first and second persons as regards referential possibilities. An often-addressed matter is whether the reference is inclusive or exclusive, that is, whether interactional partners are meant to be included within the plural first-person viewpoint or not. While referential differences are not associated with any formal variations in contemporary Spanish, they may have some correlation with patterns of choice regarding formulation, placement and functional encoding. In the following section we will further discuss the problems posed by reference and propose a classification of the manifold contextual possibilities into four basic categories.

5.2 The construction of reference

The referential versatility of the plural first person is parallel to a range of expressive possibilities beyond the subparadigm of plural first person-marked grammatical units. As exposed above, speakers often compensate for its fuzziness by formulating NPs and other coreferential elements. As against the usual specificity of the singular first person and, to some point, the singular second one (see Section 6.2 below), *nosotros* and its subparadigm have been characterized as "opaque deictic" units (Satorre Grau 2002, 355). Even if *nosotros* meant just "the speakers", it would promote a much more diffuse interpretation of referents than the singular first person does.

Interestingly, it makes it possible for speakers to construct themselves as part of human groups they do not belong to in the extradiscursive world, by way of metaphorical referential extensions that in some cases seem to be largely grammaticalized. For example, the supporter of a victorious sports team can say *Hemos ganado la copa* '(We) won the cup' even if he/she actually contributed nothing to the achievement (see also Borthen 2010 on the *representative* readings of plurals). There is even the apparent possibility for the plural first person to involve the addressee or audience but not the speaker, e.g. *¿Cómo estamos hoy?* ('How are (we) today?') as a question from a doctor to a patient (De Cock 2011). Similarly, a teacher may utter *Nos callamos* '(We) now shut up', to be interpreted by the students as a command directed at them. However, all such uses of the plural first person share the basic meaning put forth above – in all of them, the person speaking intends to include him/herself within a reference that in the extradiscursive world would just correspond to other people. Conversely, it is possible to approach a content concerning just the speaker from a plural viewpoint, e.g. *Estamos un poco mejor* '(We)'re feeling a little better', answered by the patient in the example above (see also the following subsection).

The expression vs. omission of coreferential pronouns or NPs will also influence referential interpretation to a significant extent. When no such elements are formulated, the reference will generally be fuzzier. Bare plural first-person agreement morphemes may even appear as more of expressive resources than indexical elements proper, as in examples (9) and (10). The English translations of the examples suggest that they could even be paraphrased without any personal indexations. Yet the latter have been chosen to construct discourse from a joint viewpoint whereby a coincidence between the speaker and the audience is assumed or sought; it is implied that the content concerns both *me* and *you* – whoever *you* is.

(9) Sólo los inteligentes cambian de opinión, los tontos, nunca; pero conviene al hacerlo, y más si *hablamos* de política, explicar el tránsito <Art-Ga-201204-3>
'Only intelligent people can change their minds; fools never do. However, it is advisable – much more so *when it comes to* (lit. if [*we*] talk about) politics – to explain the reasons for the change.'

(10) independientemente de que necesite asistencia / no hay un RIESgo / para:- / *podríamos* decir / para la vida ¿no? / no es como esos: golpes / en:- / en la cara <Dep-Pu-191204-18:10>
'Regardless of whether he needs assistance or not, there's been no real risk for, say (lit. [*we*] could say), for life, right? It's not like those impacts on the face.'

Conversely, overt *nosotros* will enhance the informativeness of the referent and thus direct attention towards the latter. In (11), the omission of the pronoun would be scarcely natural, given that the quoted speaker intends to emphasize that it is his political group that can offer hope to the community.

(11) "No se puede gobernar sin ofrecer porvenir y esperanza y *nosotros tenemos* un proyecto de futuro para Salamanca", afirmó Julián Lanzarote antes de dar paso al secretario regional del PP. <Not-Ga-201204-6/7>
' "You can't rule if you can't offer prospects and hope, and *we* have a forward-looking project for Salamanca", stated J. L. before giving way to the regional secretary of the PP.'

The greater referential vagueness associated with omission-indexation becomes particularly evident in a number of plural first person-inflected verbs that have become pragmaticalized as discourse markers with no referential value as such (see §5.2.4). All in all, upon examination of the 3,217 clauses with plural first-person agreement across the corpus, four major referential categories will be proposed: *speaker-blurring, audience-exclusive, audience-inclusive* and *pragmaticalized.* They all share the basic meaning of the plural first person, i.e. *more than the speaker*, but can generate different discursive-pragmatic effects in accordance with the contextual reference they are attributed. Each of the categories will now be separately reviewed.

5.2.1 Speaker-blurring

The extradiscursive reference of these uses is in fact coincident with the prototypical one of the singular first person, i.e. the specific individual speaking or writing. Of course, the plural person entails a quite different way of discursive-cognitive self-construction. While discourse may deal with personal stances or experiences, explicit orientation to the speaker's viewpoint is avoided. This is a well-known resource in domains such as scientific and academic writing – it is in fact used throughout the present book – and has traditionally been described as a *modesty* or *authorial plural*, among other labels, in different languages (Haverkate 1984, 85–87; Gili Gaya 2000, §173; Corbett 2000, 221). The so-called *majestic plural* – the *royal* "*we*" of English – can also be included in this first category, even if no tokens in the corpus are amenable to such a description.[2] Majestic plurals should in principle correlate with stressed *nos* rather than *nosotros* (Gómez Torrego 2004, 301; RAE 2009, §16.2n). However, the former pronoun is all but lost in present-day Spanish. Also, speaker-blurring uses strongly disfavor the formulation of pronouns (see Section 5.3).

In the corpus, the choice is frequent in journal opinion pieces, in accordance with its apparent association with expository-argumentative prose. Authors resort to it in order to assert personal stances and directives while avoiding straightforward self-involvement (example 12). Watched from the opposite perspective, it can help provide unidirectional written discourse with

2 Richards (2006, 4) discusses the motivations of Margaret Thatcher's famous statement "We are a grandmother!", as an illustration of how pronoun choice conditions self-perception and the management of interpersonal relationships. Some public figures in Spain show a preference for the plural viewpoint in their statements, often causing ambiguity as to whether they refer to themselves or to a wider team. This is the case with this Formula 1 driver, sharing his impressions in an interview from an external source: "*Íbamos* demasiado lentos, como todo el fin de semana. *Nos* ha faltado un poco de velocidad. *Debemos* buscar el porqué" (*Marca*, 10/9/2016) '(*We*) rode too slowly, just like during the whole weekend. (*We*) lacked some speed (lit. Some speed was missing [*on us*]). (*We*) need to find out why'.

some interactivity while avoiding explicit personalization (13); in this sense, it clearly approaches audience-inclusive uses (§5.2.3).

(12) Por si las moscas *hacemos* nuestras las consideraciones de los talleres mecánicos que sugieren que en caso de tener que ponerse en carretera mejor tomar todas las precauciones. <Art-Tr-260804-64>
'Just in case, (*we*) would like to endorse the recommendations provided by repair shops in the sense that, if one should need to take to the road, it is best to take all safety precautions.'

(13) Tampoco tiene mucho que añadir, así lo *leíamos* ayer en las páginas de este mismo periódico, a las palabras de Julián Barrio, Arzobispo de Santiago de Compostela <Art-Tr-060804-6>
'Also, he has little to add – as (*we*) read yesterday in the pages of this very journal – to the words of J. B., the Archbishop of Santiago de Compostela.'

The choice appears in radio speech as well, with seemingly diverse motivations related to the participants' strategies of self-presentation and the management of their relationships to addressees and audiences. Sometimes it may appear to be promoted by the very "modesty" cited by traditional descriptions. Example (14) shows the reaction of a broadcaster to a flattering comment explicitly addressed to him by an anonymous caller. The response is constructed from a plural viewpoint whereby B avoids taking the credit:

(14) <A> solamente llamar / para dar*le* las gracias <. . .> / por las canciones que nos *pone* / que: / estas sí que son de nuestra vida / gracias /
<B> pues m: / n- no vea usté / cómo: se lo *agradecemos* al mismo tiempo / porque / cuando alguien / reconoce que: lo que *hacemos* está medianamente bien hecho / pues es de agradecer <Var-Co-211204-13:10>
'A: Just calling to thank (*you+*) [. . .] for the songs (*you+*) play for us – these are indeed the songs of our life. Thanks. – B: Well, you+ can't imagine how grateful (*we*) are. Because whenever someone acknowledges that what (*we*) do is moderately well done, this needs to be welcomed.'

In turn, the plural can also help downplay self-involvement when the content is regarded negatively. In (15), a movie critic who had earlier complained that his Internet connection had not been working uses the plural in several consecutive clauses as he self-justifies for his lack of information about an upcoming release.

(15) de esta (película) *podemoh deci:r* / menos / porque: / no *hemoh podido hacer* como ya *hemoh ehplicado* nuestro trabajo convenientemente esta semana pero / e: *podemoh decir* que viene avalada por algunos premio:s / <Var-Co-230503-13:55>[3]
'There's little (*we*) can say about this [movie], since (*we*) have not been able to do our job under the proper conditions this week, as (*we*) explained before. Still, (*we*) can say it's backed up by a number of awards.'

As with the rest of the referential categories to be analyzed below, the pragmatic motivations behind the choice of a plural when referring to an extradiscursive individual are quite variable and not always easy to pin down. Its traditional characterization as both a "modesty" and a "majestic" resource can even seem contradictory. However, a strategy of replacing the construction of *the speaker* with that of a wider and less perceptible, therefore less salient reference is clearly at the basis of all its occurrences. It proves useful to downplay self-involvement whether the content is regarded positively or negatively. From this perspective, the "modesty" and "majestic" readings are in fact hardly incompatible; both show the interplay between grammatical encoding and self-presentation in social contexts. The phenomenon is paralleled by the (less frequent) use of plural second-person forms referring to individual addressees: depending on the context, it may seem advantageous to construct a specific interactional partner as a plurality, for example in order to downplay his/her involvement in events that are viewed as negative by the speaker (see further Section 7.2).

5.2.2 Audience-exclusive

Exclusive plurals are used to construct a human group where the speaker is included, but the addressee or audience is not (Serrano 2017a, 131–132). This is the most frequent referential variant across the corpus under study, appearing

3 The transcription system of the oral texts, while employing standard spelling, is intended to reflect phonetic features that deviate significantly from the Peninsular standard. The speaker in (15) tends to the aspiration of /s/ and other consonants in syllable- or word-final position, whence *podemoh* (*podemos*) or *ehplicado* (*explicado*). Among other phenomena, it is typical of Castilian dialects to pronounce word-final /d/ as an interdental or just elide it, which will result in the pronoun *usted* being often transcribed as *ustez* or *usté* (see especially Chapter 8).

when someone speaks or writes on behalf of him/herself and others, which is a usual situation in mass-media and advertising discourse. The power of the plural first person to signal group memberships, just as to exclude people from them, has been underscored in studies dealing with different languages, communities and interactional domains (e.g. Helmbrecht 2002; Van Knippenberg/ Ellemers 2003; Cortés Conde 2007; Serrano 2011b; Aijón Oliva 2013; Davies 2013, 189–193). Haverkate (1984, 88) characterizes exclusive uses as *class-inclusive*, meaning that "the speaker identifies his/her personal beliefs, points of view, or assumptions with those of the class of which he/she indicates or implies him/herself to be a member". The frequency of the exclusive plural in the speech of politicians has also motivated the label *partisan "we"* for this kind of use (see e.g. Blas Arroyo 2000). Another significant contribution is offered by Bell's (1984; 2001) model, where the notion of *referee* is used to denote groups external to the interaction that participants intend to identify with. Referees can strongly condition linguistic choice, their most evident effect being lack of accommodation to the audience where it could be expected.

Besides the indexation of group membership, the exclusive plural can be a resource to express the speaker's own stances while diminishing self-involvement (De Cock 2014, 23–25); therefore, the choice is hardly unconnected with the speaker-blurring uses reviewed just above. However, in this case the plural forms should be indexical of some group that can be identified within the context. Actually, many people taking part in mass-media interactions – journalists, public figures, anonymous callers or writers – are often not contextually "relevant" in themselves, but just as the representatives of a larger group, as will be observed.

In the written press, exclusive uses are typical of interviews (example 16) and of literal quotations inserted within news items and stories (17). In both of the excerpts, the role assumed by the speaker as a spokesperson for others is quite evident – in the first one the reference of the plural is even made explicit through the NP *4 o 5 empresas especializadas* '4 or 5 specialized companies'. In (17), the group is constructed as a third-person plural in the surrounding narrative context (*lo que quieren dejar claro* 'the point (they) want to make'), even if it is sensible to think that the quote must have been uttered by a single person. This is quite revealing of how the informational and argumentative goals of media texts interact with choices for participant construction – in this context, the people in question are only considered interesting as a group, not as individuals.

(16) En Salamanca sólo *trabajamos* 4 ó 5 empresas verdaderamente especializadas, si bien tampoco existe una gran demanda de estos productos. <Ent-Ad-121203-17>
'Only 4 or 5 really specialized companies (*we*) work in Salamanca, although it is true that there is not a great demand of this kind of products.'

(17) Lo que *quieren* dejar claro es que "todo *lo hacemos* de manera desinteresada, *colaboramos* porque *nos* gusta". <Rep-Ad-170504-15>
'The point (*they*) want to make is that [*quoting*] "(*We*) do it all in a selfless way; (*we*) collaborate because it pleases (*us*) to." '

In constructions with a coreferential NP such as (16), the latter tends to be placed before the verb, i.e. at the prototypical position of the subject in declarative clauses, as can also be observed in (18) below. It can also be left unexpressed if it is already activated in the context due to mention in some previous clause, as in (19). In this particular stretch, the coreference between *el Ayuntamiento* 'the Town Council' and *queremos* '(we) want' is inferable from the fact that the person speaking is introduced as a member of that institution. All the examples suggest the need for speakers to delimit the human group indexed by plural first-person morphemes whenever such delimitation is perceived as useful for the adequate interpretation of the content.

(18) Lograba que *sus nietos* lo *pasásemos* todos bomba, sin ningún grito, tan solo favoreciendo y creando una atmósfera adecuada. <Art-Ga-290104-5a>
'She would make it possible that *her grandchildren* (*we*) all had a whale of a time, with no need to shout, just by creating and promoting an adequate atmosphere.'

(19) Según indica a este periódico la concejala responsable, Cristina Klimowitz, "*el Ayuntamiento* ha asumido personalmente el programa de apoyo a la familia y *queremos* impulsarlo" <Not-Ga-310104-11b>
'As pointed out to this journal by the councilor in charge, C. K., "*the Town Council* has personally taken over the family support program, and (*we*) want to promote it." '

The choice of exclusive plurals also has clear repercussions on self-presentation and the management of relationships between participants, most clearly in spoken discourse. In (20), when requesting further personal information from a phone caller, the broadcaster uses an exclusive plural. Even if a referentially individual interpretation would also be possible, the speaker seems to be assuming the role of spokesperson for the audience of the program. This, in turn, promotes a view of her question as motivated by commonly shared rather than personal interest. After some pause, B provides the information requested.

(20) <A> ¿y qué estabas haciendo Dani? /
<B> na aquí / currando /
<A> ah currando: / [¿nos po- /]
<B> [sí <ininteligible>]
<A> *¿nos podemos* enterar dónde:? //
<B> e:n un almacén de forja <Mus-Di-251104-13:15>
'A: So, what were you doing right now, Dani? – B: Just here, at work. – A: Oh, at work. – B: Yeah [unintelligible]. – A: So may (*we*) know where? – B: At a metal workshop.'

More generally, audience-exclusive plurals in the speech of radio broadcasters, just as in that of politicians and some other public figures, often seem to have the dual function of constructing them into a demarcated group – the radio station or the team they belong to; their political group or association – and avoiding the singular first-person viewpoint (Serrano/Aijón Oliva 2013). This is illustrated by (21) and (22), respectively showing typical uses in opening and closing sequences of radio programs where a contrast is established between the plural first person and the displaced second plural one denoting the audience.

(21) también les *contaremos* los detalles / de la nueva: edición de la *Navidad Mágica* un proyecto / de ocio para jóvenes: y niños <Inf-Pu-171204-13:45>
'(*We*)'ll also give (you guys+) details about the new edition of *Magical Christmas*, an entertainment project for teenagers and children.'

(22) *nos vamos* a despedir de ustedes deseando / que tengan buen fin de semana / y les *esperamos* ya saben el próximo lunes <Var-Co-230503-14:00>
'(*We*)'re going to say goodbye (to you guys+), wishing (you guys+) a nice weekend, and as (you guys+) know, (*we*)'ll be waiting (for you guys+) next Monday.'

In general, the pragmatic effects of exclusive plurals are most notorious when they are used to highlight self-insertion in a specific human group the audience is not part of – in other words, when group insertion or demarcation is the dominant value in the context. In turn, when their primary intention is to diminish self-involvement, they approach speaker-blurring plurals.

5.2.3 Audience-inclusive

As happens in most Western Eurasian languages (Bickel/Nichols 2005), Spanish morphology does not supply any formal means to distinguish between plural references excluding the addressee or audience and those including them. In either case, the reference can of course go beyond the specific individuals interacting to encompass larger and often fuzzy groups. Vagueness is a particularly obvious feature of audience-inclusive plurals, which can even denote all human beings and other entities, as well as acquire a discursive value whereby there is no discernible reference as such (Posio 2012; Pavlidou 2014; see also the following subsection on pragmaticalized uses). Even if this is not the most frequent referential variant across the corpus, it is indeed the one with the highest contextual versatility. Its possible pragmatic motivations beg for detailed discussion.

Inclusive *nosotros* is usually not aimed at delimiting a particular human group – this being a characteristic function of exclusive uses – but rather at getting the attention and collaboration of the audience through their involvement by means of grammatical indexation. It thus constitutes a basically intersubjectivizing choice (De Cock 2016) and can prove useful in genres exploiting the features of conversational discourse, such as music programs (examples 23, 24). In the first excerpt, the broadcaster addresses a series of questions to her nonspecific audience, which she individualizes through the singular second person. In the last clause, she switches to a plural first person whereby herself and the assumed listener come together. The reference in (24) is a more diffuse one, apparently subsuming the speaker within the audience at large.

(23) hola: // ¿qué tal: / *te* fue el: menú? ¿estuvo rico? / ¿bien? ¿todavía *estás* saboreándolo? / bue:no pues *compartimos* el café juntos <Mus-Ci-230903-16:05>
'Hi there. How was your lunch (*to you*)? Did it taste good? Was it OK? Are (*you*) still savoring it? Well, (*we*) can share coffee together.'

(24) después de sorprender*nos* y muy gratamente además / con su versión del *Unchained Melody* de los Righteous Brothers / Gareth Gates / *n:os* presenta el tema que da título a su nuevo disco: <Mus-Ci-230903-16:55>
'After surprising (*us*), and quite pleasantly indeed, with his version of *Unchained Melody* by the R. B.'s, G. G. is presenting (*us*) with the song that gives its title to his new album.'

When constructing inclusive first-person groups, speakers will always be presupposing or seeking some coincidence with the addressee or audience, which can be understood as an alignment of discursive-cognitive viewpoints. This is obvious when a clearly personal stance is expressed, as in (25), where the writer sarcastically states *Ya podemos dormir tranquilos* '(We) can now sleep well', alluding to the whole local community that is affected by public health policies. In (26), participant A – a radio broadcaster conducting a section on movie releases – shows some insecurity when expressing a judgment about some popular performers, as suggested by the final question tag. Instead of *me parece* 'it seems (to me)', she chooses *nos parece* 'it seems (to us)', thus practically forcing the acquiescence of her specific addressee, who is the one holding the status of movie expert in this interaction.

(25) Mientras el Hospital Clínico pierde prestigio a nivel nacional y los médicos ven cómo empeoran sus condiciones de trabajo, la consejería prepara un completo cuestionario, con el fin de mejorar la atención a los ciudadanos. Ya *podemos* dormir tranquilos. <Art-Ad-200804-4>
'As the Clinical Hospital keeps losing its prestige at a national level, and physicians watch their working conditions get ever worse, the Department is preparing a comprehensive questionnaire in order to improve citizen care. (*We*) can now sleep well.'

(26) <A> se titula *Relaciones* / *confidenciales* / con: Al Pacino y Kim Basinger de entrada / *n- n- nos* parece que son buenos actores [¿no?]
<B> [sí una] Kim Basinger recuperada ya no como mito sexual / (por e)jemplo: en *Ocho millas* / que ya: / ha recup- / e: ha: / tomado: e: con la edaz / una: / entidaz como actriz que antes yo creo que no tenía <Var-SE-300503-19:50>
'A: Its title is *People I know*, and features A. P. and K. B. In principle it seems (*to us*) that they are good performers, right? – B: Yes. This is a K. B. that has made her comeback as less of a sex symbol, for example in *8 Mile*, and that with age has acquired the acting prestige she lacked before.'

Viewpoint alignment makes it natural that the plural first person should be a frequent resource for the modalization of directive acts, as in the proposed example *Nos callamos* '(We) now shut up', addressed by a teacher to their students, or the suggestion by A – formulated as a question – in (27) below. The answer given by B is also interesting, using a plural that might seem to refer just to himself, since it is he who is going to give the good news; however, in this context the plural is easier to interpret as inclusive of A, given that both are talking in front of an implicit audience, i.e. the listeners of the program.

Inclusion may also have been favored by an intention to share involvement in a positively-regarded content.

(27) <A> *¿dejamos* lo: burocrático administrativo / y *nos centramos* en lo deportivo?
<B> sí / o bueno / antes que / en lo deportivo deportivo deportivo / que es decir los entrenamientos del Salamanca <. . .> *vamos* a dar: / bueno una buena noticia que Montero ha sido de n:uevo convocado / por la selección española / subdiecinueve <Dep-Co-080104-14:40>
'A: Shall (*we*) leave bureaucratic, administrative issues aside and shall (*we*) get to sports ones? – B: Yes, but well, before issues related to sports proper – which here means the training sessions of the Salamanca club – (*we*)'re going to give some good news: Montero has been called up by the under-19 national team again.'

Actually, the potential of the plural first person for the management of interpersonal relationships becomes most obvious when it does not suggest an unfolding of the speaker's own cognitive viewpoint, but rather the other way around, i.e. when the person speaking uses it to involve him/herself in some content that in principle concerns only the other – including the need to do something. So-called addressee-oriented plurals (e.g. *How are we today?*) suggest that the speaker "shares" the content, so their intention is still inclusive even if the extradiscursive reference is not.

In the corpus, the adoption of an inclusive viewpoint for contents that specifically concern others appears occasionally as an indirect way to formulate commands or requests. The speaker assumes part of the responsibility for the task he/she is asking others to do, thus appears to relieve them from it (28, 29). In the second example, the broadcaster asks a reporter standing on the soccer pitch to narrate what he can see on the touchline. In both excerpts there is a suggestion of shared involvement, aimed at mitigating a directive on the part of someone who has the right to make it. Besides, the present tense in the verbal nuclei (*repasamos, nos damos*) helps construct the actions as mutually accepted facts rather than as one-way commands.

(28) David Sierra / *repasamo:s:* cómo ha ido la jornada en segunda división: <Dep-Co-221104-14:40>
'D. S., (*we*) are now going through the results in the second division.'

(29) e:n la banda calientan ya varios hombres Jorge: *nos damos:* e / o:tro: paseo por esa zona: <Dep-Pu-191204-18:05>

'Several men are already warming up near the touchline. Jorge, (*we*) now take a walk around that zone.'

In other contexts where the speaker does not make a command or request, viewpoint alignment through inclusive plurals can also reveal an intention not to suggest superiority. The movie critic in (30) talks about *nombres y apellidos que nos sonarán más* ('first names and family names that should be more familiar (to us)'), constructing himself as part of an expectably non-specialist audience that is likely to choose movies (partly) based on the stars featuring in them. Second-person plural choices like *que os/les sonarán más* 'that should be more familiar (to you guys)' might in turn be perceived as somewhat patronizing.

(30) e:l director / francés / George / Sluizer / e: dirige / a: gente: / co:n nombres y apellidos que *nos* sonarán más / como Federico Luppi Icíar Bollaín / o Gabino Diego <Var-Co-230503-13:55>
'Here the French director G. S. is in charge of people with first names and family names that should be more familiar (*to us*), such as F. L., I. B. or G. D.'

Finally, referential blurring leads to the basically discursive uses of the plural whereby, rather than denoting any discernible group, it becomes a rhetoric device that helps structure expository or argumentative discourse, always with the intention to suggest alignment between the speaker and any possible audience. This is particularly characteristic of written texts such as opinion pieces (see 25 above). The plural first person seems to be perceived as an adequate perspective for highly elaborated texts combining exposition with persuasive intent, as is also clear in (31).

(31) No generalizo en el poder judicial, en el que aún creo, pero *necesitamos* más cirujanos para extirpar determinados tumores que amenazan por reventar la confianza popular en el sistema. <Art-Tr-241104-4>
'I'm not trying to generalize about the judiciary, in which I still believe, but (*we*) need more surgeons to remove certain tumors that are threatening to wreck the people's confidence in the system.'

Examples like this one suggest that, while both exclusive and inclusive plurals have a potential for argumentation, their pragmatic motivations are quite different. Whereas the former make it possible to associate a stance with a group relevant in the context – with pronoun expression and placement helping modulate pragmatic meaning; see Section 5.3 – inclusion can set up the presupposition that the audience shares that stance (Gardelle/Sorlin 2015, 13). A plural construction used as an epistemic modalizer, such as *como (todos) sabemos* 'as (we all) know' (example 32), presupposes that everyone agrees on some content that need not be common knowledge, much less have been convincingly demonstrated. In fact, the participant in (33) seems to acknowledge the risk of this choice being interpreted as manipulative by subsequently adding the caveat *desde mi punto de vista* 'from my point of view'. Still, he later resumes the argumentation through other inclusive plural forms.

(32) hay e:n:- / como *sabemos* en España muchos clubes (de fútbol) / que están dirigidos / por / personas / e:n:- / que no sienten los colores del club sino que van únicamente a hacer negocio <Dep-On-080104-15:25>
'In Spain there are, as (*we*) know, many [soccer] clubs under the administration of people who don't feel the spirit of the club, but are only concerned about doing business.'

(33) Salamanca: / como *todos sabemos* es la: ciudaz: universitaria más importante de- / de España desde mi punto de vista / y: *tenemos* que mantenerlo porque:: / ya que *tenemos* poco / en Salamanca: en cuestión de trabajo / la universidaz / es un: sitio muy importante / para que la gente pueda segui:r desarrollando su actividaz <Var-Pu-281204-12:25>
'Salamanca, as (*we*) all know, is the most important university town in Spain, from my point of view. And (*we*) need to preserve this status because, since (*we*) don't have much in Salamanca when it comes to work, the university is an essential place for people to keep on pursuing their activities.'

The lack of formal differences between exclusive and inclusive uses results in their distinction not always being straightforward. Speakers can shift between them across short stretches and sometimes in a quite subtle way. In (34), the initial complaint by someone writing on behalf of a supposedly exclusive group – those who everyday *utilizamos* '(we) take', lit. 'use' a certain route – is followed by an inclusive plural (*tengamos* '(we) should have') subsuming the whole population and implying that everyone is affected by the poor condition of public infrastructures.

(34) ¿Qué pasa, que estos señores que trabajan allí, tienen más derechos que las personas que *utilizamos* diariamente esta ruta alternativa comiéndonos los baches? ¿Cómo es posible que no puedan bachear la carretera hasta Babilafuente? Todo política. Señores, habrá que esperar a organizar una vuelta

ciclista para que así la arreglen, parece mentira que en pleno siglo XX <*sic*>, *tengamos* estas infraestructuras tercermundistas <Car-Ga-190604-6b>
'So the fellows working there have more rights than the people who (*we*) daily take this alternative route, suffering all the bumps? How come they can't patch the road up to Babilafuente? It's all a matter of politics. Sirs, it will be necessary to wait until a cycling tour is organized to see it repaired; it's hard to believe that, well into the 20th [*sic*] century, (*we*) should have such third-world infrastructures.'

It appears that referential variants form a continuum in real usage, inclusion of the audience being itself a gradual matter (De Cock 2011, 2763). This results in the possibility to formalize other taxonomies by taking different features into account. In Serrano/Aijón Oliva (2013, 420–422), an intermediate category between exclusion and inclusion was proposed, encompassing exclusive uses that could be interpreted as *empathic*. Empathy was grammatically operationalized as the simultaneous indexation of the first and second persons in the verbal nucleus – one as the subject and the other as a central object. This would be the case with examples (21) and (22) above, which illustrate quite frequent strategies in the opening and closing sequences of radio broadcasts. At the other extreme, inclusive uses with a mainly discourse-structuring function are quite close to the pragmaticalized ones to be surveyed in the following subsection.

5.2.4 Pragmaticalized

The last category is proposed here as a particular extension of the previous one, given that pragmaticalized plurals can never be interpreted as excluding the audience. At the same time, they are not referential in a strict sense. A number of plural first person-inflected verbs are used as discourse markers and conversational fillers, among them *digamos* 'let's say', *vamos* 'we go/let's go', *vamos a ver* 'we're going to see/let's see' and *esperemos* 'let's hope/hopefully'. At least in some contexts, they appear as fixed, syntactically independent units wherefrom no human reference is recoverable, even if from an isomorphic perspective they must retain the basic meaning of all plural first persons. It is generally impossible to formulate coreferential pronouns or NPs in adjacency to them. Being a sort of inclusive plurals, they also share the possibilities of this choice for argumentative discourse, albeit in a quite subtler way.

The marker *digamos* (Santos Río 2003, 337) is used in expository and argumentative discourse to adduce something that may not be totally exact, but can be considered sufficiently accurate for the point to be made (35). The plural first person implies the assumption that the audience could have used the same words. In (36), the writer humorously deautomatizes the marker by replacing it with singular first-person *digo* 'I say', admitting that the content exposed is just a personal assessment and need not be generalizable to the readership. Also, whereas in the first example *digamos* appears as a syntactically independent insertion within oral discourse, in the second one it governs a complement clause, indicating a less fixed use.

(35) yo he leído el periódico desde pequeño: / e: afortunadamente: mis padres: / me:- me enseñaron / y me educaron en ese sentido / Y / conocía: / *digamos* el: escenario de todo esto <Var-SE-300503-19:20>
'I've read the newspaper since I was a child. Fortunately, my parents taught me and trained me in that sense, and thus I was already familiar with, *say*, the setting for this all.'

(36) *Digamos* (*digo*) que hoy cualquiera quiere escribir en voz alta, hasta el punto de que no son precisamente pocos los que, sin ningún pudor, se lanzan al vacío <Art-Ga-121203-5b>
'*Let's say* – (*I*) *say* – that these days everyone feels like writing out loud, to the point that more than a few just leap into the void without any shame.'

There is a negative variant of the construction, namely (*y*) *no digamos* 'let alone', lit. '(and) let's not say', whose pragmatic meaning is scarcely connected with that of the affirmative one. It is used as an emphasizer, introducing an element that in some sense surpasses what was previously mentioned – which was already regarded as remarkable.

(37) El mayor problema de cualquier escritor –*y no digamos* de un comentarista de la actualidad– es la soledad con la que prepara su labor. <Art-Ga-091204-5a>
'The biggest problem for a writer – *let alone* a news commentator – is the isolation in which they need to do their job.'

(38) Aunque tampoco entonces habrá museo propiamente dicho, porque antes se habrá de formar una colección mínima, lo que obviamente lleva su tiempo *y no digamos* su dinero. <Art-Tr-201204-64>
'Even after that, this won't be a museum proper, since it would still be

necessary to gather a minimal collection of works, which obviously takes time, *let alone* money.'

The other most clearly pragmaticalized unit is *vamos* ('(we) go/let's go') (Portolés 2001, 143; Polanco Martínez 2013). It has a range of discursive-pragmatic functions – reformulation, explanation, intensification – all of which are founded on cognitive alignment. While in (39) the speaker uses *vamos* in order to better explain what he means by *los estudiantes de Farmacia* 'the Pharmacy students', in (40) reformulation has a primarily intensifying intention – it is implied that *not only* does the participant promise, but he can swear as well.

(39) hay / algo / que: sí me gustaría decir de lo que me han dicho los: estudiantes de Farmacia *vamos* la delegación que ha venido (en su nombre) <Inf-Pu-021204-13:50>
'There's something I'd like to say about what the Pharmacy students told me – *I mean*, the delegation that came to me [on their behalf].'

(40) yo les prometo a ustedes / *vamos* se lo juro que no está bien decirlo / que ya no hablamos más de política <Var-Co-230503-13:50>
'I promise you guys+ – *indeed*, I swear it to you guys+, even if this may not be quite right – that we won't be talking about politics anymore.'

The association of these units with reformulation or further elaboration explains why most tokens should be found across radio formats containing stretches of conversational argumentation. They are in turn less expectable in written texts, although it is possible to find occasional instances of *digamos* in opinion pieces and letters, as shown by some of the examples above.

Vamos a ver 'let's see', lit. '(we)'ll see', just like *vamos* alone, has a variety of pragmatic functions that correlate with different degrees of pragmaticalization and semantic blurring. Aside relatively literal cases where the verbal nucleus governs a lexical or clausal object denoting what will be *seen*, i.e. checked or discovered (41), there are others where the construction is syntactically independent and shows mobility across utterances. It can then be used to indicate the beginning of an expository or argumentative stretch (42) or as a filler amidst on-the-fly spoken narration (43).

(41) *vamos a ver* cómo está: la agenda informativa de esta jornada <Inf-Co-241104-8:40>
'*Let's see* what the news agenda has for this day.'

(42) *vamos a ver* lo que no(s)otros entendemos por *yogur* / es: la leche: agria: s- vamos / que se dice: vulgarmente: / y que:: bueno pues tiene una serie de componentes y digamos que está: VIVA: la leche <Var-On-080104-13:25>
'*Now*, what we usually mean by *yoghourt* is sour milk, I mean, so it is commonly called. And which has, well, a number of components and is, say, living milk.'

(43) rodeado de contrarios terminó perdiéndola / vuelve a la carga el Elche / *vamos a ver* / Afek caracolea / tra:ta de salir <Dep-Pu-191204-18:40>
'Surrounded by his rivals, he finally yielded the ball. The Elche team now strikes back. *So*, Afek revolves, he's trying to get out.'

Finally, *esperemos* 'let's hope', coming from an imperative form, has a clear argumentative potential insofar as it does not only express a desire, but apparently obliges the audience to share it, even if semantic blurring precludes a directive interpretation as such. While it can govern a syntactic object, usually in the form of a complement clause (44), in more pragmaticalized uses it functions as a modalizer with positional freedom (45).[4]

(44) Sin ir más lejos, la Roma recibió recientemente dos goleadas del Real Madrid en la Liga de Campeones. *Esperemos* que continúe la racha con la Juventus. <Art-Ga-201204-5>
'As it happens, the Roma club recently suffered two crushing defeats from Real Madrid in the Champions League. *Let's hope* that the streak will continue against Juventus.'

(45) volveremo:s: la próxima semana: / el jueve:s: e:n: el apartado: de consumo: / con otras noticias: e: / *esperemos* / de: interés / para todos ustedes <Var-On-080104-13:30>
'We'll be back next week, on Thursday, with our section on consumer information, bringing – *hopefully* – interesting pieces of news for all of you guys+.'

In the corpus, 170 tokens of plural first-person verbs were classified as pragmaticalized. The categoricity of pronoun omission, while being coherent with their lack of referential capacity, makes them of little use for our analyses of pronoun

4 More detailed descriptions of *digamos, vamos* and other pragmaticalized plural first-person forms can be found in Portolés (2001), Santos Río (2003) and Fuentes Rodríguez (2009).

formulation and placement. There is also no variability in functional encoding, all pragmaticalized constructions being of subject agreement. All this contrasts with singular first-person forms such as *creo* '(I) think', *digo* '(I) say' or *me parece* 'it seems (to me)', which still admit the formulation and variable placement of pronouns, and are not so clearly deprived of referential capacity (see Section 4.2). Given these differences, the following quantitative analyses will not take pragmaticalized plural first persons into account.

5.3 Variable expression and placement of pronouns

Being the grammatical person with the largest number of verbal indexations altogether (3,047 excluding pragmaticalized tokens), which is no doubt related to its referential and pragmatic versatility, the plural first person is also among the ones with the lowest scores of pronoun formulation, having 9.4% of this variant altogether (Table 5.1).[5] The choice is somewhat more frequent in contexts of subject encoding, as happens with the singular first person (Section 4.3) and others to be reviewed. This would seem to contradict the ideal association between subject encoding, pronoun omission and cognitive salience, but is explainable on discursive-pragmatic grounds.

Table 5.1: Expression vs. omission of plural first-person pronouns.

	Subject (*nosotros*)		**Object (*a nosotros*)**		**Total**	
	#	%	#	%	#	%
Expression	246	9.9	41	7.4	287	9.4
Omission	2,245	90.1	515	92.6	2,760	90.6
Total	2,491	81.8	556	18.2	3,047	100

In no less than 168 (58.5%) of the 287 tokens of expression, the formulated element is not the pronoun *nosotros* – or a coordination between singular *yo/a mí*

5 Throughout the analysis it should be borne in mind that the term *pronouns* conventionally includes lexical NPs and relative heads in coreference with plural first-person forms. Their consideration as functionally analogous to pronouns marks a difference with previous studies such as Aijón Oliva/Serrano (2013) and Serrano/Aijón Oliva (2013), where only actual occurrences of *nosotros/as* were considered cases of pronoun expression.

and some other element – but a third-person NP or the head of a relative clause. We could expect expression to be primarily associated with audience-exclusive referential uses. Serrano/Aijón Oliva (2013, 412, 419) find that overt *nosotros* in subject contexts is associated with relatively delimited human groups, especially when they exclude the addressee or audience. Also, as pointed out in Section 5.1, the agglutination *nos-otros* was originally used to demarcate audience-exclusive references as against the more diffuse *nos*, eventually displacing the latter and taking up all of its referential possibilities.

Given that the referential variants proposed can be suspected to behave differently, their respective frequencies of pronoun formulation are shown in Table 5.2. It turns out that exclusive uses exceed inclusive ones by a mere 1.4%. Even so, if the results are watched from the perspective of the total tokens, the 171 cases of formulated exclusive plurals represent 59.6% of this choice – exclusive plurals in general accounting for just 54.9% of the database. This still suggests some divergence between referential types that will become more evident through qualitative analysis.

Table 5.2: Expression vs. omission of plural first-person pronouns and referential category.

	Expression		Omission		Total	
	#	%	#	%	#	%
Speaker-blurring	5	4.5	107	95.5	112	3.7
Exclusive	171	10.2	1,502	89.8	1,673	54.9
Inclusive	111	8.8	1,151	91.2	1,262	41.4
Total	287	9.4	2,760	90.6	3,047	100

Speaker-blurring uses, i.e. those whose extradiscursive reference is just the individual speaking or writing, are the ones with the strongest tendency to omission, with just 5 tokens of overt *nosotros*. This is understandable insofar as expression would draw attention towards an apparent human plurality that does not exist as anything else than a discursive resource – and the audience is assumed to know it. This choice is favored by the pragmatic conventions of particular textual genres, whereby an explicitly personal viewpoint is dispreferred (see back the examples in §5.2.1).

As for inclusive plurals, it must be noted that most tokens of expression (67 of 111, i.e. 60.4%) correspond to generalizing NPs such as *todos* 'all', *todo el mundo* 'everyone' or *nadie* 'no one'. Therefore, in inclusive contexts expression is usually not intended to delimit a group, as it is in exclusive ones, but rather to emphasize that the content concerns all – or none – of the members. In both (46) and (47), the content is assumed to be or have been valid for all of Spanish society, even if this may not be true.

(46) Hace años, no muchos, cuando *decíamos* España *nos sentíamos* parte *todos*, ahora, en cambio, al decir esta misma palabra se autoexcluyen catalanes, gallegos, vascos, navarros, valencianos… <Art-Ad-290704-5>
'Not so many years ago, when (*we*) said "Spain", (*we*) *all* felt part of it. Now, in turn, when the same word is uttered, people from Catalonia, Galicia, the Basque country, Navarra, Valencia… exclude themselves.'

(47) *A nadie* se *nos* han ido de la cabeza las dramáticas imágenes de los atentados del 11-M <Art-Ga-070404-3a>
'*No one* (*we*) have ever gotten (lit. *To no one* [*us*] have ever gone) out of our heads the dramatic images of the 11-M terrorist attacks.'

Therefore, an association can still be posited of inclusive uses with omission on the one hand, and exclusive ones with expression on the other, even if this has little impact on mere quantitative data and only becomes evident through the observation of contextual usage. Expression always makes a referent come under the focus of attention, thus enhances its informativeness (§1.3.2). The reference of audience-exclusive plurals is usually more clearly demarcated, but it is expression itself that arguably contributes to such a demarcation. Even when it is *nosotros* and not a lexical NP that is formulated, the choice will entail the suggestion that the audience should track a contextually relevant referent. In (48), after uttering the personal pronoun, the speaker adds the apposition *los políticos* 'politicians', with some pause in between. This suggests an intuition that hearers may need further help in identifying the reference.

(48) puede ocurrir / cualquier cosa: / y supongo que estará ocurriendo / ¿eh? / menos: que el Ayuntamiento / al final / haya hecho una concesión administrativa en BAJA temeraria / ¿eh? / por dos razones fundamentales: / primero porque no se *nos* ocurre *a nosotros* / *los políticos:* <Inf-SE-180603-14:10>
'Anything can happen, and I guess it is happening, right? – anything except for the Town Council to make an administrative concession in a situation of abnormally low tender, right? This for two basic reasons. First, because such an idea would never occur *to us, politicians*.'

Expression in exclusive contexts can also help clarify the identity of the group when it is not so evident that the speaker be part of it. In (49), a street reporter takes up the role of spokeswoman for *the listeners*, including herself in a group she does not belong to – she asks her interviewee to describe what he is disguised as, obvious as it is that she can see it. Rather than claiming explicit-addressee status, she is constructing herself as the representative of an external group that is demarcated through the expressed NP.

(49) una estatua humana que está descansando <. . .> ¿de qué:- / de- / de qué va disfrazado? cuénte*nos*lo: *a los oyentes* <Var-SE-230903-13:15>
'Here is a human statue that is taking a rest. What are you+ disguised as? Tell (*us*) *the listeners.*'

In press and radio interviews there is often variability in the choice of singular vs. (exclusive) plural first persons on the part of interviewees, which reveals a tension between different strategies of self-construction. Many people responding to interviews are introduced as representatives of a certain group – and this is tacitly accepted to be the main reason why they are interviewed. However, they are still individuals who may at any point feel compelled to convey personal stances, or be asked to do so by journalists. In (50), the chief of the university sports division discusses the economic problems faced by his department using plural forms, subsequently developing his own view of things with singular ones. In both cases, expressed pronouns help signal the viewpoint adopted.

(50) –¿Qué intenta decir?
–Que si *nosotros* encontramos un patrocinador que se haga cargo del equipo de rugby *seguimos* adelante. Si no lo *hallamos* en breve, no podría seguir en esta categoría.
–¿A qué se debe el incremento de la deuda?
–A que se crearon necesidades que no iban acordes con el presupuesto de la universidad para ello. La filosofía que *yo* planteo es que el deporte universitario federado tiene que estar sostenido por jugadores universitarios. <Ent-Ad-170504-7>
'A: What are you+ trying to say? – B: That if *we* can find a sponsor that takes over the rugby team, (*we*)'ll go on with it. If (*we*) don't find it soon, it will not be possible to stay in this division. – A: What is the reason for the increase in debt? – B: The generation of necessities that exceeded the budget of the university for this. The philosophy *I* advocate is that federated college sport needs to rely on college players.'

Whether in exclusive or inclusive contexts, the pragmatic motivations of plural first-person pronoun expression are analogous to those observed in the analysis of the singular. Besides contributing to referential demarcation, the focusing of attention on a referent makes it possible to highlight its involvement in the content. For example, it can help emphasize the virtues of a company or product in advertising discourse, as can be observed in (51), from a radio commercial where *nosotros* is formulated in three parallelistic question-answer pairs. Preverbal placement is also a quite coherent choice in a context where the firm presents itself as being the ideal solution for the needs of customers. Note that the singular second-person subject, constructing a nonspecific audience as an individual, is in turn systematically omitted. This helps establish the latter as the most contextually salient participant and his/her viewpoint as the dominant one. A situation is constructed where a person who needs something comes across a company that has just that to offer.

(51) *¿necesitas* muebles? / *nosotros* / l:os *tenemo:s* / todo:s / *¿necesitas* proyectos? / *nosotro:s* / l:os *tenemos* todo:s / *¿necesita:s* / financiación? / *nosotros* / *tenemos* la solución <Anu-Di-200503-12:55>
'Do (*you*) need furniture? *We*'ve got it all. Do (*you*) need design projects? *We*'ve got them all. Do (*you*) need financing? *We*'ve got the right solution.'

In inclusive contexts, always entailing the alignment of viewpoints, the speaker can also formulate *nosotros* with the aim of intensifying both his/her and the audience's involvement, even when both are often constructed within a much larger and more diffuse plurality. In (52), a participant in a debate encourages his partners and the implicit audience to move together with him in a particular direction – a more responsible attitude of adults as to what children are allowed to see and do – uttering three parallelistic clauses as in (51) above, but in this case opting for the postverbal placement of the pronouns. This choice is parallel to informative focalization; the meaning could be paraphrased as 'if it's us that change' and so on, contrasting the plural first-person referent with the subsequent *nuestros hijos* 'our children'.

(52) si *cambiamoh nosotros* / si *modifiCAmoh nosotros* si *luchamoh nosotro* / nuestros hijos también van a cambiar / porque van a seguir modelos <Var-Pu-211204-12:35>
'If *we* change, if *we* modify things, if *we* fight, our children will also change, because they're going to follow our models.'

Through the analysis of variable formulation it has already been possible to make some comments on pronoun placement, whose variants help modulate the meanings associated with expression in general. The data in Table 5.3 suggest quite striking tendencies in this regard, particularly if subject-encoding contexts are compared with object-encoding ones.

Table 5.3: Preverbal vs. postverbal placement of plural first-person pronouns.

	Subject (*nosotros*)		**Object (*a nosotros*)**		**Total**	
	#	%	#	%	#	%
Preverbal	192	78	16	39	208	72.5
Postverbal	54	22	25	61	79	27.5
Total	246	85.7	41	14.3	287	100

While the 246 subject tokens – representing 85.7% of the total cases of expressed referents – show the expectable preference for preverbal placement, in the context of object encoding it is postposition that accounts for 61% of the tokens. Even if the figures in this column are small, it seems evident that plural first-person objects are inclined towards a positional variant that is rare with the singular first person in either syntactic function (see Section 4.3). Upon examination of the examples, it turns out that most of them are clause-final pronouns or NPs in transitive clauses where speakers intend to emphasize the patienthood of a human group they construct themselves into, in sharp contrast with the agency and autonomy associated with preverbal subjects and with first- and second-person referents in general. That is, the high rate of postposition is connected with an atypical frequency of contexts where plural first-person referents approach the prototypical features of accusatives, including semantic patienthood – sometimes in psychological-verb contexts, as in (53). In (54) there is a functionally dative context where the speaker recounts personal criticism directed at himself and a fellow party member by a political opponent. There is thus still the suggestion of harmful behavior.

(53) para hablar / precisamente de eso: / de algo que: *nos* preocupa *a todos los aficionados salmantinos / a todos los aficionados de la Unión Deportiva Salaman:ca* la situación económica <Dep-On-080104-15:20>
'In order to talk precisely about that, about something that worries *us, all the Salamanca supporters, all the fans of the U. D. S. team* – the financial situation.'

(54) los proyectos más sólidos / que ha utilizado para con Salamanca han sido <. . .> hablar: de: sesenta mil velas que quiere poner*nos a: Fernando y a mí* <Var-Co-230503-13:20>
'The soundest proposals he has made for Salamanca come down to [. . .] talking about sixty thousand candles he'd like to dedicate (*to us*) *to Fernando and me.*'

In turn, plural first-person objects approaching the dative prototype, particularly those accorded the semantic roles of cognizer of experiencer with *gustar*-type verbs (Section 2.4), understandably prefer preposition when expressed. The construction is most often used to convey the opinions or discuss the situation of some audience-exclusive group the participant is speaking for, as in the following excerpts.

(55) Enrique Battaner recibió a una comisión de cinco estudiantes a los que, como informó uno de ellos a *El Adelanto*, "nos dijo que a Educación y *a nosotros nos* debe una fiesta porque hemos ido a la *manifa* sin bebidas y agradece nuestro comportamiento". <Not-Ad-031204-10>
'E. B. met with a commission of five students to whom – as one of them told *El Adelanto* – "he said that to the Faculty of Education and *to us* he owes a feast because we attended the demonstration without any drinks, so he acknowledges our behavior." '

(56) bueno / pue:s *nosotros::* se *nos* ha acabado el tiempo así que mañana *volvemos* / a partir de las dos y media <Dep-Co-221104-15:00>
'Well, *we*'ve run out of time (lit. *we, to us* time has ended), so (*we*)'ll be back tomorrow from 2:30 p.m.'

In (56), the topicalization of *nosotros* is particularly evident in the absence of the object marker *a*. Given the noticeable lengthening of the final /s/, suggesting hesitation, it is possible to assume that the speaker opted for object encoding once the pronoun had been formulated; anyway, this does not prevent the referent from being highly topical.[6] Some similar examples with the singular first person, where the pronoun in coreference with the clitic is not preceded by *a* but rather adopts the form of a subject in an

6 The controversial point would in any case be whether this element is actually integrated in the clause or rather functions an independent topic. However, we do not usually attempt to differentiate between left-dislocated elements and discursive topics, since in oral discourse there are often no clear indicators – e.g. a perceptible pause or intonational change – that help

apparently ungrammatical construction (as in *yo me gusta* 'I (to me) it is pleasing', *yo me parece* 'I (to me) it seems'), have been discussed in Sections 2.4 and 4.4 as illustrations of the scarce prototypicality of first- and second-person objects or, in other words, their functional and cognitive proximity to subjects.

Finally, regarding the positional tendencies of the different referential variants (see Table 5.4), the most significant fact is the comparable preference of audience-exclusive plurals for preverbal placement, with 77.8% of this variant against 64% with inclusive uses. This is easy to put in connection with the results obtained with the singular first person. The preverbal expression of subjects, which we have characterized as combining semantic agency with relative informational focalization, is a coherent choice in expository and argumentative contexts where speakers assert the positions held by the contextually relevant groups they construct themselves as part of. This also explains the usually higher percentages of expression in subject-encoding contexts (see the following section).

Table 5.4: Preverbal vs. postverbal placement of plural first-person pronouns and referential category.

	Preverbal		Postverbal		Total	
	#	%	#	%	#	%
Speaker-blurring	4	80	1	20	5	1.7
Exclusive	133	77.8	38	22.2	171	59.6
Inclusive	71	64	40	36	111	38.7
Total	208	72.5	79	27.5	287	100

Examples (57) and (58) illustrate the pragmatic values of preverbal expression. In the first one, the very formulation of *nosotros* right after a clause where it had been omitted suggests some referential shift. It is possible to think that the preceding *no podemos permitir* '(we) cannot allow' actually alluded to a wider, possibly inclusive human plurality. The uses in the second excerpt are clearly audience-exclusive ones, exposing the stance held by a political party.

make a decision. In the absence of marked intonation, preverbal elements are always endowed with topicality (see back §1.3.1).

(57) No hay marcha atrás y no *podemos* permitir el consumo de alcohol en la calle. En esto *nosotros* no *podemos* ceder <Not-Ad-031204-10>
'There is no turning back and (*we*) cannot allow alcohol consumption on the streets. On this point *we* cannot yield.'

(58) *nosotros* hemos sido / especialmente / coherentes y lo *mantenemos* / en decir que: / el patrimonio que está depositado en los museos / y en los archivos de España / en todo el territorio del Estado / es algo que se tiene que preservar <. . .> *nosotros* defendemos la unidaz / y la *defendemos* como un patrimonio de todos <Inf-On-301204-13:55>
'*We* have been particularly coherent, and (*we*) stand by our position, in saying that the cultural heritage lodged in Spain's museums and archives, all across the national territory, is something that needs preserving. [. . .] *We* defend its integrity, and (*we*) defend it as a heritage of us all.'

In turn, the more balanced results with inclusive plurals are coherent with the usually lower perceptibility of the referents constructed through this choice. It can be concluded that the more specific the human group at issue, the more expectable it will be for its coreferential pronouns to be formulated at preverbal rather than postverbal positions.

5.4 Functional encoding

Table 5.5 displays the percentages of subject vs. object encoding in combination with the different variants of expression and placement. The plural first person parallels the strong preference of the singular one for subject encoding, even surpassing it by nearly two points (81.8 against 80.1%). As in that case, the general scarcity of object encoding makes it particularly interesting to analyze the possible motivations for the latter choice.

In spite of the low percentage they represent, there are 556 plural first-person object indexations across the corpus. As pointed out in the previous section, there is often emphasis on the patienthood of the referent, even if inherent salience can result in detachment from the prototypical features of objects. In (59), starting with a topicalized pronoun, the speaker alludes to situations where his political group is the target of external attacks. They are subsequently encoded as subjects when recounting what happens when it is they who talk about their opponents. Despite the change in function and semantic role, there is always an intention to present the referent as the damaged party. Patienthood is to be interpreted more metaphorically in contexts of object pronoun omission such as (60),

Table 5.5: Functional encoding of plural first persons.

	Omitted		Expressed preverbal		Expressed postverbal		Total	
	#	%	#	%	#	%	#	%
Subject	2,245	90.1	192	7.7	54	2.2	2,491	81.8
Object	515	92.6	16	2.9	25	4.5	556	18.2
Total	2,760	90.6	208	6.8	79	2.6	3,047	100

where someone humorously recalls the attitude of elder people towards youngsters and their musical tastes in the 60s.

(59) *a nosotros* / y digo a todos a la gente del PP <. . .> se *nos* / insulta se *nos* injuria y calumnia de una manera / (ab)solutamente atroz / no *decimos* nada / no *decimos* nada / ahora m: / *salimos* un día *alguno de nosotros* diciendo "mecachis en la mar" / y *somos* unos incultos unos insultadores / unos descerebraos <Var-Co-230503-13:15>
'*Us* – and I mean all of us, the people at the PP [. . .] – people insult, offend and slander (*us*) in absolutely heinous ways. But (*we*) don't answer, (*we*) just don't answer. Now if someday *anyone of us* (*we*) should dare to go like "Oh darn!", (*we*) will turn out to be uneducated, offensive and brainless people.'

(60) empezaron los yeyé:s y la música aquella moderna: y bueno *nos* ponían- / e: la gente mayor *nos* ponía verdes: e de ello / en el periódico salieron algunos escritos diciendo que las piedras / de la Plaza Mayor se sonroJAban: de la música aquella <Var-SE-011204-13:30>
'Then came the sixties with all that modern pop music, and elder people would call (*us*) every name in the book. The newspapers published some pieces saying that even the stones at the Major Square would blush when hearing that kind of music.'

Radio broadcasters frequently encode themselves and their team or station as a plural object, while the audience is encoded as the subject of the same clause (example 61). The co-occurrence within a verbal nucleus of a first-person clitic and a second-person verbal ending, or vice versa, has been analyzed as a grammatical manifestation of empathy (cf. Serrano/ Aijón Oliva 2013). However, in these contexts, object self-encoding can also be viewed as a grammatical reflection of the subordinate position these professionals tend to assume towards their audience (see further Section 9.6). In the excerpt, the second-person subject is explicitly presented as someone who *chooses* to listen. (62) illustrates a functionally dative context where the broadcaster, again speaking on behalf of her team – but also, apparently, on that of the audience of the program – asks the interviewee to state his views on the issue at hand.

(61) hablamos: ahora de música / que es lo que: / bueno / que ese es el motivo principal supongo por el que tú eliges escuchar*nos* ¿no:? <Mus-Ci-230903-16:15>
'Now let's talk about music, which is, well, is the main reason, I guess, you normally choose to listen (*to us*), right?'

(62) olvidándonos: de: que no / TIEne / competencias en esta materia: / sí lo tiene: la Concejalía de:- de Cultura pero: / me parece que: / e: sería interesante la opinión que *nos* pudiera aportar: <Var-On-080104-13:05>
'Forgetting for a while that you+ have no competence on this subject – since it corresponds to the Culture Department – it seems to me that any opinion you+ could provide (*us*) with should be an interesting one.'

Therefore, the audience-exclusive groups speakers construct themselves into are sometimes presented as the patients or recipients of externally-initiated actions. However, the analysis of functional encoding according to referential types (Table 5.6) shows that exclusive uses are actually the ones with the strongest preference for subject encoding (83.4%). This combination also offers the most favorable conditions for preverbal pronoun expression (see 57 and 58 above), usually in argumentative discourse.

In turn, it is inclusive and speaker-blurring plurals that have comparably higher percentages of object encoding (respectively 20.5 and 20.2%). Most examples of inclusive objects appear across oral (e.g. 53 above) and written argumentative discourse (63, 64). This choice helps the individual suggest that the facts described affect both him/her and the whole audience; in the corpus this is a recurrent strategy in contexts of criticism directed at the administration, political parties or other factual powers. By way of cognitive alignment, opinion piece authors can suggest alliance with the audience against an external enemy, as in these excerpts.

(63) Pero algo que atenta, aún más, contra la inteligencia del colectivo, es la utilización torcida de ciertas palabras; palabras impropias, inadecuadas y

premeditadamente usadas con el único objetivo de confundir*nos*. <Art-Ad-121203-5a>
'But something that is even more insulting to the intelligence of the community is the distorted use of certain words; improper, inadequate words that are intentionally chosen with the only goal of misleading (*us*).'

(64) Si esta política refleja la austeridad que *nos* venden un día sí y otro también nuestros munícipes, que venga Dios y lo vea. <Art-Ga-221203-3>
'If these policies are inspired by the austerity that our administrators are trying to sell (*us*) everyday, then I'm a donkey.'

Table 5.6: Functional encoding of plural first persons and referential category.

	Subject		Object		Total	
	#	%	#	%	#	%
Speaker-blurring	89	79.5	23	20.5	112	3.7
Exclusive	1,395	83.4	278	16.6	1,673	54.9
Inclusive	1,007	79.8	255	20.2	1,262	41.4
Total	2,491	81.8	556	18.2	3,047	100

The other most significant source of object tokens for the plural first person is *gustar*-type verbs, where the tension between functional encoding and salience becomes evident – unlike prototypical accusative or dative contexts, they strongly favor the omission or preverbal placement of pronouns. These verbs are expectably dominant with audience-exclusive references; the person speaking exposes the stance of the group he/she represents (see 55 above). In turn, they are rare in inclusive contexts. Performing cognitive alignment in processes such as are described by these verbs could suggest the attribution of a personal stance to the audience. In (65), the writer makes a moral assessment through an inclusive plural that draws on the seemingly safe assumption that everyone wishes to be respected by others.

(65) la educación y el sentido del deber impelen a respetar escrupulosamente a los demás, al igual que *nos* gusta que *nos* respeten <Car-Tr-031104-6>
'Education and sense of duty compel one to scrupulously respect others, just as (*we*) like it (lit. it pleases [*us*]) when others respect (*us*).'

In turn, it is interesting to note that *gustar*-type verbs do occur with some frequency in contexts of speaker-blurring reference. The plural person and the object-encoding verb are choices respectively contributing to the desubjectivization of the viewpoint and the minimization of personal responsibility (see further Chapter 9). (66) and (67), with *parecer* 'to seem' and *ocurrirse* 'to occur', are stretches where radio broadcasters intend to influence the behavior of the audience, respectively through the suggestion to visit an exhibition and some advice on public conduct. The participant in the second excerpt later switches to subject encoding – still within the speaker-blurring plural viewpoint – in order to give an example.

(66) desde luego *nos* parece / que: la esposición / pues e: / puede despertar el interés incluso de aquellas personas / más allá de lo que es el ámbito / de: los propio:s arquitectos <Var-Co-050204-12:45>
'Truly, it seems (*to us*) that this exhibition can even arouse the interest of anyone beyond the field of architecture proper.'

(67) por lo tanto se *nos* ocurre / una especie de: sugerencia de consejo / e:viten tirar / nada encendido / *estamos* pensando en el cigarrillo por la ventanilla del coche <Var-Co-230503-13:20>
'Therefore, there's some suggestion that occurs (*to us*) – avoid throwing away anything on fire. (*We*)'re thinking of those cigarettes thrown out the car window.'

However, most constructions with speaker-blurring plurals in expository and argumentative discourse encode the referent as subject. These include discourse-structuring communication verbs (*decir* 'to say', *comentar* 'to comment') and psychological verbs with an epistemic modalizing function (*creer* 'to think', *imaginarse* 'to imagine, to suppose'). The plurals in (68) and (69) are largely discursive resources serving the demands of the textual genres they appear in.

(68) ganó: / como *decíamos* el Cádiz en casa / y m: como visitantes e aparte del Salamanca / ese uno tres: ante el Málaga / ganando también el Éibar: / que: continúa líder <Dep-Co-221104-14:45>
'As (*we*) were saying, the Cádiz team won at home. As for visitors, leaving aside Salamanca, who defeated Málaga one to three, Éibar won as well, thus remains on the lead.'

(69) se están montando las caseta:s / pa:ra la feria del libro antiguo y de ocasió:n / ya lo *comentábamos* aye:r / e: *nos imaginamos* que probablemente

ya maña:na o pasado el jueves comiencen a llegar / los libreros <Var-SE-230903-12:50>
'The stands are being installed for the old and used book fair, as (*we*) already remarked yesterday. (*We*) suppose that tomorrow or the day after, that is on Thursday, booksellers will probably start coming in.'

As also observed across the present chapter, referential categories form a continuum in discourse, which means that plural first persons can be ambiguous between individual and audience-exclusive references, just as they can be between exclusive and inclusive ones. Ambiguity reflects the fact that referential identification is sometimes not necessary for the adequate development of the communicative act. This is especially true in media discourse, where people – either journalists or other types of participants – often avoid what could be perceived as excessive subjectivity by constructing themselves as part of larger, often scarcely specified groups. Significantly, it is audience-exclusive plurals that take the lead as regards subject encoding, even surpassing the singular first person in this respect. They also have the highest percentage of preverbal pronoun formulation among the referential variants. All this suggests that many plural choices respond to the strategy of extending the singular first-person viewpoint towards a wider, less subjective one. Speakers often find it advantageous to downplay self-involvement by constructing themselves as groups, whether the latter do exist in the extralinguistic world or are just pragmatically-motivated discursive resources (see further Sections 9.4 and 10.4 on the stylistic implications of grammatical person choice).

5.5 Summary

The plural first person appears as an especially versatile communicative choice in Spanish media discourse. It constructs a type of direct participant whose viewpoint necessarily goes beyond that of the individual speaking or writing. Such cognitive extension is at the core of its meaning, which can be paraphrased as *more than the speaker*, and differentiates it from the singular first person. Even in contexts where the actual extradiscursive referent is only that individual, the choice of the plural entails some blurring of the latter, which in pragmatic terms reduces self-involvement, thus promotes stylistic desubjectivization. Referential fuzziness can in turn prompt the formulation of third-person NPs or relative heads that contribute to reference delimitation and can be considered functionally and pragmatically analogous to personal pronouns.

Apart from the uses we have termed speaker-blurring, plurals can construct relatively specified human groups from which the addressee or audience is excluded, as well as audience-inclusive ones with varying degrees of specificity. Inclusion is used to perform a cognitive alignment of speaker and audience viewpoints, to the point that plural morphemes can function as a basically discursive convention that helps provide expository and argumentative discourse with some interactional orientation. There are also highly pragmaticalized verb forms used as discourse markers, such as *vamos* or *digamos*, that have lost referential capacity and do not allow for formal variation regarding the formulation and placement of pronouns. However, even in these cases plural first-person morphemes retain their basic meaning and help speakers suggest that both themselves and the audience are involved in the content of discourse.

The quantitative patterns of variation are largely coincident with those of the singular first person, with pronoun omission and subject encoding being strongly preferred. Also, when pronouns are formulated, they tend to be placed before the verbal nucleus. However, there is a substantial difference between subject- and object-encoding constructions in the latter regard. Preverbal expressed subjects are associated with argumentative contexts where the stances or deeds of a (usually audience-exclusive) group are exposed. In turn, expressed plural objects show an atypical preference for the clause-final position, often displaying the semantic patienthood and informative focalization associated with the accusative prototype – even if many of the contexts are functionally dative ones or, in any case, promote metaphorical interpretations of events. This often reveals argumentative strategies whereby speakers highlight some damage or inconvenience suffered by a group they include themselves in. In other contexts where patienthood is not an evident semantic feature, object encoding can suggest that speakers and their groups assume a subordinate position as against the audience – which will in turn be encoded as subject – in order to secure the approval of the latter. Finally, the objects of *gustar*-type verbs usually approach the prototypical features of subjects, i.e. pronoun omission or preverbal formulation. The analysis of corpora from different communicative domains would obviously help check whether the data discussed here are representative of more general tendencies in the use of plural first persons for the construction of the speaker and other participants.

6 The singular second person: *the addressee*

6.1 The subparadigm and its meaning

This chapter and the following one will be respectively devoted to the singular and plural prototypical second persons. In turn, Chapter 8 will jointly address the singular and plural *displaced* second persons, meaning *usted/ustedes* and their (third-person) morphematical subparadigms used to construct addressees and audiences in discourse. Given that we will be dealing with four different grammatical persons that in standard English would correspond to just one subparadigm (*you*), in the translations of examples four different forms will be conventionally used: *you* (prototypical singular second person), *you guys* (prototypical plural second person), *you+* (displaced singular second person) and *you guys+* (displaced plural second person).

The Spanish prototypical singular second-person subparadigm is represented by the pronoun *tú*. When encoded as a subject, this person is unequivocally identifiable in most contexts thanks to the verbal ending -*s* adjoined after the root and the TMA morphemes (examples 1, 2). An exception to this is the perfective simple past, using the ending -*ste* (3), to which – due to analogy with the rest of the subparadigm – the morpheme -*s* is occasionally added (*escuchaste-s*) in spontaneous speech and on the part of less-educated speakers, with no clear geographical restriction (Renwick Campos 2007, 311).

(1) (tú) escuch- -a- -s
you listen THEME-V 2ND.SING
'You listen.'

(2) (tú) escuch- -a- -rá- -s
you listen THEME-V FUT 2ND.SING
'You will listen.'

(3) (tú) escuch- -a- -ste
you listen THEME-V 2ND.SING.PAST
'You listened.'

The imperative lacks morphematical realization; it is also the form with which the formulation of the subject pronoun is less expectable: *escucha* 'listen!' This makes it often homonymous with the singular third person in the present simple: *él escucha* 'he listens'. Apart from this, the second person is never isomorphic with either

https://doi.org/10.1515/9783110643442-007

the first or the third one in the standard paradigm (see also §1.3.1a). In negative hortative clauses, subjunctive forms rather than imperative ones need to be used, e.g. *no escuch-es* 'don't you listen'.

The stressed object pronoun is (*a*) *ti*, from the Latin dative TIBI, also used after any preposition indexing oblique and adjunct functions, with the exception of the amalgam *contigo* < CUM TE-CUM (see Section 4.1 on *conmigo*). The corresponding object clitic is *te*, coming from the Latin (stressed) accusative TE. As with the first persons, formal distinctions between the object prototypes have been lost, both *ti* and *te* being used in functionally accusative contexts (4) just as in dative ones (5). Also, due to the grammaticalization of the clitic as a verbal agreement morpheme, its formulation is mandatory whenever the second person is encoded as a central object, while the stressed pronoun is variably expressed.

(4)	(a ti)	no	te	expuls-	-a-	-rá-	-n
	to you	not	2ND.SING.CL	expel	THEME-V	FUT	3RD.PL
	'They won't expel you.'						

(5)	(a ti)	no	te	gust-	-a-	-rá-	-n
	to you	not	2ND.SING.CL	please	THEME-V	FUT	3RD.PL
	'You won't like them', lit. 'They won't please you.'						

The subparadigm as described above is not of general use across the Spanish-speaking domain. Approximately one third of the population, distributed in different zones of Central and South America, regularly practices *voseo* (see e.g. Benavides 2003; Bertolotti 2015). In this system, the stressed subject and object pronoun is *vos* – from Latin plural second-person VOS – and some verbal tenses are conjugated differently, with the stress displaced from the root to the morphemes, e.g. *vos escuchás* instead of *tú escuchas* 'you listen'. Nevertheless, *te* remains the object-agreement morpheme. Example (6) from the corpus is an interesting excerpt of a radio commercial advertising an Argentinian restaurant. The two characters in the dialogue mimic many phonetic, grammatical and lexical choices intuitively associated with the dialects of the Southern Cone. These include characteristic intonation, the aspiration and elision of syllable- and word-final /s/, the colloquial interjection *che* 'hey', and *voseo* in all pronouns and verbs: imperative *escuchame* (instead of *escúchame* 'listen to me'), present *podés* (*puedes* 'you can'), etc. While the text surely reveals a highly stereotyped view of Argentinian Spanish, the exploitation of commonplace dialectal or social features is known to be a usual strategy in advertising (e.g. Bell 1992; O'Sullivan 2013).

(6) <A> ¡che *vo:!* / *ehcucha::me* / en el Rancho Asador Argentino *voh podeh* dihfrutar todo loh díah de un menú / basado en la carta: / solo por nueve con ochenta euros
<B> ¿y qué me *desih* de la exelente carta de pehcados a la bra:sa? <Anu-Di-200503-13:15>
'A: Hey *you*! Listen to me. At R. A. A. *you* can enjoy a daily menu based on the carte for just 9.80 euros. – B: And what would (*you*) say about their excellent menu of grilled fish?'

Latin nominative and accusative VOS is at the origin of Peninsular Spanish *vosotros* and its associated clitic *os* (see Section 7.1 below). However, already in that language it started to be used when addressing single individuals – initially the Emperor – as a more respectful form than singular TU, mirroring the "majestic" use of the plural first person (Marrón 2011, 60–61). As exposed by Lapesa (1981, §95), during the 15th and 16th centuries Spanish had a threefold address system which comprised *tú*, *vos* and *vuestra merced* 'your mercy', the latter form eventually evolving into *usted* (see Chapter 8). The three subparadigms were organized along a scale of formality or respect towards the addressee, with *tú* being mostly used with children and servants, *vos* with people considered to be roughly equal to the person speaking, and *vuestra merced* with those of higher status. However, such a system proved rather unstable; European varieties as well as many American ones came to drop *vos* out, while others – mainly in Central America and the Southern Cone – progressively dispensed with *tú*.

The basic meaning of the singular second person will be paraphrased as *the addressee*. It explicitly designates a participant as the one discourse is produced for and constructs this participant as individual, i.e. not as a plurality. The notion of *addressee* is hardly equivalent to those of *hearer/listener* or *reader*, just as *the speaker* does not mean the individual speaking or writing (Section 4.1; see also Serrano, in press b, for a delimitation between *hearer* and *addressee*). This is particularly evident in mass-media communication, where, given its public nature, everyone can in principle act as a hearer or reader. At the same time, however, not everyone will be an addressee proper; this status will be granted by the speaker through the second-person grammatical encoding of a certain contextual reference.[1] Therefore, the role of addressee can be

1 Bell (1984, 159–160), together with the communicative role of *addressee*, distinguishes those of *auditor, overhearer* and *eavesdropper*, depending on the extent to which they are involved in the interaction. Even if all these kinds of participants can exert a significant influence in discourse construction – radio broadcasters, even when addressing specific individuals, are also speaking for a nonspecific audience they can hardly disregard – it is obvious that person

considered a creation of the speaker (De Cock 2014, 26). As in the case of the latter, it needs to be primarily analyzed as a discursive-cognitive construction. Like many plural first persons reviewed across the previous chapter, it can actually appear as much of a convention, as happens in advertising and other forms of argumentative or persuasive discourse. However, and although it may often seem that second-person forms in media discourse are directed at anyone listening or reading, there will always be some kind of target addressee (see further §6.2.2 on nonspecific references).

Therefore, among the communicative rights entailed by the status of *speaker* is the option to construct anyone else as *the addressee* and make the latter participant salient as against external entities. Through the subparadigm of *tú*, the participant will also be granted individuality – irrespective of extradiscursive features – thus higher perceptibility than they would enjoy if constructed as a plural audience. In example (7), a broadcaster referring to a specific listener carries out a transition from the third person to the second one. This shows the multifaceted nature of participants in radio discourse – first she talks to the audience about somebody, then she turns the latter into her explicit addressee. It is also worth noting the persons she successively chooses to encode herself – the third one when figuring the thoughts of the other, then the *plural* first one when directly addressing him, avoiding a straightforwardly subjective viewpoint.

(7) seguro que *estaba* diciendo "¡ay que *se ha olvidado* de poner mi canción!" / no: lo que pasa que *estamos* esperando / el momen:to: / para poner esa canción de Ismael Serrano que *nos pedías* <Mus-Di-200503-12:35>
'Sure (*he*) was like "Oh man, (*she*)'s forgotten to play my song!" Nope – it's just that (*we*) are waiting for the right time to play that song by I. S. (*you*) asked (*us*) for.'

Finally, the status of addressee, just as that of speaker, understandably entails a set of communicative rights and duties. It will be the responsibility of this participant to co-construct discourse by interpreting meaning at all possible semiotic levels, as well as – in interactional contexts proper – by exchanging communicative roles with other participants, sometimes even having to compete for them, as evidenced by conversational turn-taking strategies. While singular first- and second-person grammatical forms necessarily construct the speaker and the addressee as cognitively distinct entities, it is true that in actual communication

forms need to be primarily analyzed from the viewpoint of the reference they denote in some context.

these are dynamic roles that emerge from constant re-negotiation. Also, in a sort of reverse process of audience-inclusive plurals, the individual speaking can choose to construct him/herself as part of the reference of *tú*, in speaker-inclusive uses (§6.2.3). However, even in such cases there will be the implication that what is said concerns (primarily) the addressee rather than the speaker.

6.2 The construction of reference

The referential possibilities of the singular second person are intuitively wider than those of the singular first one. Its uses beyond the specific reference of the participant listening or reading are mostly coincident with the ones pointed out in the analysis of *yo* (Section 4.2), but in this case they appear to be rather more frequent and conventionalized. This would also suggest that *the addressee* as a cognitive construction has lesser perceptibility than *the speaker*, which strongly tends to be associated with the actual person speaking. In the following discussion we will propose four referential categories, based on the observation of media discourse: *specific* – the referent is an individual whose existence is known by the speaker; *nonspecific* – the referent is anyone who may be listening or reading, but usually with certain preferential characteristics; *speaker-inclusive* – the referent is in principle anyone, including the speaker; and *pragmaticalized* – appearing in a number of verbal units used as discourse markers or fillers with no referential capacity or formal variation, but whereby the basic cognitive meaning of the second person is still constructed.

6.2.1 Specific

The prototypical extradiscursive reference of the singular second person is a specific human entity addressed by someone in some communicative situation. As noted above, being chosen as the addressee grants a participant a high degree of salience, but at the same time entails a communicative and social engagement whereby significant tasks are imposed on that participant. The power of speakers to construct their interactional partners by way of second-person choice is evident in all radio programs where the primary responsibility for discourse production is placed on a broadcaster who can, in turn, decide when and for how long others are allowed to participate. Vocatives and question tags (example 8), as well as second-person grammatical encoding in deontic utterances (9), are the elements commonly used to signal the points where someone else's intervention is expected. They are turn-yielding devices that simultaneously specify the identity of the addressee and recognize his/her right to become the speaker from that point on.

(8) <A> *Martín* / más en torno: a la reunión de esta tarde que está prevista a las ocho *¿no?* /
<B> así es: <Dep-Co-080104-14:40>
'A: *Martín*, let's say something more about this evening's meeting, which is scheduled at 8 p.m., *right?* – B: That's it.'

(9) <A> ¿tenemos noticias de la gastronomía que hace mucho que m: no nos *cuentas* nada? / *cuéntanos:* /
<B> bueno pues tenemos e: / dos buenas noticias: <Var-SE-300503-19:40>
'A: Do we have any news on gastronomy? – it's been long since (*you*) last told us something. (*You*) tell us. – B: Well, we do have two pieces of good news.'

The specific addressee is always relevant for the construction and organization of discourse, not just because he/she can trigger strategies of linguistic accommodation or differentiation (Giles/Coupland/Coupland 1991; Bell 1984; 2001), but also because the contributions of speakers in interactional situations can hardly be understood without taking into account the ones previously made by others, as well as the kind of relationships existing between the participants. The recognition of the addressee's previous utterances is often a relevant strategy, as in the following excerpt, which shows the recurrent use of partly conventionalized constructions such as *lo que has comentado* ('as (you) have noted'). This suggests the inextricable link between the notions of speaker and addressee. In this context, the second person can also be considered a resource for viewpoint alignment, given that the person speaking explicitly assumes the other's words as his own.

(10) y en: torno a los otros dos r:- / equipos salmantinos / pues lo que *has comentado* que no se juegan prácticamente nada <. . .> la gente que se está jugando algo tanto por arriba como por abajo: / pues tiene que:- / que jugar a la misma hora decir / lo que *has comentado* del Ciudá Rodrigo / que n:o solo se acaban ahí: las esperanzas de: ascenso sino que: / habrá también que estar muy pendiente de los equipos que puedan ascender de la tercera a la segunda división B <Dep-SE-210504-15:25>
'And as regards the other two Salamanca teams, as (*you*) have noted, they have basically nothing at stake. [. . .] All those who are still competing for something, either at the top or bottom positions, need to have their games scheduled at the same time. And also, as (*you*) have noted regarding the C. R.

team, their hopes of promotion do not end here – we need to wait and see what happens with those teams that can be promoted from the third to the second-B league.'

In less interactional media contexts, such as those of letters to the editor of a journal, the writer can also construct a specific addressee through second-person morphemes, often in co-occurrence with choices aimed at simulating interaction, such as vocatives or questions (11). Also, in opinion pieces, characterized by wide stylistic variety and strong literary elaboration, someone can write to him/herself as if he/she were someone else, as in (12). The examples suggest that all situations with a specific addressee – and, as we will see below, also those with nonspecific ones – tend to imitate the interactivity of face-to-face conversation to some extent.

(11) Dije en una opinión personal que para algunos quitar iones sodio es como quitar lentejas, y de eso no me apeo. *Pedro*: ¿A que <lo primero> es más complejo? ¿A que esos iones no *te* los *llevas* a casa para guardarlos debajo de la cama para no romper el equilibrio? <Car-Ga-300604-6>
'As a personal opinion, I said that for some people removing sodium ions is like removing lentils, and I won't retract it. *Pedro*, isn't it true that [the former] is more complex? Isn't it true that (*you*) wouldn't take the ions home and put them under the bed so as not to destroy the balance?'

(12) Nada, que no Miguel, que *te estás* metiendo en charcos que *te* van a acabar salpicando. Que *tú* lo que *tienes* que hacer es escribir de publicidad, que es de lo que realmente *sabes*. <Art-Ad-170504-5>
'No way, Miguel – (*you*)'re just getting into trouble and it'll end up splashing (*on you*). What *you* should do is write about advertising, which is what (*you*) really know about.'

6.2.2 Nonspecific

Unlike specific references, which are prototypically associated with face-to-face conversation, this second category is tightly linked to mass-media, advertising and public discourse in general. It is thus expectably the most frequent one across the corpus. Media formats are addressed to a plural and most often unknown audience, whose members can nonetheless be constructed as an individual participant through the choice of singular second-person forms.

Curiously enough, if the people in the audience were individually known to the speaker, the plural second person would be the expectable choice, in order to indicate that they are all being addressed at the same time (see further Section 7.2). Diffuse as the nonspecific reference may prove, certain kinds of preferential addressees are always assumed, which in media theory are conceptualized as *target* audiences (Kelley/Jugenheimer 2008, 36–40). These are defined by psychosocial features related to e.g. gender, age or socioeconomic status. Their influence on linguistic choice in the media has been extensively analyzed from different perspectives (e.g. Bell 1984; 1991; 2001; Cutillas 2003; Coupland 2001; 2007, 150–154).

This referential category is best illustrated by radio commercials. Nonspecific *tú* is intended to be taken by any possible addressee as denoting just him/herself, even if this is of course a mutually accepted genre convention. Deontic utterances suggesting face-to-face interactivity, such as questions and invitations, are common (example 13). In turn, in commercials adopting the structure of a dialogue among two or more characters, most second-person forms are understandably specific – even if these characters are of course not "real" people, but rather social archetypes the target audience is expected to identify with (see also Section 4.2 on polyphony in the media). In (14) we can even perceive some referential overlapping, since the three characters are supposedly talking to one another, but some of their lines clearly adopt the form of advertising messages aimed at the audience, as in *llévate* '(you) get' and *te regalan* 'they'll give (you)'.

(13) ¿*quieres* elegir? / ¿vivienda en bloque / o chalet adosado:? / en este momento / Altamira *te* ofrece con la mejor relación / calidad precio: / m:ás de doscientas cincuenta opciones / para que *encuentres* / la vivienda que *estás* buscando / *infórmate* ya <Anu-On-080104-13:30>
'Do (*you*) want to have options? An apartment or a terraced house? Altamira is now offering (*you*) more than 250 options with the best price-quality ratio, so (*you*) can find the place (*you*)'re looking for. (*You*) ask for information now.'

(14) <A> ¿y tú? / ¿dónde *vas* a pasar estas Navidades? /
<B> en Intesa <. . .> *llévate* gratis un móvil multimedia /
<A> ¿dónde *dices*? /
<C> en el Grupo Intesa: /
<B> ¡ah! y además / *te* regalan el quince por ciento de tus llamadas / durante tres meses <Anu-Pu-211204-12:20>

'A: What about you – where are (*you*) spending this Christmas? – B: At Intesa. [. . .] (*You*) get a multimedia cell phone for free. – A: Where did (*you*) say? – C: At the Intesa Corporation. – B: Oh, and they'll also give (*you*) a 15% discount on your calls during three months.'

In other formats like music programs, the singular second person helps broadcasters construct an individual addressee with whom a closer relationship is suggested. In (15), the expressed subject pronoun in *si tú quieres* 'if you want to' highlights the involvement of the virtual conversational partner. (16) presents a very similar use by a different broadcaster. Both excerpts suggest that the choices used for the construction of a nonspecific addressee are often hardly different from those employed with specific ones, including metadiscursive comments that build on previous contributions (*como te decía* 'as I was telling you') or invitations (*siempre que tú lo quieras* 'as long as you want it that way'). Questions and requests with second-person indexical forms are among the most usual resources for the suggestion of interactivity.

(15) nos volvemos a encontrar / tan solo si *tú quieres* / ¿mañana sobre la una? / ¿*te* va bien:? ¿es buena hora? / pues hasta entonces <Mus-Ci-230903-18:00>
'We'll meet again – only if *you* want to – tomorrow around one? Does it suit (*you*)? Is it a good time? Well, see you then.'

(16) *mira* como *te* decía / treinta y seis <sic>años</sic> / para que se nos: marche: un año más / y yo también espero pasar mi Navidaz junto a ti / siempre que:: / *tú* lo *quiera:s* <Mus-Di-251104-10:50>
'*Look*, as I was telling (*you*), in thirty-six years [*sic*] another year will be gone. And I hope I can spend my Christmas with you, as long as *you* want it that way.'

Nevertheless, nonspecific *tú* is not equally frequent in all radio genres; neither is its displaced second-person counterpart *usted*. While in contexts such as the ones discussed the individuation of the audience is perceived as a profitable strategy, talk magazines and news reports seem to incorporate the convention that plural forms – *vosotros* and, especially, *ustedes* – are more adequate (see the following chapters).

It must also be emphasized that there are no formal or functional differences between specific and nonspecific *tú*, and that the usual grammatical choices and pragmatic meanings are very similar in either case – even if the lack of real interaction and feedback necessarily results in such strategies being imitative when the audience is unknown. This also seems coherent with the fact that nonspecific forms are to be conventionally interpreted by each individual member of the audience as specifically addressed to him/her. The distinction between both categories can thus be made only on the basis of knowledge about the interactional circumstances under which choices are made; different discursive genres can favor different referential interpretations.

Consequently, other features of the communicative situation – e.g. the time slot where a program is broadcast, the topic and purpose of discourse, as well as the very linguistic and semiotic choices made, starting from *tú* vs. *usted* as forms of address (see discussion in Chapter 8) – can help delineate the types of addressees that are primarily targeted. Actually, nonspecific *usted* can be a much more expectable choice depending on the textual genre and the types of relationships speakers intend to develop.

In spite of the nonspecific character of the reference in the cases reviewed across this subsection, it should be obvious that a participant is constructed through interactional strategies that clearly resemble those employed with specific addressees. However, the following category is a referentially more diffuse one and tends to appear in different contexts.

6.2.3 Speaker-inclusive/objectivizing

This is a particularly interesting use of the singular second person that is also found in English, French and many other languages (see e.g. Coveney 2003; Gast et al. 2015). In this case, speakers intend to refer not just to some actual or expected interlocutor, but to anyone with certain characteristics or who might find him/herself in a certain situation, including – and often especially – themselves. This use of the second person is often termed *impersonal* (Hidalgo Navarro 1996–1997; Guirado 2011; Posio 2016, among many others); however, the label is probably not the most adequate one for a resource based precisely on the exploitation of a grammatical *person* and its meaning. Other traditional characterizations such as *generic* or *nonspecific* can also be misleading, the latter being more appropriate for second-person forms addressed to unknown and potentially wide audiences, as it is used here. Other authors have approached the phenomenon as a *defocusing* strategy (Haverkate 1984, 131; Bidot Martínez 2008), considering that it helps move the deictic center away from the direct participants. In line with the referential shifts described for other first and second persons, it can be labelled *speaker-inclusive* (cf. Fernández/Táboas 1999, 1732) or *objectivizing* (Serrano/Aijón Oliva 2012; 2014), the latter term being aimed at capturing its fundamental stylistic effect, as will be discussed below. Examples (17) and (18) are proposed as preliminary illustrations.

(17) Cuando *ves* el problema de una familia con un niño oncológico, *piensas* que los tuyos son unos problemas ridículos. <Ent-Ga-190604-20>
'When (*you*) watch the problems of a family with a cancer-ill child, (*you*) come to think that your own problems are ridiculous.'

(18) yo siempre he dicho ¿no? que si: no *disfrutas* jugando mejor no *juegues* / porque::- / porque no *te* van a salir las cosas ni aunque *quieras* <Dep-Co-221104-14:50>
'I've always said it, right? That if (*you*) don't enjoy playing, (*you*) better not play. Because things won't work out (*on you*), no matter how much (*you*) want them to.'

In both of them, speakers expose personal stances or experiences from a second-person viewpoint. The speaker-inclusive referential interpretation is facilitated by the co-occurrence of grammatical choices such as imperfective verbal tenses – most notably the present simple, promoting a universal or gnomic reading of the content – as well as temporal, conditional or causal particles like *cuando* 'when' in (17) or *si* 'if' and *porque* 'because' in (18). Features like these are characterized by Hernanz Carbó (1990, 175) as *genericity inductors* (see also Fernández/Táboas 1999, 1734–1737; RAE 2009, §16.2u). They offer a good instantiation of the notion that meanings are usually not constructed through a linguistic choice alone, but through the co-occurrence of different linguistic and semiotic ones. Given that there are no formal differences among the referential categories of the singular second person, it is the context as a whole that will make the participants select some referential interpretation as more relevant than other possible ones.

In previous studies adopting a discursive-cognitive approach (Serrano/Aijón Oliva 2012; 2014; Serrano 2013b; Aijón Oliva/Serrano 2014), such uses of the second person were labelled *objectivizing*, given their relationship with the reduction of stylistic subjectivity (see especially Section 9.1 below). They need to be understood as a strategy to displace the viewpoint of discourse from the speaker towards the addressee. The participants avoid the subjectivity associated with the singular first person, presenting the content as something that may actually concern their interlocutor (Siewierska 2004, 212; Huang 2011, 401). However, they will usually add some contextual cues, i.e. the genericity inductors already cited, in order to make it clear that it does not concern him/her alone. The phenomenon is connected with others such as the choice of the plural first person, most evidently in its audience-inclusive uses (§5.2.3), but of course cannot be considered equivalent to it from an isomorphic perspective. Given that the stylistic notions of subjectivity, intersubjectivity and objectivity need more detailed discussion – to be developed in the final chapters of this book – for now we will usually employ the more descriptive *speaker-inclusive* label for the referential uses at hand.

It is worth stressing that such uses are not only frequent when exposing ideas that could be easily accepted as common knowledge – for example, when talking about such a universal topic as weather (19) – but also when recounting clearly personal experiences. In (20), an urban artist is asked about the possibilities of achieving financial stability with his job. The use of the second person in his answer implies that his experience can serve as an example to others.[2]

(19) es cierto que el mundo cambia / pero la climatología últimamente: también / e: // tan pronto *tieneh* que salir en manga corta y *te achicharras* / como *tienes* que sali:r / con un abriguito por si acaso / y paraguah porque va a llover <Dep-SE-210504-15:35>
'It's true that the world changes, but so does the weather nowadays. Either (*you*) have to go out in short sleeves and still (*you*) get scorched, or (*you*) need to take an overcoat just in case, together with an umbrella, because it's going to rain.'

(20) –¿Cómo consigue uno ganarse la vida con esto?
–Hay que trabajar el nombre, tiene que sonar bien para diferenciarse, no vale un nombre cualquiera. Luego, la gente *te* conoce en cuanto *empiezas a introducirte* en el ambiente y *te* van llamando a raíz de otros trabajos que han visto tuyos. <Ent-Ga-020604-16>
'A: How can one make a living out of this? – B: It is necessary to craft your name, it needs to sound good in order to stand out; not any name will work. Then people get acquainted (*with you*) as (*you*) start entering the scene, and they begin to call (*you*) thanks to other works of yours they've seen.'

In the second example it is interesting to observe the co-occurrence of several grammatical constructions that promote so-called *impersonal*, i.e. objective readings: together with the repeated use of the second person, there are instances of the nonspecific third-person pronoun *uno* 'one', usually interpreted as referring to the speaker or the addressee (García 2009, 146; Guirado 2011), as well as of the

2 Wales (1996, 79) transcribes some examples where English *you* has a similarly subjective or egocentric orientation.

deontic construction *hay que* 'it is necessary to' + infinitive. Beyond their particular meanings, they all help suggest that personal experience is being transferred to a wider human reference in order to endow it with general validity.

For the same reason, and in line with speaker-blurring uses of the plural first person (§5.2.1), speaker-inclusive *tú* might be intuitively described as a "modesty" strategy when it seems aimed at avoiding what could be perceived as self-flattery. In fact, Posio (2016, 6) finds that speaker-inclusive second-persons are a characteristic choice of interviewees as against participants in spontaneous conversations. In our view, this is partly because interviewees in the media are often reminded or forced to acknowledge their own personal achievements, which can be perceived as harmful to their image. (21) is a short excerpt from an interview where the choice is recurrent, as are explicit recognitions by the speaker that the credit is also due to others.

(21) –¿Y vale la pena tanto esfuerzo?
–Por supuesto. Y no sólo a nivel personal. También a nivel profesional *recibes* una gran recompensa. <...>
–Después de casi dos décadas de docencia en Salamanca, ¿diría que ha creado escuela?
–Cuando *llevas* una actividad docente muy centrada inevitablemente *haces* escuela. Pero el mérito no es sólo mío; hay que atribuírselo a un equipo docente muy conjuntado y comprometido con su trabajo. <Ent-Ga-201204-13>
'A: Is the effort worth it? – B: Definitely. And not just at a personal level. In professional terms (*you*)'re also highly rewarded. [...] – A: After nearly two decades of instructing in Salamanca, could you+ say you+'ve created a style? – B: When (*you*) pursue a constant academic activity, (*you*) cannot but create a style. But it's not just me who deserves the credit; it must be attributed to a strongly coordinated and committed work team.'

The stretch also shows how the interviewer indexes the addressee through *usted* third-person morphemes, while the interviewee resorts to *tú* with a speaker-inclusive reference. Actually, a participant can simultaneously use *usted* to address his/her specific interlocutor and *tú* with a speaker-inclusive value (Fernández Ramírez 1986, 48). This is a clear indicator of the degree to which the latter choice is conventionalized – it can hardly be taken by participants being addressed with *usted* as a violation of socio-interactional norms.

Conversely, when the content is perceived as negative or potentially controversial, the choice will help avoid its explicit association with the person speaking, as in (22), where a local politician performs a transition from the audience-exclusive plural *hemos metido la pata* '(we)'ve made some blunders' to speaker-inclusive *dependes de otros* '(you) depend on others' and other second-person indexations.

(22) hemos tenido estas dificultades / en algunas / por- / por impericia nuestra / por- porque hemos metido la pata y en otras porque *dependes* de otros / y cuando *dependes* de otros como antes esplicaba en política / es lo peor que *te* puede pasar <Var-Co-230503-13:10>
'We've experienced these difficulties, in some cases because of our own lack of skill, because we've made some blunders, and sometimes because (*you*) depend on others, and when (*you*) need to depend on others, as I explained before, it's the worst that can happen (*to you*) in politics.'

However, the association of some personal content with a wider reference including the addressee is a pragmatic strategy that may always be contested. As happens with inclusive *nosotros* (see Chapter 5, examples 32 and 33), speaker-inclusive *tú* can be a resource for manipulation when it is aimed at presenting personal views as commonly accepted facts. In (23), a citizen calling to a radio program complains that the rest of stations do not allow free expression. It is not difficult to perceive the potential of the co-occurrence of several choices – objectivizing *tú*, present tense, temporal particles – to instill the notion in the audience that cutting off callers with dissenting views is common practice in those radio stations, even though the speaker is probably just drawing on personal experience. While she does not explicitly involve her interlocutor in the content – as would be the case with a perfective tense promoting a specific reading, e.g. *cuando empezaste a decir algo* 'as soon as (you) started saying something' – she takes it for granted that such content might be predicated of others and not just of herself.

(23) desde luego es en la Única cadena / que se: puede hablar / porque en las otras / (en) cuanto *empiezas* a decir algo de esto / *te* cortan <Var-Co-230503-13:50>
'Truly, this is the only station where one can speak freely. In all others, as soon as (*you*) start saying something of this sort, they cut (*you*) off.'

In sum, the use of the singular second person with a speaker-inclusive reference is a recurrent strategy whereby participants desubjectivize some personal stance or experience, implying that it might also be attributed to the addressee. It appears to be a highly conventionalized and recognizable use, usually appearing in different contexts from those of the referential variants previously discussed. Also, as will be observed in Section 6.3, it notably diverges from them as regards patterns of quantitative variation.

6.2.4 Pragmaticalized

Finally, a number of verbal forms with second-person subject or object indexation have become fixed as discourse markers or conversational fillers. As also noted with regard to pragmaticalized plural first persons, no reference as such is identifiable in these cases; however, they are still second-person inflected verbs and necessarily retain the capacity to construct *the addressee* as a discursive-cognitive notion. Their occurrence is an indication that the speaker takes the other into account for the construction of discourse; they can thus be described as *alterity markers* (Martín/Portolés 1999, 4171). While they are common in spontaneous conversation, across the corpus we have only collected 68 tokens that can safely be included in the category of pragmaticalized uses, most of them expectably appearing in radio discourse.

Among the most recurrent units are the originally imperative forms *oye* 'hear, listen' and *mira* 'look'. They have been classified as pragmaticalized whenever it is clear from the context that the person speaking is not really commanding or asking someone else to look or listen to anything. The process of fixation of these forms has been parallel to one of semantic bleaching from their literal sensorial meaning towards epistemic and textual uses (De Cock 2014, 67–72). In turn, the focus on the addressee, or perhaps more accurately on communication itself, is a crucial motivation for their use. *Oye* helps attract the addressee's attention and is often used as a turn-taking device; in (24) it appears as much of an interjection used to convey interest for the preceding contribution and start building on it. The pragmatic function of *mira* in (25) is a similar one; however, in this case it is the conversational marker *pues* that is used to regain the turn even before A has finished speaking.

(24) <A> hasta el vivi:r es malo <entre risas>para la saluz / porque: c- <...> a medida que vas viviendo</entre risas> / pue:s: / vas teniendo más: probabilidades de que te quede menos
<B> *oye* no no es mala frase esa ¿e:h? / vivir es / MAlo para la saluz / vaya / vaya vaya frase / di- digna casi casi de Woody Allen <Var-SE-230903-13:20>
'A: Even living is bad for your health [*laughs*], for as you grow older it is more likely for you to have less time ahead. – B: *Hey* (lit. Listen), that's not a bad line at all. Living is bad for your health. Yo, what a line – it could almost have been uttered by W. A.'

(25) <A> pues a lo mejor habría que hacer / (una campaña con pegatinas de) pies / o mano:s / y en cada uno de ellos / poner una partida presupue-s<entre risas>ta[ria / y a lo mejor-</entre risas>]
<B> [pues *mira* no estaría] mal / porque no saldría muy caro esto: al: Consistorio ¿no? <Var-On-281204-13:15>
'A: Well, it might be a good idea to launch [an awareness campaign] using foot and hand [stickers], each of them containing a budget item, and maybe this way – [*laughs*] – B: Well, *hey* (lit. look), that would be no bad thing, and it wouldn't be so expensive for the Town Council, right?'

One of the clearest indicators of pragmaticalization is the occurrence of these forms in contexts where the addressee or audience is being regularly indexed through a different grammatical person, i.e. plural *vosotros* or the displaced second persons. This was actually the case in both (24) and (25) above, even if the transcribed stretches do not contain any examples of audience indexation. In (26) we can observe that while the specific addressee is constructed through *usted* and correlative third-person morphemes, the speaker does not utter *oiga* '(you+) listen' but *oye*. The form is not to be taken as a literal command on the addressee, but as a discourse marker, in this case used to draw a conclusion from the preceding statements.

(26) pues si a *usté le* ha tocado más de cinco mil euros / que *sepa* que la Agencia Tributaria *le* va a investigar • *le* va a investigar / no solamente el premio *le* va a investigar todas / sus finanzas todo lo que *tenga* / l:o cua:l / pue:s *oye* a lo mejor hay que pensárselo si a uno le interesa que le toque o no <Var-On-080104-13:15>
'So if (*you+*) have won more than 5,000 euros, (*you+*) need to be aware that the Tax Agency is going to investigate (*you+*). Not only will they investigate the prize, but also all of your finances, everything (*you+*) have. So, *hey* (lit. listen), perhaps one might want to consider whether it is desirable to win the lottery.'

Another originally imperative form, *anda* 'walk, go' is used in contexts where the speaker urges the addressee to do something. It usually co-appears with other imperative forms with a more literal deontic interpretation and functions as a phatic reinforcing marker, roughly meaning 'come on!' (27). In turn, its co-occurrence with different second persons is less acceptable than in the cases of *oye* and *mira*, which suggests a lower degree of fixation. There is a different, more clearly pragmaticalized use of *¡anda!* as an interjection conveying surprise or disappointment (cf. Tanghe 2013 on interjections derived from motion verbs), of which there are no examples in the corpus.

(27) <A> mis padres se han comprado un coche que corre como un avión / <B> pues los mí:os / se han comprado un chalet / en Urbanización Fontana / ¡*anda*! / ¡mejora eso! <Anu-Co-280803-22:45>
'A: My parents have bought a car as fast as a plane. – B: Well, mine have bought a house at U. F. *Come on* (lit. Walk)! Beat that!'

Finally, other apparent imperatives show oscillation between the omission and expression of the second-person subject, in parallel with the extent to which involvement of the addressee is sought. This is the case of *fíjate* (*tú*) 'mind you', lit. 'observe, note' and *vete* (*tú*) *a saber* 'who knows', lit. 'go and learn'. In example (28) there are several choices contributing to the suggestion of interactivity in a monologic context, including yet another token of *oye* as well as the question tag *¿no?* 'right?' In (29), *vete tú a saber* is immediately followed by another pragmaticalized second-person construction, namely *quieras que no* 'like it or not; anyway'. All this suggests that pragmaticalized uses are indeed frequent in conversation, even if the usually scarce interactivity of radio discourse results in low occurrence rates.

(28) Juanes que yo no sé qué problemas tiene con el móvil o que no le quieren coger el teléfono / pero el caso es que cada vez que llama como que nunca encuentra a nadie *oye* pobrecillo ¿no? / *fíjate* / le vamos a tener que dar nuestro teléfono: <Mus-Di-200503-12:25>
'As for J., I don't know if there is some problem with his cell phone or it's just that people don't want to answer, but the fact is that whenever he calls he can't find anyone, *hey* (lit. listen), poor him, right? *Mind you* (lit. Observe), we'll have to give him our number.'

(29) ya: / pensando un poco en el mes de septiembre o para aquellas e: / personas / e que están trabajando / que han: tenido sus vacaciones / o que no las tienen hasta los meses de sepTIEMbre o: / *vete tú a saber* / pues *quieras que no* / pensar en el fin de semana y tener dos días por delante siempre <. . .> se lleva un poquito mejor <Mus-40-220803-13:10>
'We're already thinking of September. Or else, for those people who are working now, who are already back from vacation, or who won't be taking leave until September or even later – *who knows* (lit. go and learn), well, *anyway* (lit. like it or not), thinking of the weekend and those two free days ahead always [. . .] makes things a little more bearable.'

There are also object-encoding second-person pragmaticalized constructions. They generally appear to be less fixed than the preceding ones, and extradiscursive reference is often still discernible, in accordance with the fact that object agreement is altogether less generalized in Spanish – recall that all the plural first-person constructions we classified as pragmaticalized were subject-encoding ones (§5.2.4). First, *ya te digo*, lit. 'I'm already telling (you)', as is usual with psychological and communication verbs, has a more literal meaning when the nucleus heads an embedded clause resuming something previously said (30). In turn, in clearly pragmaticalized contexts it functions as a conversational marker with positional mobility. It conveys emphatic agreement with what someone else has uttered, implying that it is so true or appropriate that the speaker him/herself could have said it. (31) contains the only token in the corpus that seems amenable to the latter description; the broadcaster uses it to endorse the message of the song just aired.

(30) el número:: (de jugadores) bueno pues:- / pues a veces se me queda un poco corto pero:- / pero *ya te digo* que no:- no tengo preocupación: <Dep-On-080104-15:10>
'About the number [of players], well, sometimes it does fall kind of short, but *I'm already telling you* that I'm not really worried.'

(31) ¡*YA / te digo*:! / que si en la vida / todo puede cambiar: lo que hoy: / ves: e totalmente ne:gro / O: de un tono grisáceo: mañana puede estar: / rosado: / o azu:l: <Mus-Di-251104-10:35>
'*Indeed!* (lit. I'm already telling you!) Everything in life can change. What you see completely black or grayish today, may look pinkish or bluish tomorrow.'

Like many other pragmaticalized constructions, *ya te digo* is tightly associated with face-to-face conversation, where interlocutors continuously feed each other back with metadiscursive comments containing participant-indexical morphemes. There are other object-encoding constructions also involving the verb *decir* 'to say' and having similar pragmatic functions. *¿Qué te iba a decir?*, lit. 'What was I going to tell (you)?' is used to take the turn and/or as a transitional sequence towards an issue that is seen as scarcely connected with the previous one, as in (32). Another recurrent construction is *no te digo*, lit. 'I don't tell (you)'. When governing an embedded clause, it often appears as a variant of the rhetoric figure of preterition or paralipsis, i.e. the apparent refusal of the speaker to address some issue when he/she is in fact calling attention upon it. Its meaning is thus connected with that of plural first-person *no digamos*

(§5.2.4). In (33), the sports commentator suggests that if the foul had been made on a different player, the reaction of the latter would have been rather more aggressive, to the point that he prefers not to mention it – which he is of course doing. In other contexts, of which there are no instances in the corpus, *no te digo* is used as more of an emphatic interjection.

(32) <A> (o) sea un partido para: / r:oda:r / e: / a la: subdiecinueve [<risas> / ¿e:h?]
<B> [<risas> / no sé:]
<A> a: la subdiecinueve / *¿qué te iba a decir?* una cosa /
<B> no sé /
<A> bonito ayer lo de Francia: y: / B- Brasil ¿verdá:? <Dep-SE-210504-15:15>
'A: So this will be a game for the under-19 team to get some warmup, right? [*laughs*] – B: [*laughs*] I don't know. – A: The under-19 ones. *What was I going to tell you?* Err. . . – B: I don't know. – A: It was beautiful yesterday with France and Brazil, right?'

(33) y: Afek / porque es un pedazo de pan ¿eh? / pero:- / pero: le hacen eso a:- / a Aurelio o a Cañas / y *no te digo* la que se prepara <Dep-Pu-191204-18:35>
'And anyway, Afek has a heart of gold, right? But if they'd done the same to Aurelio or Cañas, *I won't tell you* what would have happened.'

Finally, there are also constructions with the verb *parecer* 'to seem' and a second-person (dative) object. Originally coming from attributive constructions like *parecer bien, mal*, etc. 'to seem good, bad', where the second-person referent would be the experiencer, in a more pragmaticalized use the predicate adverb or adjective is omitted and implicitly included in the verb, yielding a meaning of positive evaluation: *si te parece* Ø 'if it's OK with you', lit. 'if it seems (to you)'. In other words, *parecer* becomes equivalent to *parecer bien* 'to seem good' and similar to *gustar* or *agradar* 'to please'. The expression often appears as a conversational marker indicating deference to the other, but to which a reaction is not really expected. In (34), it appears amidst a conversation between two broadcasters. The construction can also be formulated as an inviting question: *¿te parece?* 'is it OK with you?', lit. 'does it seem to you?' (35).

(34) hablamos de deportes *si te parece* y es que: el equipo nacional: la selección española juega hoy a partir de las ocho: <Mus-40-220803-11:40>
'Let's talk about sports, *if you will* (lit. if it seems [*to you*]), since the Spanish national team is playing today from 8 p.m.'

(35) <A> algu:nas (películas) te han gustado: otras no ahora nos lo cuentas vamos primero con los estrenos *¿te parece*? /
<B> perfecto <Var-SE-300503-19:45>
'A: Some [movies] you liked, some you didn't. You'll tell us in a minute. Let's start with the latest releases, *if you will?* (lit. does it seem [*to you*]?) – B: Perfect.'

It is important to note that, whereas the corresponding first-person constructions with *parecer* usually have an epistemic modalizing value – (*a mí*) *me parece* was approached in Section 4.4 as an alternative to (*yo*) *creo* in argumentative discourse, the cognitive difference between them being related to the unequal degrees of salience associated with subject vs. object self-encoding – the use of *te parece* in contexts such as the ones reviewed is most often deontic, requesting the other's agreement or at least suggesting that his/her opinion on the issue is taken into account.

Despite their syntactic and discursive-pragmatic interest, pragmaticalized second-person constructions in the corpus – accounting for 49 subject-encoding tokens and 19 object-encoding ones – will not be considered across our quantitative analyses, given that most of them do not admit formal variation and their respective token numbers are generally rather low. We will in turn analyze the three remaining referential categories – specific, nonspecific and speaker-inclusive – in order to elucidate the relationships between their discursive-pragmatic values and their patterns of variation.

6.3 Variable expression and placement of pronouns

Table 6.1 presents the general data of pronoun expression vs. omission for the singular second person with either type of functional encoding. The rates of expression are notoriously low, particularly in object-encoding contexts, with just

Table 6.1: Expression vs. omission of singular second-person pronouns.

	Subject (*tú*)		Object (*a ti*)		Total	
	#	%	#	%	#	%
Expression	92	8.7	7	2.6	99	7.4
Omission	965	91.3	266	97.4	1,231	92.6
Total	1,057	79.5	273	20.5	1,330	100

2.6%. This score is in fact among the lowest ones obtained with any grammatical person. Several hypotheses can be put forward to explain this, which will need to be discussed through the examination of contextual usage. We will observe that, just like in the case of plural first persons (see Section 5.3), the strong tendency to omission of singular second-person pronouns has much to do with referential fuzziness in many contexts.

If the data are broken into the three referential categories considered, the results are as shown in Table 6.2. There is an evident decrease in pronoun formulation as the reference constructed in discourse moves from a specific addressee towards nonspecific audiences – these being the most frequent ones across the corpus – and ultimately to speaker-inclusive uses, with just 7 tokens (2.8%) of pronoun expression, all of them subject-encoding ones. However, even with specific referents the percentage of expression (12.7%) is roughly half that of the singular first person (24.2%), i.e. there is a clear divergence between them as regards the quantitative patterning of pronoun expression vs. omission.

Table 6.2: Expression vs. omission of singular second-person pronouns and referential category.

	Expression		Omission		Total	
	#	%	#	%	#	%
Specific	61	12.7	420	87.3	481	36.2
Nonspecific	31	5.2	571	94.8	602	45.3
Speaker-inclusive	7	2.8	240	97.2	247	18.5
Total	99	7.4	1,231	92.6	1,330	100

On the one hand, the comparably strong preference of second-person pronouns for omission could be taken as an argument in support of the higher salience associated with the second person in Spanish. An apparent counterargument is the fact that the choice becomes more frequent the more general, thus less perceptible the reference is. It must be borne in mind that omission is not necessarily connected with high salience; it can also suggest cognitive unimportance, in the sense that speakers avoid focalization on its possible reference (see also §1.3.1, as well as Section 9.5 below). In turn, hypotheses based on functional compensation would emphasize the unambiguous grammatical specification of the verbal ending -s and the clitic *te*, which usually renders the formulation of *tú* and *a ti* unnecessary. This explanation is also far from satisfactory since, as we have already observed, many instances of pronoun expression can hardly be seen as motivated by referential disambiguation, most evidently with the singular first person – and, as for the plural first one, speakers will most often formulate a third-person NP rather than (*a*) *nosotros* if they really intend to demarcate the referent. As in other cases, detailed contextual examination seems necessary to unveil the pragmatic motivations of the patterns found.

First, it seems obvious that the participants in the corpus are seldom prompted to highlight the addressee's involvement in the content through pronoun formulation; much less so when the latter is not a specific individual. But this could hardly be due to the fact that the addressee is already indexed by inflectional morphemes. We can suspect the influence of socio-interactional norms and tendencies whereby it is considered preferable not to bring the other under the focus of attention, unless there is some pragmatic motivation to do so. This should concern not just specific but also nonspecific second persons, which in media discourse are to be conventionally interpreted by each listener or reader as specifically addressed to them. In (36) and (37) we can respectively observe the recurrent omission of pronouns with specific and nonspecific references. In both cases, the viewpoint of the addressee clearly dominates discourse progression, with no competition from other participants, which makes the former highly salient and is coherent with systematic subject encoding and pronoun omission.[3]

(36) con las mejores atletas del continente además / *hicistes* la carrera perfecta porque: / si *hubieras:* e:: *realizado* otra estrategia seguramente no *hubieras conseguido* esa medalla / sin embargo *hicistes* e: / digamos el guión / idóneo el guión: ideal / para / e: lograr: e / ese metal <Dep-On-141204-15:25>
'Competing with the best athletes in the continent, (*you*) ran the perfect race, since if (*you*) had adopted a different strategy, (*you*) probably wouldn't have won that medal. However, (*you*) followed, say, the perfect script, the ideal script in order to achieve that prize.'

(37) si todavía no *tienes* tu invitació:n / a qué *estás* esperando: / *pásate* por aquí por la calle Veracruz: / n:úmero do:s / o: directamente: / *te puedes*

3 The presence of more than one referent in the context is also a decisive factor in the encoding of third-person referents, as shown by Arnold/Griffin (2007). In narrative discourse, there is a preference for lexical NPs instead of pronouns when more than one character has appeared in the preceding context, irrespective of whether there is actual risk of ambiguity.

acercar: / por: La Española / o: / por El Puerto de Chu:s: <Mus-Di-251104-14:00>
'If (*you*) still don't have your invitation, what are (*you*) waiting for? (*You*) just come around here, that is 2 Veracruz Street, or else (*you*) can directly drop by La Española or El Puerto de Chus.'

With respect to speaker-inclusive or objectivizing contexts, where pronoun omission approaches categoricity in the corpus, it could be hypothesized that expression is perceived as somewhat contradictory when the intention is to generalize the content as applicable to anyone. In (38), the views of the speaker on a particular soccer team are generalized through second-person inflected and present-tensed verbs in a conditional construction. Singular second-person agreement would itself be among the linguistic features promoting a generic reading, while overt pronouns would disfavor it.

(38) es un equipo: que tiene: mucha calidá <...> y: bueno / con:- / con posibilidades de:- de:- como todos de que si: *enganchas* un par de partidos o tres pues *te metes* arriba ¿no? / entonces / esa es un poquito la:- la:- / la visión que tengo de ellos <Dep-Co-080104-14:55>
'It's a high-quality team [...] and well, with chances – just like all others – that, if (*you*) can connect two or three wins in a row, (*you*) can go up in the chart, right? So this is basically the view I have of them.'

However, previous studies show that the strong preference for omission with this referential category is not common to all varieties of Spanish. In Serrano/Aijón Oliva (2012), significant divergences were found between the corpus under analysis and one of Canary Islands conversational speech. The latter actually yielded higher percentages of pronoun expression with speaker-inclusive uses than with the rest – no distinction between specific and nonspecific references was drawn. A similar divergence between Peninsular and non-Peninsular varieties had previously been detected by Cameron (1993), studying corpora from Madrid and Puerto Rico. The author explored the possibility that the results be due to the supposed referential ambiguity caused by the loss of word-final -*s* in Caribbean dialects, i.e. to functional compensation, with inconclusive results. On the other hand, Serrano/Aijón Oliva noted that the texts in the Canarian corpus, besides having a stronger interactional orientation – they were all face-to-face spontaneous conversations – often suggested the development of more subjective styles through first- and second-person pronoun formulation. This would also be the case with example (39), where speaker-inclusive *tú* is formulated twice as the speaker tries to involve the addressee in her line of reasoning. The pragmatic meanings of grammatical choices should be thought to remain the same across geographical zones, social groups and communicative domains and situations. However, each of these will tend to exploit some choices and their meanings over others, in connection with particular cultural values and socio-interactional norms (see Section 1.2 on the controversy about meaningful variation across linguistic varieties).

(39) hay veces: que a lo mejor la báscula marca igual / pero: *tú has perdido* volumen <. . .> si un día / que *tú te pases* / ¡no pasa na:da! / un día / realmente los días de- / de comi:da / son: / dos / tres <Var-On-080104-12:45>
'There are times when the scale keeps returning the same figure, but *you* have lost some volume. [. . .] I mean, if *you* overeat one day – it's OK! One day. There are actually just two or three real overeating days.'

The meaning generated by pronoun formulation in this speaker-inclusive example actually reflects the prototypical association between this choice and specific references. While the 481 specific tokens represent just 36.2% of the total second-person indexations, they account for 61.6% of the overt pronouns. In other words, *tú* and *a ti* are usually linked to the existence of a specific participant that is known to the speaker. These are the situations where the meanings of expression can be made the most of, for example when contrasting the referent with other ones in the context, as in (40). It is interesting to note that here such contrast is only established between the subject pronouns and not between their respective objects. It would have been possible to formulate the object pronouns as well (i.e. *yo te doy* a ti *una moneda, pero tú me das* a mí *un beso*) but the result would prove somewhat redundant, given that the referents – the speaker and the addressee – are already in clear contrast.

(40) "Me acerqué: ¡Eh! ¿Me das una moneda?. . . Ella caminaba deprisa, pero se paró y me miró: Bueno, *yo te voy* a dar una moneda, pero *tú me das* un beso" <Art-Ga-171104-3b>
'I approached her: "Hey! Will you give me a coin?" She was walking quickly, but she stopped to look at me: "OK, *I*'ll give (*you*) a coin, but *you* must give (*me*) a kiss." '

In the case of the singular second person, expression has an obvious potential for the management of identities and interpersonal relationships, based on its association with participant involvement. It can contribute to the development of either a positive or a negative image of the addressee, in connection with how the content is evaluated by the speaker. In the excerpts from a radio interview in (41), the interviewer first highlights the winning streak his interlocutor is going through, then points out the fact that earlier times were not as easy. In both contexts, there is initial expression of the preverbal subject pronoun. Probably due to the features of media communication, it is rare to find overt second-person pronouns in clearly pejorative contexts; when this happens, there is often an evident tongue-in-cheek intention, as in B's utterance in (42): *tú de eso no tienes ni idea* 'you have no clue about that'. It is A that flatters his interlocutor through the repeated formulation of *usted* (see further Section 8.3).

(41) *tú* ahora no *pareces* tener techo / *sigues* crecien:do y crecien:do y siendo: / m cada día / e: m:: pues mejo:r <. . .> las vueltas que da la vida / m: / e:n cualquier persona y:- y en un futbolista pues también ¿no? / que *tú llegaste* / aquí a la Unión Deportiva Salamanca *volviste* al fútbol nacional: *volviste* al equipo unionista / m: poco más que por:- e: / por la comida como suele decirse <Dep-Co-080104-14:45>
'*You* seem to have no limits right now; (*you*) keep on growing and growing and improving day after day. [. . .] It's funny to see the twists that life takes for anyone, and also for a soccer player, right? Because *you* came here to the U. D. S. team, (*you*) came back to national soccer, back to the Unión team, with few prospects other than putting food on the table, as they say.'

(42) <A> yo puedo decirle a alguien que / m: voy a: intentar meter la bola en el hoyo diecisiete // claro / *usté:* / m: [*tiene* la- / tiene la- /]
<B> [¡pero si *tú* de eso no *tienes* ni idea:!] / [/ claro de eso no *tienes* ni idea]
<A> [pueh por eso / *usté tiene*] la ventaja / de: decir lo mismo / pero con la garantía de que *usté* las *mete*: de un: solo golpe <Var-Co-230503-12:55>
'A: I can tell anyone that I'm going to try and hit the ball into hole 17. Now, *you+* have. . . – B: Hey, but *you* have no clue about that! Sure, (*you*) have no clue about that. – A: That's it. So *you+* have the advantage that (*you+*) can say the same, but with the guarantee that *you+* can get it in with just a stroke.'

Many other cases of pronoun expression appear as discourse-organizing – but not totally fixed – markers that build on previous contributions of the addressee, thus carry out viewpoint alignment in a different way as is done through plural first-person indexations. For the same reason, they can be quite indicative of interpersonal relationship management in conversation. Dialogic radio sequences contain abundant variants of resuming constructions such as *como tú has dicho* 'as you just said' (43) or *como tú dices* 'as you say' (44).

(43) vaya la gran victoria que consiguieron aye:r / las chicas en:: La Fuente de San Luis en::- / en Valencia / porque el Perfumerías como *tú has dicho* se impuso al Ros Casares <Dep-Co-221104-14:50>
'Yo, what a great victory our girls achieved yesterday at La Fuente de San Luis, in Valencia. Because the Perfumerías team, as *you* just said, defeated Ros Casares.'

(44) hacer un buen programa infantil / como cualquier otro poquit- / o:- / pro:- / buen programa / cuesta / dinero / Y: / e: calentar un poquito las neuronas / ¿e:h? / para hacer unos programas / como *tú dices* antes ha:bía unos programas preciosos <Var-Pu-211204-12:30>
'Making a good TV program for children – just as any sort of good program – takes some money and a little bit of brain racking, right? This in order to make such programs. As *you* say, in the past there used to be gorgeous programs.'

Finally, pronoun expression with nonspecific references generates analogous pragmatic meanings as with specific ones, basically associated with emphasis on personal involvement, e.g. when urging the audience to make a decision (example 45; see further discussion of subject encoding in the following section). Again, overt pronouns also appear in situations of informative focalization such as those of contrast between referents, generally the speaker or his/her relevant group vs. the addressee. In (46), *tú*, having been omitted in the initial clauses, needs to be formulated when opposed to audience-exclusive *nosotros*.

(45) *puedes* aprender peluquería por correspondencia / por Formación Profesional / en Boss Hair / *te* enseñamos peluquería y estética / con: garantía:s / con es:periencia / en grupos reducido:s / y personalizado:s <...> *TÚ* decides: <Anu-Ci-030903-13:15>
'(*You*) can learn hairdressing through correspondence or through occupational training. At B. H. we'll teach (*you*) hairdressing and aesthetics with guarantees, with expertise, in small and customized groups. [...] *You* decide.'

(46) si lo que *buscas* es una tienda donde encontrar / u:na variedad de láminas de todos los estilos / con un amplio taller / que *te* ofrezca un servicio

inmediato de enmarcación: / *busca:s:* / Po:r Amor al Arte: / *tú* / *pones* la idea / *nosotro:s* / el marco <Anu-On-141204-13:40>
'If (*you*)'re looking for a shop containing a wide variety of posters of all styles, with a large workshop offering (*you*) immediate framing service, (*you*)'re looking for P. A. A. *You* supply the idea, *we* supply the frame.'

Table 6.3, restricted to the 99 tokens of expressed singular second-person pronouns, shows their distribution regarding preverbal vs. postverbal placement. The token numbers in the different tiles, particularly those corresponding to object encoding, are rather small; even so, it may be worth noting that 3 out of 7 object pronouns are postposed to the verb. Given that preverbal subjects with either a specific or nonspecific reference are strongly dominant (77 tokens), it does not seem necessary to further analyze the quantitative patterning of placement according to referential categories. Interestingly, the general 81.8% of preposition falls 9.3 points below the frequency of this variant with singular first-person pronouns (91.1%) while it exceeds that of plural first-person ones (72.5%) by exactly the same figure.

Table 6.3: Preverbal vs. postverbal placement of singular second-person pronouns.

	Subject (*tú*)		Object (*a ti*)		Total	
	#	%	#	%	#	%
Preverbal	77	83.7	4	57.1	81	81.8
Postverbal	15	16.3	3	42.9	18	18.1
Total	92	92.9	7	7.1	99	100

Preverbal placement helps highlight the relationship between the referent and the content of the utterance. As already shown through some of the preceding examples, it can help develop either a positive or a negative image of a specific addressee. It also appears in discourse-organizing constructions that build on previous contributions of an interlocutor. As regards referentially nonspecific contexts, the choice appears occasionally in radio commercials, where it emphasizes the agency of the customer, constructed as a subject-agent with the power to choose or do something (see also 45 above). This is further suggested by its frequent co-occurrence with volitional verbs such as *querer* 'to want', *elegir* 'to choose', *decidir* 'to decide', etc. In (47), the emphatic pronunciation of the pronoun is indicative of the fact that this variant combines some features associated with salience – the referent has an agentive or in any case autonomous role – and others associated with informativeness – the referent is placed under the focus of attention.

(47) ve:n a Idea: / ¡n:o *te arrepentirás:*! / en agosto / *TÚ* ganas: <Anu-SE-110803-17:10>
'Come to Idea – (*you*) won't regret it! In August, *you* win.'

In turn, the observation of the 18 tokens of postposition supports the general characterization of this variant as associated with higher informativeness and lower autonomy. As pointed out, 3 out of 7 object pronouns are postverbal. However, even with subjects it is possible to perceive the enhancement of informativeness when the pronoun appears as the last constituent. In the preceding example, the alternative *ganas tú* would have promoted a contrastive reading that does not seem so coherent with the context – the intention is to highlight the autonomy of the addressee, not to differentiate the latter from other referents. In (48), taken from an opinion piece with religious content and strong literary elaboration, the writer uses a cleft construction – a focalizing grammatical device in itself – in order to specify the identity of the addressee. Much the same happens in the attributive clause at the end of the excerpt. It must be noted that in both cases, and unlike what happens in the English translation, *tú* forces second-person subject agreement in the verb – which shows the salience of the addressee even when the syntactic configuration is aimed at enhancing its informativeness.

(48) *Fuiste Tú*, Señor, quien *escribiste* recto con renglones torcidos. Había querido *echarte* para ser dueño y no *permitiste* tanta osadía. <. . .> nace un amor sincero, limpio y sano que serena los ánimos, me hace libre y vuelvo a enamorarme de un valor que no corrompe el tiempo. Ese valor *eres Tú*, mi Dios <Art-Ga-310104-4>
'It was *You*, Lord, (*you*) who wrote straight with crooked lines. I intended to oust (*you*) and become the master, but (*you*) didn't suffer such insolence. [. . .] A true, clean and healthy love is born that soothes spirits, makes me free, and once again I fall in love with a wealth that is not corrupted by time. That wealth is *You*, my God.'

In other contexts, postverbal subject pronouns can even approach the patienthood prototypically associated with accusative objects, as in (49), where a journalist comments on a soccer player's being the usual target of his coach's scolding. This is of course compatible with the usual focalization and contrastiveness entailed by this position – in this case, the player is singled out from the rest of his team. However, lack of autonomy will be more evident in object-encoding contexts such as (50), where the broadcaster, while yielding the turn to her nonspecific addressee, implicitly recognizes that she is the one who will allow others to come on air and participate.

(49) ¿no:- / no *piensas* que está como:- / tiene demasiada fijación en ti:? // pare (ce) que *te* las *llevas* todas *tú* <Dep-On-080104-15:20>
'Don't (*you*) think he's got, like, a fixation with you? It seems that it's always *you* [postv.] that gets bashed.'

(50) ¡ay! / ¡si es que yo no puedo jugar! / vale // doce minutos: sobrepasamos de la una del mediodía / y: por qué yo no puedo jugar / porque: / evidentemente: *te* voy a dejar *a ti* <Mus-Di-251104-13:10>
'Oh, but it turns out I can't compete! OK. It's now 12 minutes past 1 p.m. And why can't I compete? Obviously, because I'm going to let *you* do so.'

In another example of object pronoun postposition such as (51), a sarcastic pejorative intention can be interpreted in B's degrading his addressee to the clause-final position, focusing on him in order to highlight the unlikelihood of his being invited to a major social event. This configuration also contrasts with that of the previous turn, where A had encoded himself as a topicalized object, extracted from an embedded clause up to the beginning of the utterance.

(51) <A> *a mí* es una auténtica pena que no *me* hayan invitao (a la boda real) / <B> <risas> <entre risas>s:í / *te* van a invitar *a ti*</entre risas> <Dep-SE-210504-15:55>
'A: *Me*, it's a real shame they didn't invite [to the royal wedding]. – B: [*Laughs*.] Oh yes, they might as well have invited *you*.'

There are very few examples in the corpus of clause-intermediate postposition of *tú* or (*a*) *ti*. As exposed in Section 4.3 regarding the singular first person, this particular variant results in some defocusing of the referent as against clause-final placement, while the content is presented as a mutually accepted fact. In (52), the speaker opts for this configuration when referring to a previous contribution of the addressee. Neither semantic agency nor discursive informativeness are prominent meanings in the context. Even so, the differences with the preverbal-subject alternative (*tú has sacado* 'you brought up') seem to be quite subtle.

(52) el bien público sin duda: mayor / puede ser en muchos casos / el de aprender / hoy en día en un mundo / absolutamente globalizado y absolutamente interconectado / puede ser el de aprende:r a lo mejor mejor: / *has sacado tú* el ejemplo de las lenguas / puede ser aprender inglé:s <Var-Pu-211204-12:55>
'What can be most beneficial for the population is often to learn – in an absolutely globalized and absolutely interconnected world as today's – it can be to learn, maybe – *you* [postv.] just brought up the issue of languages – it can be to learn English.'

In sum, second-person pronoun formulation is altogether rare in the corpus. However, neither hypotheses assuming the higher salience of this person against the first one, nor those based on the unambiguity of second-person morphemes, can fully account for the results. These rather seem to be connected with the high frequency of nonspecific referents in media discourse; but even with specific ones – which account for most tokens of pronoun expression – it is obvious that focusing on the addressee is most often avoided, probably following general socio-interactional norms. Expression happens when there is an intention to highlight the addressee's involvement in the content, either as responsible for it or, more rarely, as the recipient of externally-initiated actions. The pragmatic values of this choice are further modulated through variable placement in the clause, with preposition usually enhancing the autonomy of subject-encoded addressees. On the other hand, postverbal placement can suggest patienthood and lack of autonomy, but such features are rarely attributed to addressees across the corpus – the situation is partly different with those constructed through displaced *usted* (see Section 8.3). What clause-final placement does systematically reveal is high informativeness, as observed in (48) above, where the intention of the writer is a clearly flattering one, as well as (49) and (50), with different motivations.

6.4 Functional encoding

Many of the considerations exposed in the preceding section concern the functional encoding of addressees in some way. Table 6.4 shows the percentages of subject vs. object encoding across the corpus, classified according to the formal variants discussed above. As in the preceding chapters, subject encoding is strongly dominant. While in this case the general percentage of the choice falls slightly below 80%, the result is not quite apart from those of the singular and plural first persons (respectively 80.2% and 81.8%).

Table 6.4: Functional encoding of singular second persons.

	Omitted		Expressed preverbal		Expressed postverbal		Total	
	#	%	#	%	#	%	#	%
Subject (*tú*)	965	91.3	77	7.3	15	1.4	1,057	79.5
Object (*a ti*)	266	97.4	4	1.5	3	1.1	273	20.5
Total	1,231	92.6	81	6.1	18	1.3	1,330	100

Also, Table 6.5 shows the token numbers and percentages for each referential category. Specific references are expectably the ones with the strongest preference for subject encoding (80.5%); there is a slight but progressive decrease in this choice as the referential scope widens. Thus speaker-inclusive uses, being the ones with the highest rate of pronoun omission, are also the least inclined to subject encoding. However, this may seem scarcely consistent with the fact that plural first persons, being the epitome of referential variability, show a higher rate of subject encoding (81.8%) than both singular first and second ones – as exposed, this is mainly due to the dominance of audience-exclusive uses, usually entailing higher perceptibility than inclusive ones. For now, we can at most conclude that the co-occurrence of different grammatical choices can yield quite variable results as regards participant construction, which will be a basic principle for the stylistic analyses to be developed in Chapters 9 and 10.

Table 6.5: Functional encoding of singular second persons and referential category.

	Subject (*tú*)		Object (*a ti*)		Total	
	#	%	#	%	#	%
Specific	387	80.5	94	19.5	481	36.2
Nonspecific	477	79.2	125	20.8	602	45.3
Speaker-inclusive	193	78.1	54	21.9	247	18.5
Total	1,057	79.5	273	20.5	1,330	100

From a discursive perspective, it seems coherent for the singular second person to have a lower frequency of subject encoding than both of the first ones, given that the viewpoint of addressees is in principle less likely to dominate discourse as against that of the speaker or the group the speaker constructs him/herself as part of. Even so, in contexts such as a second-person narrative or argumentative stretch, the addressee can remain a central participant – ideally, the subject – across successive clauses (see example 36 above). Interestingly, this kind of situation is more usual with speaker-inclusive references, whereby it can be assumed that people are actually thinking of themselves even if constructing their own viewpoint as a second-person one. This is the case with the dialogue in (53), where many instances of both subject and object encoding can be observed. As usual, speaker-inclusive *tú* co-occurs with genericity inductors like conditional particles, as well as other desubjectivizing constructions such as *se está pagando* 'one is paying'.

(53) <A> es un engaño / e:n definitiva / es (de)cir si: e: se está pagando por un servicio que no *recibes* /
<B> sí / y ade[más / sí]
<A> [y si *haces* la] reclamación / y no *te* contestan /
<B> e:sactamente / o:- / o: *dejas* / de abonar el servicio que no *recibes* / y *te* amenazan / co:n *retirarte::* / el servicio ¿no? <Var-Co-230503-13:50>
'A: In short, it is a hoax, I mean, if one is paying for a service (*you*)'re just not getting. – B: Yes, and besides… – A: And if (*you*) submit a complaint and they don't even bother to answer (*you*). B: Exactly. Or if (*you*) stop paying for the service (*you*)'re not getting, and then they threaten (*you*) with cutting the supply, right?'

As for *gustar*-type verbs – which are one of the main sources of first-person object encoding in the corpus – they prove relatively infrequent with the singular second one. These verbs could entail the attribution of personal assessments to interlocutors who have not pronounced themselves on the issue at hand, thus threaten interpersonal relationships. This also explains why they should usually appear in non-declarative contexts such as questions and hypothetical clauses with an inviting function, most typically in advertising discourse and with a nonspecific reference. In (54), the addressee is encoded as an object across four consecutive clauses; two of them have nuclei of this type, namely *gustar* and the idiom *hacer ilusión* 'to excite, to tickle one's fancy', while the others encode the addressee as a beneficiary dative object and the audience-exclusive first person as the subject that can provide some service. In the similar context of (55), there is alternation between second-person object encoding with *gustar* and subject encoding with *querer* 'to want, to feel like'.

(54) si *te* gusta bailar: / *te* esperamos este sábado en La Rocina: / y si además *te* hace ilusión: conseguir un jamón / o un: televisor: / en La Rocina *te* diremos: / cómo: <Anu-To-080803-11:55>
'If (*you*) like (lit. if it pleases [*you*]) to dance, we'll be waiting (*for you*) this Saturday at L. R. And if it excites (*you*) to win a cured ham or a TV, at L. R. we'll tell (*you*) how to.'

(55) ¿que *te* gusta el mundo Disney? / en: La Hacienda está la fiesta del Pato Donald y compañía: / y si lo que *quieres* es algo relacionado con el mar / en: Gatsby está tu fiesta marina: <Anu-40-120803-11:20>
'So (*you*) like (lit. it pleases [*you*]) the world of Disney? At L. H. there's a party with Donald Duck and company. And if (*you*) rather feel like something related to the sea, there's your sea party at G.'

Actually, 3 of the 4 tokens of preverbal object pronouns obtained appear with *gustar*-type verbs in non-declarative clauses where the speaker inquires about some taste or wish of the addressee. In (56), the formulation of *a ti* in A's question helps involve B in the content, indicating that it is her viewpoint that matters. This is reinforced through the formulation of preverbal *tú* in a subsequent turn. As in other cases, the alternation in functional encoding suggests the cognitive proximity of the human objects of psychological verbs to subjects (see back Sections 3.3 and 4.4).

(56) <A> oye: / *¿a ti te* gusta Camela? /
<B> mucho /
<A> ¿mucho:?
<B> mucho
<A> *tú quieres* ir al concierto / totalmente gratis: <Mus-Di-251104-13:15>
'A: Hey, do *you* like C. (lit. does C. please *you*?) – B: Indeed. – A: Indeed? – B: Indeed. A: So *you* want to go to the concert totally free.'

The occurrence of these verbs with speaker-inclusive references is rare across the corpus, which suggests that these are not perceived as adequate contexts for the generalization of contents, again because they would implicitly attribute the addressee stances or feelings that are actually those of the person speaking. (57) is an example with *gustar*; in this case, straightforward generalization is avoided through a modal auxiliary (*te podrá gustar* 'he may please you') and temporal delimitation (*un día* 'some day') indicating that the event is not necessarily seen as a recurrent one, i.e. that people need not like this player all the time, since the point being made is a different one.

(57) *te* podrá gustar o no / un día porque *dices* "bua: hoy Lupi / no está acertao" / pero este es de los que se vacía / y de loh que suda la camiseta / a base de bien <Dep-Co-080104-14:45>
'(*You*) may like him (lit. He may please [*you*]) or not some day; (*you*) may say "Nah, today L. is not sharp"; but he is indeed one of those who give it all and sweat it off.'

Finally, in the preceding chapters we pointed out the interest of observing the distribution of central functions in clauses where the first and second persons are simultaneously indexed. Which participant is encoded as the subject and which one as the object will have some repercussion on how each of them is cognitively constructed as well as on the kind of relationship that is established between them. As also noted, there is some tendency of broadcasters and advertisers to encode the addressee as subject and themselves or their groups as an object, particularly when expressing requests or invitations, as in (58) and (59). In the second example, the plural first-person referent evolves from object to subject in the last clause, where the intention is to suggest the effort made by the company – in this case, their extended opening schedule.

(58) nos vamos acercando: / a la una y media / vámono:s: / a por uno de los destacados antes / *dame* apenas un minuto y regresamos / con: *Veinte de enero* <Mus-40-220803-13:25>
'We're approaching 1:30 p.m. Let's go for one of our top entries. (*You*) give (*me*) just a minute and we'll be back with *Veinte de enero*.'

(59) todo a los mejores precios / además *podrás* visitar nuestra exposición de pintura y obra gráfica catalogada / *ven* a *vernos* / *cerramos* tarde <Anu-To-160503-18:40>
'Everything at the best prices. Besides, (*you*) will have the chance to visit our exhibition of catalog paintings and graphic works. (*You*) come to see (*us*) – (*we*) close late in the evening.'

In turn, when it is the speaker or a first-person group that is constructed as the subject, the verb will usually indicate deference, e.g. *invitar* 'to invite', *esperar* 'to wait for' or *regalar* 'to give' (example 60; see also 54 above). In contexts with a referentially specific addressee, there are also frequent metadiscursive comments with a first-person subject and a second-person object enhancing interactivity, such as *te voy a decir una cosa* 'I'll tell (you) something' in (61).

(60) al realizar tu compra: / *te regalamos* un descuento del / CINco por ciento: / s:ólo / durante el mes de agosto: <Anu-SE-110803-17:10>
'When making your purchase, (*we*) give (*you*) a 5% discount. Only during the month of August.'

(61) yo también s:oy positivo ¿eh? / pero *te* voy a decir una cosa / perdona / el noventa y cinco por ciento de loh presoh // han sido / NIños / agredidos / en su infancia <Var-Pu-211204-12:35>
'I'm also optimistic, right? But I'll tell (*you*) something – just a second. 95% of prisoners have been abused when they were children.'

In sum, the encoding of the singular second person as subject in media discourse often suggests a strategy to indicate that the addressee – either a specific or nonspecific one – has the capacity to do or choose something, which has evident advantages for broadcasting and advertising discourse. At the same time, the encoding of the speaker or his/her group as an object of the same verb will suggest the adoption of a subordinate position towards the addressee. When the functions are reversed, the first-person subject-agent is presented as rendering a service to the second-person object-beneficiary (see further discussion of functional encoding and the stylistic dimension of *responsibility* in Section 9.6). Other instances of second-person object encoding are of *gustar*-type verbs, usually appearing in deontic utterances such as questions and offerings. Also, in interactions with a specific addressee, both the subject and object encoding of the latter are frequent in metadiscursive comments that help organize conversation and emphasize involvement. A general tendency can be inferred to accord high salience to the addressee – in coherence with the high frequency of second-person pronoun omission – which is perceived as profitable in most situations.

6.5 Summary

The addressee is a discursive-cognitive construction entailing a set of communicative rights and duties for some participant chosen by the speaker to be the explicit recipient of discourse. The main resources for its construction in Spanish are *tú* and its corresponding subparadigm of singular second-person forms. In media discourse, these are most often referentially nonspecific; they help individualize a target audience to whom some expectable psychosocial features are attributed. The very choice of *tú* instead of other second persons to be reviewed below is indicative of a certain ideal addressee, as well as of the kind of interpersonal relationships speakers intend to develop with the latter. Its use is aimed at suggesting interactivity within communicative situations that are themselves scarcely interactive; it is usually accompanied by pragmatic strategies closely resembling those of face-to-face conversation, including vocatives and deontic utterances such as questions and requests. Together with specific and nonspecific references, we have distinguished speaker-inclusive uses, whereby the speaker constructs a stance or experience that is primarily related to him/herself as applicable to the other. Finally, a number of pragmaticalized constructions function as discourse markers or conversational fillers. Irrespective of their referential scope, all cases of singular second-person indexation imply a recognition of the existence of the addressee and of the latter's role in the construction and interpretation of discourse.

The analysis has shown that the meanings of the different formal and functional choices – expression, placement, functional encoding – are the same as with the singular and plural first persons. However, their contextual repercussions will of course be conditioned by the peculiarities of the singular second person, implying a particular way to construct the other. The relatively high frequencies of formulation and preverbal placement of *yo* are not reproduced by *tú*, save in contexts such as advertising, where it is often implied that the addressee has the capacity – even the responsibility – to do something that will be profitable to him/her. In general terms, participants in media discourse prefer second-person pronoun omission and thus avoid highlighting the addressee's involvement in the content. This is even more usual when the referent is not a specific interlocutor, and especially in speaker-inclusive contexts, reflecting not just the referential fuzziness of the latter, but also probably the fact that people are primarily thinking of themselves when opting for them.

Going back to the question of whether it is the first person or the second one that is inherently more salient, we have found some evidence in support of the former hypothesis, such as the lesser referential variability of *yo* forms – which most often denote just the individual speaking, suggesting high perceptibility as against the frequent fuzziness of *tú* – as well as their higher percentages of subject encoding and especially of preverbal pronoun expression. It is also true that the singular second person is rather more inclined to omission; but, as noted above, the result is partly due to the strong preference of speaker-inclusive uses for this formal variant. Most of our findings thus point to the speaker and its prototypical way of discursive construction – *yo* and its subparadigm – as being associated with the highest salience. Be it as it may, what we can safely conclude from the analysis is that speakers often accord higher contextual salience to their addressees as against themselves, in order to secure their cooperation and achieve communicative goals. Therefore, even though each linguistic choice can be inherently associated with some degree of salience vs. informativeness, it is always necessary to consider the particular context and the goals pursued within it in order to develop a complete picture of the cognitive construction of the participants.

7 The plural second person: *the audience*

7.1 The subparadigm and its meaning

Vosotros/vosotras is the plural second-person pronoun used in both subject and object contexts. It resulted from the agglutination of the Latin pronoun VOS and indefinite *otros/otras* 'others', which started to be used in order to demarcate a specific group within the audience. *Vosotros* had already become common usage in Spain as of the earlier decades of the 16th century (Keniston 1937, 7.127) and probably was the model for plural first-person *nosotros*. In turn, *vos* – which was used not just with plural audiences, but also with certain types of individual addressees – was progressively abandoned. It has survived, though, as the singular second-person pronoun in American varieties practicing *voseo* (see the discussion in Section 6.1). Also, as an accusative pronoun it evolved into the object clitic *os*.

Plural second-person subject agreement is realized through the verbal ending *-is: cantá-is* 'you guys sing', *viniste-is* 'you guys came'. The only exception is the imperative, using *-d: escucha-d* 'you guys listen!'[1] The latter is often replaced with other consonants or just elided in spontaneous speech, Spanish having relatively few words ending with *-d*. In northern and central Peninsular varieties such as the dominant ones in the corpus, it is often articulated as an interdental (García Mouton/Molina Martos 2015, 277–280). In spontaneous speech it is also commonly realized as *-r*, whereby it becomes homonymous with the infinitive. This probably has to do with construction overlapping – the use of a deontic infinitive in instructional texts and signboards is customary, e.g. *empujar* 'push', written on a door. However, the solution is considered nonstandard (Gómez Torrego 2004, 424). In negative hortative clauses, subjunctive forms rather than imperative ones need to be used: *no escuch-éis* 'don't you guys listen!', as happens with the singular second person. Examples (1) and (2) illustrate the use of the pronouns and bound morphemes of the subparadigm.

(1) (vosotras) cant- -á- -is muy bien
you guys.FEM sing THEME-V 2ND.PL very well
'You guys sing very well.'

1 As already pointed out, in the English versions of the examples plural second-person indexations will be conventionally translated as *you guys*.

https://doi.org/10.1515/9783110643442-008

(2)

(a vosotros)	os	d-	-a-	-n	dinero
to you guys.MASC	2ND.PL.CL	give	THEME-V	3RD.PL	money

'They give you guys money.'

In contemporary Spanish, *vosotros* and its subparadigm are mostly restricted to Peninsular varieties, Canarian and American ones resorting to *ustedes* (see Chapter 8) in any context of plural second-person encoding. However, the traditional Peninsular forms have for centuries been taught in schools and used in formal and literary discourse across the Spanish-speaking domain (Frago Gracia 2011, 56–62), thus are likely to retain social prestige, at least in some communities. Serrano (in press a) finds a tendency of many speakers in the Canary Islands to use the alien forms in newer communicative domains such as social networks. In principle it would seem easy to explain this as reflecting the popular view of northern and central Peninsular dialects as more "prestigious" or "correct" than those of the islands. However, and more interestingly, the author observes that speakers resort to *vosotros* morphemes when personal closeness or intimacy are prominent values in the interactional context. That is, if they draw upon grammatical forms strange to their vernacular variety it is not in order to express formality or distance – as would be more expectable, following typical sociolinguistic tendencies (see e.g. Álvarez Muro/New 2003; King/Nadasdi/Butler 2004) – but rather to highlight the opposite values, which seems more difficult through *ustedes*. Speakers of varieties lacking the distinction between a prototypical and a displaced second person can thus find it useful to incorporate such a distinction in order to widen their repertoire of discursive-pragmatic resources.

As was also exposed with regard to the plural first person (Sections 5.1, 5.2), the pronoun *vosotros/as* is not the only stressed element that can be formulated in coreference with plural second-person verbal morphemes. Rather, speakers will often demarcate the reference through lexical elements, sometimes in coordination with singular second-person pronouns. In (3), *tu coche y tú* 'your car and you' triggers plural second-person agreement in the nucleus *agradeceré-is* '(you guys) will appreciate'. In (4), the clitic *os* is coreferential with the postverbal third-person NP *a todos* 'to all', also a frequent choice in audience-inclusive first-person contexts.

(3) el más completo / PUENte de lavado en Salamanca / encerado / al:ta presión / espuma aztiva / ven a probarlo / *tu coche y tú* l:o *agradeceréis* <Anu-Pu-281204-12:20>
'The most complete gantry car wash in Salamanca. Wax-up, high-pressure technology, active foam. Come and try it – *your car and you* (*you guys*) will appreciate it.'

(4) *os* deseo: unas felices fiestas *a todos:* <Dep-On-141204-15:15>
'I wish (*you guys*) happy holidays *to all.*'

Another procedure for reference delimitation is the formulation of a relative head introducing an embedded clause with plural second-person subject or object agreement. In (5), *que* 'who, that' functions as the subject of the subordinate verb and is coreferential with the preceding NPs *todas las personas, instituciones* 'all the people, institutions'. In (6), the reference of *los que* 'those who' is delimited by the embedded clause itself. This clause in turn functions as the subject of the main verb *sabéis* '(you guys) know', which has plural second-person inflection as well.

(5) Gracias a *todas las personas, instituciones...* que *habéis hecho* posible la celebración de estos actos en favor de los más pobres. <Car-Ga-190604-6a>
'Thanks to all the people, institutions... who (*you guys*) have made it possible to carry out these activities in support of the poorest.'

(6) no quiero defraudar a nadie / y: *los que* me *conocéis* y: yo creo que en Salamanca me conoce: bastante gente / *sabéis* cómo soy <Dep-Co-080104-14:35>
'I don't want to disappoint anyone. And those who (*you guys*) know me – and I think there are many people in Salamanca who know me – (*you guys*) know how I am.'

The plural second person is by far the least frequent one in the corpus analyzed. This does not necessarily mean for it to be a rare choice in other communicative domains – it can a priori be considered as usual for the construction of plural audiences in Peninsular Spanish as *tú* is for that of singular addressees. Rather, its low rate of occurrence is probably an effect of the types of communicative situations featured in the corpus and the socio-interactional norms and tendencies prevailing in them. *Vosotros* is generally restricted to radio programs where broadcasters construct a nonspecific audience as a plurality rather than as an individual; but even in these contexts the alternative *ustedes* – traditionally seen as more "formal", "polite" and appropriate for public situations – is often preferred. *Vosotros* is relatively frequent in music programs targeted to a predominantly young or middle-aged audience (example 7), as well as in advertising discourse with analogous targets (8), even if *tú* is more usual in both genres, suggesting the preference for addressee individuation. The latter example is also interesting because the speaker is mimicking a popular TV personality of Cuban origin; however, the imitation focuses on phonetic and prosodic features, while he indexes the audience with *vosotros* morphemes, these being hardly expectable in an actual American speaker.

(7) bueno para aquellos que: / *salgáis* cara al fin de semana: / *o:s* recomiendo que hoy día ventitrés (Juanes) está / e:n Almería en el recinto ferial <Mus-40-220803-12:15>
'So, for those who (*you guys*) are going out on the weekend, I recommend (*you guys*) that today, the 23rd, [Juanes] will be in Almería, at the exhibition grounds.'

(8) <imitación de acento cubano> ¡eh colega:s! / en Capitólium / ehte verano la noche *oh* confunde: / *venid* a lah mejoreh fiehtah del verano / en: Capitólium <Anu-40-220803-11:00>
'[*Imitating Cuban accent*] Hey dudes! This summer at C., the night is gonna confuse (*you guys*). (*You guys*) come to C. for the best summer parties!'

In other words, in the domain of mass communication the plural second person appears to face tough competition from choices perceived as pragmatically and socially more advantageous, either because they help individualize the addressee – in the case of singular persons *tú* and *usted* – or because they are perceived as more "formal" – in the case of displaced *usted* and *ustedes*.

The basic discursive-cognitive meaning of this person will be paraphrased as *the audience*. This needs to be understood as a quite different notion from that of *the addressee* (Section 6.1) rather than just a plural variant of it. By choosing the plural second person, speakers do not just assemble a number of individual recipients, even if this might seem to be the case in particular contexts. They actually construct a plurality discourse is explicitly produced for, none of whose members is cognitively singled out from the rest. This plurality can also subsume referents external to the interaction, even inanimate ones (recall *tu coche y tú* 'your car and you' in example 3). The plural second person replaces the meaning of individuality that is inherent to the singular with that of groupness. Of course, it will be useful to take into account whether the entities gathered within the audience in a given context are specifically known to the speaker (see the following section). For now, the point to be made is that, when making this choice, people intend for all possible interlocutors, and sometimes even for beings that would hardly qualify as such, to be constructed as cognitively equal.

Also, it cannot be considered a mere second-person counterpart of *nosotros*. While the meaning of the latter has been formulated as *more than the speaker* (Section 5.1), it is not so evident that *vosotros* can be paraphrased as "more than the addressee". In most contexts, the speaker has a discernible extradiscursive reference, but still can opt to construct him/herself as a plurality through the plural first person. In turn, *vosotros* is rarely the result of widening the reference of a specific addressee. This is obvious in public situations as those of media communication. If there exists such a specific participant – e.g. in press and radio interviews – the possibility for speakers to oscillate between the singular and plural construction of the other may give rise to interesting pragmatic effects, as will also be discussed below.

7.2 The construction of reference

The extradiscursive referential possibilities of *vosotros*, just as those of all plural persons, are quite wide. In this case it would be of little use to put forward an exclusive/inclusive distinction as has proven to be crucial with the plural first person, since the individual speaking can hardly be included within the reference, while the specific interlocutor, provided there is one, will always be.[2] Speaker self-exclusion makes *vosotros* a less referentially diffuse choice than the plural first person; actually, it is seldom found in clearly pragmaticalized uses as are recurrent with the latter (§5.2.4), but rather retains its deictic-anaphoric capacity across contexts. We will distinguish three referential categories in media discourse: *specific* – all entities within the audience are identifiable by the speaker; *semispecific* – there are both identifiable and non-identifiable entities; and *nonspecific* – there is a virtual audience whose actual members are unknown to the speaker but will usually be attributed some ideal psychosocial features, i.e. a target audience.

7.2.1 Specific

This is the only referential type that would adjust to an "aggregate of individual addressees" interpretation. The speaker addresses an audience whose members

2 This statement may be disputed considering the (rather restricted) possibility to extend the reference of speaker-inclusive singular second persons to a plurality, e.g. *Cuando te peleas con un amigo, normalmente intentáis arreglarlo* 'When (you) quarrel with a friend, (you guys) normally try to sort things out'. However, as the example suggests, a previous singular indexation is almost indispensable for this interpretation to be feasible. There are no plural second-person tokens in the corpus that can be classified as speaker-inclusive.

are all known to him/her and are assumed to be listening or reading. While this might be a usual situation in face-to-face interactions, it can hardly be expected to be the dominant one in media discourse, obtaining only in interviews, conversations or debates with more than two participants. However, even in such contexts *ustedes* is by far preferred. (9) is an example where the moderator of a debate simultaneously addresses the three political representatives taking part in it. The choice of *vosotros* rather than *ustedes* is coherent with the fact that all of them are around 30 years old and feature as spokesmen for the youth divisions of their respective parties. However, the interaction itself is scarcely conversational, with the moderator usually addressing just one participant at a time through singular forms, and getting the same sort of response from them. A different kind of context providing some tokens of specific second plural persons is that of recorded clips from press conferences, where someone talks to a group of reporters (10).

(9) ¿se ha politizado demasiado el asunto (del Archivo de la Guerra Civil) / cómo lo *veis*? <Var-Pu-281204-12:50>
'Has the issue [of the Civil War Archives] grown too politicized? What do (*you guys*) think about it?'

(10) lo que sí *o:s* puedo decir / porque tenemos mucha esperiencia de estos viajes es que efectivamente / cuando: ves un:- / un avión de una línea aérea / e:m: / desconocida / y: un modelo / desconocido / pues desl- / desde el primer momento hay una desconfianza <Inf-SE-300503-19:15>
'What I can indeed tell (*you guys*), since we do have broad experience with this sort of flights, is that, when you spot an aircraft belonging to an unknown airline and an unknown model, there is a certain wariness from the beginning.'

The fact that specific plural audiences must be more usual in communicative domains outside the media is evidenced by (11), from a letter written by a Spanish Civil War prisoner to his wife and daughter, as transcribed in a journal story about a commemorative exhibition. As pointed out, the choice of *vosotros* is an indication that both addressees are constructed as equal and that the content concerns both of them. Also, the recurrence of first- and second-person indexations across the text enhances its interactivity (see further Section 9.3).

(11) *Tened* la seguridad absoluta de que soy inocente hasta la saciedad. No tengo nada de qué arrepentirme, si no es de no haber huido, y *confiad* en que *os* quiero <. . .> Sólo *os* repito que no *tenéis* motivo para *avergonzaros* de nadie. <Rep-Ad-070404-53>

'(*You guys*) can be absolutely sure that I couldn't be more innocent. I have nothing to regret, except not having fled; and (*you guys*) can rest assured that I love (*you guys*). [. . .] I can only repeat (*to you guys*) that (*you guys*) have no reason to feel ashamed before anyone.'

Some radio commercials containing scripted dialogue also reflect the customary use of *vosotros* forms when indexing a group of friends, as done by C in (12). He rapidly shifts to a singular second-person viewpoint that is ambiguous between a speaker-inclusive reference – meaning to expose what *anyone*, including himself, normally does – and a nonspecific one – meaning to tell the audience what *they* need to do.

(12) <A> ¿y dónde vamos? /
<B> tú lo flipas eso sí que es una preguntita: /
<C> ¿pero *estáis* bobo:s? sin discusión *comienzas* la noche en la Apotheka: / donde hay una marcha alucinante <Anu-40-120803-11:45>
'A: So where shall we go? – B: Now that's a good question, dude. – C: Hey, are (*you guys*) dumb? There's no question that (*you*) need to start your evening at A., where the party is awesome.'

7.2.2 Semispecific

The second referential category is rather more usual in media discourse. Semispecific references characterize situations where someone is featured as the representative of a relatively delimited group the speaker does not belong to, and whose other members are not present. Nowikow (1994, 285) views these uses as constructing a *heterogeneous* audience ("you + others"), as against the *homogeneous* ones represented by specific plurals ("you + you + you, etc."). Semispecific contexts are thus the ones where the plural second person could be paraphrased as "more than the addressee" and, in fact, the occurrence of this referential variant in media interactions tends to mirror that of audience-exclusive *nosotros*.

People interviewed in the press or radio often shift between two different kinds of identity – they are individuals and can/should be treated as such, but their being featured in these kinds of situations is in many cases justified by the fact that they represent a human group, e.g. an association, institution or political party. This has striking reflections on the choice of second persons by those who address them, with frequent shifts between the singular and plural viewpoints. In (13), a journalist interviewing a soccer player first uses *tú* when asking a personal question, then *vosotros* when inquiring about the everyday life of his team. The responses by the player adjust to the person chosen in either case.

(13) – La afición por el fútbol, ¿*te* viene de familia?
– *Me* viene sobre todo de mi padre que fue jugador del Ciudad Rodrigo. Llegó a jugar en Tercera División.
– ¿*Soléis* ir todos los jugadores a los partidos?
– En mi equipo *somos* 22 y normalmente van todos. <Ent-Ga-171104-54>

'A: Did love for soccer come (*to you*) from your family? – B. It came (*to me*) mostly from my father, who played at the C. R. team. He got to play in the third division. – A: Do all players (*you guys*) usually attend the games? – B: There (*we*) are 22 players in the team, and normally everyone attends.'

Similarly, in (14) a radio broadcaster interviewing a basketball player alternates between the plural and singular second persons, as he moves from discussing the prospects of her team in a competition to assessing her personal feelings about it. Again, her answers accordingly shift from the plural to the singular viewpoint.

(14) <A> ¿qué consigna:s *os* ha dado: José Ignacio Hernández? es decir / para: / esta competición en la que hay que: jugar: / al ciento diez por cien cada partido / e: ¿cómo hay que salir a la pista? /
<B> bueno de momento hay que darlo todo en cada partido ¿no? / *tenemo:s:-* / bueno / *tenemos* que ir paso a paso primero: / superar este partido <. . .>
<A> *oye* / ¿*te has* llevado algún amuleto / quizás la medalla de: bronce que *conseguistes* en el e- / EUropeo para:- / bueno / para poder estar en la final: / *te has* llevado algún tipo de::-? /
<B> no: no *me he llevado* nada: <risas> / nada nada / *yo creo* que- / bueno en esas cosas: / no *creo* mucho <Dep-On-080104-15:25>

'A: What instructions has J. I. H. given (*you guys*)? I mean, for this competition in which one needs to be at 110% in each game. How should one take to the court? – B: Well, at present it is necessary to give one's all in each game, right? (*We*) need, well, (*we*) need to go step by step, and start by winning this game. [. . .] A: Hey (lit. Listen), did (*you*) take any amulets with you, maybe the bronze medal (*you*) won at the European Championship, in order to reach the final? Did (*you*) take anything? – B: No, (*I*) took nothing [*laughs*]. Nothing, nothing. *I* think, well, (*I*) don't really believe in such things.'

In situations of this sort, it is also possible to view plural forms as a strategy to avoid singular ones, if the latter might excessively highlight the involvement of a specific addressee. In other words, we could speak of an *addressee-blurring* variant of the plural second person, in line with speaker-blurring uses of the plural first one (see §5.2.1), even if in this case the strategy seems to be much less widespread and conventionalized. In (15), a soccer player reacts to the words of a journalist in a press conference by generalizing the viewpoint to journalists at large (*me preguntáis* '(you guys) ask me'), apparently relieving the individual posing the question from personal responsibility. Also, in (16) a broadcaster makes a request to an interviewee, but does so through a plural, implying that the fulfillment of his wishes is not just the latter's responsibility. Shifts from the singular to the plural can be observed whenever some content is generalized to a group the interviewee can be constructed into.

(15) me *preguntáis* que si hablo que si no hablo / yo soy un jugador más en: treno y: / se acabó <Dep-SE-210504-15:45>
'(*You guys*) ask me whether I talk or don't talk. I'm just one player, I do my training and that's all.'

(16) la reunión yo ehpero que sea tremendamente positiva / y: m / hombre / ojalá fuese definitiva / mucho me temo que no pero que en cualquier caso / que hoy Rafa / *deis* pasos de verdaz / IM:portantes / y clarificadores / en el futuro de la Unión Deportiva Salamanca <Dep-Co-080104-14:30>
'I hope the meeting will be hugely positive – well, I wish it could even be conclusive. I'm afraid it won't, but in any case, R., I hope that today (*you guys*) will take real steps, important and clarifying ones, towards the future of the U. D. S. team.'

As observed in examples (13) and (14), the participants tend to imitate the singular vs. plural choices made by others in previous turns. In particular, the tendency of broadcasters to construct themselves with plural first-person forms – which depending on the context will favor either a speaker-blurring interpretation or an audience-exclusive one – is parallel to some preference on the part of their interlocutors to construct them through plural second persons whose extradiscursive reference is often diffuse. In (17), an interviewee is talking about the works of a renowned architect to whom an exhibition has been devoted. The plural object indexation in the last clause, appearing within a metadiscursive construction (*como os acabo de decir* 'as I just told (you guys)'), may denote the people present at the studio, which would make it specific, or else the latter plus the listeners to the program, thus semispecific. In either case, it is a significant choice as against the singular *como te acabo de decir* 'as I just told (you)', whereby the interviewer would be individualized as addressee.

(17) en España pues tiene mucha:s- / muchas obras / realmente en Andalucía / porque: él: / trabaja mucho en ese entorno Sevilla / Cádiz / e: Jerez etcétera / pero bueno / y luego en Madriz / como: *os* acabo de decir <Var-Co-050204-12:45>
'Well, there are many works of his in Spain; actually in Andalusia, since he usually works around that region: Seville, Cádiz, Jerez, etc. And then also in Madrid, as I just told (*you guys*).'

Also, in (18) the broadcaster reads the text of an email requesting that a particular song be aired. Even if the sender might have addressed him alone through the singular – as happens in other similar messages – her choice of the plural is a recognition that the broadcaster's identity in this context is hardly detachable from that of the station or team he represents. It is also interesting to observe his subsequent response, where he oscillates among three different addressees or audiences – first he mentions *Marta* and *Laura* as a specific plural audience, then shifts to the singular in *recuerda* '(you) keep in mind', apparently denoting *Marta* alone in connection with her praise of the program, and finally formulates a *vosotros* pronoun that should be understood as semispecific, referring to *Marta* (and her friend) together with the rest of the audience. If the latter choice were meant to denote just the two friends, the feminine form *vosotras* would have been more coherent – note also the preceding adjective *atentas* – even if it is not rare to address *vosotros* to an all-female audience, also in line with the gender-unmarked use of *nosotros*.

(18) "hola me llamo Marta y quería *pediros* / si *podéis* poner la canción de Nika *Ser yo* <...> y dedicársela / a Laura una amiga que la QUIEro mucho / muchas gracia:s un beso: y me encanta vuestro programa" pue:s Marta / L:aura / atentas / que llega: / este fantástico: tema / y *recuerda* que este programa si es bueno / es gracias *a vosotros:* <Mus-40-220803-13:10>
'"Hi, my name is Marta and I'd like to ask (*you guys*) if (*you guys*) can play Nika's song *Ser yo* [...] and dedicate it to Laura, a friend I love so much. Many thanks, kisses and I love your program." Well, Marta, Laura, stay tuned because this great theme is coming. And (*you*) keep in mind that, if this is a good program, it is only thanks *to you guys*.'

7.2.3 Nonspecific

Most uses of the plural second person across the corpus have a clearly nonspecific reference. They appear in radio programs where broadcasters address their target audience and, more rarely, in journal pieces where the readership is indexed by the writer. Anyway, as pointed out, it is a dispreferred choice outside the particular genre of music programs. Other radio formats tend to opt for the more "polite" *ustedes* treatment or, in the case of commercials, for either of the singular persons *tú* and *usted*. Contexts with a nonspecific audience are in fact the ones where speakers have the broadest margin of choice between the singular and plural subparadigms, basically depending on how they intend to construct their unknown listeners (Aijón Oliva 2018b). On the other hand, with specific references the plural will be necessary as long as all addressees are constructed as cognitively equal; with semispecific ones, the oscillation between the singular and the plural is parallel to the construction of the specific addressee as an individual vs. as a representative of a particular group, as discussed in the preceding subsection.

The choice of *vosotros* and its subparadigm is indicative of some expectations regarding media audiences. This concerns not just the psychosocial values attached to the prototypical second persons as against the displaced ones – whereby the former are in principle more adequate to address e.g. younger listeners seeking entertainment contents, which explains their association with music programs – but also those arising from the comparison with singular *tú*. The choice of the plural instead of the singular in example (19) may have been favored by the fact that the broadcaster first alludes to some unfruitful attempts of listeners to win some prize by singing a song, then urges the rest of the audience to do better. A nonspecific audience – future competitors – thus seems to merge with a specific one – the previous ones – in this choice.

(19) YA *os deberíais* de saber la letra de sus cancione:s / no me *hagáis* lo de aye:r / <risas> <Mus-Di-251104-13:20>
'By now (*you guys*) should know by heart the lyrics to their songs. Don't (*you guys*) let me down like yesterday [*laughs*].'

As exposed, the plural second person helps dispense with the meaning of individuality and exploit that of groupness, constructing listeners as a collectivity for which discourse is produced. However, it is obvious that contemporary mass-media communication and advertising usually tend to highlight individual values, in some contradiction with their inevitable view of consumers as an anonymous crowd. This also explains the growing desire of people for visibility through newer formats, including social-network profiles and customized websites (Holmes 2005, 100–101). For the same reasons, it is hardly surprising that the plural second person should be the least common one in media discourse. Even when it is chosen to construct nonspecific audiences, it constantly alternates with singular nonspecific *tú*; in (20), this happens across two contiguous and syntactically related clauses.

(20) volveremo:s / el lunes / después de *Anda ya del verano* / con más propuesta:s / con más novedades / y donde / e / *os* <sic>invitamos</sic> / que este sábado / s:i no *te desconectas* de la radio / Toni Aguilar ofrecerá / el cambio de la lista <Mus-40-220803-14:00>
'We'll be back on Monday, just after *Anda ya del verano*, with further suggestions, with new releases. And we remind (lit. invite) (*you guys*) that on Saturday, if (*you*) don't switch off from the radio, T. A. will present the new hit list.'

Such alternation may in fact reveal peculiar conventions of media communication at stake. The habit of some radio professionals to regularly use nonspecific plurals may result in a tendency to construct even specific individuals through nonspecific plural second persons, as already suggested with regard to example (18). The same broadcaster, early on in the program, had already referred to the request as if it had come from the whole of the audience instead of a specific individual:

(21) y un tema que pondremos a partir de la una / el tema de máxima actualidat el sínguel promocional de Nika que también nos *pedíais* / a: través del meil <Mus-40-220803-10:10>
'And there's a song we'll play from 1 p.m., the hottest song right now, that is Nika's promotional single, which (*you guys*) also asked us for by email.'

Finally, and unlike what happens with some of the persons previously analyzed, there do not seem to be clearly pragmaticalized plural second-person constructions used as conversational fillers or discourse organizers. We could at most cite *si os parece* 'if you guys like', lit. 'if it seems (to you guys)', clearly analogous to the singular *si te parece*, sometimes used as a tag to request the other's approval (see §6.2.4). The corpus contains just a couple of tokens, such as this one from the debate quoted in (9) above, where the moderator addresses the other three participants simultaneously. However, she immediately switches to a singular viewpoint by means of a vocative addressed to one of them:

(22) terminamos *si os parece:* Manuel: e: / con que nos *cuentes:* en / qué temas: a nivel municipal a nivel (de) Salamanca está trabajando la juventud de Izquierda Unida <Var-Pu-281204-13:00>
'We'll finish now, *if you guys like*, M., with (*you*) telling us about the issues concerning the town, concerning Salamanca, that the young members of I. U. are now working on.'

The fact that this tag needs to be used with audiences to which *vosotros* – not *ustedes* – is regularly addressed shows that the clitic retains its referential capacity and the construction has not achieved the degree of fixation of others, such as those formed with *tú* that even appear with interlocutors treated with *usted*. All tokens of plural second-person subject or object indexation will therefore be included in the subsequent quantitative analyses.

7.3 Variable expression and placement of pronouns

The scarcity of plural second-person indexations in the corpus – 149 tokens – makes it unlikely that a significant number of instances of expressed *vosotros*, or of coreferential elements delimiting their contextual reference, can be obtained. In fact, there are just 10 cases of expression in subject encoding contexts and 2 in object encoding ones, as shown in Table 7.1.

Table 7.1: Expression vs. omission of plural second-person pronouns.

	Subject (vosotros)		Object (a vosotros)		Total	
	#	%	#	%	#	%
Expression	10	10.8	2	3.6	12	8.1
Omission	83	89.2	54	96.4	137	91.9
Total	93	62.4	56	37.6	149	100

The general percentage of expression (8.1%) falls between those of the plural first person (9.4%) and the singular second one (7.4%), which might be taken as a reflection of the fact that this person shares one grammatical feature with each of them – respectively plural number and second person. With respect to variation across the referential categories distinguished (Table 7.2), there is not a clear association of either syntactic variant with any of them, although specific referents, having just 3 tokens of expression, achieve the highest percentage of this choice (9.7%), as was also the case with the singular second person. In turn, nonspecific contexts have a very slight advantage over semi-specific ones. The token numbers are too low for safe conclusions to be drawn.

Table 7.2: Expression vs. omission of plural second-person pronouns and referential category.

	Expression		Omission		Total	
	#	%	#	%	#	%
Specific	3	9.7	28	90.3	31	20.8
Semispecific	4	7.3	51	92.7	55	36.9
Nonspecific	5	7.9	58	92.1	63	42.3
Total	12	8.1	137	91.9	149	100

The general dominance of omission is probably favored by the fact that, as already suggested when discussing examples (18) and (21), the plural second person often appears to be more of a convention of broadcaster speech in radio genres than a referential device proper. This implies yet another similarity with the plural first person (see Section 5.3), whose even wider referential possibilities are reflected on a slightly higher rate of omission as well. There is an audience whose existence needs to be assumed for media broadcasts themselves to make sense, and whose virtual members are expected to have some predominant psychosocial features – which partly motivate the very choice of *vosotros* as a way of address instead of *ustedes* or the singular persons – but whose actual identity as well as their effective participation are often scarcely relevant. On discursive-pragmatic grounds, there seems to be little justification for the explicit formulation of a participant whose extradiscursive reference is so diffuse. *Vosotros*, together with displaced *ustedes*, represents the traditional view of media communication as the unidirectional transmission of contents to a wide audience, as against the individualization suggested by their singular counterparts. In (23), there is some contrast between the specificity of the audience-exclusive first person – in this case referentially demarcated through a prepositional phrase – and the fuzziness of the audience indexed by the second-person clitic.

(23) todos los vierne:s / en la noventa y seis punto nueve / *nos* gusta / *a:delan: taros:* / n:uevos artistas nuevas canciones <Mus-40-220803-10:05>
'All Fridays, at the 96.9 point of the dial, (*we*) like to give (*you guys*) updates on new artists and new songs.'

The use of plural second-person morphemes is quite conventionalized in opening, transitional and closing program sequences, as suggested by the example. Broadcasters acknowledge the fact that radio discourse is produced for the consumption of an audience, framing it within a supposedly interactional situation. Second-person indexation is especially recurrent in the context of leave-taking, as a means to engage the audience for the following program and usually in alternation with *tú* forms (see 20 above).

In turn, the very few cases of expression are clearly motivated by the need for referential disambiguation. Only in 3 of the 12 tokens is *vosotros* the formulated element; in all others, it is a lexical NP, a relative head/clause or a coordination between singular *tú* and some third-person element. When these are used for the construction of a nonspecific audience, the latter becomes demarcated to some extent, as in (24), where the speaker introduces a gender distinction among listeners through the coordinated indefinites *muchas y muchos*. *Vosotros* is formulated as an adjacent phrase to them.

(24) un poquito de tambor: de rizmo: / que llega el fin de semana y *mucha:s y muchos de vosotros vais* a salir <Mus-40-220803-10:45>
'A little bit of drums, of rhythm, since the weekend is coming and *many* [fem. and masc.] *of you guys* will be going out.'

As discussed across the preceding chapters, all cases of pronoun expression entail some informative focusing on the referent, which explains why they should necessarily suggest some delimitation of the latter as against the fuzziness associated with omission. The enhancement of informativeness can in turn reveal different pragmatic motivations. One of the two cases of formulation in an object-encoding context, transcribed in (25), shows how a contrast is established between the second-person audience and the first-person audience-exclusive group, which makes the formulation of both pronouns only natural (*ni a vosotros ni a nosotros* 'to either you guys or us'). It must be noted that, while both of them appear in coordination, the coreferential clitic adjoined to the verb is second-person *os* and not – as general grammatical rules would have it in cases of first- and second-person coordination – first-person *nos*. The reason is probably that *vosotros*, appearing closer to the verb, has imposed its grammatical features on the agreement morpheme.

(25) si no *aceptáis* esto / *os* ponemos una ley *os* q- / ponemos un consejo / que tenga un poder mucho más / coercitivo / e: / pero que entonces a lo mejor no *os* gusta ni *a vosotros* ni *a nosotros* <Var-Pu-211204-12:35>

'If (*you guys*) don't accept these conditions, we can set up (*on you guys*) a law or a council with a much greater coercive power, and neither *you guys* nor *we* might like that (lit. that might not be pleasing to either *you guys* or *us*).'

With regard to preverbal vs. postverbal placement, the very low token number also hinders the reliability of quantitative analysis. Still, the general preference of first- and second-person forms for preposition is reproduced: of the total 12 cases, 9 (75%) are preverbal, all of them appearing in contexts of subject encoding. The only postposed plural second-person subject is the one in (26), where both informative focalization of the referent and some pejorative intent can be perceived. A soccer player answering the questions of reporters during a press conference – a specific-audience context – tries to detach himself from A's suggestion that he does not work hard enough. He makes it clear that it is only *you guys*, i.e. journalists, that hold such a view – note in passing the apparently addressee-blurring value of the plural. As is usual in contexts where different referents and their respective stances are put into contrast, just after the formulation of *vosotros* there is a preverbal *yo* that highlights the involvement of the speaker in a more positively-regarded sort of behavior.

(26) <A> parece que lo del trabajo es la frase tuya / trabajar trabajar / pero no debes hacerlo mucho <entre risas>porque-</entre risas> /
<B> bueno: eso lo *opináis vosotro:s* eso: e: / *yo vengo* entreno y: lo hago lo mejor posible <Dep-On-080104-15:20>
'A: It would seem that hard work is your motto. Hard work, hard work. But you don't seem to practice it much [*laughs*], since... – B: Well, that's what *you guys* [postv.] think. *I* come here, do my training and try to do my best.'

The preverbal placement of subject pronouns to suggest the agency and responsibility of the referent with regard to the content – whether the latter is viewed by the speaker as positive or negative – is illustrated by (27), where a positive image of a specific audience – a group of friends calling to the station in order to participate in a contest – is constructed by emphasizing their salience within the event; they have won tickets for a concert and are thus entitled to them. At the same time, the preverbal subject seems to exploit the contrastive potential of pronoun expression in general; this particular group is singled out from the whole of the audience.

(27) alguien que me dé / los datos: e / porque *vosotros tenéis:* / esa en:trada para ir totalmente gratis al concierto de Camela <Mus-Di-251104-13:15>

'Someone please give me your contact details, since *you guys* just got that ticket to attend the C. concert totally for free.'

This is a similar strategy as was observed regarding the preverbal placement of the singular second person in radio commercials (see Section 6.3), even if in the latter contexts the reference is of course nonspecific. The placement of the subject pronoun before the clause nucleus highlights agentivity, which is perceived as pragmatically advantageous when the speaker is offering the audience the possibility to do or acquire something. The management of pronoun placement in contexts of offer or request will be further discussed in relation to *usted* and *ustedes*, which present some special complications regarding this feature of choice (see Section 8.3).

Postposition, associated with the highest degree of informativeness, tends to occur in contexts where the second-person referent enters a contrast with some other one, as is the case in (25) above. When the variant appears in non-contrastive contexts, it can reveal different motivations. In example (28), repeating (4) above, the object NP *a todos* 'to all' is formulated in order to highlight the general scope of the dative-beneficiary object, rather than to demarcate a particular group. As pointed out in Section 5.3, a large proportion of plural first-person expression tokens in inclusive contexts are also realized through NPs including the form *todos* or other generalizing expressions.

(28) *os* deseo: unas felices fiestas *a todos:* <Dep-On-141204-15:15>
'I wish (*you guys*) happy holidays *to all.*'

7.4 Functional encoding

As shown in Table 7.3, the plural second person is encoded as a subject in 62.4% of its occurrences as a central clause function. This is a low score in comparison with those of the persons reviewed so far, all of which are around 80%. On the other hand, it is quite in accordance with the result for the displaced plural *ustedes* (see Section 8.3). This can be seen as a reflection of the relatively low perceptibility of plural, most often nonspecific media audiences in comparison with the types of references associated with the first persons – where the speaker is always included, even if the plural can be referentially rather diffuse – as well as with the singular second ones, prototypically used to construct specific interlocutors.

The suggestion that it should be less expectable for unknown human audiences to be accorded the function of subject is confirmed when observing the

Table 7.3: Functional encoding of plural second persons.

	Omitted		Expressed preverbal		Expressed postverbal		Total	
	#	%	#	%	#	%	#	%
Subject (*vosotros*)	83	89.2	9	9.7	1	1.1	93	62.4
Object (*a vosotros*)	54	96.4	0	0	2	3.6	56	37.6
Total	137	91.9	9	6.1	3	2	149	100

distribution according to referential types (Table 7.4). Whereas subject encoding is clearly dominant with specific references, and more so with semi-specific ones, in nonspecific contexts it is object encoding that accounts for more than half of the tokens (57.1%). Together with the data for the singular second person, where specific referents take the lead in subject encoding (Section 6.4), this shows that, the fuzzier the extradiscursive reference of interlocutors, the less likely these are to be encoded in the syntactic function associated with the highest salience.

Table 7.4: Functional encoding of plural second persons and referential category.

	Subject (*vosotros*)		Object (*a vosotros*)		Total	
	#	%	#	%	#	%
Specific	23	74.2	8	25.8	31	20.8
Semispecific	43	78.2	12	21.8	55	36.9
Nonspecific	27	42.9	36	57.1	63	42.3
Total	93	62.4	56	37.6	149	100

Anyway, the basic meanings associated with subject vs. object encoding can be exploited with all kinds of references. Speakers will highlight the responsibility of the audience – even a nonspecific one they are not really interacting with – through subject encoding. Example (29) shows a discourse-organizing construction (*como ya escuchasteis ayer* 'as (you guys) heard yesterday') whereby the speaker recapitulates some content that had been exposed the day before, granting the audience an active role in resuming it. Of course, the responsibility bestowed on listeners is more evident when actions proper – generally of a communicative nature – are attributed to them. (30) is another example of how an action carried out by a specific person is extrapolated to the audience as a whole (see again 18 and 21 above).

(29) el Salamanca pue:s: / viene de caer / pero como y:a: *escuchasteis* ayer / a:l técnico maragato de la Unión Deportiva Salamanca l:os cambios no tienen por qué venir / precedidos de un: e mal resultado <Dep-SE-210504-15:40>
'Well, the Salamanca team is coming home from a defeat, but, as (*you guys*) heard yesterday from the Maragato [i.e. from the Maragatería region in northern Spain] coach of the U. D. S., team changes need not follow from bad results.'

(30) bien vamos a por otra de esas: / peticione:s / que nos *hacéis* por medio del teléfono <Mus-Di-200503-11:50>
'OK, let's go ahead with one more of those requests (*you guys*) make us over the phone.'

However, the tendency to conceive the audience as a (passive) receiver of media contents results in object encoding being dominant in nonspecific contexts. In radio discourse, broadcasters tend to view themselves or their work team as informing the public rather than interacting with them, and this in spite of the frequent second-person indexations aimed at suggesting interactivity. This is evidenced by recurrent discourse-organizing comments where the plural second person is almost invariably encoded as the object (example 31). Also, in the relatively scarce radio commercials where the audience is constructed through *vosotros* forms, the same distribution of roles can be observed (32). Note, however, the presence of a singular second-person subject at the beginning of the stretch (*encontrarás* '(you) will find'), showing the tendency to attribute higher salience to audiences when they are constructed as individual addressees, as reflected in the much higher rate of subject encoding with *tú* as against *vosotros* (79.2 vs. 42.9% in nonspecific contexts).

(31) mañana: *os* contamo:s lo más: interesante: de: / el fin de semana / que va a ir por esos parámetros que al principio *os* apuntábamos <Dep-SE-210504-15:40>
'Tomorrow we'll give (*you guys*) the most interesting details about the weekend, which will follow the lines we sketched out (*to you guys*) at the beginning.'

(32) *encontrarás* el diseño más actual: a los mejores precios / ¡ah! y lo más importante / a partir de la talla cuarenta y seis / hasta la setenta / *os* espero en la calle Caleros <Anu-On-291104-13:45>
'(*You*)'ll find the latest designs at the best prices. Oh! And most importantly, going from sizes 46 to 70. I'll be waiting (*for you guys*) at Caleros Street.'

As has been repeatedly observed, the choice of a certain syntactic function to encode others is hardly understandable without simultaneously considering the one speakers accord themselves or the groups they construct themselves into. Depending on the kinds of contextual identities and interpersonal relationships developed, there will be a stronger or weaker tendency of speakers to grant their audience the salience associated with subject encoding (see further Section 10.6).

7.5 Summary

The pronoun *vosotros* and its subparadigm are used for the construction of *the audience*, understood as a plurality of which no individual member is cognitively more salient than any other, and where entities external to the interaction can also be subsumed. These forms are at present mostly restricted to Peninsular dialects, while the rest of varieties use displaced *ustedes* to construct any sort of plural audience. Furthermore, in Peninsular media discourse it is altogether an infrequent choice, other second persons – *tú, usted, ustedes* – being preferred depending on the context. Even so, participants in radio genres such as music programs and commercials can profit from its discursive-pragmatic values. Its choice will also have particular pragmatic and social repercussions as against that of the displaced plural *ustedes*, just as happens between both singular second persons (see also the following chapter).

Three referential variants have been proposed: specific, semispecific and nonspecific. The first one is the least frequent in media communication, quite unlike what might be expected in e.g. spontaneous conversation. Semispecific uses are especially interesting insofar as *vosotros* often alternates with the singular second person in interviews and debates, which is indicative of shifts between the construction of the addressee as an individual participant and as the representative of a wider human group. In some contexts they suggest an addressee-blurring intention, in line with speaker-blurring uses of the plural first person. The alternation between the singular and plural persons is also significant in nonspecific contexts, showing different ways to construct a group of virtual, unknown addressees in broadcasting and advertising.

Even though the general scarcity of plural second-person tokens has hampered the possibility of reliable quantitative analysis, the detailed observation of examples confirms that the meanings of variable pronoun expression and placement, as well as of subject vs. object functional encoding, are also exploited with this person. The different variants result in the development of different communicative roles for the audience and relationships between the latter and the speaker. Pronoun expression enhances the discursive-pragmatic meanings associated with informativeness, helping put different participants and their respective stances into contrast, particularly in the clause-final position. For its part, subject encoding highlights the responsibility attributed to the audience, according it a more agentive role in the event at stake. However, the nonspecificity of media audiences, together with their usual perception as passive receivers of contents – even if media communication has grown increasingly interactional in the last decades (Elleström 2010) – result in a comparably high rate of object encoding with the plural second person. This points to the relevance of referent perceptibility as the most basic level of discursive-cognitive salience.

8 The displaced second persons: *addressees and audiences far away*

8.1 The subparadigms and their meaning

Besides the prototypical second persons, there is another set of singular and plural forms used in Spanish for the discursive-cognitive construction of addressees and audiences. *Usted* and *ustedes* involve an apparent contradiction between grammatical form and extradiscursive reference that places them halfway between the third person – considering their formal features – and the second one – considering the kinds of participants they are meant to construct, i.e. addressees and audiences (Aijón Oliva/Serrano 2013, 112–113). As will be observed across this chapter, their functional patterns show a tendency to become grammaticalized as a special person type (see also García 2009, 49–52), not exactly assimilable to either the second or third ones.[1] They originated in the deferential treatment *vuestra merced* 'your mercy' and its plural (Penny 1993, 138), these being lexical NPs correlating with third-person verbal morphemes. In spoken discourse they evolved through different variants – *vuesarced, vuested*, etc. – until *usted* and *ustedes* became standardized around the 17th century (De Jonge 2005).

The reflection of social organization and processes on grammatical structure has been analyzed in different languages (Lapesa 2000, 316; Siewierska 2004, 215–228; Gardelle/Sorlin 2015, 10). In present-day Portuguese, third-person NPs *o senhor/a senhora* 'the gentleman/the lady' are conventionalized as forms of treatment (Silva Menon 2000). Actually, the preceding chapters have shown how the choice among grammatical persons and numbers is largely conditioned by the way people intend to construct themselves or their interactional partners, as in speaker-blurring plural first persons or speaker-inclusive second persons (§5.2.1; §6.2.3). For the same reason, rather than just socially "polite" or "respectful" second-person forms – as they still tend to be characterized, often for the sake of understandability (e.g. De Cock 2014, 5, 29) – *usted* and *ustedes* are person choices that make it possible for speakers to cognitively construct others in a particular way (Serrano 2017b, 89), and whose motivations and repercussions are basically different from those of *tú* and *vosotros*.

1 In the English translations, all pronominal formulations and morphematical indexations of the singular second person will be conventionally identified as *you+*, and those of the plural as *you guys+*.

https://doi.org/10.1515/9783110643442-009

The following examples will make it possible to observe how subject and object agreement is realized. There are no gender distinctions across the sub-paradigms except for (third-person) accusative clitics, such as *la* in (2).

(1) (usted) escuch- -ó
you+ listen 3RD.SING.PAST
'You+ listened.'

(2) (a usted) no la llam- -a- -rá- -n
to you+ not 3RD.SING.FEM.ACC.CL call THEME-V FUT 3RD.PL
'They won't call you+ (fem.).'

(3) (ustedes) cant- -a- -n muy bien
you guys+ sing THEME-V 3RD.PL very well
'You guys+ sing very well.'

(4) (a ustedes) les d- -a- -n dinero
to you guys+ 3RD.PL.DAT.CL give THEME-V 3RD.PL money
'They give you guys+ money.'

As also observed with the plural first and second persons, it is possible for displaced plural verbal morphemes to appear in coreference with third-person NPs or relative heads. However, in this case the examples are rather scarce in the corpus. It is frequent to find the quantifier *todos* 'all of' preposed to *ustedes* and denoting a nonspecific audience, but these cases will be included among those of pronoun formulation. Also, in (5) there is a coordination between singular *usted* and a third-person NP that necessarily yields plural third-person verb agreement, in contrast with *tu coche y tú* 'your car and you' in example (3) of Chapter 7.

(5) Por último, le diré que deduzco que *ni usted ni su marido han asumido* que éste fuera destituido de su cometido democráticamente en un comité por mayoría absoluta. <Car-Ad-041104-10>
'Finally, I'll tell you+ I can infer that *neither you+ nor your husband* have [3rd pl] accepted the fact that he was democratically removed from office by an absolute majority of the committee.'

Actually, third-person NPs could easily prove referentially ambiguous in such contexts. In the absence of contextual information, an utterance like *Los futbolistas son gente sana* 'Soccer players are healthy people' could equally be interpreted as including *ustedes* or just an external group. In the former case, it would be more expectable for speakers to avoid the potential ambiguity by formulating *ustedes* followed by the NP as an apposition: *Ustedes los futbolistas son gente sana* 'You guys+ soccer players are healthy people'. Even if there are no examples of the latter construction in the corpus, throughout this chapter we will repeatedly observe that *usted* and *ustedes* have much higher rates of formal expression than any other first- and second-person pronouns, which would seem easy to connect with strategies of referential disambiguation.

Our analysis is based on a central-western variety of Peninsular Spanish, which means that the distinction between a prototypical and a displaced second person holds in both the singular and plural subparadigms. This is not the case with most dialects of Spanish outside the Peninsula, which show such a distinction in the singular, i.e. *tú/usted* or *vos/usted* – or sometimes a tripartite *tú/vos/usted* system, as in areas of Chile, Ecuador and Colombia (Penny 1993, 139) – while the plural is always *ustedes*. This does not imply for the latter person to have a different inherent meaning in these varieties; it is still a third-person grammatical subparadigm used for the construction of the audience. However, it is not in contrast with a different, prototypical second person, which must have some repercussion on the dynamics of person choice and its interpretation. As pointed out in Section 7.1, speakers of some varieties lacking the subparadigm of *vosotros* use it occasionally in order to convey meanings that prove difficult to construct in a system where *ustedes* is generalized.

Shifts between the prototypical and displaced second persons actually go much farther across dialects. In the southwest of Spain it is usual for the pronoun *ustedes* to appear in coreference with verbal morphemes pertaining to the subparadigm of *vosotros*, e.g. *ustedes tenéis* 'you guys+ have' (Fontanella de Weinberg 1995–1996, 154), causing an apparent discordance as against either *vosotros tenéis* or *ustedes tienen*. Also, some American varieties tend to generalize *usted* with individual addressees, even in familiar and intimate contexts, at the expense of prototypical *tú* or *vos*.[2] These can in turn come to be perceived as alien forms and be used only with strangers or outsiders to the community (cf. Álvarez Muro/New 2003), reversing the more usual socio-interactional pattern. Therefore, generalizing statements concerning the social meanings of the second persons in Spanish should be avoided, even if the approach adopted in this study assumes that the basic discursive-cognitive meanings of linguistic elements need to be present in all varieties of a language, however much the motivations and effects of their choice can be affected by different cultural settings and contextual conditions.

2 A similar process has occurred in wide areas of Brazilian Portuguese, where third-person *você* is preferred with all kinds of interlocutors (Campos/Rodrigues-Moura 1998, 177).

The peculiarities of these subparadigms appear to strongly influence their functional behavior, which tends to mirror that of the prototypical second persons in a number of ways. *Vuestra merced* and its plural have clearly evolved into personal pronouns and thus are unlikely to be seen as lexical units by present-day speakers. Also, when encoded as central objects, these persons behave in a similar way to that of the prototypical second ones, even if other features still reveal their hybrid status between the second and third persons. Object marking with *a* is categorical in either dative or accusative contexts: *Les agredieron *(a) ustedes* 'They attacked [to] you guys+'. Clitic agreement could also be considered mandatory. However, the omission of the morpheme is still marginally acceptable in contexts of postverbal pronoun formulation, revealing the persistence of third-person features. Example (6) shows one of two such cases found across the corpus. It should be pointed out that in both of them the referents are nonspecific audiences whose relatively low perceptibility might facilitate lack of agreement.

(6) Ø saludamos *a todos ustedes* que nos / sintonizan a través de la radio a todos uste:des / que: nos sintonizan / también / en Internet <Var-SE-230903-12:30>
'We now say hello to *all of you guys+* who tune in to us through your radios, together with all of you guys+ who tune in through the Internet.'

Also interestingly, while these persons can in principle distinguish between accusative and dative case in object clitics – *lo* and *la* vs. *le*, together with their respective plurals – addressees and audiences are categorically constructed through the dative forms in the corpus. (7) is an example of *le* used to index a female interlocutor in a supposedly accusative context, namely as the central object of *invitar* 'to invite'. The tendency of *usted* and *ustedes* to correlate with *le* and *les* in any contexts of object encoding has also been documented in other varieties, although to rather different degrees (Uruburu Bidaurrazaga 1993, 159; Paredes García 2015, 188). It is undoubtedly connected with the perception of dative clitics as "polite" choices (Lorenzo Ramos 1981; DeMello 2002), given that they cognitively construct others as relatively autonomous and thus scarcely affected by verbal events (Aijón Oliva 2006b). It also suggests a tendency to reproduce the behavior of the first and prototypical second persons, where case distinctions were lost many centuries ago.

(7) yo *le*:- / *le*: m:: / invitaba / a- quizá: / a desarrollar políticas municipales de aYUda para que: (contratar mujeres) no sea tan gravoso <Var-On-281204-13:15>

'I was actually (3rd sing dat cl) inviting (*you+*) to, say, develop local support policies, so that [hiring women] wouldn't be so expensive.'

We will paraphrase the meaning of *usted* as *the addressee far away* and, consequently, that of *ustedes* as *the audience far away*. Their choice entails the construction of a viewpoint removed from both that of the speaker and that of the prototypical addressee or audience. However, our use of *far* instead of *farther away* is intended to avoid the suggestion that they should receive their meaning from a comparison with the prototypical second persons. It is obvious that Spanish speakers are usually aware that there are two basic forms of address at the grammatical level – as evidenced e.g. by everyday requests for interlocutors to "change the treatment" (Blas Arroyo 2005, 313–314) – and it is often inevitable to view either person as a choice against the alternative possibility, as should have become evident across the preceding chapters. However, a scientific approach to linguistic variation makes it necessary to analyze each choice according to its inherent meanings and its contextual effects, not necessarily in comparison with alleged alternatives (see Sections 1.1, 1.2). The raison d'être of *usted* and *ustedes*, just as that of *tú* and *vosotros*, is the fact that they make it possible to construct others in discourse. The relevant point to be made is that their choice concerns not just social deixis (Levinson 1983, 89–92), that is, the marking of social statuses and relationships, but rather affects the whole perception of others, even in physical terms – it is not unreasonable to expect participants using *usted* in face-to-face conversation to typically keep some distance from each other. The use of third-person forms to index interlocutors represents a strategy of cognitive detachment from them. Such a view is coherent with more traditional, intuitive descriptions of *usted* and *ustedes* as signaling "distance"; however, it makes it possible to reinterpret this notion in discursive-cognitive terms. This way it can be applied to any level of meaning construction, transcending approaches based on psychosocial evaluations in particular Spanish-speaking communities.

Also, the choice between *tú* and *usted* – which is among the most popular topics in Spanish sociolinguistic research; see Blas Arroyo (2005, ch. 9), Kluge (2010) and Fernández/Gerhalter (2017) – concerns the identity of addressees just as much as the contextual self-identity speakers intend to construct (Aijón Oliva 2012; Raymond 2016; see also Section 10.4 below). When selecting some grammatical subparadigm to index others in discourse, participants will be defining a shared system of communicative rights and duties. More importantly, they will be implicitly asserting their right to use that form in that particular context towards those particular addressees. All this is reflected on the quantitative and qualitative usage patterns of *usted* and *ustedes*, as will be observed.

8.2 The construction of reference

Even though *tú* and *usted* are viewed by common speakers and traditional grammatical descriptions as alternative possibilities of address, and the differences between them as restricted to intuitive psychosocial dimensions such as "distance" vs. "familiarity" or "power" vs. "solidarity", their respective referential possibilities are not identical, which further suggests that they have inherently different meanings. *Usted* shows the specific and nonspecific uses of the prototypical second person, but is not so clearly amenable to speaker-inclusive ones (§6.2.3). It has also given rise to pragmaticalized constructions that are not mere equivalents to those formed with *tú*, even if several of them are based on the same verbal lexemes. As for plural *ustedes*, its basic referential types do coincide with those of *vosotros*, i.e. specific, semispecific and nonspecific (Section 7.2), but the construction of such references will of course be conditioned by its cognitive peculiarities. Given the differences between the singular and the plural, we will separately examine their patterns of contextual usage. Across the discussion we will also point out some interesting facts regarding the effects of their choice as against that of the prototypical persons.

8.2.1 *Usted*

As happens with *tú*, the prototypical reference of the displaced singular second person is a specific individual that is known to the speaker, but that through this choice is cognitively constructed as being at a (physical, social and cognitive) distance from the latter. Examples (8) and (9) have respectively been taken from a written-press interview with a local artist and a radio one with a soccer coach.

(8) *Usted es* salmantino y *ha expuesto* aquí en numerosas ocasiones. ¿*Se siente* respaldado por el público? <Ent-Ga-121203-12>
'*You+* are from Salamanca and (*you+*) have had many exhibitions here. Do (*you+*) feel supported by the public?'

(9) si es así como *usted dice* / con esa propuesta que- / m que *ustez* a su vez / e: *cree* que- / que es la que ofrece / el:- el Tarrasa / y la que hace la Unión Deportiva Salamanca / resulta que podemos ver un: partido / M:UY agradable <Dep-Co-080104-14:25>

'If things are as *you+* say, with this style of play that *you+* think the Tarrasa team is proposing, together with that of the U. D. S. team, it appears we may end up seeing a very nice game.'

Journalists in newspaper and radio interviews usually opt for *usted* in order to construct their addressees. The prototypical second person is in turn mostly restricted to younger interviewees, as well as to those with whom interviewers intend to suggest familiarity for some reason. Significantly, media professionals regularly exchange the latter treatment among themselves. This suggests that *usted* is as much a socially "polite" choice as a marker of outwardness – it is normally addressed to those who do not professionally belong to the sector of media communication (see further Section 10.4). Such a view is supported by examples like (10), where a radio broadcaster uses *tú* when interviewing a journalist who has published a book. The choice would have been hardly expectable if she had not highlighted the professional ascription of her guest at the beginning of the sequence (*un compañero periodista* 'a fellow journalist').

(10) <A> el autor es un: compañero: / m: periodista que es Ignacio Francia: buenas tardes Ignacio: /
<B> hola / buenas tardes:
<A> gracias po:r estar aquí ya sé que *estás:* / con: gripe y que *has hecho* el: esfuerzo de: acompañarnos: <Var-SE-300503-19:20>
'A: The author is a fellow journalist whose name is I. F. Good evening, Ignacio. – B: Hello, good evening. – A: Thanks for being here; I know (*you*) have the flu and still (*you*)'ve made the effort to be with us.'

Nonspecific uses of *usted* are intended to construct target audiences as individuals, as happens in radio commercials or in calls for participation in a program. The very choice of this grammatical person will suggest certain types of intended addressees, as well as the development of certain contextual identities for speakers and their groups. (11) is an instance of addressee construction through *usted* in advertising. In (12), the broadcaster utters a sort of slogan (*La Cope le escucha* 'Cope Radio is listening (to you+)') that simultaneously acts as a signal for the beginning of a telephone conversation. In cases like the latter, the formal and cognitive closeness between specific and nonspecific uses is clearly taken advantage of. The referent that had been nonspecific to the broadcaster when uttering the slogan rapidly becomes specific to him – and to the whole audience – when the anonymous caller takes the turn.

(11) *l:e* vamos a contar: / algo / que *le* interesa: // si *está* buscando una cocina / que esté fabricada solo pensando en usted / *tiene que acercarse* a la fábrica y las esposiciones de Nífar: <Anu-To-180603-19:00>
'We're going to tell (*you+*) something that will interest (*you+*). If (*you+*) are looking for a kitchen made with only you+ in mind, (*you+*) need to come around to the factory and exhibitions at N.'

(12) <A> porque no solo es / e: motivo: / e de: / manifesta:r la queja correspondiente sino también pu(e)s / tal vez la alabanza el comentario en torno a temas de actualidá lo que *usted quiera* / el teléfono es el <...> / la Cope *le* escucha //
<B> hola buenos días / mire / soy: una ciudadana / m: de aquí de Salamanca <Var-Co-050204-13:00>
'A: Because it is not just due complaints that are expected here, but maybe also praises, comments about current topics – well, anything *you+* may want to say. Our number is [...] Cope Radio is listening (*to you+*). – B: Hello, good morning. Look, I'm a citizen of Salamanca...'

On the other hand, there are no clear cases of *usted*, at least in the corpus analyzed, with the speaker-inclusive or objectivizing reference that characterizes the prototypical second person in many contexts (see, however, Bidot Martínez 2008, 73; León-Castro Gómez 2014, 53–58). The rarity of this variant might be taken to indirectly support our statement in §6.2.3 that objectivizing *tú* is above all a projection of the speaker onto the domain of the second person, given that it would be scarcely expectable for most speakers to address themselves with *usted* – the latter being a form so clearly laden with socio-structural meanings.[3] All this is obviously connected with the higher inherent salience of the prototypical second person as against the displaced second one. There are still a few examples where it would be possible to argue that the speaker is using the displaced second person with a generalizing referential value; however, in these cases it seems almost necessary for speakers to be using *usted* with their

3 This can be put in connection with an often-noted fact: worshippers rarely if ever address God with *usted* (Blas Arroyo 2005, 300) or with any other "formal" choices such as high languages or varieties in situations of diglossia (Gal 1979, 121). Besides obvious explanations based on emotionality and intimacy, we suspect a perception that the use of *usted* requires the acceptance of some social structure and conventions that make little sense when talking to some entity that is not a member of human society – in a fictional context, it would also be hardly expectable for people to address a talking animal or an extraterrestrial with *usted* (see, however, RAE 2009, §16.15v on apparent uses of *usted* with animals around the Río de la Plata).

addressees – whether they are specific or nonspecific ones. This makes it disputable that the displaced second person be really a resource to objectivize a content that concerns the speaker personally. The excerpt in (13) – a segment of which was already discussed in §6.2.4 – is interesting because, together with several tokens of *usted* forms with an ambiguous reference, there are also cases of the third-person pronoun *uno* 'one', as well as of clearly speaker-inclusive *tú* in the last clauses.

(13) si *ustez:* / *le* toca la loterí:a:: o: un premio importante / que ahora ha habido / sorteo que en Salamanca no ha caído mucho pero bueno / pues si *a usté le* ha tocado más de cinco mil euros / que *sepa* que la Agencia Tributaria *le* va a investigar • *le* va a investigar / no solamente el premio *le* va a investigar todas / sus finanzas todo lo que *tenga* / l:o cua:l / pue:s oye a lo mejor hay que pensárselo si a *uno* le interesa que le toque o no / <risas> / <entre risas>-porque le va: a investigar </entre risas> / e: si *tiene usté* un negocio / pue:s el negocio entero / entonce:s: e:: esto es un hecho nuevo / porque anteriormente: la loterí:a / realmente *podrías* incluso: / no aparecer por ninguna parte y nadie se enteraba de que *te* había tocao <Var-On-080104-13:15>
'If *you+* win the lottery or any important prize – there's been a draw recently, with little earnings for Salamanca, but still – if (*you+*) have won more than 5,000 euros, (*you+*) need to know that the Tax Agency is going to investigate (*you+*). They will not only investigate the prize, but also all of your finances, everything (*you+*) have. So, hey, perhaps *one* might want to consider whether it is desirable to win the lottery. [*laughs*] Because, if *you+* are running a business, they'll investigate the whole business. This is a new situation, since in the past (*you*) could just vanish after winning the lottery and nobody would know (*you*) had won it.'

Finally, there are a few displaced singular second-person constructions used as pragmaticalized conversational markers. The most common ones are *mire* (*usted*), lit. 'you+ look' and *oiga* (*usted*), lit. 'you+ listen', with the pronoun postposed to the verb when formulated. These imperative forms of the physical perception verbs *mirar* and *oír* have followed a path of desemantization, acquiring meanings related to mental perception and communication (see also §6.2.4 on the second-person forms *mira* and *oye*). Even when not used referentially, i.e. when they are not meant to construct a specific or nonspecific addressee, they help reinforce argumentative discourse by implicitly acknowledging the existence of the other as inherent to communication. In most cases, as in (14) and (15), it is possible to perceive that the people speaking – respectively an interviewee and a broadcaster – are imitating the dynamics of a virtual debate with an opponent that would be addressed through *usted*.

(14) ¿qué ideología tiene / el: / hacer una buena pavimentación de la Avenida Champagnat por ejemplo / o de: la Avenida de Federico Anaya? / p(ue)s e: no • *mire usté* / m: hacerlo / bueno bonito y barato / y que moleste muy poco la obra a los vecinos <Var-Co-230503-12:55>
'Is it a matter of ideology to carry out a good paving work of the Champagnat or Federico Anaya avenues, for example? Well, *look*, it is not. What matters is just to make it good, beautiful and cheap – and to bother the neighbors as little as possible.'

(15) ha:ce: / pues algunas sema:nas pues estábamos todos muy preocupados / por la calidaz / del agua de Salamanca / que mientras el Ayuntamiento negaba la evidencia / *oiga* los demás es que: bebíamos el agua nos sabía mal: / y: olía mal <Var-SE-230903-13:55>
'Well, some weeks ago we were all rather worried about the quality of water in Salamanca. While the Town Council kept denying the evidence, *hey*, the rest of us were drinking water that just tasted bad and smelled bad.'

Notably, while these constructions admit both the omission and the postverbal expression of the pronoun, *mire usted* appears to be more pragmaticalized in the latter configuration – this variant even became a sort of stereotype characterizing the speech of a former Prime Minister of Spain (cf. Blas Arroyo 2000) and is used several times by the speaker in (14) across the interview – while the contrary happens with *oiga*. The variant *oiga usted* is more likely to be interpreted as an attention call to a specific addressee, although this may depend on the context. No cases were found in the corpus.

Another construction based on a verb of perception is *ya ve usted*, lit. 'you+ (postv.) already see', used in conversation as an evidential modalizer (Santos Río 2003, 649) and often suggesting that the content dealt with is e.g. curious, surprising or outrageous. However, it is again generally found in contexts where someone is already being addressed with *usted* – as is the interviewer in (16) – which shows that pragmaticalization is far from complete and it probably retains its referential function. As in other cases, there is an analogous variant with the second person, namely *ya ves* (*tú*), although the latter does not appear in the corpus.

(16) Uno de sus habitantes, Francisco Matilla, lleva 50 años viviendo en La Vega. "La casa me costó 40.000 pesetas de las de entonces, *ya ve usted*, y ahora se pagan más de 150.000 euros, sin incluir la reforma". <Rep-Tr-230804-11>
'One of the neighbors, F. M., has lived in La Vega for 50 years now. "The house cost me 40,000 pesetas in that time, *you+ see*, and now they're being sold for more than 150,000 euros, refurbishment not included." '

8.2.2 *Ustedes*

As regards the displaced plural person, its referential possibilities are apparently much the same as those of *vosotros* (Section 7.2), including specific, semispecific and nonspecific uses. The social and pragmatic factors involved in the choice between both persons also appear to mirror those concerning the singular ones, e.g. the construction of identities for both the speaker and the audience, ingroup vs. outgroup demarcation and relationship management. However, *ustedes* is a rather more frequent choice than *vosotros* across the corpus, in accordance with the public nature of the texts and the socio-interactional conventions of the genres analyzed.

Specific audiences, i.e. those whose members are all individually known to the speaker, are the least frequent ones and can sometimes be ambiguous. The politician in (17), being jointly interviewed by the conductor of the program and a regular collaborator, uses this person when simultaneously addressing both of them; however, it is not clear whether he intends to include the audience of the program as well, which would make the reference a semispecific one. In public communication, the nonspecific audience is always present, even if just as an implicit addressee. The potential ambiguity of the reference can thus be taken advantage of for different purposes, as has also been observed with other persons.

(17) ¿*ustedes* saben lo que significa entra:r / a tomar posesión de un cargo público: / de un cargo político: / a una corporación como es una diputación provincial / e: / m / con / la mayoría absoluta / tu grupo político: / y salir / absolutamente N:ADA? <Var-Co-230503-12:40>
'Do *you guys+* know what it's like to be just about to take office in a public corporation such as a provincial council, with your political group holding an absolute majority, and to come out of the session with absolutely nothing?'

As we know, semispecific contexts allow for a "more than the addressee" interpretation of the plural. The frequent shifts between this person and the singular one across interviews and other dialogical interactions make it possible to perceive the dual construction of participants as individuals and as representatives of (external) groups, as was also discussed regarding the choice between *tú* and *vosotros*. As also noted there, shifts can even suggest addressee-blurring strategies with contents perceived as troublesome, usually because they might be understood as personal criticisms. In example (18) we can observe one of the first questions in an interview with the president of a neighborhood federation that holds a critical stance towards the town mayor's policies. The interviewer opts for the singular viewpoint when asking about his personal motivations to take up the post.

(18) –¿Qué *le* mueve para ser presidente de la Federación?
–Esto hay que llevarlo en el corazón. Y tener unos maestros como los *he tenido yo*, como Víctor Pedraz. <Ent-Ad-031104-9>
'A: What motivates (*you+*) to be the president of the Federation? – B: This needs to be in your blood. It is also thanks to such good mentors as *I*'ve had, such as V. P.'

Conversely, a subsequent turn of the interviewer is constructed from the plural viewpoint when suggesting that the scarce political involvement of most citizens may respond to inadequate propagandistic strategies on the part of the federation. As is also usual, the answer mirrors the choice of the plural viewpoint (see further Section 9.4 on subjectivity vs. objectivity in connection with person choice).

(19) –Quizá no *sepan* transmitir.
–*Tenemos* que estar más en los medios de comunicación. Es la vía de llegar más a la opinión pública. *Nosotros hacemos* infinidad de cosas que no trascienden porque lo *vendemos* mal. <Ent-Ad-031104-9>
'A: (*You guys+*) may have a problem of communication. – B: (*We*) need to increase our media exposure. That's the way to get to public opinion. *We* do countless things that pass unnoticed just because (*we*) don't publicize them enough.'

Expectably, the most frequent referential values of displaced plurals in media discourse are nonspecific ones. *Ustedes* is the usual choice in written genres such as opinion pieces and letters to the editor whenever writers index the readership of the journal, which is itself an infrequent strategy; in (20), it reveals a humorous or sarcastic intention. In turn, radio anchors regularly use this person for the construction of their audience in magazines, sports programs and news reports (21).

(20) Si hay que romper, *háganme* caso, mejor hacerlo con un apretón de manos y un beso si se puede. Además de ser más civilizado, y hasta tierno, es mucho más económico <Art-Ga-230804-3>
'If breakup is inevitable, (*you guys+*) follow my advice – it's better to do it with a handshake and, if possible, with a kiss. Besides being more civilized, and even touching, it's much cheaper.'

(21) tengo que *recordarles:* que es la primera entrevista que le hacemo:s / después: de las eleccione:s pasadas / celebrada:s / en la capital salmantina / a la una *les* dejaremos con las noticias nacionales e internacionales <Var-On-080104-12:45>
'I need to remind (*you guys+*) that this is the first time we're interviewing him since the last election held in Salamanca. At one o'clock we'll leave (*you guys+*) with the national and international news.'

Ustedes does not seem to admit speaker-inclusive referential uses – again in line with *vosotros* – nor does it form clearly pragmaticalized constructions. An exception to the latter might be *miren* (*ustedes*), lit. 'you guys+ look', with an optional postverbal subject, in parallel with singular *mire* (*usted*). However, its contexts of occurrence do not suggest a high degree of formal fixation and desemantization. It is used to explicitly call the attention of the audience, apparently retaining its referential capacity; actually, it would be scarcely coherent to use it with individual addressees. The few tokens of the construction in the corpus have pronoun omission, as in (22). Other expressions resembling discourse organizers and evidential markers appearing in radio texts are *ya ven* (*ustedes*), lit. 'you guys+ already see' and *ya saben* (*ustedes*), lit. 'you guys+ already know' (23). However, given that they allow variable subject expression and do not seem to lack contextual reference, they have been included into nonspecific uses for the subsequent quantitative analyses.

(22) hablaremos de- / m: de la Unión Deportiva Salamanca / de lo que puede suceder esta tarde / o no <...> *miren* esta tarde / los sesudos barones de

la Unión Deportiva Salamanca SAD / se reúnen / en CÓN:clave / para ver / qué: hacer <Dep-Co-080104-14:30>
'We'll talk about the U. D. S. team and what may or may not happen this evening. [. . .] *Look*, those thoughtful barons of the U. D. S. sports society are having a meeting this evening in order to decide what to do.'

(23) que tengan buen fin de semana / y les esperamos *ya saben* el próximo lunes / ¡bueno! / el domingo / que tenemos programación: / especial <Var-Co-230503-14:00>
'Have a nice weekend and we'll be waiting for you guys+, *as you guys+ know*, on Monday. Well, actually on Sunday, as we're having special programming.'

In general, while *usted* and *ustedes* can be used in most of the communicative contexts where *tú* and *vosotros* appear, they show significant peculiarities such as the difficulty for *usted* to take on speaker-inclusive uses, as well as the scarce degree of pragmaticalization of most constructions used as discourse organizers and conversational markers. This can all be put in connection with their lower salience and their non-prototypical nature as second persons, whereby addressees and audiences are constructed as cognitively detached from the speaker.

8.3 Variable expression and placement of pronouns

As will be observed, the functional and cognitive peculiarities of the displaced second persons are reflected on their quantitative patterns of usage. Both the singular and plural variants display notable rates of pronoun expression, and especially of postverbal placement, as against the first and prototypical second persons. To start with, Tables 8.1 and 8.2 show the respective frequencies of expression vs. omission of *usted* and *ustedes*.

Table 8.1: Expression vs. omission of displaced singular second-person pronouns.

	Subject (*usted*)		**Object (*a usted*)**		**Total**	
	#	%	#	%	#	%
Expression	104	22.5	11	8	115	19.2
Omission	358	77.5	126	92	484	80.8
Total	462	77.1	137	22.9	599	100

Table 8.2: Expression vs. omission of displaced plural second-person pronouns.

	Subject (*ustedes*)		**Object (*a ustedes*)**		**Total**	
	#	%	#	%	#	%
Expression	67	30.6	11	9.6	78	23.4
Omission	152	69.4	104	90.4	256	76.6
Total	219	65.6	115	34.4	334	100

The general percentages of pronoun formulation – 19.2 for the singular, 23.4 for the plural – are among the highest ones obtained, falling just behind that of the singular first person (24.2%), whose special pragmatic motivations were discussed in Section 4.3. However, it should be further noted that most tokens of pronoun expression appear in subject contexts, whereas object encoding yields low rates of this variant, not quite apart from those found with the first and second persons. The atypical preference of *usted* and *ustedes* for formulation has been observed in a number of studies (e.g. Rosengren 1974, 25; Serrano 2012, 110).

A first factor that could be put forward as an explanation is the potential referential ambiguity of third-person verbal endings. As noted in Section 8.1, dative clitics, associated with animacy and definiteness, show some tendency to generalization as the only object morphemes of the displaced second person. They are thus easy to interpret as indexing addressees and audiences – which in passing may explain why expression rates are not so high in object contexts. However, this could hardly be the case with third-person verbal endings, which are regularly used to index external referents, including inanimate and indefinite ones. The following examples of subject formulation might be taken to support an explanation based on morphematic ambiguity. While pronoun expression is infrequent in written-press discourse, (24) shows this variant in a journal letter addressed to a nonspecific user of the public healthcare system. The pronoun could be aimed at precluding the interpretation of *no esté bien atendido* 'is not adequately cared for' as denoting an external referent – or even the writer him/herself, since first- and third-person forms are homonymous in this verbal tense. In (25), preverbal *ustedes* makes it clear that the writer is referring to the management of the newspaper rather than to external media.

(24) la dirección del Hospital y algunos de sus amigos sindicalistas, han decidido que sobramos personal en esta gran empresa, aunque *usted* no *esté* bien atendido, aunque no pueda *prestarle* los cuidados que como profesional sé que debería *darle*. <Car-Ga-090604-8>

'The management of the hospital and some of their friends at the trade unions have concluded that there is overstaffing in this great institution, no matter if *you+* are not adequately cared for, no matter if I cannot provide (*you+*) with the medical care that, as a professional, I know I should provide (*you+*) with.'

(25) Cuando *ustedes publicaron* en el Suplemento Dominical un reportaje de mis abuelos, Francisca Sánchez y Vicente Andrés, mi abuelo ya había fallecido. <Car-Ga-080604-8>
'When *you guys+* published a story about my grandparents, F. S. and V. A., in your Sunday supplement, my grandfather had already passed away.'

However, both examples suggest that the frontier between referential disambiguation and pragmatically-motivated emphasis on the involvement of the referent is a fuzzy one. Pronoun expression, due to its inherent association with informativeness, can be interpreted as having both effects at the same time. The detailed examination of the tokens shows that only in a few of them can disambiguation be put forward as the basic motivation for this choice. The discursive context generally makes it clear whether the intended referent is an interlocutor or an external entity; more so in oral communication, where overt *usted* and *ustedes* are however quite common. It is thus necessary to take other contextual features into account. Quite expectably, pronouns are usual in contexts where a contrast or a rapid shift between referents is carried out. While in (26) it could still be argued that overt *usted* helps avoid the potential ambiguity of the verb *decía* '(I/you+) was saying', in (27) the subject of the preceding clause was a plural first person with an unambiguous verbal ending. What the broadcaster clearly does is not to identify referents, but rather to contrast their respective stances, i.e. the usual prejudices of society – in which he includes himself – about music festivals as against the more open-minded view of his addressee. Actually, contrast turns out to be a likely explanation for the first example as well, given the subsequent token of expressed *nosotros*.

(26) eso que *usted decía* / e: n:o se sabe a qué: municipio corresponde (el establecimiento) que fue lo que *comentamos nosotros* / parece que está en terreno de nadie <Var-Co-211204-13:10>
'Just what *you+* were saying – it is not known to which municipality [the establishment] belongs, which is what *we* had pointed out. It seems to be in a no man's land.'

(27) *me* llama la atención porque *tenemos* la idea de los festivales de España como una cosa así un poco / folclórica un poco retro y *usted dice* que no <Var-SE-011204-13:30>
'This kind of strikes (*me*), because (*we*) have this notion of festivals in Spain as something, like, a bit folksy, a bit retro, and *you+* contend they're not.'

More generally, and in coincidence with the findings made with all first and second persons, pronoun formulation occurs whenever the speakers intends to put the informative focus on the addressee or audience. This entails reducing their contextual salience in order to highlight their involvement in the content, which in turn will influence the construction of participant identities and the management of relationships. The expression of subjects, particularly in the preverbal position, makes it possible to explicitly associate addressees with either positively- or negatively-regarded contents (see also Aijón Oliva/Serrano 2013, 219–221). In (28), the political group represented by the interviewee is flattered as the only one that has really improved regional infrastructure. Conversely, in (29) the town major is explicitly blamed for the cancellation of local bullfighting shows.

(28) tema de autovías / que es: m: e: un: / tema que / maneja todo el mundo "hare:mos autovías" / e / *ustedes* / de: cualquier forma / lo que sí *han demostrado* es que *son* capaces de hacerlas <Dep-Co-080104-14:50>
'Regarding highways, which is an issue where everyone is always like, "We'll build highways" – well, what *you guys+* have in any case demonstrated is that (*you guys*) are able to build them.'

(29) ¿no podemos seguir viniendo a Salamanca como siempre porque *usted* se ha enfadado con los empresarios de La Glorieta? Suena un poco a prepotencia, ¿no? <Car-Ga-070404-6a>
'So we can't keep on coming to Salamanca as always, just because *you+* have a quarrel with the entrepreneurs at L. G. square? This sounds kind of arrogant, doesn't it?'

Therefore, the expression of displaced second-person pronouns is always associated with an intention to make addressees and audiences more informative, which can have different and not mutually exclusive contextual repercussions: reference disambiguation, explicit contrast between referents and their respective stances, or emphasis on the involvement and responsibility of some participant in the events described. Also, the origin of *usted* and *ustedes* in lexical NPs probably contributes to their comparably high preference for explicit formulation (Aijón Oliva/Serrano 2013, 115).

It may also be useful to consider the possible interactions between referential type and expression vs. omission. In order not to excessively complicate the analysis, Table 8.3 collates the data for both the singular person and the plural one. However, it must be borne in mind that semispecific references can only be constructed with *ustedes*, while specific and nonspecific ones are possible with both persons. The few clearly pragmaticalized tokens of *usted* have been excluded from the counts.

Table 8.3: Expression vs. omission of displaced second-person pronouns and referential category.

	Expression		Omission		Total	
	#	%	#	%	#	%
Specific	92	27.8	239	72.2	331	35.5
Semispecific	10	27	27	73	37	4
Nonspecific	91	16.1	474	83.9	565	60.5
Total	193	20.7	740	79.3	933	100

While specific and semispecific references – the latter with relatively few tokens – have similar percentages of expression, nonspecific ones are more than 10 points below. This is coherent with the results obtained for *tú* (Section 6.3), while those of *vosotros* were not so conclusive. It seems to suggest yet again that the potential ambiguity of verbal morphemes need not be a crucial factor in pronoun formulation – there is no reason to suppose that referential disambiguation should be more necessary with specific addressees or audiences than with nonspecific ones. Quite to the contrary, in the former case speakers should more often feel compelled to explicitly mention their addressees, in order to secure their involvement and cooperation in the construction of discourse. This is evident in several of the preceding examples, as well as in (30), with the subject pronoun topicalized within an interrogative clause.

(30) ¿*ustez cree* que: / e: ha podido llamar la atención? / ¿que nos hemos fijado lo suficiente: / e:n estas huellas / que: / están repartidas por toda la ciudaz <. . .>? <Var-On-281204-13:15>
'Do *you+* think that this has attracted attention? That we have taken sufficient notice of these footprints spread all over the town?'

The discursive-pragmatic meanings associated with the expression of *usted* and *ustedes* are thus the same that have been observed with the rest of pronouns. As pointed out, their relatively high rates of formulation are probably a remnant of their secular status as lexical NPs, which correlates with the cognitive construction of addressees and audiences as "displaced" from the realm of the direct participants proper. This is hardly incompatible with any contextual interpretations that can be derived from the rise in informativeness generally associated with the formulation of referential expressions.

The most striking fact regarding quantitative patterns of *usted* and *ustedes* usage – and where their preservation of lexical features becomes most evident – is not so much their rates of formulation as those of postverbal placement when formulated (Tables 8.4 and 8.5), which clearly differentiate them from the first and prototypical second persons (see also Serrano 2014, 142–144). Postposition accounts for 39.1% of overt *usted* tokens and 61.5% of *ustedes* ones. The latter is in fact the only first- or second-person pronoun that is more often formulated after the verb than before it.

Table 8.4: Preverbal vs. postverbal placement of displaced singular second-person pronouns.

	Subject (*usted*)		**Object (*a usted*)**		**Total**	
	#	%	#	%	#	%
Preverbal	62	59.6	8	72.7	70	60.9
Postverbal	42	40.4	3	27.3	45	39.1
Total	104	90.4	11	9.6	115	100

Table 8.5: Preverbal vs. postverbal placement of displaced plural second-person pronouns.

	Subject (*ustedes*)		**Object (*a ustedes*)**		**Total**	
	#	%	#	%	#	%
Preverbal	28	41.8	2	18.2	30	38.5
Postverbal	39	58.2	9	81.8	48	61.5
Total	67	85.9	11	14.1	78	100

In previous chapters we have pointed out the usefulness of distinguishing between clause-final and clause-intermediate postverbal pronouns. This is especially evident with *usted* and *ustedes*, given their strong preference for the latter configuration, as will be observed. As for pronouns formulated in the final position, it is usually easy to perceive how referents are brought under the focus of attention through this choice. The broadcaster in (31), after recalling some argument allegedly developed by his interviewee – whom he constructs as a preverbal subject-agent – requests his confirmation that it was actually him who said so – this time formulating *usted* after the verb and followed by a question tag that is not integrated in the clause. A contrastive interpretation, i.e. "you+ and not anyone else", is favored. In (32), from a street conversation between two citizens recorded by a reporter, the subject is also focalized as the last element in the interrogative clause. Speaker B seems to correct A's audience-inclusive statement (*le votamos al alcalde* '(we) voted for the major') by specifying that it should at most be A who did so. The latter subsequently detaches herself from this assumption as well.

(31) *usté* ya *escribió* algo en ese sentido de que / algunas / ideas / no: / se pueden plantear así <entre risas>porque los edificios tienen dueño</entre risas> / ya lo *dijo usté* ¿no? <Var-Co-230503-12:50>
'*You+* already wrote something in the sense that certain proposals can't just be raised that way [*laughs*], since in the end buildings are someone's property. It was *you+* who stated that, right?'

(32) <A> hay / doscientos chavales jóvenes en el paro con carné / que los cojan // el mínimo en ningún lao / es una vergüenza <...> ¡y le *votamos* al- / al alcalde! / ¡le *votamos* / para que: / que no: [nos hagan es-]
<B> [¿le *votó usté*? /] pues / vaya desgracia /
<A> yo no / yo no <Inf-SE-300503-19:15>
'A: There's two hundred unemployed young guys with a driving license – let them be hired. No minimum services anywhere; this is shameful. [...] And (*we*) voted for the major! (*We*) voted for him so that this wouldn't happen and... – B: Did *you+* vote for him? Now that's disgraceful. – A: No, I didn't. I didn't.'

However, there are only a few examples in the corpus where *usted* or *ustedes* is clearly focalized through clause-final formulation. Their insertion between the verb and other constituents is in turn the usual solution. 37 of the 45 postverbal tokens of *usted* (82.2%) and 38 of the 48 ones of *ustedes* (79.2%) have the subject pronoun placed right after the verb and before some other constituents. More importantly, even in verbal nuclei composed of more than a lexeme, i.e. those containing aspectual or modal auxiliaries, the pronouns tend to be inserted between them, that is, right after the one that is conjugated (examples 33 and 34; see also De Cock 2014, 139; De Cock/Nogué Serrano 2017, 113–114 on this particular construction). As will subsequently be discussed, the strong tendency of *usted* and *ustedes* to appear right after the subject-agreeing verbal endings is crucial for the explanation of their patterns of choice.

(33) este programa lo hacemos todos los miércole:s en: colaboración: / con la Fa: Salaman- / con la FundaCIÓN Salamanca Ciudad de Cultura // *pueden ustedes participar* a través del telé:fono <Var-SE-011204-13:30>
'We make this program every Wednesday in cooperation with the S. C. C. Foundation. *You guys+* can come on air (lit. can *you guys+* come on air) by telephone.'

(34) el asunto de- / del Archi:vo o de la Casa Lis / bueno / to:- todas estas- / estas cosas ¿no? / que *vienen ustedes e:splicando* <Var-SE-211204-13:55>
'The issue of the Archives or that of Casa Lis, well, all these things that *you guys+* have been explaining (lit. come *you guys+* explaining).'

There are apparently a number of factors at play. It could be hypothesized that, while the lexical origin of *usted* and *ustedes* may still favor their postposition to the verb to some extent, their inherent salience as against third-person NPs or pronouns promotes their adjacency to the nucleus rather than their displacement to the position associated with the lowest salience. This is especially notorious in subject-encoding contexts. If this is combined with the capacity of overt pronouns to disambiguate references – even if the influence of potential ambiguity is often debatable – we can suspect that speakers tend to use the pronouns as morphemes formulated right after the (ambiguous) third-person verbal endings. This would be in line with the general diachronic tendency suggested by Givón (1976) in the sense that subject-agreeing verbal endings result from the evolution of postverbal pronouns, while preverbal subjects would be the outcome of the progressive syntactic integration of left-dislocated topics. In Spanish, the apparent process of incorporation of *usted*/*ustedes* to the morphematic complex at the right of the verb would represent the development of a peculiar kind of conjugation specifically characterizing the displaced second persons – which constitute themselves a peculiar subparadigm within the system of grammatical persons, for the reasons exposed across this chapter. It would make it possible for speakers to distinguish between displaced second-person verbal forms on the one hand and third-person ones with no expressed subject on the other, as illustrated by the following pair of constructed examples. In the absence of contextual information, (35b) seems easier to interpret as referring to an external individual than to an interactional partner.

(35a) Est- -á- -usted invitado a participar
be 3RD.SING YOU+ invited.MASC to participate
'You+ are invited to participate.'

(35b) Est- -á invitado a participar
be 3RD.SING invited.MASC to participate
'He is invited to participate.'

If it were demonstrated that Givón's hypothesis applies to the use of postverbal *usted* and *ustedes* in contemporary Spanish, this could also be viewed as a subject-encoding counterpart of the apparent generalization of dative clitics for the indexation of addressees and audiences in different varieties. The hybrid functional and cognitive nature of the displaced second persons would result in their tendency to develop patterns of syntactic behavior that differentiate them from both the prototypical second and the third ones with which they share formal and functional features.

The phenomenon also generates analogous pragmatic meanings to those of other persons when formulated at the right of the verb. Actually, the preceding hypothesis of postverbal *usted* and *ustedes* as coming to resemble subject-agreement morphemes is coherent with our analysis of clause-intermediate postverbal pronouns as constructing meanings not quite apart from those of pronoun omission. We will begin by considering example (36). Postverbal *usted*, while sharing the relative informativeness of all expressed pronouns, suggests some intention to avoid excessive emphasis on the referent. Its intermediate placement, which is parallel to an intermediate discursive-cognitive status, favors some interpretation that the role of the subject in the event is viewed as known or presupposed (cf. also Serrano 2012, 117–119). The broadcaster suggests that his interlocutor's stance makes perfect sense and that he fully espouses it. The formulation of the pronoun at the preverbal position, while also possible (*usted tiene toda la razón*), would favor the interpretation of personal achievement over that of shared view – thus constructing a more subjective, less intersubjective meaning (see Section 9.5). Of course, clause-final placement and its enhancement of informativeness would seem scarcely coherent.

(36) *tiene usted* toda la razón del mundo y si se limpia se limpia mal: porque- / por las quejas que tenemos <Var-SE-230903-13:50>
'*You+* [postv.] are absolutely right. There's no cleaning, and if there is, it is just badly done, given the complaints we have received.'

A similar interpretation of the overt pronoun in VSO constructions is possible in other contexts dealing with positively-regarded facts that are actually the responsibility of the speaker, who nonetheless avoids explicitly taking credit for them. This way it can be implied that a gift or invitation is something mutually known and not worth emphasizing, in order to preserve the images of both the radio station granting the gift and the person receiving it. This would be the case with *está usted invitado* 'you+'re invited' (37) or *tiene usted la palabra* 'you + have the floor' (38), the latter constituting a conventional and solemn way of yielding the turn.[4]

(37) música moderna música aztual *tiene ustez* ¿eh? / pero: de un cantautor interesante David Broza *está ustez* invitado ¿eh? <Var-SE-011204-13:25>
'Modern music, current music *you+* [postv.] have, right? But from an interesting singer-songwriter – D. B. *You+* [postv.] are invited, OK?'

(38) <A> bien / don Julián / *tiene usté* la palabra /
<B> bueno pues yo: e: / quería: / si se me permite deci:r pues: / rápidamente // que yo creo que los salmantinos deben de seguir confiando en nuestra opción política <Var-Co-230503-12:35>
'A: OK, Mr. J., now *you+* [postv.] have the floor. – B: Well, if I may and to put it in just a few words, I think the Salamanca people should keep on trusting our political option.'

The placement of subject pronouns between the verb and the objects can thus be characterized as an objectivizing resource as against both preverbal and clause-final postverbal placement (see also Section 4.3 on postverbal *yo*, as well as Section 9.5). It reduces the salience of the subject, apparently "hiding" the expressed pronoun in a position where it displays some features associated with subject-agreement morphemes. At the discursive-pragmatic level, this results in the modalization of contents as already known. There is some suggestion that those contents should naturally be accepted by all participants and are not amenable to objection.

In previous chapters it has also been shown that objectivization through grammatical means can be used by speakers in order to present personal stances as universal or common-sense facts – recall e.g. omission of singular first-

4 The functional peculiarities of *usted* are again evidenced by the fact that the postverbal formulation of *tú* is much less expectable in such contexts: ?*estás tú invitado*, ?*tienes tú la palabra*, etc. In these cases, the prototypical second person would most often opt for pronoun omission.

person pronouns, as well as of speaker-inclusive second-person ones, with verbs of cognition and communication. Again, similar pragmatic meanings can be detected when *usted* is formulated at the right of the verb. In a context where criticism is directed at the addressee, preverbal placement stresses the involvement of the latter, thus makes the criticism more straightforward (see example 29 above). In turn, postposition suggests that the content is already known by the participants, which depending on the context can prove to be a more effective strategy. In (39), the speaker takes it for granted that his partner has already understood his stance, practically hindering any possible objection from the latter. The suggestion of presupposedness is coherent with the [verb + *usted*(*es*)] pattern.

(39) lo que yo pretendía decir don Alberto que: no es cosa que *le* quiera espli-car porque la *ha entendido usté* perfectamente <Var-Co-230503-12:55>
'What I intended to say, Mr. A., is nothing I want to explain (*to you+*), because *you+* [postv.] have already understood it perfectly.'

In (40), a broadcaster formulates a hypothesis on her interviewee's being aware of a particular issue by way of a construction (*será usted sabedor* 'you+ [postv.] should know', lit. 'you+ should be a knower', the latter term being infrequent in Spanish as well) where both the postverbal pronoun and the hypothetical future tense contribute to the suggestion that the propositional content is obvious, thus that the attribution of this awareness to the addressee is readily acceptable.

(40) imagino que *será ustez* también: sabedor / de que una de las reivindicaciones que: / con la llegada del nuevo año hace esta: asociación / es algo que tiene pendiente nuestro Consistorio: <Var-On-080104-12:55>
'I guess *you+* [postv.] should also know that one of the demands of this association at the beginning of the new year is an issue that our Town Council has yet to tackle.'

While the plural *ustedes* is most often used to address a semispecific or nonspecific audience, the pragmatic effects of its postposition to the verb are analogous to those observed with the singular. The suggestion of presupposedness and the desubjectivization of discourse can be perceived in modalizing and discourse-organizing expressions such as *saben* (*ustedes*) 'you guys+ know' (41), *ya ven* (*ustedes*) 'you guys+ already see' (42), etc., all of which can be seen as partly pragmaticalized markers, but where variation in the formulation of the postverbal subject is parallel to different degrees of audience involvement.

(41) ya *saben ustedes* que ayer se celebró el "Día sin mi Coche" / popularmente conocido como / el "día sin coches" / y: lo cierto es que hay división de opiniones <Var-SE-230903-12:45>
'As *you guys+* [postv.] know, yesterday was the *Day without my Car*, popularly known as the *no-car day*, and the truth is that views are divided.'

(42) y la Falan:ge / también / convocaba un desayuno de trabajo en Garrido / para hacer balance de la cam:paña electoral // bueno pues ya: *ven ustedes* / que procuramos: e: men:cionarlos a todos: <Var-CO-230503-13:10>
'And the Falange party also held a breakfast meeting in the Garrido district, in order to take stock of the election campaign. Well, as *you guys+* [postv.] can see, we take care to mention them all.'

In sum, the atypically high rates of postverbal placement of *usted* and *ustedes*, which are most often formulated right after the clause nucleus, suggest a process of grammaticalization of these pronouns as morphemes helping differentiate a special conjugational paradigm. The discursive-pragmatic effects of the choice are analogous to those observed with other pronouns in the same constructional scheme. The involvement of the addressee or audience is reduced as against preverbal placement; in turn, the content tends to be presented as commonly known and accepted, all of which can prove useful in contexts where it seems advisable to avoid either explicit (self-)flattering or straightforward criticism.

8.4 Functional encoding

The respective percentages of subject and object encoding for the singular and plural displaced persons (Tables 8.6 and 8.7) approach those obtained with their prototypical counterparts. *Usted* is the subject in 77.1% of the clauses, not quite apart from the 79.5% score of *tú; ustedes*, with 65.6%, aligns with *vosotros* (62.4%). All these figures fall below those of the singular and plural first persons, with percentages above 80%, in accordance with the general tendency for speakers to construct themselves or the groups they include themselves into as the main viewpoint of discourse (see Sections 4.4, 5.4). Still, the differences with *tú* and *usted* are not large. Frequencies of subject encoding seem to be more connected with referential specificity – nonspecific audiences are the most usual ones with both *vosotros* and *ustedes* in the corpus – rather than with grammatical person itself. The less perceptible a referent, the less likely for it to be accorded the syntactic function associated with the highest salience.

Table 8.6: Functional encoding of displaced singular second persons.

	Omitted		Expressed preverbal		Expressed postverbal		Total	
	#	%	#	%	#	%	#	%
Subject (*usted*)	358	77.5	62	13.4	42	9.1	462	77.1
Object (*a usted*)	126	92	8	5.8	3	2.2	137	22.9
Total	484	80.8	70	11.7	45	7.5	599	100

Table 8.7: Functional encoding of displaced plural second persons.

	Omitted		Expressed preverbal		Expressed postverbal		Total	
	#	%	#	%	#	%	#	%
Subject (*ustedes*)	152	69.4	28	12.8	39	17.8	219	65.6
Object (*a ustedes*)	104	90.5	2	1.7	9	7.8	115	34.4
Total	256	76.6	30	9	48	14.4	334	100

Table 8.8: Functional encoding of displaced second persons and referential category.

	Subject		Object		Total	
	#	%	#	%	#	%
Specific	251	75.8	80	24.2	331	35.5
Semispecific	34	91.9	3	8.1	37	4
Nonspecific	396	70.1	169	29.9	565	60.5
Total	681	73	252	27	933	100

Table 8.8 shows the distribution of functional encoding according to referential categories, with nonspecific referents having a comparably low percentage of subject encoding (70.1%). Still, they are just 5.7 points below specific addressees and audiences, while semispecific referents are strikingly differentiated from them both, reaching 91.9% of subject encoding. The result is

somewhat puzzling if it is borne in mind that semispecific uses always involve the plural *ustedes*, which should cause a lesser tendency to subject encoding. The token number of this referential type – with just 3 cases of object encoding across the whole corpus – is probably too small to be representative, but anyway it will be necessary to go deeper into its peculiarities.

As observed in Section 7.4, despite the constant evolution of media communication towards more interactional formats and the proliferation of information sources, the traditional notion of audiences as massive crowds receiving the contents generated by a few professionals and corporations is still influential, particularly in older media such as the written press and the radio. This notion is probably accountable for the relatively high rates of object encoding with nonspecific referents. Most of the tokens appear in radio magazines and news reports, with verbs of communication whose subject is a singular first person denoting the broadcaster or – more often – a plural first person denoting his/her station or work team. In (43), the broadcaster introduces herself as a third-person subject, then shifts to a plural first-person viewpoint with a reference-demarcating prepositional phrase (*desde Cope Salamanca*). In turn, the audience is encoded twice as a displaced plural object through the clitic *les*.

(43) muy buenos días *les* habla <. . .> e desde Cope Salamanca *les* avanzamos a esta hora de la mañana las previsiones informativas más destacadas de esta jornada <Inf-Co-241104-8:45>
'Good morning, this is [. . .] speaking (*to you guys+*). At this time of the morning, from Cope Salamanca (*we*)'re giving (*you guys+*) a flash of the top news headlines of today.'

In turn, when there is some intention to involve the audience in the co-construction of discourse, subject encoding becomes dominant. The same broadcaster of the preceding example, in a subsequent stretch dealing with the weather, invites listeners to look out the window in order to check what she is saying.

(44) nada más que *se asomen* a la ventana / m *verán* que persiste la niebla un día más y la temperatura a esta hora / es de: / entre / UN grado bajo cero y cero grados <Inf-Co-241104-8:45>
'As soon as (*you guys+*) look out the window, (*you guys+*) will see that one more day the weather remains foggy, and the temperature at this time is between -1 and 0 degrees [Celsius].'

The higher responsibility associated with subject encoding is coherent with the occurrence of this choice whenever broadcasters request the participation of the audience, generally by suggesting they call the station and contribute their comments, complaints and suggestions. In (45) there are several tokens of subject encoding with both the singular and plural persons, showing the usual oscillation between addressee and audience construction in broadcasting speech. It is also interesting to compare the usual postposition of the second-person subject in an invitation (*tienen ustedes el teléfono* 'you guys+ [postv.] have our number') with its preposition in a hypothetical clause (*si usted considera* 'if you + consider') whose content is not taken for granted.

(45) *tienen ustedes* el teléfono y *pueden hacer* uso de él / cuando *gusten* / en cualquier momento porque hay un contestador nos *dejan* ahí: el: / comentario: / e / que: no: / *se crean ustedes* que nosotros siempre estamos en posesión de la verdaz o sea que si *usté considera* que hemos dicho algo / fuera de: lugar / pues / no *tiene* más que llamar a ese teléfono <Var-Co-211204-13:20>
'*You guys+* [postv.] have our number and (*you guys+*) can use it whenever (*you guys+*) wish to, at any moment, because there's an answering machine. (*You guys+*) can leave us your comments there, since *you guys+* shouldn't believe that we're always in possession of the truth. So, if *you+* consider that anything we may have said is inappropriate, well, (*you+*) only have to call that number.'

When it comes to interactions with specific addressees, functional encoding shows analogous pragmatic values to those observed with *tú* (Section 6.4). *Usted* and *ustedes* subjects sometimes appear in clauses where the speaker or his/her group are simultaneously encoded as central objects, suggesting the audience is accorded a more active role that includes the basic right to speak and be listened to, as recognized through partly pragmaticalized turn-yielding constructions such as *dígame* '(you+) tell (me)' (see also Chapter 4, example 44). In (46), B grants speaker status to A through the same expression. The latter participant, after uttering the conversational marker *mire* '(you+) look', seems to accept that status by encoding herself as the subject and her interlocutor as the object in *le voy a decir* '(I)'ll tell (you+)'.

(46) <A> buenas tardes
<B> ho:la *¡dígame!* /
<A> pues *mire* e:s sobre esta señora que ha hablao del Gran Hotel que tiene toda la razón <...> porque *le voy* a decir que son: / sesenta y tres familias y las que van al Monterrey son TRES p- / empleaos / TRES <Var-SE-211204-13:55>

'A: Good afternoon. – B: Hi. (*You+*) tell (*me*)! – A: Well, (*you+*) look, it's about this lady who just talked about the Gran Hotel, well, she's absolutely right. [...] Because (*I*)'ll tell (*you+*) that there are sixty-three families there, and only three of them are going to be hired at the Monterrey.'

As also noted with regard to the prototypical second persons, the displaced second ones are rarely encoded as the objects of *gustar*-type verbs. As we know, this kind of syntactic-semantic context represents a reversal of the prototypical association between objects and lower salience – it is the human cognizer or experiencer that is encoded as the syntactic object – which makes OVS the unmarked ordering and partly explains the high frequencies of preverbal placement obtained with first- and second-person object pronouns. Its practical absence with *ustedes* is coherent with the fact that the latter person is the only one that apparently prefers postverbal placement when encoded as an object. It is also rare for speakers to attribute a personal stance or feeling to individual addressees; when this happens, it is usually done in the form of a question or hypothesis. Also, in (47), the interviewer presents such a kind of stance as a fact in the past, probably based on older statements made by the interviewee. 5 of the 8 preverbal *usted* object tokens in the corpus actually have *gustar*-type verbs.

(47) –*A usted le* gustaba el barcelonista Sergio.
–Sí, pero me ha dicho Beguiristain que hay problemas y no pueden desprenderse de delanteros. <Ent-Ga-121203-49>
'A: *You+* used to like (lit. *To you* pleased) the Barcelona player S. – B: Yes, but B. told me there are some problems and they cannot dispense with any strikers.'

Finally, the strong preference of semispecific uses of *ustedes* for subject encoding is also related to the discursive and interactional contexts where they typically appear, namely written-press interviews where journalists inquire about the activities of the company or group represented by the interviewee. This is almost invariably made through the encoding of the second person as the clause subject, as in (48) and (49). As is usual in these contexts (see §7.2.2; §8.2.2), the answers tend to reproduce the plural number of the questions, showing the self-construction of speakers as groups. In turn, *gustar*-type and other kinds of verbal lexemes encoding human participants as objects are uncommon in such interviews.

(48) –¿Desde cuándo lleva funcionando esta empresa en Salamanca y a qué *se dedican* exactamente?
–*Llevamos* en este sector desde el año 1966. Nuestra actividad esencial se basa en el sector de la música <Ent-Ad-121203-18>
'A: How long has this company operated in Salamanca and what do (*you guys+*) exactly do? – B: (*We*)'ve been in the sector since 1966. Our activities are essentially centered on the music sector.'

(49) <A> *quieren ustedes* además que (el alcalde) intervenga en los plenos / cosa que: no hace: / m m:ás que / para cosas muy determinadas ¿no? <. . .>
<B> lo *vamos* a seguir haciendo / *vamos* a seguir: / pidiendo s:u opinión en temas que sean de relevancia para la ciudaz <Inf-SE-180603-14:20>
'A: *You guys+* [postv.] also want [the mayor] to speak in the Town Council meetings, which is something he does only in quite specific occasions, right? [. . .] – B: (*We*)'ll keep doing it. (*We*)'ll keep asking for his opinion on any issues that may be relevant for the town.'

8.5 Summary

The Spanish displaced second persons show a number of functional and cognitive peculiarities derived from their intermediate status between the prototypical second and third persons. While *usted* and *ustedes* are commonly described as second-person pronouns, they correlate with third-person subject and object morphemes that construct addressees and audiences as physically, socially and cognitively detached from the speaker. This is coherent with their traditional, intuitive characterizations as address forms indicating "distance", "formality" or "respect". While their behavior clearly tends to resemble that of the persons indexing the direct participants – as evidenced by e.g. the categoricity of object marking with *a*, the near-categoricity of clitic agreement and the apparent tendency to the loss of case distinctions in clitics – at the same time they display atypical patterns such as a marked preference for the postposition of subject pronouns to the verb, in the fashion of inflectional morphemes. This makes it possible to envisage the development of a special conjugational subparadigm, in parallel to a particular way of participant construction that is essentially different from those of other grammatical persons.

Although communicative choices need not be studied in comparison with supposed alternatives – as is most often done in studies of linguistic variation – it is often difficult to overlook the fact that, in Peninsular Spanish, *usted* and *ustedes* are marked choices as against prototypical *tú* and *vosotros*. However, such markedness largely depends on the communicative domain and situation, with a good number of press and radio genres clearly preferring the displaced persons (see further Section 9.4). Also, they are not necessarily equivalent as regards their referential possibilities. While singular *usted* can construct either specific and nonspecific addressees, in the corpus it is not used with the speaker-inclusive reference characterizing many indexations of the prototypical second person. In turn, *ustedes* is similar to *vosotros* in its potential to construct specific, semispecific and – most often in the corpus – nonspecific audiences. There are few constructions with either *usted* or *ustedes* that can be considered clearly pragmaticalized, pronoun expression and placement being still variable in most of them.

Both persons have comparably high rates of pronoun expression, and especially of postverbal placement, which could be viewed as a functional vestige of the lexical origin of the stressed forms. However, their striking tendency to appear immediately after the verb suggests a functional analogy with subject-agreement morphemes, which may also be favored by the potential ambiguity of third-person verbal endings. As exposed with other pronouns, the VSO pattern indexes an intermediate status between salience and informativeness and helps present the content as presupposed and commonly accepted. When it comes to functional encoding, *usted* and *ustedes* respectively align with the prototypical singular and plural second persons. The lower percentages of subject encoding with both plural persons are largely related to their usually fuzzier references. The encoding of audiences as objects is more usual when the latter are nonspecific and communication is viewed as unidirectional, with no intent to accord listeners any responsibility in the construction of discourse. Conversely, it is usual for radio broadcasters to construct their specific interlocutors as subjects and assume a subordinate position with regard to them, for example in turn-yielding contexts.

The preceding five chapters have been devoted to the separate study of the different first and second persons of Spanish. Many of the findings exposed make it possible to infer that these persons, with their variable contextual references and syntactic possibilities, are used by people taking part in media interactions to develop communicative styles – understood as semiotic systems linking discursive-cognitive and contextual meanings – that are perceived as advantageous for the achievement of personal and professional goals. We have already pointed out a number of facts regarding the stylistic values of choices, which as will be seen can be formalized along a general continuum between subjectivity and objectivity. The different features of syntactic choice considered in the present study – person indexation, person choice, pronoun expression and placement, functional encoding – can in turn be analyzed as concretions of that continuum according to more specific stylistic dimensions, such as involvement or responsibility. For these reasons, in the remaining two chapters of this book we will more systematically explore the construction of styles, respectively through the consideration of linguistic choice across textual genres and across participant identities in media communication.

9 The construction of style across textual genres

9.1 Linguistic choice and sociocommunicative style

Cognitive sociolinguistics has recently emerged as a research paradigm that aims at analyzing linguistic variation from both the cognitive and social perspectives, seeking to provide a more comprehensive understanding of the construction of meaning and its variation across contexts (Pütz/Robinson/Reif 2014; see also Croft 2009; Hollmann 2013). From another point of view, the aim of cognitive sociolinguistics would be to extend the focus of research from individual cognition towards social or collective cognition (Kristiansen/Dirven 2008). In spite of its view of language structure as usage-based and of meaning as experiential in nature, the truth is that mainstream functional and cognitive linguistics has rarely taken into consideration the social and cultural values shaping communicative events in specific human communities – just as most sociolinguistic research, due to its disregard for differences in meaning, has squandered the chance to achieve theoretical adequacy (Section 1.2). The dual cognitive and social nature of language stems from its being the most fundamental resource for both the organization of human thought and its communication to others; therefore, a theoretical frame that can systematize the relationship between both facets appears as a desirable goal.

We may say that the preceding analyses of the first and second persons in Spanish media discourse are of a cognitive sociolinguistic nature, inasmuch as the linguistic choices under study have been simultaneously viewed as constructing discursive-cognitive meanings and as realizing communication among people across social contexts. In the last two chapters of this book it is our intention to go deeper into the parallel construction of the cognitive scene – i.e. any particular event as developed in cognition – and the social context where communication takes place. Linguistic choices related to the first and second persons will be seen as meaningful resources with the power to carry out such a parallel construction. Also, we will propose *style* as the fundamental notion whereby both domains are connected, and the features of variation and choice analyzed as revealing particular dimensions of style.

It is first necessary to attempt an approximation to what should be understood by style. The term will be used to encapsulate the construction of meanings through semiotic – in our case, primarily linguistic – choices *in particular sociocommunicative contexts*. The underlining of the last segment is intended to emphasize the fact that style begs for a social approach, even if the latter may

https://doi.org/10.1515/9783110643442-010

turn out to be different from those usually characterized as sociolinguistic. However, the definition is also partly tautological in the sense that no linguistic choice can be made *outside of a particular sociocommunicative context*. As famously pointed out by Labov (1972, xiii), every linguistic theory or practice is necessarily social, even those not intended to be. The important point to be inferred for the present investigation is that linguistic choices are meaningful at a variety of levels, including so-called extralinguistic, i.e. sociodemographic and situational ones (see also Section 1.1). Perhaps more accurately, they contribute not just to the construction of "internal" meanings, but also to that of sociocommunicative contexts as well as of the personal and social identities of those who take part in them. These are all facets of meaning that need not be excluded from scientific analysis.

Research on linguistic variation has traditionally drawn a distinction between its interspeaker (*social*) and intraspeaker (*stylistic*) axes, that is, between the patterning of linguistic choices in relation to sociodemographic speaker groupings – according to age, gender, ethnicity, socioeconomic status, educational achievement and so on – and the behavior of each individual speaker across different communicative situations – often ordered along a general formality-informality scale. Mainstream variationism always granted primacy to the social axis, with the aim of describing general patterns of linguistic variation and change in speech communities (Chambers 2003, ch. 1; Patrick 2006). Even analytical frames devoting special attention to linguistic style, most significantly Bell's audience design model (e.g. 1984; 2001), have tended to view variation across communicative situations as subsidiary to that existing across social groups. In turn, in recent times the focus of interest has progressively moved to the ways speakers use language in different communicative contexts, as a means of achieving transactional, relational and identity goals. This change is parallel to a shift from structure to use, as well as from speech to speaking (cf. Zenner/Kristiansen/Geeraerts 2016, 40 and references therein). Contrary to Bell's proposal, Finegan and Biber's (1994; 2001) model of register variation views the social axis as subordinate to the stylistic one. This view is based on the reasoning that the range of expressive possibilities available to a speaker will be derived from the range of communicative situations he/she has access to. As already discussed in Chapter 1, their hypothesis echoes significant points of Bernstein's (1971) as well as Lavandera's (1978; 1984) approaches to variation and choice, as the authors themselves acknowledge.

Irrespective of whether it is social or situational variation that is given theoretical primacy, the very distinction between axes of variation and the discussion about their relative ordering reveals the persistence of structural views of both language and society, whose usefulness from a functional and cognitive perspective as adopted here is at most limited. The sociolinguistic categories handled usually appear as intricately mixed in human communities; social and situational variation are actually part of a continuum (Serrano/Aijón Oliva 2013, 410–411). It is however true that any sociolinguistic approach to variation and choice probably entails some degree of simplification, particularly whenever supposedly discrete social and situational categories are isolated for the sake of quantitative analysis. This amounts to saying that it is probably impossible to fully overcome the structuralism of variationist sociolinguistic studies, at least in an investigation with a quantitative component.

On the other hand, it is indeed possible to make research more realistic through the consideration of culture- and domain-specific categories formulated through ethnographic observation. In the investigation to be carried out, communicative situations will be reformulated as *textual genres* (see the following section), and speaker groups as *socioprofessional identities* (see Sections 10.1, 10.2). These notions need to be viewed as dynamic and co-constructive. Genres require the enactment of certain participant identities to be recognized as such – e.g. the *judge*, the *attorney*, the *advocate* and the *accused* in a trial – just as such identities can be partly or totally deprived of sense if taken out of the appropriate situation. Neither facet of stylistic construction will be thought to have primacy over the other, even if the general organization of the corpus according to genres might lead to assume that it is the latter that condition the rest of situational features, including participant identities – and in fact this is the case to a certain extent. In media communication, genres are the basic formats whereby discourse is packed and offered to audiences. However, as will be observed, many of these genres – and particularly oral ones – are quite eclectic formats allowing for a wide degree of stylistic variation, just as participants can shift from one type of identity to another, depending on their communicative goals and on the way interactions unfold.

In short, style is a complex phenomenon that is best described as the intersection of cognition, language and society. The basic discursive-cognitive notions handled across this book – salience and informativeness – have been seen as undetachable from linguistic choices – grammatical person, functional encoding, variable expression and placement – as well as from their pragmatic effects when projected onto particular contexts – emphasis, contrastiveness, presupposition and so on. Now it is also necessary to analyze the connection between all elements involved in variation and the social milieu where language is put to use; in other words, to investigate why the variable distribution of non-synonymous constructions across genres and identities can at the same time be indexical of social meanings, following the basic principle that choice is meaningful at all possible "internal" and "external" levels. In order to adequately frame the analysis of the first and second persons as elements of stylistic construction, some further theoretical notions will need to be developed in the following subsection.

9.1.1 Subjectivity, intersubjectivity and objectivity

The investigation will start from the hypothesis that the stylistic values of linguistic choices can be characterized according to a discursive-cognitive-social, i.e. stylistic continuum from *subjectivity* to *objectivity*, as already proposed in Aijón Oliva (2013, 585–587), Aijón Oliva/Serrano (2013, 146–150) and other works adopting the same approach. The present study will further incorporate the systematic consideration of *intersubjectivity* as an intermediate notion, as well as assume that the proposed continuum need not be a single or unitary one; rather, different linguistic choices can result in different stylistic characterizations or dimensions. A particular dimension of the general stylistic continuum will in fact be associated with each of the phenomena under study.

The notion of subjectivity encapsulates the tendency to build discourse from the viewpoint of the direct participants, and particularly that of the speaker (see e.g. Langacker 1987, 131–133; Croft/Cruse 2004, 62–63; Traugott 2010, 31–33). Conversely, the detachment from personal viewpoints will endow discourse with higher objectivity (Albentosa/Moya 2000; Farrar/Jones 2002, 6). Actually, any choice displacing the viewpoint of discourse from that of the speaker, such as the use of a second person instead of a first one, can be considered objectivizing (Serrano/Aijón Oliva 2012; 2014). From a functional-cognitive approach, these abstract notions need to be seen as undetachable from the linguistic choices enacting them across discourse – as manifested in the very terms *subject* and *object*. They are also clearly connected with “subjective” vs. “objective” interpretations of discourse and of those producing it in the non-specialized sense of the terms, whose relevance in public communication hardly needs emphasizing.

For its part, intersubjectivity will be understood as the construction of discourse from a shared viewpoint, normally as an extension from that of the speaker towards that of a wider human group where the addressee or audience will ideally be included (cf. Nuyts 2006, 14; Sidnell 2010, 12). In this sense, choices such as audience-inclusive *nosotros* (§5.2.3) and speaker-inclusive *tú* (§6.2.3) are often motivated by a clear intersubjectivizing intention. They imply desubjectivization with respect to clearly subjective choices – prototypically the singular first person – but, being still participant indexations, are also at a distance from the pole of objectivity. Actually, the restriction of the present investigation to the realm of the first and second persons will make it difficult to talk about objectivity proper, except perhaps in discursive contexts where personal indexations are altogether suppressed. For the same reason, *desubjectivization* would appear as a more accurate term to describe the stylistic meaning of choices intended to reduce subjectivity while not being objective in themselves. Of course, its difference with *objectivization* is basically one of perspective.

The degree of subjectivity vs. objectivity of discourse can hardly be independent of the values simultaneously constructed by co-occurring semiotic systems. In sociocommunicative contexts, subjectivity is associated with features such as orality, interactivity, self-involvement and argumentation. In turn, the opposite features – literacy, lack of interaction, self-detachment, information or exposition, etc. – are characteristic of objective styles. Oral communication is prototypically more subjective than writing (see e.g. Dahl 2000, 58; Vázquez Rozas/García-Miguel 2006). It is little wonder that scientific and academic prose should usually be written in the third person, with rare if any first- and second-person indexations (Biber/Conrad/Reppen 1998, 149–153). That not all communicative domains and textual genres are equally inclined to subjectivity vs. objectivity is even an intuitive fact. This also comes to support one of the principles posed from the beginning of the present study, and which is of capital importance if a truly scientific approach to style is to be developed: if variation is not just formal but also meaningful, the external covariations of any linguistic choice should somehow be related to its internal meanings. In other words, the frequent association of certain linguistic forms with certain social groups and communicative situations should be explained with regard to what those forms are able to construct in speakers' cognition, and not just as a manifestation of – presumably haphazard – psychosocial evaluations.

Subjectivity, intersubjectivity and objectivity will thus be seen as inherently connected with the viewpoints adopted by speakers for the construction of discourse, in which the choice of grammatical persons and their ways of formal and functional encoding no doubt play a major role. The development of styles based on these dimensions can and should be approached from both quantitative and qualitative perspectives. As we will have the chance to observe across the analysis, it is not infrequent for media genres and participant identities to be apparently subjective on account of some linguistic choices and apparently objective as regards others. This is because each linguistic feature reveals a particular facet of the subjectivity-objectivity continuum; it is their joint action that gives rise to a specific sociocommunicative style. Thus the description and explanation of styles will be more accurate the more linguistic choices and their inherent meanings are taken into account.

9.1.2 Stylistic features considered

Obviously, there are multiple features of grammatical choice that can be analyzed in connection with the construction of textual genres and participant identities. The present investigation will focus on phenomena related to the first and second persons as discussed across the preceding chapters. We have considered six different grammatical subparadigms, each one with a variety of referential possibilities and with three basic features of syntactic variation, namely pronoun formulation, pronoun placement within the clause, and subject vs. functional encoding. The detailed consideration of each choice with each person, across the ten textual genres and four types of socioprofessional identity to be distinguished, would of course take up another entire book. It will thus be necessary to limit quantitative observation to the most significant facts and complement them with the qualitative discussion of recurrent contextual uses, in order to lay the bases for further research on style from a functional-cognitive approach. We will now briefly review the four features to be analyzed: participant indexation, person choice, variable expression and placement of pronouns, and functional encoding. While the last two of them have been studied separately for each person across the preceding chapters, the other two involve the choice among all persons, which is why they have not been raised until the meanings and functional peculiarities of each of them have been made clear.

a) *Participant indexation.* Actually, the first matter of variability regarding the first and second persons is the very fact that speakers can either construct them into discourse or not. This first feature concerns the overall amount of first- and second-person indexations through subject- or object-agreement morphemes adjoined to verbal nuclei, across the different textual genres and types of participant identity in the corpus. We will start from the hypothesis that the frequency with which the direct participants are indexed in discourse is a significant stylistic feature, with more frequent indexations enhancing subjectivity, as against less subjective discourse where first- and second-person marks tend to be suppressed. Instead of calculating percentage scores, as has been done throughout the preceding chapters, the kind of analysis proposed begs for a methodological approach based on normalized or *absolute* frequencies (Macaulay 2009, ch. 7; Aijón Oliva/Serrano 2012; 2013, 64–67). These result from the consideration of how many times a particular choice, in this case person agreement morphemes, occurs against an independent measure, in this case word number (see further Section 9.3 for a more detailed exposition of the methodology).

b) *Person choice.* A more accurate stylistic characterization of communicative situations and speaker groups can be achieved by considering the respective normalized frequencies with which the different grammatical persons are indexed in discourse. The singular first person will be deemed to entail the highest degree of subjectivity, explicitly associating discourse with the viewpoint of the speaker; in turn, the displaced second persons, correlating with third-person morphemes and thus displacing discourse to the realm of external entities, will be placed closest to the domain of stylistic objectivity within the subparadigms under study. In between there are other grammatical persons that, at least in some of their uses, are clearly associated with intersubjectivity, such as the plural first one in its speaker-blurring and audience-inclusive uses, as well as the singular second one when it is meant to include the speaker. The relative dominance of some grammatical persons over others will reveal stylistic differences associated with the particular features of textual genres and participant identities. Even if this is clearly a complex feature of variation that would merit a much more extensive investigation, here we will try to uncover the most significant patterns of choice and their connections with sociocommunicative styles.

c) *Variable expression and placement of pronouns*. Starting from the discursive-cognitive characterizations we have attributed to each of the three main variants, i.e. omission, preverbal placement and postverbal placement (see especially §1.3.3; §2.3.3), as well as the pragmatic repercussions of their contextual usage, we will analyze whether they are unequally distributed across textual genres and participant groups, thus whether they could be viewed as stylistic features in the communicative domain under study. The preverbal placement of pronouns has been shown to grant their referents – most evidently the speaker – both the salience of the position associated with subject-agents and the relative informativeness of explicit formulation, which results in an enhancement of their involvement in the content of discourse. This variant will thus be hypothesized to represent the highest degree of subjectivity among the variants. In turn, postverbal placement and omission of the pronouns should entail successive steps towards intersubjectivity and objectivity. It will however be necessary to consider these relationships in detail, given the different dimensions involved.

d) *Functional encoding*. Finally, it will be interesting to ascertain whether genres and speaker identity types also differ as to their tendency to encode the direct participants in subject vs. object functions. In this case, the very etymological relationship between *subject* and *subjectivity*, just as between *object* and *objectivity*, offers some clue on the expectable stylistic distribution of syntactic functions. According a participant the syntactic function of subject – again, most clearly when it is the speaker him/herself – will enhance the agency or responsibility of the latter in the content, resulting in higher subjectivity (see e.g.

Section 4.4 on subject vs. object encoding with psychological verbs). However, this fourth and last feature of choice is also a quite complex one and includes many more specific aspects that could be assessed in connection with style construction; the inquiry will necessarily be restricted to the most revealing patterns of choice observed.

The quantitative and qualitative analysis of each of these features will make it possible to infer a more specific dimension of the subjectivity-intersubjectivity-objectivity continuum, in order to better characterize the kinds of styles constructed in media communication. The adequacy of such dimensions could in turn be tested by considering other features of linguistic variation and different communicative domains in future research.

9.2 The study of variation and choice across textual genres

Genres are culture-specific communication formats that are recognizable by the members of a human community, and that entail some expectations regarding participant roles, goals, topics and other features of the communicative situation, but also regarding linguistic forms themselves (Swales 1990, 45–58). They usually promote the development of discursive patterns for linguistic features (Ariel 2008, 62), thus are a significant source of variation. Previous research has resulted in better understanding of the relationship between formal choices and the development of socially recognized types of discourse or of communicative activity. This relationship must be viewed as a bidirectional one – genres establish some kind of communicative behavior as expected or preferable; however, speakers will often have some margin of freedom to exercise creativity and change some aspect of the situation through their choices.

There are a number of previous studies on variation and genre that offer some guidelines for the present one. In an application of Biber's (1995) multi-dimensional approach to Spanish discourse, Biber et al. (2006) describe six functional dimensions manifested in a wide range of grammatical phenomena and along which textual genres are organized. Travis (2007), in a more sociolinguistically-oriented study, considers the relationship between genre and the expression of first-person subject pronouns in spoken Spanish, showing how topic continuity promotes pronoun omission and is more characteristic of highly preplanned and thematically structured discourse. Dumont (2016) is a monographic study on the construction of third-person referents in two spoken genres, namely spontaneous conversation and narrative. It shows the stronger inclination of narrative discourse to high transitivity, with referents more often being accorded agent and patient roles. In line with Travis's study, conversations turn out to have higher rates of full NP expression, as a result of more frequent changes in topic and of lesser shared knowledge between the participants. These and other investigations have unveiled some facets of the relationship between linguistic choices related to person and the construction of textual genres, which is also the subject of this chapter.

The written-press and radio sections of the MEDIASA corpus are divided into five different textual genres each, whose basic socio-interactional features will subsequently be exposed. The selection and characterization of the genres result from our own detailed observation of local media communication in the Spanish town of Salamanca (see further Aijón Oliva 2006a, ch. 3). While the two subcorpora have practically the same extension – some 150,000 words each – the respective word counts of the genres within them are rather unbalanced. This way of configuration was adopted for the sake of representativeness, given the rather disparate space usually occupied by different types of texts in journal issues, as well as the unequal airing time accorded to different program formats in radio programming schedules. However, normalized frequencies according to word number will facilitate comparison when the features under study are not viewed as composed of different alternatives.

The written-press subcorpus has a total 150,582 words. It is divided into the following textual genres:

a) *News items* (59,651 words). This is the most prototypical and frequent type of text in the local written press. They are authored by (sometimes uncredited) journalists and their goal is to provide information about recent events, their causes and consequences, as well as the people involved in them. They are known to typically dispose informations from the most to the least relevant ones, i.e. following an inverted-pyramid structure. These texts should ideally limit themselves to the transmission of information; the intromission of the writer's viewpoint is not generally expected. However, the interpolation of quoted statements amidst the narrative can sometimes cause a significant change in stylistic orientation according to the subjectivity-objectivity continuum. These are often transcriptions of spoken discourse where people expose personal stances and first- and second-person indexations are more likely to appear.
b) *Stories* (30,314 words). Being also written by journalists and with a dominance of the informational and narrative functions, their stylistic features should expectably approach those of the preceding genre. Still, they are differentiated from the latter by their usually greater length and welth of details; together with the main text body, they usually offer additional materials such as images, graphics, or even interviews. Also, the issues dealt with are not necessarily recent news and can include social trends

and matters of everyday life. This is patent from their very headlines, often lacking a verb: *Verano, tiempo para el amor* 'Summer: a time for love' <Rep-Ga-230804-14>; *Los últimos nómadas* 'The last nomads' <Rep-Ga-031104-10>. All this could make it more expectable to find some features associated with subjectivity, but in most cases these will again be limited to transcriptions of oral discourse.

c) *Opinion pieces* (30,128 words). This being a general label encompassing subgenres such as *articles* and *columns*, it denotes argumentative texts written – either on special request or as fixed sections of the newspaper – by people considered to have some kind of social or intellectual prestige. They constitute short essays, never exceeding the boundaries of a page, and can cover quite varied topics, from political and social affairs to recollections and anecdotes, but which will always be approached from a more-or-less personal, argumentative perspective. Opinion pieces also allow for a wide range of expressive choices, often showing strong literary elaboration through comparisons, metaphors or wordplays, just as they can imitate conversational and sometimes even coarse language.
d) *Letters to the editor* (15,201 words). Their wide variety of possible topics and the dominance of personal viewpoints make this genre similar to opinion pieces. The differences are mainly related to the kind of identity displayed by their authors – in this case they are not socially prominent people collaborating with the newspaper, but rather particular, sometimes anonymous citizens who want to express their stances on a certain issue or inform about facts that may be of interest to the rest of the community. Letters also tend to be much shorter than articles, and newspaper editors will sometimes abridge them for the sake of space saving. For the same reason, they need to be more straightforward, with scarce digressions and a narrower variety of expressive resources; they also occasionally contain (arguably unintentional) nonstandard constructions.
e) *Interviews* (15,288 words). The last genre distinguished in the written-press section is related to oral communication, since the texts result from the transcription of previously recorded conversations between an interviewer and someone that is considered of potential interest to media audiences. Of course, interviews are fundamentally different from spontaneous conversations, speech turns being rigidly distributed as question-answer pairs. Besides, their process of conversion into written language can cause alterations in grammatical constructions and lexical choices, particularly in the sense of eliminating repetitions, reformulations and clearly oral features. Interviews often appear as independent texts, but can also be featured as supplementary material to wider texts such as stories.

With regard to the radio subcorpus, it comprises 151,995 words and includes the following genres:

a) *News reports* (18,155 words). These quite short programs, usually with a running time from 5 to 15 minutes, include previously written or scripted informational texts that are read aloud by one or more broadcasters. They can thus be considered functionally similar to written-press news items (see above). Just as the latter, reports are generally expected to limit themselves to the transmission of informational contents and avoid personal viewpoints. However, also in line with written news texts, the frequent insertion of excerpts from recorded interviews or press conferences can cause the appearance of first- and second-person indexations. Also, news segments proper are framed by introductory, transitional and closing comments by broadcasters where they often index themselves, their workteams and/or the audience of the program (see e.g. Chapter 8, example 43).
b) *Talk magazines* (62,483 words). This is the genre taking the greatest word share in the corpus, due to the relative length of the programs and the fact that – in contrast with music ones – they are heavily based on spoken interaction. They are what in more technical terms would be called *generalist* magazines, in contrast to *sectorial* ones such as those devoted to sports or music (see below). Actually, talk magazines are a relatively loose format where many different kinds of materials can be featured, including news segments, interviews, debates, sections for citizen participation, songs, movie reviews, etc. In spite of this – or perhaps for the same reason – they seem to be recognized as a differentiated genre. In most stations they are conducted by the most prominent broadcasters among their staff and aired during the morning and noon hours, which suggests a predominantly female and mature target audience. Still, other magazines broadcast in the evening and more specifically focusing on economic or cultural matters are aimed at different kinds of audiences.
c) *Sports programs* (35,226 words). This modality of sectorial magazines is mainly concerned with the world of soccer, given the massive popularity of this sport in Spanish society, but occasionally pay attention to other ones. Programs tend to combine recent news and information on upcoming competitions with personal argumentation by broadcasters, as well as interviews to sportspeople and other individuals working within the sector. They are most often aired in the afternoon, and a male target audience is obviously assumed, most broadcasters being male as well. Special editions, most often on weekends, are devoted to the live commentary of soccer games, of which the corpus contains an example (see also §1.3.3).

d) *Music programs* (20,901 words). This other type of magazine has the greater average length, even if its word share in the corpus is relatively small, given that programs mostly consist of successions of songs and brief remarks on them. Still, other kinds of materials can be featured, including news segments, interviews or contests. Most music programs have a young or middle-aged target audience. As will be noted across the analysis, they are singled out by their strong interactional orientation – even if the programs are often scarcely "interactional" in themselves. The focus on the transmission of information that dominates many instances of the preceding genres is replaced by a tendency to exploit interpersonal meanings, which is undetachable from linguistic choices.
e) *Commercials* (15,230 words). Their inclusion in the corpus and in the present investigation is motivated by the peculiarities of advertising discourse and its interest for studies of variation across communicative contexts. However, it must be pointed out that they are not exactly a *genre*, at least in the sense of the preceding ones – i.e. radio formats that can include a wider or narrower variety of textual materials. Rather, commercials are only short recorded clips, generally appearing within or between radio programs, and usually with no transitional sequences. Most of them are aimed at persuading listeners to purchase products or services; the corpus also contains occasional instances of institutional advertising as well as of political propaganda. They can have quite different target audiences depending on their content; however, those audiences will generally be coincident with those of the programs they appear within.

From the preceding characterizations it is easy to conclude that radio genres, leaving aside the special case of commercials and perhaps that of news reports, are conceptually and stylistically more heterogeneous than written-press ones. Rather than text types proper, they constitute general formats where different kinds of texts and interactions can appear. As pointed out, our classification is the result of direct observation over an extended period, and is mainly based on the recurrent ways in which radio contents are presented to audiences, rather than on discursive features themselves. An alternative division of the materials into textual sequences – e.g. informational stretches, recorded clips, interviews, debates, phone calls, etc. – would also have been possible, but would in turn have given rise to other difficulties. The types of sequences to be distinguished and the criteria followed to characterize them would probably entail arbitrary decisions. Also, in actual radio communication, different types of sequences usually appear intermingled; in other cases, there are transition stretches that would also be difficult to categorize for quantitative analysis. In turn, starting from the most recurrent radio formats as they are offered to the public appears as a more objective criterion, even if it will probably result in a less straightforward patterning of the linguistic choices across genres, and will make it necessary to complement general quantitative results with the observation of possible stylistic variability among different sequences within programs.

9.3 Participant indexation

As exposed in §9.1.2, the first feature of stylistic construction to be analyzed, and which shows notorious differences among media genres, is the total frequency of first- and second-person indexations through (subject or object) verbal agreement morphemes. In this case we will not take into account whether there is omission or expression of personal pronouns, but just whether there is morphematic indexation of some direct participant in the verbal nucleus. Discourse will be stylistically more subjective the more indexical marks of the speaker or other participants are formulated across it. In turn, the absence of such marks will mean a displacement from the pole of subjectivity and towards that of objectivity. The proposed correlation between frequency of participant indexation and the stylistic continuum is schematized in Figure 9.1.[1]

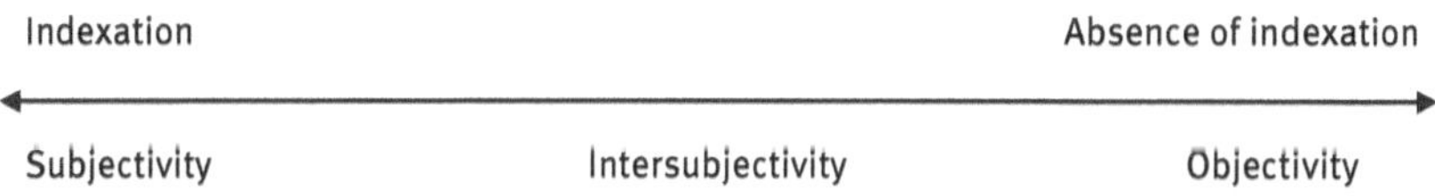

Figure 9.1: Participant indexation along the stylistic continuum.

For each genre in the corpus we will calculate the normalized frequency of person indexations per 1,000 words. That is, the number of tokens in each genre will be multiplied by 1,000 and then divided by its total number of words, in

1 As will be discussed, the status of intersubjectivity in this and other stylistic continua is not so clear. The avoidance of first- and second-person indexations across discourse can in principle respond to either an intersubjectivizing intention – if aimed at promoting the co-construction of discourse with the audience – or an objectivizing one – if intended to altogether detach the viewpoint of discourse from the direct participants. A list of normalized frequencies such as we are going to present will be of little use unless complemented with the discussion of what those frequencies mean for the construction of textual genres in actual instances of usage.

order to obtain comparable data across the genres (Aijón Oliva/Serrano 2012, 86; see also Biber/Conrad/Reppen 1998, Methodology Box 6). The choice of 1,000 as the basis for normalization – rather than e.g. 100 or 10,000 – seems most adequate considering both the reduced size of the corpus and the low frequency of the features under study in some textual genres. It will generally make it possible to obtain frequencies above 1; at the same time, all genres contain enough portions of 1,000 words for the counts to be representative. The results are displayed in Table 9.1. The respective total frequencies for the written-press and radio subcorpora are also presented in the table, in order to facilitate a general comparison between basic communicative modes, even if the continuous nature of the literacy-orality dimension should be evident from the very characterizations of some genres – e.g. interviews, radio news reports – in the preceding section.

Table 9.1: Frequency of participant indexation according to textual genre.

Genre	Word count	First- and second-person forms	Frequency per 1,000 words
News items	59,651	221	3.7
Stories	30,314	201	6.6
Opinion pieces	30,128	678	22.5
Letters	15,201	458	30.1
Interviews	15,288	611	40
Press total	150,582	2,169	14.4
News reports	18,155	382	21
Talk magazines	62,483	2,773	44.4
Sports programs	35,226	1,302	37
Music programs	20,901	977	46.7
Commercials	15,230	823	54
Radio total	151,995	6,257	41.2

Actually, the difference between both sections of the corpus is a notorious one, radio discourse expectably showing a much higher frequency of participant indexations (41.2 against 14.4 tokens per 1,000 words). In fact, roughly three quarters of the total cases appear in this subcorpus, which translates into its normalized frequency almost tripling that of the press. However, it must be noted that there are also wide differences inside each subcorpus, and that some written genres actually surpass some oral ones – e.g. journal interviews have a higher frequency than either radio news reports or sports programs – which makes it necessary to further examine the motivations for the different results.

First, it is possible to suspect the relevance of the oral vs. literate stylistic dimension considered by Biber et al. (2006, 12) to be involved in Spanish genre variation, and which has first- and second-person pronouns among its many characterizing features. According to the authors, higher frequencies of participant indexation correlate with greater proximity to the prototype of oral communication. This dimension relates to more specific communicative features such as informational vs. interactional orientation, as well as the degrees of speaker self-involvement and of discourse pre-planning, all of which are also manifested in the genres under study. This is of course not meant to say that all written discourse is highly informative and scarcely interactive. The two genres with the lowest frequencies of person indexations are written news items and stories, which are indeed the ones closest to the literate prototype. They are oriented to the transmission of (objective) information, and despite their urgency – particularly in the case of news items – they can be considered to be highly pre-planned. For these reasons, the adoption of a third-person viewpoint is almost inescapable; first- and second-person indexations are only expectable in quoted statements inserted within the narrative or exposition, usually conveying personal stances and experiences of the main actors or the groups they include themselves in (example 1). Also, in stories dealing with everyday matters is it possible to find occasional instances of inclusive plural first persons produced by journalists themselves. In (2), the writer builds on a general belief – "modern societies are materialistic" – that no one is expected to challenge, and thus does not seem to threaten the objectivity demanded by this genre.

(1) A pesar de todo, prefirió no revelar los resultados de los contactos hasta que exista un acuerdo firme. "Lo que *quiero* decir a los ciudadanos es que *tenemos* el mismo interés que ellos en encontrar un lugar adecuado, y nuestra intención es dar una solución rápida al problema", manifestó. <Not-Ad-290104-16>
'Even so, he would rather not reveal the results of the contacts made until a final agreement is reached. "What (*I*) want to tell the citizens is that (*we*) are just as interested as they are in finding an adequate location, and it is our intention to find a rapid solution to this issue," he stated.'

(2) La sociedad consumista en la que *vivimos* hace que muchas personas se equivoquen y piensen que la compra de una mascota viva no es muy

diferente a la de un pantalón o un juguete: una simple cuestión de dinero. <Rep-Ad-071204-12>
'The consumerist society (*we*) live in causes many people to wrongly think that buying a living pet is not very different from buying pants or a toy, i.e. just a matter of money.'

All in all, strong pre-planning seems scarcely explanatory as a stylistic dimension, given that it is common to all written-press genres, including opinion pieces and letters to the editor, both of which have considerable frequencies of participant indexation (respectively 22.5 and 30.1). Quite unlike news items and stories, with their strongly desubjectivized presentation of information, these are mainly argumentative texts where writers expose personal stances through first-person indexations (3) and often, especially in letters, also address specific people through prototypical or displaced second-person ones (4).

(3) no *me* conforta que sepamos que han dado su vida en defensa de unos ideales, *me* asusta y estremece pensar en las Navidades que esperan a las familias de estos españoles asesinados <Art-Ga-221203-5a>
'It doesn't comfort (*me*) to know that they gave their lives in defense of some ideals; it scares (*me*) and makes me tremble to imagine the sort of Christmas holidays that await the families of these murdered Spaniards.'

(4) No *se preocupe* si algún descerebrado –seguro que existe– *le* dice que sus ideas estaban en el PP, no *le* conteste, no merece que *distraiga* tiempo a su trabajo. <Car-Ga-310104-6>
'Don't (*you+*) worry if some brainless folk – there must be some – tells (*you+*) that your positions were those of the PP; don't (*you+*) answer, there's no point in (*you+*) taking time away from your duties.'

From the perspective of both the oral-literate and the informational-interactional continua, it seems understandable that interviews should achieve the highest score (40) of participant indexation among written-press genres. As pointed out, these texts usually result from the transcription of previously recorded oral interactions. The editing of the materials, whereby clearly oral features are often removed or modified in order to adapt the text to the conventions of written discourse, does not seem to significantly affect the stylistic feature under study – but of course a comparison with the original spoken interactions, to which we have no access, would be necessary in order to certify this. There may also be some difference in this respect between the types of interviews respectively labelled *thematic* and *profile* in media jargon. While the former are aimed at collecting information on some topic from an expert in the field, which can result in scarce personal indexations, the latter focus on the personality of a prominent figure and tend to be stylistically quite subjective, as the one in example (5). Note, in passing, the different persons chosen by each participant to address the other – *usted* by the journalist, *tú* by the interviewee, which probably reveals different speaker self-perceptions (see further Section 10.4).

(5) – Y en el fondo, tampoco es que *le* apasione el fútbol.
– Pues no *vas* muy desencaminado. *Yo* todo esto lo *hago*, no por el fútbol en sí, sino por la ciudad, que es lo que más *quiero* y a la que *tengo* la obligación moral de ayudar. <Ent-Ga-121203-49>
'A: And after all, it's not like (*you+*)'re passionate about soccer. – B: Well, (*you*)'re not way off-track. (*I*)'m not doing all this for the sake of soccer, but for that of the town, which is what (*I*) love most and (*I*)'m morally obliged to help.'

In the radio subcorpus there are two genres whose normalized frequencies fall below those of press interviews: sports programs (37 indexations per 1,000 words) and, especially, news reports (21 indexations). The latter case is easily explainable, given that radio news broadcasts mostly consist of previously written texts that are read aloud for the audience. Participant indexations – usually plural ones, referring either to the broadcaster and his/her workteam or to the audience – are restricted to opening, transitional and closing sequences, often with a discourse-organizing function (example 6). They can also occur within inserted clips from recorded interviews, press conferences or speeches (7), i.e. samples of discourse extracted from a different kind of situation, quite in line with quoted segments in written news pieces (see 1 above). As for sports programs, they have similar interactional conditions, although the occasional presence of two or more broadcasters who dialogate between themselves, as well as the more frequent insertion of interviews, result in their frequency of person indexation approaching the average 41.2 tokens of the radio subcorpus.

(6) *se lo contábamos* en titulares / el equipo de gobierno del Ayuntamiento de Salamanca ha presentado hoy un nuevo material informático / que reúne las declaraciones / m:ás importantes realizadas por / Pepe y Pesoe: <Inf-Pu-171204-13:50>
'As (*we*) were telling (*you guys+*) in the headlines, today the government team at the Salamanca Town Council has released new digital materials compiling the most significant statements made by the PP and the PSOE.'

(7) <A> dice / que el esfuerzo de la J:unta: en este ámbito / comienza a dar sus frutos:
<B, grabación> en primer lugar / que todo el mundo conozca las herramientas que *tenemos* a disposición de:.- / de la protección civil / fundamentalmente el uno uno dos / que *entendemos* que es e: la pieza clave en la coordinación <Inf-SE-301104-14:15>
'A: He says the efforts made by the regional government in this area are starting to pay off. – B (*recorded*): First of all, everyone should be aware of the tools (*we*) have at our disposal for civil protection, basically the 112 phone number, which, the way (*we*) see it, is the key element for coordination.'

In turn, radio commercials show the highest frequency of participant indexation among all spoken and written genres (54 tokens per 1,000 words), which in principle seems difficult to explain as a reflection of orality, interactivity or scarce pre-planning – the texts are of course written and carefully edited before being read aloud, with no possibility for the audience to react on the fly. Rather, the figure is mainly due to the fact that commercials are not programs, i.e. extended discursive formats, but rather very short clips with high condensation of the message, and where participant indexation is recurrently put at the service of persuasive goals, even if the contextual conditions are scarcely interactional themselves. As pointed out in §8.2.1, it is usual for second-person indexations – either prototypical (*tú*) or displaced (*usted*) ones – to appear across these texts, together with plural first-person ones denoting the company or group assuming responsibility for the message, as in (8). Thus, while there is not real interactivity with the addressee, there is indeed the *suggestion* of interactivity through typically oral stylistic features such as recurrent personal indexation. The same happens with the genre achieving the second-highest frequency in the corpus, namely music programs. Whereas most of the time there is just a broadcaster talking unidirectionally to an unknown audience, indexations of both participants – the latter most often constructed as an individual addressee – are widespread (9).

(8) trein:ta días únicos con trein:ta artículos irrepetibles / con un trein:ta por ciento de descuento: / los *tienes* en tu casa: / en: treinta hora:s / y *te damos* / trein:ta semanas para paga:r / sin intereses: <Anu-To-080803-12:15>
'Thirty unique days with thirty unrepeatable items, and with a 30% discount. (*You*)'ll have them at your home in thirty hours, and (*we*)'ll give (*you*) thirty weeks to pay interest-free.'

(9) a:y que esto no iba a ser lo mismo: si no *te tuviera* a mi vera / en estos momento:s / *te presentamo:s* en exclusiva en Cadena Dial Salamanca: / el NUEvo disco de nuestro Juan Mari / Montes sí como lo *estás* escuchando: <Mus-Di-200503-12:10>
'Oh, this just wouldn't be the same if (*I*) didn't have (*you*) by my side. At this moment (*we*)'re exclusively introducing (*you*) to the new album by our J. M. M. Yes, just as (*you*)'re hearing.'

Although, as we have observed, there are several sociocommunicative dimensions involved in the quantitative patterning of participant indexations across media genres, from the preceding analysis we can conclude that *interactivity* is the notion that can more accurately characterize the stylistic value of this feature of linguistic choice in the corpus analyzed. Media genres – whether they are written or oral, as well as more or less pre-planned – show an increase in first- and second-person indexations whenever there is an intention to suggest the existence of interaction between the direct participants, and whether such interaction is actually carried out between specific, mutually known interlocutors or not. A high level of interactivity is most often correlative with argumentative and persuasive goals, as in opinion pieces, letters to the editor or commercials. In the case of broadcasters in music programs or talk magazines, it helps enact a more interpersonal kind of relationship with the audience. In Figure 9.2, the ten genres under study have been ordered from the one with the highest frequency of first-

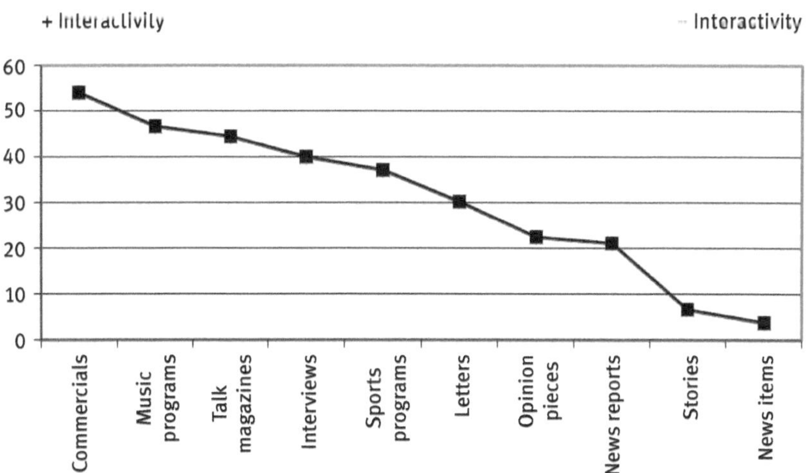

Figure 9.2: Media genres and interactivity (based on frequency of first- and second-person indexations).

and second-person indexations – radio commercials – to that with the lowest one – written news items.

Largely informational, written or read-aloud texts such as news items, stories and radio news reports, according to the dimension of interactivity, are farthest from the pole of subjectivity. While literacy and pre-planning are dimensions typically correlating with lesser interactivity, thus subjectivity, the figure makes it clear that such a correlation is hardly a systematic one. Radio commercials, also being heavily scripted texts, obtain the highest frequency of participant indexations, which is coherent with their strongly persuasive orientation. The remaining genres fall at different points between the poles, which suggests that they also allow for a wider margin of choice regarding interactivity. It is most important to underline the fact that this notion is a *stylistic* one in the sense that it is constructed through linguistic choice; in other words, a certain kind of communicative situation that is scarcely interactional in itself can nevertheless have a high frequency of participant indexations, suggesting that in such a situation it proves advantageous to construct a highly interactive style. As will be seen, the relative ordering of the genres can be quite different according to other phenomena, which justifies the consideration of a variety of stylistic dimensions within the general subjectivity-objectivity continuum. While some genres tend to stick to a certain kind of choices – e.g. news reports and stories to objectivizing ones – others produce quite variable results according to the features considered.

9.4 Person choice

Our next hypothesis is that genres will also be differentiated according to the frequency with which each particular grammatical person is indexed within them. The analysis of person choice can provide a more accurate stylistic description than mere participant indexation, given that grammatical persons help establish a certain viewpoint in discourse, which will have repercussions on its degree of subjectivity vs. objectivity. As done with the previous feature of choice, we can propose an ordering of the persons considered in this study along the general continuum (Figure 9.3).[2]

The singular first person, used to construct the speaker and usually having the individual speaking or writing as its extradiscursive referent, is considered to

2 See similar proposals in Aijón Oliva (2013, 587) and Posio (2016, 6), as well as De Cock (2014, 237), even if the latter considers a wider variety of stylistic dimensions and linguistic phenomena.

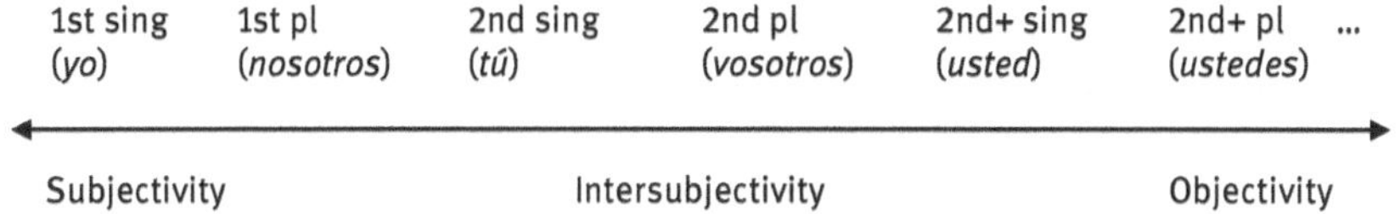

Figure 9.3: Grammatical person choice along the stylistic continuum.

be associated with the highest subjectivity. In discursive contexts characterized by a first-person viewpoint, the content will need to be interpreted as attached to the personal circumstances of the speaker, whether it is actions, processes or states that are described. The plural first person, even if basically subjective – particularly in its audience-exclusive uses – always entails the broadening of the speaker's viewpoint towards a wider human group. When the audience is included in the reference, the choice can be considered intersubjective, since it pursues a cognitive alignment with other participants (see §5.2.3). The singular second person is also intersubjective in the sense that it entails for the speaker to assume the viewpoint of the addressee; in speaker-inclusive uses of this person, there is often a notorious intention to desubjectivize the content by apparently attributing it to the other while still sharing it (§6.2.3). The remaining persons under study are progressively closer to the pole of objectivity. In the plural second one (*vosotros*), the speaker, with rare exceptions, can no longer be referentially included; as for the displaced second persons, they are halfway between the second and third ones. As discussed in Chapter 8, the basic cognitive meaning of these choices is the displacement of addressees and audiences away from the speaker; they are thus objectivizing in comparison with the prototypical second person.

On the other hand, plural persons are always less subjective than the corresponding singular ones, since they construct participants as part of wider groups, thus help avoid the adoption of individual viewpoints. The desubjectivizing power of *nosotros* as against *yo* was discussed in §5.2.1; similarly, the construction of an audience through either *vosotros* or *ustedes* is inherently less subjective than that of an individual addressee. Even so, objectivity proper can only be achieved through the adoption of third-person or impersonal viewpoints, which are not specifically addressed in this study. And even in such cases different constructions will most probably result in different degrees of objectivization.

In any case, Figure 9.3 is just an ideal model of what in real usage will appear as a rather heterogeneous range of possibilities. It could be argued that *usted*, often denoting a specific addressee, might be no less (inter)subjective than the singular second person in the same context – although it rarely allows for speaker-inclusive uses. Similarly, *tú*, when addressed to a specific participant, may seem more subjective than audience-inclusive *nosotros*. Therefore, the proposed ordering is based solely on the inherent meaning of each person as described across the preceding chapters. It is also obvious that subjectivity can be further nuanced through simultaneous choices such as intended reference, formal configuration and functional encoding (see the following sections), all of which correlate with variations in referent salience.

Table 9.2 shows the absolute frequencies per 1,000 words of each of the six grammatical persons in each of the genres considered, as well as their respective total scores in the written and oral sections of the corpus.

Table 9.2: Frequency of each grammatical person according to textual genre.

Genre	1st sing	1st pl	2nd sing	2nd pl	2nd+ sing	2nd+ pl
News items	1.4	2	0.2	0	0	0
Stories	3.2	2.6	0.5	0.3	0.1	0
Opinion pieces	9.7	9.4	1.8	0	1	0.6
Letters	12.4	10.6	1.3	0.4	4.6	0.9
Interviews	17.9	10.9	3.5	0.2	6.8	0.8
Press total	6.2	5.4	1	0.1	1.4	0.3
News reports	4.8	11.9	0.6	0.2	0.7	2.8
Talk magazines	14.7	19.9	2.9	0.6	3.4	2.9
Sports programs	15.6	11.1	7.9	1	0.2	1.1
Music programs	7.7	18.5	17.8	2.4	0.2	0.2
Commercials	2.8	10.9	26.5	0.4	12.2	1.2
Radio total	11.6	15.8	8.2	0.9	2.8	1.9

The heterogeneity of the results obtained merits some detailed analysis. The singular first person is altogether the most frequent one in the written-press subcorpus (6.2 indexations) and in each of its specific genres, except for news items, where it is slightly surpassed by the plural first one. Its frequencies are quite higher in the more argumentative genres – opinion pieces and letters – and especially in interviews. The three of them seem to naturally allow for the construction of individual speakers expressing personal stances and experiences; style will thus be closer to the pole of subjectivity than in the more informational genres. The very act of writing an opinion piece for a journal tacitly grants the author the right to speak for him/herself, as in (10). Basically the same can be said of people agreeing to do an interview (11).

(10) *Me temo* que tampoco *digiero* bien el triunfalismo ante los datos del paro del mes de julio. *He visto*, leído y oído opiniones varias al respecto. *Me* parecen sensatas la mayoría de ellas, menos las de los políticos. <Art-Tr-060804-6>
'(*I*)'m afraid (*I*) can't easily digest the triumphalism about the unemployment figures in July. (*I*) have seen, read and heard various opinions in this regard. Most of them seem reasonable (*to me*), except for those of politicians.'

(11) – ¿Habrás recibido muchas felicitaciones?
– Muchas. *He recibido* mucho apoyo, sobre todo de Arturo, mi profesor. *Me* gusta ver cómo la gente aprecia la poesía, porque *veo* literatura en la vida cotidiana de cada persona. <Ent-Ga-030604-18>
'A: You surely have received a lot of compliments? – B: A lot of them. (*I*)'ve received a lot of support, especially from A., my teacher. It pleases (*me*) to see how people appreciate poetry, since (*I*) can see literature in the everyday life of each person.'

In turn, the plural first person is the second most usual choice in all written genres except for news items, where it surpasses the singular. As we know, informational genres tend to be very low in the dimension of interactivity; provided there is any sort of participant indexation, it is usually of speakers themselves or their audience-exclusive groups amidst quoted segments, showing the construction of a first-person extended viewpoint (12), much like in interviews.

(12) "Hace un mes el Rectorado *nos* pidió un plano sobre el espacio físico que *ocupábamos*. Aún no *hemos recibido* una respuesta", señala Purificación Galindo, directora de este Departamento <Not-Ga-121203-9>
' "A month ago, the University governing board asked (*us*) to submit a plan of the physical space (*we*) occupied. To date (*we*) have received no answer", states P. G., head of this department.'

Argumentative written genres oscillate between the audience-exclusive and inclusive uses of *nosotros*. Authors of letters to the editor often write on behalf of a particular group in which the audience is not necessarily included (example 13). However, the power of inclusive *nosotros* to suggest the alignment of viewpoints with the readership also makes it a useful choice in the same genre. Thus, in (14), after expressing a personal acknowledgment, the writer involves both herself and the readers in her plea for stronger social commitment.

(13) Hoy, con motivo del Día de Terapia Ocupacional, *queremos* dar a conocer nuestra profesión. Para ello *hemos preparado* carteles explicativos que estarán colocados en las distintas facultades. <Car-Ad-171104-6a>
'Today, on the occasion of Occupational Therapy Day, (*we*) want to publicize our profession. With this goal (*we*) have elaborated explanatory posters that will be on display at the different schools.'

(14) *Quiero*, una vez más, agradecer la importante labor de la Casa de los Pobres durante todo el año, y ojalá *todos aprendiéramos* de esas personas que dedican parte de su tiempo libre a ayudar a los demás. <Car-Ga-200804-6a>
'Once again (*I*) want to thank the House of the Poor for their continued work throughout the year, and I wish *we all* would follow the example of those who devote part of their free time to helping others.'

Therefore, singular and plural first persons are the most expectable kinds of participant indexation in the written press. As regards the singular second person, its use is rare, with the understandable exception of interviews. In the remaining genres, most tokens are speaker-inclusive, that is, they express personal contents and stances that are intersubjectivized through this grammatical choice, as evidenced by the quoted segments in (15).

(15) Beatriz Santiago acoge con resignación la lesión que ha obligado a cambiar sus planes: "*puedes* entrenar y competir menos", señala. Según Santiago, "si *haces* rodajes largos se *te* irrita y *te* molesta". <Not-Tr-041104-58>
'B. S. resigns herself to the injury that has forced her to change her plans: "(*You*) cannot train and compete as much", she states. According to S., "If (*you*) go a long way, it becomes irritated (*on you*) and bothers (*you*)." '

As for referentially specific contexts, *usted* is usually considered to be a more appropriate treatment than *tú*, as becomes patent when observing the respective frequencies of both persons in letters and interviews. Unless there is the suggestion of previous acquaintance or of coincident group affiliation between the participants, the public nature of the interactions as well as their often contentious orientation lead most authors to opt for the displaced second person. In interviews this can happen even with quite young interviewees, such as the supermarket cashier in (16) (compare, however, with 11 above, where a teenage student was addressed with *tú*). *Usted* is generally perceived as enhancing the social status of the addressee, as well as the seriousness of the interaction altogether (Blas Arroyo 2005, 298–300).

(16) – ¿Alguna vez *ha tenido* la tentación de cobrarle mal a alguien?
– No, porque yo sería la primera afectada. <Ent-Ga-260804-17>
'A: Have (*you+*) ever felt tempted to charge anyone more than due?
– B: No, because I'd be the first one to bear the brunt.'

Person choice across radio genres responds to partially different conditionings. The singular first person is still a quite frequent choice – with scores expectably higher than those of some written genres – which suggests that the construction of an overtly subjective style is expectable in some situations. However, only in sports programs is it the most frequent one, which can be put in connection with their argumentative orientation; anchors and collaborators are often expected to express personal stances, in contrast with e.g. news reports or even talk magazines. In commercials, both *tú* and *usted* surpass *yo*. This is again indicative of the strongly persuasive orientation of advertising discourse (see the preceding section).

In the remaining radio genres, speakers often elude self-encoding and opt for a plural viewpoint whereby they construct themselves into a wider group – the radio station, an association, a political party, etc. (see also Bull/Fetzer 2006, 14–15). The greater exposure of speakers before their audiences and the frequent need to seek agreement with others result in some preference for the plural, either with exclusion or inclusion of the audience. Both referential possibilities are exploited in (17), as is patent across the successive instances of *tenemos* 'we have', whose intended reference oscillates between the whole population of the town and the team of the radio station, or perhaps just the broadcaster in a speaker-blurring use of the plural person.

(17) no *podemos ajustarnos* / a:l eslogan: / del más que ayer / pero menos que mañana / porque / m: / hoy / efectivamente *tenemos* / MÁS temperatura que ayer / pero no va a ocurrir eso mañana / hoy *tenemos* que decirles que *tenemos* una jornada: / plenamente veraniega muy calurosa: <Var-Co-230503-13:20>
'(*We*) cannot adjust to the "more than yesterday but less than tomorrow" motto, because today (*we*) indeed have a higher temperature than yesterday, but it won't be the same tomorrow. As for today, (*we*) have to tell you guys+ that (*we*) have a fully summer day, a very hot one.'

As regards the second persons, *tú* achieves high scores in both music and sports programs, but it does so under different conditions in either case. While in the former genre it is regularly addressed to the nonspecific audience (18), in the latter one it is almost categorically used to construct specific participants, either partner journalists (as in 19) or interviewees. These examples show that second-person indexations are always correlative with some increase in interactivity, and usually go together with indexations of the speaker, highlighting the co-constructed nature of discourse. The connection between the different stylistic dimensions under study is often quite evident.

(18) si lo que *necesitas* es una: / dosis de energía extra puesto que *estamos* en el: otoño ya: y parece que las temperaturas van a bajar / bueno pues: / *prepárate* a escuchar esto <Mus-Ci-230903-16:30>
'If it is an extra dose of energy that (*you*) need, given that (*we*)'re already in fall and it seems that the temperature is going to drop, well, (*you*) get ready to hear this.'

(19) <A> antes de: continuar adelante / ¿*has: felicitado* a tu madre hoy? /
<B> m: sí: bueno cuando me::- esta mañana / a primera hora *me he levantado* y *he dicho* "mamá felicidades" pero bueno si eso la *felicito* otra vez /
<A> cumpleaños de mamá no es: todos los días así que *aprovecha* / *te doy:* unos segundos: <Dep-SE-210504-15:20>
'A: Before moving on – did (*you*) compliment your mother today? – B: Yes, well, when (*I*) got up this morning (*I*) said "Happy birthday, Mom". But anyway, (*I*) could compliment her again now. – A: It's not Mom's birthday every day, so (*you*) go ahead. (*I*)'ll give (*you*) a few seconds.'

Therefore, the use of *tú* – or, more rarely, *vosotros* – to address the nonspecific audience is practically restricted to commercials and music programs. The other three genres will opt for the displaced second persons, and especially the plural one. Both (20) and (21) are typical examples of closing sequences using this person, respectively taken from a news report and a talk magazine (see also Section 8.3 on constructions like *saben ustedes*).

(20) información: local: / también la *tienen* en Localia Televisión: / que *tengan* buena tarde <Inf-SE-180603-14:30>
'(*You guys+*) also have the local news at Localia TV. (*You guys+*) have a good evening.'

(21) mañana / ya *saben ustede:s* / que: abriremos / esa: Radio de la Memoria / a su llamada y participación / la Plaza: / como escenario / de nuestros / r: ecuerdos <Var-SE-230903-14:00>
'Tomorrow, as *you guys+* know, we'll open the Radio of Memory to your calls and contributions. The Square will be the setting for our memories.'

It is remarkable that it should be *tú* and *ustedes*, pertaining to different grammatical persons and numbers, that prove to be the most usual choices to address nonspecific audiences in radio communication. The explanation may lie in the fact that they represent opposite values within the domain of second persons, regarding cognitive proximity and individuation of the addressee. When there is an intention to suggest good rapport and intimacy – as is often the case in music programs – *tú* will help construct every potential listener as an individual addressee. In turn, when it is personal detachment and professionalism that are considered more advantageous for the attainment of communicative goals, speakers will resort to *ustedes* as if addressing a plural audience in a formal setting (see Aijón Oliva 2018b on the choice among the second persons in broadcasters' speech). Finally, as pointed out in §8.2.1, the distribution of usage contexts between *tú* and *usted* with specific addressees in radio communication often suggests group demarcation – *tú* is the typical choice between professionals of journalism (see again 19), while the displaced second person is the unmarked treatment with participants displaying any other kind of identity (see further Section 10.4).

The conclusion of the preceding inquiry into person choice and style construction is that genres can be distinguished according to their tendency to construct discourse from the viewpoint of the speaker, from that of the addressee/audience, or from a joint one; this is the stylistic dimension we will term *viewpoint orientation*. In Figure 9.4, the ten genres have been disposed over a triangular area by taking into account the dominant grammatical persons within

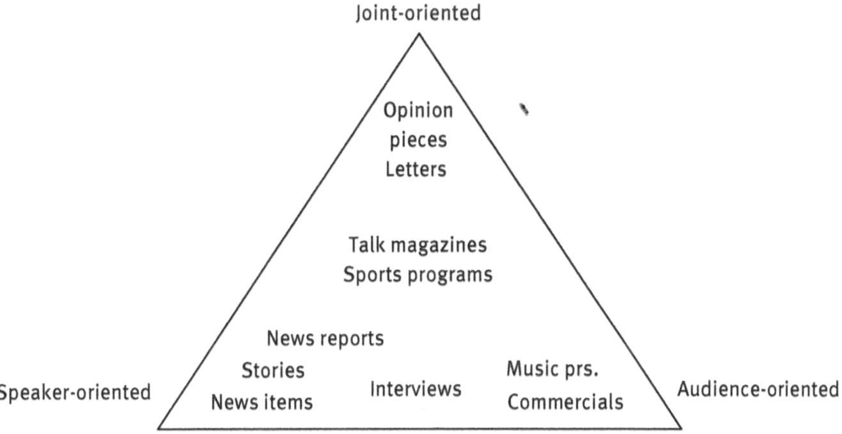

Figure 9.4: Media genres and orientation towards speaker, audience or joint viewpoints (based on the respective frequencies of grammatical persons).

each of them: singular and audience-exclusive plural first ones (speaker-oriented), audience-inclusive plural first and speaker-inclusive singular second ones (joint-oriented) and speaker non-inclusive second ones altogether (audience-oriented). Of course, the figure only aims at reflecting the most usual tendency in each genre; any of the three types of orientation might be adopted in some context for certain communicative purposes.

This dimension provides a partially different, more complex view of the subjectivity-intersubjectivity-objectivity continuum. While genres like news items, stories and news reports are strongly inclined to objectivity – given their general scarcity of participant indexations – at the same time they can be considered speaker-oriented in the sense that, when such indexations do occur, they are usually first-person ones excluding the audience. In turn, primarily argumentative genres such as opinion pieces and letters occupy the domain of joint orientation; discourse is aimed at constructing a shared viewpoint, resulting in the frequent choice of persons where both the speaker and the audience can be included, i.e. the plural first one and the singular second one. Music programs and commercials are genres where the consideration of the audience, either specific or nonspecific, is paramount; second persons not including the speaker are dominant in them. As for interviews, they are harder to situate in any particular vertex, given the neatly different communicative roles accorded to each of the participants – interviewers need to construct an audience (addressee)-oriented style, while interviewees are usually expected to be speaker-oriented. This makes it sensible to place this genre in an intermediate zone between speaker- and audience-viewpoint orientations. Finally, talk magazines and sports programs are located at the central area of the triangle, meaning that the three types of orientation can coexist within them. Their usual combination of informational, argumentative and conversational sequences is reflected in frequent and varied person indexations.

The possibilities for the study of person choice and its stylistic values have hardly been exhausted with the preceding discussion. It would be necessary to further consider the use of third persons and impersonal clauses, as well as to analyze other types of texts and communicative domains, in order to develop a theoretical model of such a complex and relevant area of variation and choice.

9.5 Variable expression and placement of pronouns

The choices related to the formal configuration of the clauses will help unveil yet another dimension of stylistic construction. Let us start by summing up the discursive-cognitive interpretations of the different variants as have been developed through quantitative and qualitative analysis throughout this book. The morphematic indexation of a referent without its explicit formulation is indicative of salience; such a referent is considered by the speaker to be activated in the context and straightforwardly inferable by the audience (example 22a). However, omission can also be aimed at avoiding emphasis on the involvement of a participant in the scene, which results in the apparent paradox that this variant is typical of both highly salient referents and unimportant ones. The difference is that, in the latter case, it will generally not correlate with indexation in the verbal nucleus (22b). In turn, the explicit formulation of pronouns or NPs is associated with informativeness, more so if the referent is not simultaneously indexed in the nucleus. In these cases, the speaker considers it necessary to make the referent explicit in discourse, with different possible communicative goals (22c).

(22a) Lo estoy escribiendo (omission with indexation: salient)
'I'm writing (it).'

(22b) Estoy escribiendo Ø (omission without indexation: unimportant)
'I'm writing.'

(22c) Estoy escribiendo un libro (expression: informative)
'I'm writing a book.'

Salience and informativeness are further modulated through the placement of expressed elements. Preverbal placement is prototypically associated with subject-agents. Being the usual position of discourse topics, it entails a significant degree of salience, which is however nuanced by the informativeness associated with expression, resulting in an enhancement of agency and involvement. In turn, clause-final placement is the prototypical choice with object-patients that are lowest in salience and highest in informativeness. Finally, clause-intermediate postverbal placement is a particularly complex choice with less neat values regarding salience and informativeness: seemingly "hiding" the referent behind the verb, it avoids both the agency associated with the preverbal position and the informational focalization and semantic patienthood that characterize the clause-final one, thus approaching the values of omission-indexation.

How does this all relate to the subjectivity-intersubjectivity-objectivity continuum? We can start by posing a connection between referent expression and higher subjectivity, given that this variant reinforces the association between the content of discourse and the participant in question. This will of course be especially evident with the singular first person, which, in spite of its inherent salience, has notably high rates of pronoun formulation in comparison with most others, as exposed in Section 4.3. The highest degrees of subjectivity would be associated with the preverbal placement of first- or second-person pronouns, whereby their referents will be endowed with both agency and informational focalization. The rest of the variants will represent successive steps away from the pole of subjectivity, going from postverbal placement – with its clause-final variant entailing higher subjectivity than the clause-intermediate one – to pronoun omission, which will be seen as the most desubjectivizing alternative regarding first- and second-person formal configuration (see Figure 9.5). It is however difficult to elucidate what the specific domain of intersubjectivity should be, since this appears to be strongly dependent on the grammatical person chosen. In clauses where the speaker or the addressee are indexed, intersubjectivity will be favored by syntactic variants reducing the informational focalization of the participants, i.e. clause-intermediate postverbal placement or omission. In fact, we have observed that intersubjective choices such as speaker-inclusive *tú* have a strong preference for pronoun omission in the corpus (Section 6.3). Therefore, intersubjectivity should be placed closer to the pole of omission; as in other cases, this happens because the proposed continuum is a partial one where the grammatical choices associated with objectivity proper, i.e. third-person and impersonal constructions, are not considered.

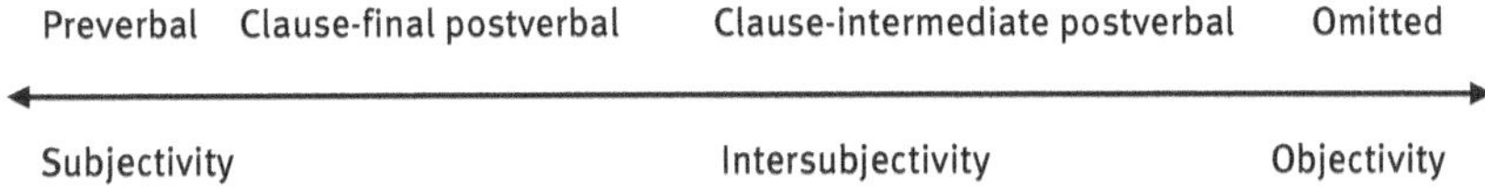

Figure 9.5: Variable expression and placement of pronouns along the stylistic continuum.

Given that the goal in this case is to ascertain which of the formal variants are dominant in each textual genre, we will calculate their respective percentages rather than their normalized frequencies. In other words, the total amounts of participant indexations handled in the preceding sections will now be classified according to the formal configurations they respond to. Table 9.3 shows the results.

Pronoun omission is by far the most frequent variant in all written and spoken genres, often approaching or exceeding 90% of the tokens. This reflects the inherent salience of first and second persons, which are left unexpressed in the absence of any motivation to contextually provide their referents with informativeness (see Section 3.2). However, there is still a difference of more than 5 points between the radio subcorpus (83.8%) and the press one (89%),

Table 9.3: Variable expression and placement of pronouns according to textual genre.

Genre	Preverbal		Clause-final postverbal		Clause-intermediate p.		Omitted	
	#	%	#	%	#	%	#	%
News items	11	5	4	1.8	1	0.4	205	92.8
Stories	11	5.5	4	2	0	0	186	92.5
Opinion pieces	54	8	13	1.9	11	1.6	600	88.5
Letters	45	9.8	4	0.9	15	3.3	394	86
Interviews	59	9.7	4	0.7	2	0.3	546	89.3
Press total	180	8.3	29	1.3	29	1.3	1,931	89
News reports	44	11.5	3	0.8	9	2.4	326	85.3
Talk magazines	470	16.9	40	1.4	90	3.2	2,173	78.4
Sports programs	203	15.6	24	1.8	9	0.7	1,066	81.9
Music programs	76	7.8	9	0.9	19	1.9	873	89.4
Commercials	20	2.4	0	0	0	0	803	97.6
Radio total	813	13	76	1.2	127	2	5,241	83.8

suggesting some association between pronoun expression and spoken discourse. Radio commercials, consisting of previously written texts, achieve the highest percentage of omission. On the other hand, talk magazines, where conversational sequences are relatively frequent, have the lowest score for the same variant. The phenomenon thus offers a different perspective of the information-interactivity continuum than was provided by participant indexation (Section 9.3).

In most varieties of written discourse, whether they are intended to be read or listened to, emphasis on the direct participants is perceived as unnecessary or scarcely expectable. This is coherent with our characterization of pronoun omission as associated with stylistic objectivity – or, more accurately, with de-subjectivization. Argumentation in written texts like opinion pieces, even when constructed from a clearly personal viewpoint, tends to avoid excessive self-involvement through omitted-subject epistemic modalizers such as *creo* '(I) think' (example 23). Pronoun expression enhances the informativeness of the referent and thus emphasizes their relationship with the content of the utterance. The stronger pragmatic weight or assertiveness conveyed through overt subject pronouns (Davidson 1996; Stewart 2003; see Section 4.3) is connected with an increase in this choice whenever speakers are expected to expose their own views and, crucially, to contrast them with those of others. In the spoken debates occasionally featured in talk magazines, the need to assert one's positions results in frequent pronoun expression, most often in the preverbal position (examples 24, 25). In the latter excerpt we can also observe the positional interplay of preverbal first-person pronouns with other topical elements in the clause (*todas las cadenas yo creo que* 'all TV channels I think that'; *a mí eso me parece* 'to me this seems'. Subject and object pronouns are used as conversational markers emphasizing the presence of the speaker.

(23) El partido de Aznar no acudió a la manifestación. *Creo* que hizo muy bien, pues sólo faltaba que en mitad de la marcha empezaran –como ya ha pasado varias veces con anterioridad– a llamarles asesinos. <Art-Ga-070404-3a>
'A.'s political party was not present at the demonstration. (*I*) think they did the right thing, since they could well have expected others – as has already happened several times – to start calling them murderers.'

(24) no forzosamente tiene que ser un niño violento / si: / está: / m: viendo imágenes violentas / pero *yo creo* que / como bien dice aquí mi compañero / algo queda / y no solamente ya estamos hablando: / de:- de:- de los programa:s / violentos y de las series estamos hablando de los mismos informativos <Var-Pu-211204-12:35>
'A child does not necessarily have to become violent by watching violent images, but *I* think, as my colleague has rightly put it, that there is always something that remains. And we're not just talking about violent programs and series – we're even talking about news broadcasts.'

(25) todas las cadenas / *yo creo* / que son: demasiado generosos / en / imágenes / violentas <. . .> un niño / se queda / pegadito a:- a- / a- al televisor / o una de dos / o t- / se <sic>familiaricia</sic> de tal forma / con la violencia / que ya le parece algo norMAL / y *a mí* eso *me* parece horroroso: ¿eh? <Var-Pu-211204-12:40>
'All TV channels *I* think they are way too abundant in violent images. [. . .] A child will get stuck to the TV, and he may end up being so familiar with violence that he will see it as an everyday thing. And *to me* this seems dreadful, you know?'

The two variants of postverbal placement are always scarce, and even nonexistent in some genres. Also, their respective percentages in the written and oral subcorpora are not quite apart (1.3% vs. 1.2% for clause-final pronouns, 1.3% vs. 2% for clause-intermediate ones). This suggests that the relevant stylistic contrast is the one established between omission and preverbal expression, i.e. the extreme variants in Figure 9.5 above, which are more usual and display greater frequential variability across modes and genres. The intermediate discursive-cognitive values of postverbal pronouns result in less clear stylistic characterizations. Even so, there are differences between the variants distinguished. As for clause-final placement, prototypically associated with object-patients and informational focalization, we have observed it is rare with first- and second-person pronouns. The choice is basically restricted to contexts of referent contrast, and to narrative stretches where actions affecting some participant are recounted (see e.g. Chapter 4, example 34). In turn, clause-intermediate postverbal placement is sometimes found when speakers express a personal stance but seem to avoid excessive self-commitment to it. In (26), the choice is followed by an instance of subject omission with the same verb, *suponer* 'to suppose, to guess' and coappears with other resources enhancing intersubjectivity, such as question tags. All this indicates that the speaker is trying to avoid the suggestion that he should intend to impose his own view.

(26) las negociaciones entre su representan:te: o él: y:- y: el club pues / tienen que ser rápidas ¿no? porque: *supongo yo* que: los clubs- / el mercado: d- está totalmente abierto ¿no? y el que ponga pues más dinero *supongo* que Róber / sobre todo q- / más que: más dinero / el que le dé minutos Róber: / ahí se irá <Dep-SE-210504-15:50>
'The negotiation between his agent or he himself and the club must be quick, right? Because *I* [postv.] guess that the market is totally open now, right? And those who offer him more money, (*I*) guess that R. – well, and rather than more money, those who offer him more playing time – R. will end up going with those.'

It is also interesting to observe that most written genres prefer the placement of postverbal pronouns at the clause-final position rather than at clause-intermediate ones, while the contrary happens with three of the oral genres. This could be indicative of a more regular tendency of written discourse to adjust to the prototypical discourse progression, from better-known to lesser-known information; but it also suggests that the choice of clause-intermediate placement is especially typical of conversational discourse. The latter intuition is reinforced by the fact that nearly two thirds of the total tokens of the choice (90 out of 156) appear in a single genre, namely talk magazines. Most of them are cases of the displaced second persons *usted* and *ustedes*, which apparently tend to get fixed at this position for the reasons that have been discussed in Section 8.3. Examples (27) and (28) further illustrate the use of overt pronouns performing the function of making the addressee or audience present in discourse while avoiding the attribution of excessive involvement to them. In the second one we can observe the usual correlation between postverbal *usted* or *ustedes* and invitations or offerings.

(27) toda la música en todos los ritmos / toda la música de / todas / las épocas / se da cita / en el punto del dial: donde *está usted* ahora <Mus-To-251104-17:35>
'All music in all styles, all music of all times, comes together at the point of the dial where *you+* [postv.] are right now.'

(28) no sé si había más llamadas / no / pero sí *tienen ustedes* el teléfono y *pueden* hacer uso de él / cuando *gusten* <Var-Co-211204-13:15>
'I'm not sure if there were still any calls on hold – no. Anyway, *you guys+* [postv.] do have our number and (*you guys+*) can use it whenever (*you guys+*) want to.'

Another significant detail is the very low rates of clause-final and especially clause-intermediate postverbal pronouns in written-press interviews (respectively 0.7 and 0.3%). This may seem contradictory with the fact that most of these texts result from the transcription of oral interactions. What is more, the percentage of pronoun omission in interviews (89.3%) slightly surpasses the general one of the written subcorpus (89%) when it could be expected to be lower. What these figures may be suggesting is that the formulation of pronouns in general, and particularly right after the verbal nucleus, is perceived as typical of conversational discourse and not so adequate for texts to be read. Thus, while transcription strategies do not seem to greatly affect the absolute frequency of participant indexations (see back Section 9.3), they may in turn promote the occasional suppression of overt subject or object pronouns perceived as clearly conversational. This results in omission and preverbal expression accounting for 99% of the tokens in transcribed interviews. In (29), the possible ambiguity of third-person verbal endings in the interviewer's questions does not trigger the formulation of *usted*.

(29) – ¿Cómo *afronta* su participación en los Juegos Olímpicos?
– Con mucha ilusión y muchas ganas de estar ahí. Son mis primeros Juegos y *estoy* muy contenta.
– ¿*Se encuentra* a pleno rendimiento?
– Sí, *me encuentro* bien aunque este año *he jugado* muchos torneos. <Ent-Ga-120804-64>
'A: How are (*you+*) facing your participation in the Olympic Games? – B: With great excitement and looking forward to being there. These will be

my first Games and (*I*)'m so happy about it. – Are (*you+*) at your full potential? – B: Yes, (*I*) feel well, even if (*I*)'ve played many tournaments this season.'

We could also suspect that the peculiarities of interviews as a genre, with their fixed distribution of speech turns, results in pronoun formulation being generally unnecessary. Perhaps the same could be said of radio commercials, showing the highest frequency of omission across the corpus (97.6%). First- and second-person forms can even be considered a part of the discursive conventions of this genre – there is always someone who explicitly offers or recommends something to someone else. The usually nonspecific reference of addressees and audiences may also have something to do with the strong dominance of omission. In example (30) we can observe abundant first- and second-person inflected verbs with no overt subject or object pronouns.

(30) *¿estás* vendiendo tu piso o buscando casa en Salamanca? / si *necesitas* ayuda: *ven* a conocernos / *tenemos*: mucho que *ofrecerte* <...> *recuerda* / Gestión Inmobiliaria / es la solución rápida / cómoda y fácil / a tus necesidades inmobiliarias / *te esperamos* <Anu-On-291104-13:15>
'Are (*you*) trying to sell your apartment or looking for a home in Salamanca? If (*you*) need help, (*you*) come to meet (*us*). (*We*) have a lot to offer (*you*). [...] (*You*) remember: G. I. is a quick, convenient and easy solution to your accommodation needs. (*We*)'re waiting (*for you*).'

From the preceding discussion we can conclude that the most significant stylistic dimension correlating with variable pronoun expression and placement is the degree of *involvement*, i.e. the emphasis on the relationship between some participant and the content of an utterance. Actually, this has been our interpretation of the pragmatic meanings of pronoun formulation and placement in the analyses of the preceding chapters. As all other dimensions of sociocommunicative style, involvement is undetachable from salience and informativeness themselves. The explicit formulation of first- and second-person pronouns, as well as their placement in discursively prominent positions – mainly the preverbal one – is associated with a degree of informational focalization; understandably, this is most usual in communicative contexts with potentially competing referents, that is, in those approaching the features of conversation. This means that involvement is often connected with other dimensions such as interactivity; in more interactive discourse, the participants will tend to be constructed as more involved. However, this is hardly a rule, as shown especially by radio commercials, which turn out to be highest in interactivity and lowest in involvement. In spite of their frequent suggestion of interaction with the virtual listener, they are clearly unidirectional texts to which the audience can only answer through their subsequent behavior as consumers. This is reflected in a very low rate of pronoun formulation.

If we restrict the characterization of this dimension to the two variants that have proved to be more frequent and stylistically differentiated, i.e. preverbal placement and omission – which would be respectively associated with the highest and lowest degrees of involvement, thus of subjectivity – media genres can be ordered as in Figure 9.6. They have been disposed from lowest to highest percentage of pronoun omission; as can be seen, the columns representing preverbal placement follow the opposite progression, with the only exception of press interviews, which slightly surpass opinion pieces in both omission and preverbal placement. This is because, as pointed out above, the two variants of postverbal placement are almost nonexistent in interviews.

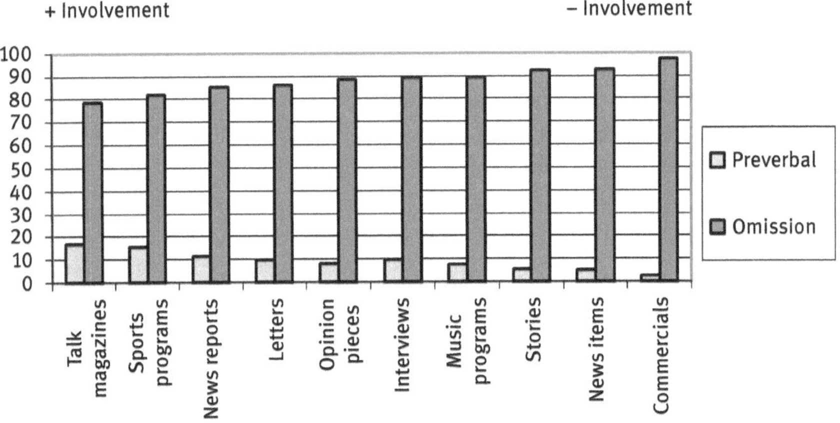

Figure 9.6: Media genres and interactivity (based on preverbal placement vs. omission of first- and second-person pronouns).

There are other, less expectable results such as that of radio news reports, which according to other dimensions are stylistically close to the written informational genres, i.e. news items and stories (see the preceding sections), but as regards involvement are situated closer to talk magazines and sports programs. This is primarily due to the notorious change in style caused by the insertion of recorded clips from oral interactions where personal stances are exposed. Also, the frequent formulation of *ustedes* in opening, transitional and closing sequences contributes to a lower percentage of omission. In turn, music programs are relatively distanced from the pole of subjectivity, again in line with commercials – they are characterized by a highly *interactive* but scarcely *involved* style. Most of the speech in this genre is produced by individual broadcasters who comment on the songs aired, read news or discuss cultural issues. As pointed out, genres need not behave in the same way according to all stylistic features related to the subjectivity-objectivity continuum; rather, the combination of different scores in different dimensions is arguably what helps shape the prototypical style of each genre.

9.6 Functional encoding

The last feature of choice that has been addressed in our analyses of the different first- and second-person subparadigms is the allocation of syntactic functions within the clause. We started from the hypothesis that subject encoding, understood as agreement between the verbal endings and a certain referent, entails for the latter to become the main participant of events, prototypically the agent. This is particularly obvious when a third-person referent remains an omitted subject for a number of successive clauses, reflecting a high degree of contextual activation (see the empirical illustration in §1.3.3). It is little wonder that the direct participants as well as animate, definite referents in general should generally be better candidates for subject encoding, and that this functional choice should be strongly dominant with the first and second persons. This also makes it especially interesting to analyze the motivations for the rarer cases of object encoding (see also Sections 3.3, 4.4 and 6.4). It is possible to hypothesize that functional encoding, just as the features considered in the preceding sections, is endowed with sociocommunicative values and can play some part in the construction of textual genres and participant identities; in other words, that it can be used by speakers as a stylistic resource.

In this case, we can propose an association – which in fact holds at the very etymological level – between subjects and subjectivity, as well as between objects and objectivity. In other words, those communicative situations where the direct participants are more often encoded as subjects – this choice helping enhance their salience – can be characterized as stylistically more subjective. This is schematized in Figure 9.7.

Nevertheless, given that the selection of a certain syntactic function – here understood as a way of verbal agreement – involves the simultaneous preference for a wide range of non-categorical formal and semantic choices (see Chapter 2), including the features of variable formulation and placement addressed in the preceding section, it would be complicated to analyze the results for each

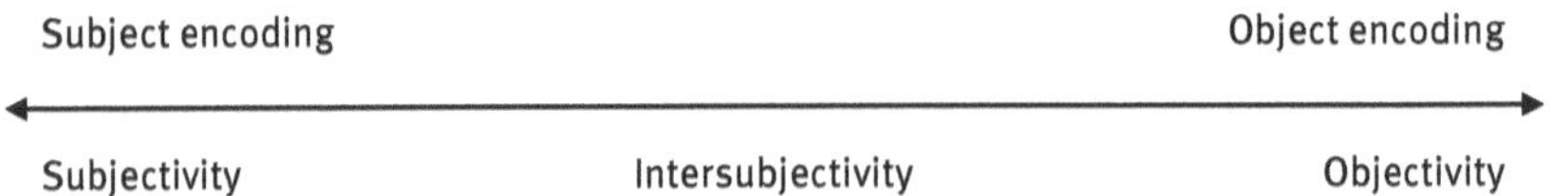

Figure 9.7: Subject vs. object functional encoding along the stylistic continuum.

grammatical person and genre in the corpus. More so if we bear in mind that most clauses in Spanish have more than one central participant, which means that the encoding of a referent in a syntactic function will restrict the range of functions available to other referents present. For these reasons, our inquiry will only explore the general distributional patterns of subject and object encoding and show their most significant connections with the communicative demands of different genres. Further information on the quantitative patterning and contextual repercussions of either choice with each person can be found in the corresponding sections of the preceding chapters. Table 9.4 displays the general percentages of subject vs. object encoding for the first and second persons in each genre, as well as the general ones in the written-press and radio sections of the corpus.

Table 9.4: Subject vs. object encoding according to textual genre.

Genre	Subject		Object	
	#	%	#	%
News items	178	80.5	43	19.5
Stories	157	78.1	44	21.9
Opinion pieces	494	72.9	184	27.1
Letters	346	75.5	112	24.5
Interviews	499	81.7	112	18.3
Press total	1,674	77.2	495	22.8
News reports	302	79.1	80	20.9
Talk magazines	2,271	81.9	502	18.1
Sports programs	1,096	84.2	206	15.8
Music programs	717	73.4	260	26.6
Commercials	675	82	148	18
Radio total	5,061	80.9	1,196	19.1

First, there is a slight advantage of 3.7 points in subject encoding for the radio subcorpus. If constructing a referent as the clause subject is parallel to an enhancement of its salience, it seems understandable that communicative situations closer to the pole of orality should have a stronger tendency to accord this function to the direct participants; conversely, prototypical written discourse would tend to deal with third-person entities. However, the internal differences within each subcorpus are probably more revealing than the general figures. We have already discussed the main contextual conditions associated with the dominance of participant subject encoding in oral discourse, such as the contrasting of stances in argumentative discourse and the use of first-person *yo* as a turn-taking device (see especially Section 4.3). The preverbal subject form acts as an indicator that some referent, most often the person speaking, constitutes the viewpoint from which the subsequent discourse is to be constructed and interpreted. Some of the more involved genres – i.e. those that achieved the highest frequencies of preverbal pronouns in Section 9.5 – also tend to have percentages above 80% of subject encoding, as is the case with talk magazines and sports programs in the radio subcorpus. The analyses in the preceding chapters have shown that choices from different levels such as subject encoding and preverbal placement often act together for the construction of certain pragmatic meanings.

Still, it is far from evident that functional encoding can be systematically associated with involvement or any other of the stylistic dimensions proposed in the preceding sections. For one thing, news items, which are closest to the prototype of informational discourse, have 80.5% of subject encoding, a percentage not far from those of the leading genres. Also, news reports, being in many respects a radio counterpart of written-press news, score 79.1%, a figure quite above those of written argumentative genres – opinion pieces and letters – as well as that of music programs. Finally, radio commercials – which are strongly subjective as regards participant indexation and strongly desubjectivized as regards pronoun expression – surpass all other genres in subject encoding, except for sports programs. It thus seems necessary to pay closer attention to the contextual conditions in which the choices are usually carried out, and particularly to the semantic roles accorded to the different participants.

What most of the genres with high rates of subject encoding have in common is the fact that speakers expose personal stances and assume responsibility for them, in clauses with a singular or plural first-person subject. This characterizes both interviews in the written press (example 31) and those featured in talk magazines and sports programs (32). Besides, it is the usual choice in recorded clips inserted in radio news reports, as well as in quoted segments within press news items (33).

(31) *Soy* profesor aquí en Salamanca y en verano *me traslado* a Carrara para realizar allí las esculturas y trabajar con los artistas italianos, en mi

opinión los mejores. Así *puedo* escoger personalmente el mejor mármol. <Ent-Ga-121203-12>
'(*I*)'m a teacher here in Salamanca, and every summer (*I*) travel to Carrara in order to create sculptures and work with Italian artists, who are in my opinion the best ones. This way (*I*) can personally select the best marble blocks.'

(32) *no(s)otros pensamos* que *somos* gente:- gente de fiar / e: gente / creíble / e: gente que tiene credibilidá / porque lo que: *decimos* e: cuatro años antes / pues *solemos* cumplirlo <Var-Co-230503-12:35>
'*We* believe that (*we*) are trustworthy people, credible people, people who have credibility, because what (*we*) promise four years in advance, (*we*) normally fulfill.'

(33) Juan Andrés González afirma sentirse "como en un sueño, por fin lo *he logrado*, aunque aún casi no *me hago* ni a la idea" <Not-Ga-260804-37>
'J. A. G. states that he feels "just like in a dream – at last (*I*) did it, although (*I*) still can't convince myself of it all." '

In all of these cases, speakers tend to place themselves at the center of attention and maintain their status as subjects across successive clauses. The orientation to the speaker's viewpoint that we proposed as a characterizing stylistic feature of some of these genres in Section 9.4 is obviously related to their comparably high rates of subject encoding. This choice can however be combined with speaker-blurring or audience-exclusive plurals in order to downplay self-involvement or, as in the case of (32), highlight membership in a group such as a political organization (see §5.2.1; §5.2.2). As we know, plural first-person subjects are also quite usual in the speech of program anchors, most often denoting the staff working at the radio station and/or having a discourse-structuring function (see examples 6, 9 or 17 above).

In turn, even if altogether less frequent, the encoding of addressees as clause subjects with *tú* or *usted*, particularly when they refer to specific individuals, is also typical of relatively interactional genres and situations. As discussed in Sections 3.2 and 6.3, this choice enhances the responsibility of the addressee and can have both dignifying and pejorative intentions, depending on how the content is evaluated by the person speaking. In (34), it is easy to perceive a flattering intention in the underlining of a positive measure that the interviewee, who is encoded as an expressed preverbal subject, is apparently determined to adopt. The speaker then opts for first-person subject omission with *creo* in order to introduce another positive fact, this time presenting it as more of a belief that the interviewee – who is the one entitled to assume responsibility for it – will subsequently confirm through a plural first-person subject. Choices like these are indicative of the types of contextual identities constructed by different groups of speakers in media communication (see further Chapter 10).

(34) <A> *usté* / *puede* decir que / a:HOra / precisamente / va a haber una concejalía / ocupada del patrimonio / o en el caso de los mayores que es un amplio coleztivo / que también quiere saber hasta qué punto le van a prestar atención / *creo* que habrá una concejalía / esclusiva para mayores <. . .>
<B> en el plan de mayores / *nosotros vamos* a seguir a rajatabla / lo que ya *hemos aprobado* <Var-Co-230503-12:50>
'A: *You+* can now say that a new department is going to be devoted to the cultural heritage. Or, with regard to elderly people, who form a large group and would like to know if they're going to be paid any attention, (*I*) think there's also going to be a specific department for the elderly. [. . .] – B: As regards the plan for the elderly, *we* are going to strictly follow what (*we*)'ve already approved.'

The comparably low rates of subject encoding in opinion pieces (72.9%) and letters to the editor (75.5%) seem to be an effect of the balance between argumentation – which would indeed favor subject encoding – and the absence of real contention with others – which situates these genres farther from the pole of subjectivity. As noted in the preceding section, strong self-involvement tends to be perceived as scarcely appropriate or altogether unnecessary in written discourse with no immediate feedback. This results in some preference for *gustar*-type verbs encoding the experiencer as an object (see Sections 2.4, 4.3, 4.4). Example (35) has two tokens of *parecer* 'to seem', one in the present tense and governing an embedded clause, the other one in its attributive construction with a predicate. Of course, *gustar*-type constructions can co-appear with others encoding the writer as subject, as in (36): *me agradaría* 'it would please (me)' vs. *no he leído* '(I) haven't read'.

(35) *Me* parece verlo todavía, con el abrigo demasiado grande, la cartera llena de arañazos y arrastrando los pies. . . Nunca como ese día, *me* pareció tan dura la tarea del vendedor de libros ambulante. <Art-Ad-221104-6>
'It seems (*to me*) as if I can still see him, his coat too large, his suitcase full of scratches, and shuffling as he walked by. . . The task of door-to-door booksellers never seemed so hard (*to me*) as that day.'

(36) No *he leído* la Constitución Europea y *me* agradaría hacerlo para, así, formar comparaciones, si las hubiera, con la nuestra. <Car-Ad-131104-7c>
'(*I*) haven't read the European Constitution and it would please (*me*) to do so, in order to draw comparisons with our own, if need be.'

In the case of letters, another significant source of object tokens are the contexts where writers recount actions – often negative ones – that have been performed on them or the groups they speak for. As exposed, cases where the first and second persons approach the discursive-cognitive features of object-patients are rare across the corpus, being mostly limited to narrative stretches with a contentious intention, such as (37). Even in this case, the first-person object would have dative features, given its co-occurrence with an accusative inanimate object (*un programa de dietas* 'a meal program'). In other contexts like that of (38), the semantic role of the object is more clearly that of a receiver or beneficiary, i.e. it comes closer to the dative prototype.

(37) *Nos* han impuesto un programa de dietas para mejorar la ingesta del paciente, sin que existiera conocimiento del personal ni formación en el manejo de dicho programa. <Car-Ad-211204-6>
'They have imposed (*on us*) a meal program in order to improve the patients' food intake, with no prior notice to the staff or training in how to manage that program.'

(38) Ayer, embargado por la tristeza, <su sobrino> *me* comunicó su muerte. Y *pensé* para mí, que Miranda sin Mariano ya no sería la Miranda que con él *conocí*. La próxima Navidad *echaré* de menos la botella de aguardiente que anualmente *me* llevaba como símbolo de su cariño <Car-Ga-031104-6>
'Yesterday, overwhelmed by sadness, [his nephew] informed (*me*) of his death. And (*I*) thought to myself that, without M., Miranda would no longer be the place (*I*) once knew with him. Next Christmas (*I*)'ll miss the bottle of spirits he always brought (*me*) as a demonstration of affection.'

Together with opinion pieces, music programs have a particularly low rate of subject encoding (73.4%). Broadcasters in this genre frequently develop a subjective style through recurrent participant indexations, but, interestingly, personal responsibility is avoided to some extent through self-encoding as an object. The situation is thus similar to that of opinion pieces and letters. Again, there are occasional constructions with *gustar*-type verbs, most often with pronoun omission (example 39). Later in the excerpt there is subject encoding of the nonspecific audience, possibly with a speaker-inclusive value (*puedes* '(you) can').

(39) *me* encanta ese final / "uno más uno son siete / quién me lo iba a decir / que: / era tan fácil: / ser feliz" con una: / sonrisa *puedes* hacer feliz a un montón de gente <Mus-40-220803-12:20>
'I love that ending (lit. That ending enchants [*me*]) – "One plus one makes seven; who would have thought it was so easy to be happy". With just a smile, (*you*) can make a lot of people happy.'

However, what most instances of object encoding in music programs suggest is that broadcasters tend to adopt a subordinate status in relation to their audience, as a strategy to secure the latter's approval or collaboration. In these cases, the singular or plural second persons will be encoded as the clause subject, whereas the first person will appear as an object. In (40), the broadcaster asks the addressee to hang on the phone for a while. We can observe how the syntactic construction chosen – second-person subject, first-person object – is subsequently reversed in order to justify the request. The frequency of clauses where both the first and second persons are central participants obviously favors an increase in the percentage of object encoding, given that this is generally the less usual choice with the direct participants. Similar cases can of course be found in talk magazines and sports programs, but not as often. As with overall participant indexation, this is a suggestion that broadcasters tend to compensate for the lack of real interactivity through stylistic choices associated with subjectivity.[3]

(40) muchas gracias no *me cuelgues* que *te cojo* los dato:s ¿vale:? <Mus-Di-251104-13:20>
'Thank you so much. (*You*) don't hang up (*on me*), since (*I*) need to take your details (*from you*), OK?'

Finally, the preference of radio commercials for subject encoding (82%) is related to emphasis on the responsibility of the company or institution issuing the advertisement as well as of potential consumers, who are presented as agentive and endowed with decision power rather than as mere recipients of goods and services (example 41). However, we can also find instances of object encoding with *gustar*-type and other verbs, particularly in questions and hypothetical clauses (42). Commercials imitating spontaneous dialogue show a

3 A further source of object self-encoding is what we have termed *discursive datives*, indexing a central participant that is not prefigured in the eventive structure of the verb (see the discussion in Section 3.4). Most examples in the corpus appear across the speech of music broadcasters.

strong dominance of subject encoding, as in the comical exchange of (43), with just one token of second-person object *te* when speaker A constructs himself as the agent and B as the beneficiary.

(41) este mes *ponemos* a la venta cincuenta y seis vehículos de kilómetro cero / a precios inigualables / los mejores modelos / al mejor precio y con la mejor garantía <. . .> no lo *dude* / *venga* a Mirauto a ver las novedades y ofertas / para este mes / y n:o *se arrepentirá* <Anu-On-141204-15:20>
'This month (*we*) are putting 56 zero-kilometer vehicles up for sale, at unbeatable prices. The best models at the best prices and with the fullest cover. (*You+*) don't hesitate – (*you+*) come to M. and see our new releases and offers for this month, and (*you+*) won't regret it.'

(42) ¿*te* gusta que cuando: *vas* a comer a un restaurante: / *te* sorprendan: con una buena carta? / *ven* / a Restaurante Merino / y *comprueba* la carta tan variada y de calidad / que *te* puede ofrecer <Anu-Di-200503-12:50>
'Do you like it (lit. Does it please [*you*]) when (*you*) go to a restaurant and they surprise (*you*) with a good menu? (*You*) come to R. M. and (*you*) check the variety and quality of the menu they can offer (*you*).'

(43) <A> felicidades cariño / *te he comprado* un regalo /
<B> Manolo: / ¡*te has acordado*! / <ruido de papel> / si esto es de la tienda de las gangas /
<A> es que: / *pasaba* por allí:
<B> "*pasaba* por allí" / anda *devuélvelo* / y *vete* a la joyería de siempre <Anu-On-141204-13:05>
'A: Happy birthday, honey. (*I*) bought (*you*) a present. – B: Oh, M., (*you*) remembered about it! [*Unwraps it.*] Hey, but this is from the bargain store! – A: Erm well, (*I*) was passing by. . . – B: "(*I*) was passing by. . ." Now (*you*) go return it and then (*you*) go to our trusted jewelry store.'

The analysis of the different genres suggests that the specific dimension of the subjectivity-objectivity continuum associated with subject vs. object encoding is what can be termed *responsibility*. When the speaker or some other participant are encoded as the clause subject, they acquire some features associated with the prototypical semantic role of this function, namely that of agent. The referent of the subject will thus tend to be viewed as more active or autonomous, thus as responsible for the content of discourse, irrespective of whether it is an action proper, a process or even a state that is described. It should have been made clear that functional encoding is hardly independent of other grammatical and semantic choices, which means that in practice the proposed dimension is difficult to detach from the ones discussed in the preceding sections, and especially of involvement. As also pointed out, it would be necessary to conduct more detailed inquiries into the encoding of different grammatical persons – and their possible references – in order to understand what this phenomenon of variation and choice actually entails for the construction of style. However, this exceeds the possibilities of the present investigation. Limiting ourselves to the general data presented, genres can be ordered as in Figure 9.8, from highest to lowest degree of responsibility accorded to the direct participants. In spite of what the visual layout might suggest, it must be kept in mind that all genres have a strong dominance of subject encoding, with a range of just some 11 points between sports programs and opinion pieces. As in other cases, the inclusion of different types of third-person referents would probably result in wider differences among the genres.

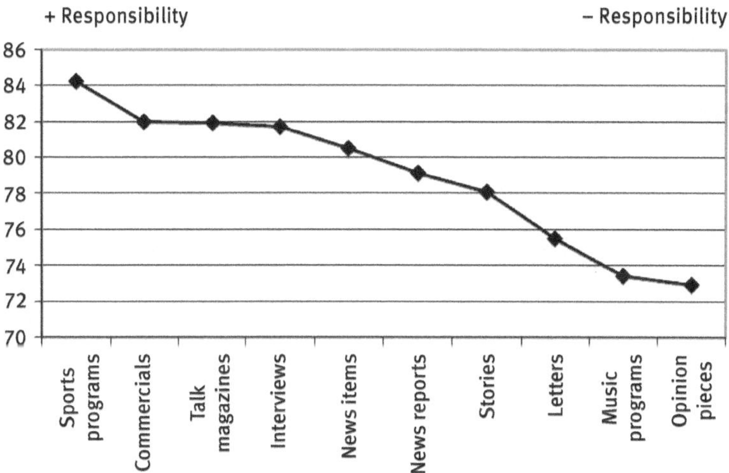

Figure 9.8: Media genres and responsibility accorded to the direct participants (based on percentages of subject encoding).

As usual, radio genres dominate the area closer to the pole of subjectivity, with only music programs coming close to the opposite end. It is especially interesting to observe what happens within the written-press subcorpus. It seems coherent for interviews to be most favorable to the dimension of responsibility, given that interviewees tend to explicitly discuss personal deeds and stances. They are followed by news items and stories, where quoted segments – containing the vast majority of participant indexations – are stylistically similar to interviews. In turn, it seems less expectable for letters and opinion pieces to be comparably low in this dimension. This is partly due to their noted preference for *gustar*-type constructions encoding the speaker as an object, thus downplaying semantic agency and presenting personal stances as more of tentative assessments. Object self-encoding is also relatively frequent in the speech of music broadcasters and to some extent of those conducting news reports, suggesting the adoption of a subordinate status as against their audiences. The remaining radio genres are strongly inclined to subject encoding.

The description and explanation of styles clearly begs for more subtle categories than the usual distinctions between oral and written, spontaneous and pre-planned, or argumentative and informative discourse, even if these and other contextual features can of course condition stylistic construction. As established from the beginning of this chapter, a scientific approach to style requires that the discursive-cognitive meanings of linguistic choices be systematically integrated with their quantitative patterning and contextual effects across sociocommunicative contexts.

9.7 Summary

In this chapter we have approached the construction of sociocommunicative styles across media genres as manifested in a variety of grammatical choices related to the first and second persons, namely participant indexation, person choice, variable expression and placement of pronouns, and functional encoding. The assumption of a general stylistic continuum from subjectivity to objectivity, with intersubjectivity as an intermediate notion, helps explain why and how styles are constructed in communicative situations. Nevertheless, this continuum has varied and complex manifestations in actual linguistic usage, and it is in fact difficult to provide a single, unitary stylistic characterization for all the phenomena under analysis. They all tend to correlate with features of communicative contexts such as orality vs. literacy or information vs. interactivity, but at the same time reveal partially different sides of stylistic construction, to the point that a given genre can respond in rather disparate ways to each of them. Which is only natural if we bear in mind that, as stated from the first chapter of this book, each grammatical choice is inherently associated with a particular meaning. For these reasons, we have proposed a different specific dimension of the general stylistic continuum for each of the features considered.

First, overall frequencies of participant indexation through first- and second-person verbal morphemes are indicative of the degree of *interactivity* of the style constructed. Perhaps surprisingly, mainly unidirectional formats of radio communication, such as commercials and music programs, are those taking the lead regarding interactivity. This shows that the latter dimension does not need to be understood as the existence of *real* interaction, but as a stylistic value that is perceived as advantageous for speakers in these genres. Person choice, understood as the frequency with which each grammatical person is indexed in discourse, proves difficult to interpret in a unified way. In general terms, it seems to reveal different *viewpoint orientations* of discourse, namely towards the speaker, the audience, or else constructing a joint viewpoint through choices like audience-inclusive *nosotros* or speaker-inclusive *tú*. As for the percentages of pronoun expression and preverbal vs. postverbal placement, it is the degree of *participant involvement* that seems to be primarily at stake. The stylistic constrast is most evident between the two most recurrent variants, namely pronoun omission and preverbal placement. The genres containing more abundant conversational sequences and where different viewpoints are often contrasted, such as talk magazines and sports programs, are usually the ones with higher percentages of the latter choice. Finally, rates of subject vs. object encoding of the direct participants – most significantly the speaker or the group he/she constructs him/herself as part of – have been interpreted as revealing the *responsibility* attributed to them with regard to the content of discourse. Strongly argumentative genres such as opinion pieces and letters to the editor turn out to have comparably low frequencies of subject encoding, often opting for *gustar*-type and other verbs encoding human participants as objects.

The differentiation of stylistic dimensions within the continuum makes it possible to explain seemingly contradictory results. For example, radio commercials, achieving the highest normalized frequency of participant indexation and a high percentage of subject encoding – both features being associated with subjectivity – also have the lowest percentage of pronoun expression, which is indexical of desubjectivization. Even the genres that appear to follow a quite systematic stylistic pattern, such as written news items and stories – usually falling farthest from the pole of subjectivity – can show less expectable results, such as their typical orientation to the speaker's viewpoint and their relative tendency to enhance participant responsibility. However, such results are largely an effect of the insertion of transcriptions of oral argumentative discourse, which, even if contemplated as part of the conventions of these genres, obviously do not conform to their prototypical style. This shows the need for qualitative analysis in order to correctly assess the quantitative results. Also, it would be necessary to extend the investigation to third-person and impersonal clauses in order to achieve a complete picture of viewpoint orientation and other proposed dimensions.

Therefore, rather than occupy a fixed position in a unitary subjectivity-intersubjectivity-objectivity scale, each textual genre can respond differently to particular facets of the stylistic continuum, associated with different linguistic features. Actually, the prototypical sociocommunicative style of a genre can only be accurately described through the joint consideration of a variety of choices that do not need to point all in the same direction, insofar as each of them will have a particular inherent meaning. The phenomena analyzed in this investigation are just a small subset of all such choices. The consideration of other ones from different semiotic codes – not just the linguistic one – would help refine the description and isolate the most relevant and explanatory dimensions involved in the construction of styles across media genres.

10 The construction of style across participant identities

10.1 Style and identity

In the general discussion of the sociocommunicative side of linguistic variation and choice in Section 9.1, *identity* was already highlighted as a key concept in contemporary sociolinguistics and related fields. While *genre* was the notion used in the preceding chapter to categorize the wide diversity of situations found across written-press and radio communication – what in more traditional terms would have been termed the "stylistic" axis of variation – in the present one it is identity that will help us characterize people taking part in media interactions and analyze how linguistic choice contributes to the construction of their selves – the "social" axis. However, by now it should be clear that, from the approach adopted here, the distribution of sociocommunicative meanings into different axes can hardly be regarded as more than a methodological artifact. Identities as we are going to define them cannot be detached from communicative situations and the goals speakers pursue within them. For this reason, most of what was exposed in the preceding chapter will need to be kept in mind across this one.

The insertion of speakers into particular social groups has been viewed as potentially conditioning linguistic choice from the earliest sociolinguistic and variationist studies (e.g. Fischer 1958; Labov 1963), to the point that it can be considered the basic justification for the social study of language from both quantitative and qualitative perspectives. The notion that there are expressive choices typical of e.g. men, women, youngsters, elderly people, higher-educated professionals or manual workers is intuitive to any member of a community, and a good deal of research has been devoted to empirically substantiating this intuition. However, the traditional and still usual characterizations of speakers according to their sex/gender, age group, socioeconomic status, educational attainment, ethnicity and so on are not necessarily what we would term *identities* from a sociocommunicative viewpoint. They rather constitute methodological constructs intended to bring some order to the apparently messy ways in which social life unfolds. An easy criticism of quantitative sociolinguistic studies is that they follow and help maintain a clearly structural, stratificational view of society, just as of communicative styles themselves (cf. Coupland 2007, 37–45; Blake 2016, 154–157). For the sake of neat statistical analysis, informants are packed into predefined, discrete categories, often based on merely physical traits. Little attention is paid to whether such categories are actually subject to any sort of

https://doi.org/10.1515/9783110643442-011

psychosocial evaluation in the community or interactional domain under study, whether they are relevant to the speakers themselves, or whether the latter would be able to detach themselves from such characterizations in particular sociocommunicative contexts and through particular semiotic choices. The focus is of course on general patterns of social distribution and ongoing processes of linguistic change, rather than on the dynamics of social microinteraction. However, it is quite evident that the speaker, as an autonomous individual whose choices contribute to the existence of variation and change, tends to get lost along the way.

Research on language and identity has helped shape a different view of what speaker group ascriptions actually entail when it comes to linguistic usage in sociocommunicative contexts. Notions such as gender, age or social status, rather than as predefined and constant features, can be viewed as meaningful choices. Just as with genres, they offer partly conventionalized and recognizable ways of self-presentation that people can modulate in order to accomplish their goals. A great deal of contemporary research on communicative style is inspired by such a notion of identity as a progressive construction of the social self, which is carried out through semiotic elements chosen from the linguistic code just as from other ones (cf. Eckert 2000; De Fina/Schiffrin/Bamberg 2006; Schilling-Estes 2006; Auer 2007; Coupland 2007; Edwards 2009; Bucholtz 2011; Potowski 2016, among many others). Bucholtz (2004, 130), building on previous contributions, encapsulates the very notion of *style* as "The use of linguistic structures to index social positioning". Also, Theodoropoulou (2014, 7) tentatively defines style as "a variable and flexible semiotic repertoire through which individuals and groups craft and index their identities to the rest of the world, depending on communication circumstances". The simultaneous reference to personal/group identities and communication circumstances is significant, and in fact the author notes the difficulty in separating *style*, *identity* and *genre* – identities are developed within discursive genres and often undetachable from them, but both are in turn based on the sets of semiotic choices called styles (see also Biber/Conrad 2009; Hernández-Campoy 2016, 33–40).

Crucially, speakers are not confined to a single, stable identity any more than they should be confined to a single linguistic variety – many people in the world can speak more than one language, but there are even more who can speak different dialects, and everyone can in fact use different styles (Edwards 2009, 3). Paraphrasing an old proverb, we could say that with each linguistic variety you get to speak, you will become a different person. Besides, and as against the tendency of quantitative sociolinguistics to attribute universal validity to its (Western-inspired) social characterizations, it is necessary to assume that identities are largely culture-and community-specific, and that their enactment will be interpreted as establishing some rights and duties for the participants, including particular ways of speaking. They are also highly dependent on the features of the communicative situation, especially when the latter instantiates a recognizable and recurrent activity. This makes it possible to reinterpret even the apparently most basic and permanent features of speakers, such as sex/gender, as features of contextual style management (Aijón Oliva/Serrano 2016).

It is of course not the intention of the present study to address all problems associated with the notion of identity and its relationship to language use, nor to solve the obvious difficulties derived from the application of a quantitative methodology to social features that are highly elusive and subject to continuous reformulation and evolution. However, at least two considerations that sum up the preceding discussion should be borne in mind for any linguistic analysis to be socially realistic. First, identities are not static, invariable features of people that condition their linguistic behavior. Speakers will tend to display some kind of identity that suits the demands of a sociocommunicative situation, but can also shift to different ones if their specific goals make it advisable to do so. This will be reflected in linguistic and any other choices aimed at constructing meanings at all possible semiotic levels. Second, identities are culture-, community- and situation-specific. They can hardly be characterized without considering the peculiarities of the sociocommunicative context under study (see further the following section), even if the ultimate goal of research should be to shape a theoretical model of identity construction across communicative domains and societies, based on general cognitive principles.

The features of grammatical choice to be analyzed in the present chapter, as well as their interpretations according to different stylistic dimensions of the subjectivity-objectivity continuum, are the same as those in Chapter 9. In order not to excessively lengthen the discussion, it will be assumed that readers are already familiar with the methodology implemented and the interpretations assigned to the different features at the discursive, cognitive and sociocommunicative levels. Again, the most crucial point to be made is that participant identities are not shaped and developed through different ways of "saying the same thing" that are only differentiated by their respective psychosocial evaluations (see Section 1.2), but rather through different ways of saying different things. In other words, speaker identities are connected with the relative preference for certain meanings over other possible ones. This means that identity is as much a cognitive construct as a social one, and that sociocommunicative meanings are an integral part of linguistic ones, which also challenges the usual distinction between "internal" and "external" meanings.

10.2 Socioprofessional identities in media communication

Participant identities in the media expectably prove hard to detach from genres themselves and their socio-interactional conventions. The fact that this is a public communicative domain where performance can usually be monitored by large groups of people results in some types of identities being highly recurrent and conditioned by specific attributions and goals. The participants are not there just for the sake of being; they are expected to do certain things and, more crucially for the present study, to *say* certain things. When speakers or writers set out to take part in some communicative format – i.e. in some genre as we have defined them – they are most often assigned a particular role that will to some extent establish what they can (or cannot) say and what they are (or are not) expected to say. The roles that can be observed across the corpus under study are of course numerous: information providers, opinion makers, debate moderators, interviewers, interviewees, phone callers, advertisers, collaborators, etc. It seems necessary to group them into a limited number of categories, just as all texts forming the corpus were previously classified as pertaining to a certain genre.

The detailed observation of the roles assumed by participants in local media interactions makes it possible to classify all speakers and writers in the corpus into four basic types of speaker socioprofessional identity. As will be discussed below, the term *socioprofessional* is aimed at reflecting the fact that these identities combine specific communicative attributions and duties in some context, i.e. roles, with more personal features that make participants qualify for those roles. The four identity types are listed and described below.

a) *Journalists and broadcasters* (182,774 words). The professionals of the media – who most often, but not always, possess a graduate degree related to the sector – are responsible for some three-fifths of the total words in the corpus. They write news items and stories, conduct interviews and host all radio programs – excluding the special case of commercials – among other occasional tasks, such as street reporting. Given their special status within the domain, they also have the power to decide on when, how and on which terms other kinds of participants are allowed to step in, or whether their contributions are to be published, in the case of the press.[1] Such a

1 These statements are only meant to hold within the limits of communicative interactions themselves. The apparent "power" of journalists and broadcasters is much of an illusion created by media formats – obviously, they are most often the employees of others who do make the fundamental decisions about participants, topics, ideological contents and so on. The present study is only concerned with communication within the media, not with the driving forces behind it.

power needs to be carefully managed, since working in the media entails a significant degree of public exposure. In fact, journalists and broadcasters, as against other identity groups, are usually expected to be polite, well-informed and ideologically neutral, even if this will also largely depend on the particular textual genre and more specific features such as the topic of discourse or the identities of other participants.

b) *Public figures* (69,380 words). The second category of participants is more heterogeneous than the previous one and could be divided into a number of subtypes, e.g. intellectuals, artists, sportspeople, entrepreneurs, spokespeople for associations, etc. What they all have in common is the fact that they do not develop their usual professional activity within the media; rather, they are only requested to participate in certain contexts, e.g. as the authors of opinion pieces or as interviewees or debaters in different genres. Their appearance is explicitly or implicitly justified by their possessing some kind of prestige or social relevance. They could be further classified as either *guests* or *collaborators*, depending on whether their contributions are incidental or rather constitute fixed sections in a newspaper or radio program. While they are often expected to be skilled and expert professionals, at the same time they are attributed greater stylistic possibilities than journalists, in connection with the frequently argumentative nature of their contributions.

c) *Politicians* (23,839 words). Obviously, this kind of identity can also be considered a subtype of the previous one. It includes those participants that are introduced in media interactions as the representatives of political parties, trade unions and other associations with explicitly political goals. If it seems advisable to detach them from the rest of public figures, it is mainly because of their peculiar socioprofessional profile in the community under study – as well as probably in most other Spanish ones. The public image of politicians has seriously deteriorated in the last decades, due to recurrent corruption scandals and the popular unease motivated by what is perceived as unfair and disproportionate social privileges (see further Kampf/Daskal 2011). Also, previous studies from different analytical approaches have revealed the often striking peculiarities of political discourse, in connection with the need to obtain the approval of the voting population (Blas Arroyo 2000; Bull/Fetzer 2006; De Cock/Nogué Serrano 2017, etc.).

d) *Anonymous individuals* (26,584 words). The final group includes participants who appear in media contexts circumstantially – much like most public figures – but who are not personally invited to do so by media professionals. Not being attributed the social relevance of speakers from the preceding groups, their social ascriptions and professional activities,

> as well as their names, sometimes remain unmentioned. Still, the label *anonymous* need not be taken in a literal sense. Their most recurrent roles in the local media are those of letter writers, callers to radio programs, or passers-by responding to the questions of reporters. It should be noted that this is a widely heterogeneous group – even more than the previous ones – from the perspective of the usual sociodemographic dimensions, i.e. age, gender or economic status, which shows yet again that identities as are understood here are tightly connected with rights and duties in specific communicative situations, rather than with predefined categories.

Kerbrat-Orecchioni (2005, 157) develops a notion of *contextual identities* quite in line with the one adopted here. They should be viewed as aggregations of features that make people qualify for playing a certain role in some context. Participants often need to enjoy a certain professional or social status in order to be assigned a role within some media format. This way, journalists should ideally hold a degree in Journalism or Audiovisual Communication – these being the specializations currently offered by most Spanish universities – in order to carry out informational tasks in present-day media. In turn, public figures are expected to have some educational or professional status that justifies their participation when a certain topic or activity is at stake. As for anonymous individuals, the pertinence of their participation can be justified by e.g. the fact that they reside in a certain part of the town where something has happened, or that they are taxpayers and want to demand something from the authorities, etc. This suggests that the identity assumed by a speaker in a context will often be hardly independent of more *static* features of speakers – i.e. the usual sociodemographic categories of variationist sociolinguistics – to the point that the neat discrimination between them can be little more than an analytical artifact.

What is more significant for the present investigation is that these roles will entail a set of communicative rights and obligations in the contexts where they are enacted, reflected in what speakers can say and do, and what they are expected to say and do. Hence these identities are largely situation-dependent characterizations, rather than inherent features of speakers, in spite of the strong ties existing between both facets of identity. The same person may adopt different kinds of socioprofessional identity, or even shift between two or more of them within the same situation, which means that there need not be a single and permanent characterization for each one. For example, while journalists are usually expected to be objective and ideologically neutral – as noted in their characterization above – in recent times there has been a growing pressure on them to adopt critical positions towards politicians (see e.g. Patrona 2011), thus to assume roles more typical of politicians themselves or of public figures. A radio broadcaster can also express concern about an everyday local matter as a letter writer or phone caller would, thus highlighting his/her personal status as a town resident instead of the professional one. Similarly, a participant initially featured as an anonymous individual can present him/herself as a specialist on the topic under discussion, automatically assuming some features of public figures, as is frequent in letters to the editor.

Anyway, in most cases these identities are part of the conventions of media genres and appear to be largely pre-assigned by the latter. Even progressive alterations will probably be interpreted in light of the primary identities established by the communicative situation. For example, political argumentation produced by a radio broadcaster is likely to sound less argumentative and more informational than if it came from a participant explicitly identified as a politician. Also, socioprofessional identities as understood here can sometimes entail a strong sense of groupness (cf. Edwards 2009, 25–27). We will observe that some grammatical choices related to the first and second persons – including that between *tú* and *usted*, as well as the varied uses of *nosotros* – can be quite revealing of the demarcation of participant groups by speakers (see especially Section 10.4 on person choice).

10.3 Participant indexation

As in the preceding chapter, the empirical analysis of style construction will start from the normalized overall frequencies of grammatical indexation of the direct participants, either through subject or object agreement morphemes. Table 10.1 shows the data for each of the four identity types distinguished.

Table 10.1: Frequency of participant indexation according to participant identity.

Identity	Word count	First- and second-person forms	Frequency per 1,000 words
Journalists	182,774	3,362	18.4
Public figures	69,380	3,109	44.8
Politicians	23,839	774	32.5
Anonymous indivs.	26,584	1,181	44.4
Total	302,577	8,426	27.8

Journalists and broadcasters are the only group whose frequency of participant indexation falls below the general one of 27.8 tokens per 1,000 words. Watched from a different perspective, while the words produced by this group represent 60.4% of the corpus, their 3,362 tokens of first- and second-person verbal morphemes account for just 39.9% of the total indexations found. As discussed in Section 9.3, the avoidance or restriction of first- and second-person forms is associated with a sociocommunicative style that tends to downplay interactivity between the direct participants and place external entities at the center of attention, thus is clearly oriented to desubjectivization. In fact, this will prove to be the regular tendency in journalists and broadcasters' style across the rest of linguistic features to be analyzed, and is consistent with the findings of previous analyses of this type of socioprofessional identity (see e.g. Aijón Oliva/Serrano 2013, 191, 196).

However, as pointed out, it is often difficult to detach identities from the situations where people take part and the tasks and goals usually attached to them. Journalists and broadcasters are typically devoted to the transmission of informational contents, which will necessarily be reflected on their patterns of linguistic choice. They are expected to construct a predominantly desubjectivized style whereby participant indexations, either first- or second-person ones, are often restricted to conventional discourse-organizing sequences, as illustrated by (1) and (2). As has been pointed out elsewhere and will be further discussed in the following section, they prefer the plural first person for self-indexation. In turn, the audience can even be constructed as an external entity by means of third-person forms, as in the second excerpt – the lexical NP and subsequent relative head indicate that it is not a displaced second person but a third one proper that is constructed – all of which makes desubjectivization more notorious.

(1) enseguida *les informamos* / de lo imprescindible de la actualidá salmantina en esta jornada de martes <Inf-Co-071204-7:55>
'In a moment (*we*) will inform (*you guys+*) about the most significant pieces of news in Salamanca on this Tuesday.'

(2) *saludamos* de nuevo a los oyentes de Punto Radio / que *nos:* escuchan: a través: / del ciento tres punto cuatro de la Efe Eme <Var-Pu-211204-12:25>
'(*We*) now say hello again to the audience of Punto Radio, who are listening (*to us*) at 103.4 FM.'

Interestingly, the tendency to avoid participant indexations on the part of media professionals does not seem to be restricted to informational discourse, which suggests that it may actually constitute more than a convention of the latter – and that stylistic choices associated with identity can be exploited across quite different genres. Although it is impossible to quantify how many times a speaker *could have* indexed a direct participant, but did not do so – and it would be scarcely justified from our approach to variation and choice; see back Sections 1.1 and 1.2 – we can find many contexts where journalists utter third-person and impersonal constructions when asking about their addressees' stances in interviews, debates and dialogical interactions in general. In (3), taken from a press interview, and (4), from a debate within a talk magazine, the speakers formulate questions to their addressees through either impersonal or passive constructions, instead of using second-person morphemes. Significantly, their interlocutors – respectively a politician and a public figure speaking for a consumer association – opt for both singular and plural first-person forms in their answers, suggesting a style more inclined to interactivity, thus to subjectivity.

(3) – ¿*Habrá* espacio para la autocrítica en el congreso?
– Siempre tiene que haber lugar a la autocrítica y *yo*, en mi informe de gestión, *voy* a decir que efectivamente *podemos* hacer mejor todavía las cosas. <Ent-Ad-131104-17>
'A: *Will there be* any room for self-criticism at the convention? – B: There always needs to be some place for self-criticism, and *I*, in my due management report, am going to make it clear that (*we*) still can do things better.'

(4) <A> *Los Lunnis* / quizá sea ese el único esPAcio (infantil) / que hay en la Dos / y por las tardes: / ¿cómo *se percibe* desde el punto de vista del consumidor:? /
<B> bueno / pue:s / cómo lo *vamos* a percibir / mal / pues que: p- / ante esa <sic>escacez</sic> / de: programas infantiles / pues qué pasa / que la audiencia infantil se traslada / a: / los / programa:s / de adultos // *yo estoy* de acuerdo / con:- / aquí con: el s- el sociólogo <Var-Pu-211204-12:35>
'A: *Los Lunnis* – this is perhaps the only program [for children], on Channel 2 in the evenings. How *is this assessed* from the point of view of consumers? – B: Well, how should (*we*) assess it? Negatively. What happens when there's such scarcity of programs for children? That the child audience switches to adult programs. *I* agree with what the sociologist here just said.'

All speaker groups other than journalists are often expected to expose their own experiences and stances, and sometimes also to contrast them with those of other participants. This results in all of them achieving quite higher frequencies of participant indexation. There is still a difference between public figures and anonymous individuals on one side, both groups having almost equal scores (44.8 vs. 44.4), and politicians, who fall below them by some 12 points. As exposed by Kampf/Daskal (2011), the growing discontent with political elites in the western world has apparently resulted in an increase – and even in the widespread acceptation – of fairly aggressive attitudes towards politicians. We can suspect that this, in turn, promotes some tendency of the latter to displace their discourse from the sphere of the direct participants, using third-person or impersonal constructions in much the same way as journalists often do.

Actually, when criticism is explicitly directed at a political opponent, it is often constructed from a third-person rather than second-person viewpoint. In (5), from a live debate, the speaker takes the reproach made by his "friend" opponent and redirects it towards the latter's political party, but does so without producing any second-person indexations. This is a frequent move in the political debates and interviews featured in the corpus, and helps avoid suggesting explicit confrontation and impolite or aggressive attitudes. Also note that an inclusive plural first person is used by the speaker at the end of the stretch, in order to present the whole citizenship as victims of the policies implemented by the party in question.

(5) mi amigo: Carlos ha hablado del tema de crispación // hombre: / crispación ahora mismo: la está generando el Partido Socialista allí donde está: / gobierne comunidades autónoma:s e / gob(i)erne el: Estado de la nació:n ahora mismo / *nos encontramos* en un: / enfrentamiento total: <Var-Pu-281204-12:40>
'My friend C. just raised the issue of social upheaval. Well, upheaval is just what the Socialist Party is producing wherever they hold the power, whether it is the regions or the whole state, the nation. Right now (*we*) find ourselves in a situation of general confrontation.'

Finally, both public figures and anonymous individuals tend to participate in contexts where indexation can be considered advantageous for the achievement of argumentative and persuasive goals. These include opinion pieces written by members of the first group (example 6), as well as letters to the editor, where contentious interaction with a specific addressee is sometimes enacted (7).

(6) "¡Dios mío! –*me digo* aterrado–, con lo que cuesta escribir y la esperpéntica autopista editorial está llena de conductores suicidas. . .". Pero llegó el miércoles y *me derrumbé* hasta desear *quemarme* a lo bonzo en la plaza de Santa Eulalia <Art-Ga-121203-5b>

' "Oh my God!," (*I*) say to myself in panic. "Writing is such a difficult task, and yet this bizarre highway of publishing is full of suicidal drivers." Then came Wednesday and (*I*) collapsed to the point of wanting to burn (*myself*) to death at S. E. Square.'

(7) Como devorador de cine que *soy, tengo que decirle* que no *he encontrado* todavía una película extranjera que *me* haga llorar <...> *Me* molesta que gente como usted intente poner el cine políticamente de su lado <Car-Ad-290704-6a>
'As the movie devourer (*I*) am, (*I*) must tell (*you+*) that (*I*) have yet to find a foreign movie that makes (*me*) cry. [...] It bothers (*me*) when people like you+ try to use cinema for political gain.'

The people speaking in radio commercials, given that they represent companies and institutions, have been included within public figures – with the exception of characters in fictional dialogue, showing the features of anonymous individuals – which also contributes to that group's having the highest normalized frequency of first- and second-person indexations (example 8). It is usually suggested that those in charge of an establishment, constructed as an audience-exclusive plural, invite addressees to take advantage of what they offer.

(8) el: mejor ambiente latino de Salamanca: la música que *tú bailas* / y las bebidas más exóticas <...> l:unes martes y miércoles / por tu consumición a partir de las nueve / *te regalamos* una clase de salsa: <Anu-Di-251104-10:50>
'The best Latin atmosphere of Salamanca, the music that *you* dance and the most exotic drinks. [...] On Monday, Tuesday and Wednesday, when ordering your drink from 9 p.m., (*we*)'ll treat (*you*) with a salsa lesson.'

As we know, normalized frequencies of participant indexation are mainly associated with the stylistic dimension of interactivity. Figure 10.1 shows the progression from anonymous individuals and public figures – whose contextual identities are characterized by a strong tendency to index the direct participants, usually in connection with argumentative and persuasive goals – to journalists – who tend to suppress first- and second-person indexations, except in rather conventionalized contexts such as opening, closing and discourse-organizing sequences. For their part, politicians occupy an intermediate position along the scale, suggesting that they elude excessive interactivity, even if this result was in principle more difficult to predict. Nevertheless, the following sections will show that the style associated with this identity type can prove quite subjective regarding other specific dimensions, which underlines the need to take into account a variety of linguistic choices and their meanings in order to make stylistic analysis more accurate.

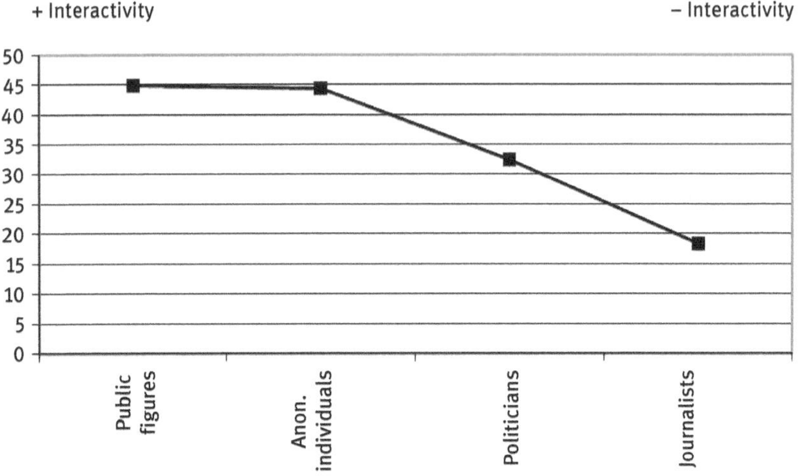

Figure 10.1: Participant identities and interactivity (based on frequency of first- and second-person indexations).

10.4 Person choice

The separate analysis of the six grammatical persons under study also reveals differences among the identity types distinguished, some of which have already been hinted at in the preceding section. Table 10.2 shows the absolute frequency of each grammatical person in the discourse produced by each of the participant groups.

Table 10.2: Frequency of each grammatical person according to participant identity.

Identity	1st sing	1st pl	2nd sing	2nd pl	2nd+ sing	2nd+ pl
Journalists	3.5	7.8	4.2	0.5	1.5	1.4
Public figures	16.6	15.1	8.5	0.4	3.5	0.6
Politicians	12.9	17.1	0.8	0.1	1.3	0.2
Anon. indivs.	22.2	12.7	4.5	0.7	3.3	1
Total	8.9	10.6	4.6	0.5	2.1	1.1

We will first pay attention to the main patterns of choice between the singular and plural first persons, which in most cases account for the great majority of tokens. In the discourse of journalists, the frequency of the plural first person more than doubles that of the singular (7.8 against 3.5). These speakers tend to avoid explicit self-indexation by constructing themselves into either exclusive or inclusive plurals – sometimes also speaker-blurring ones – depending on the requirements of the situation. Politicians, despite their considerable normalized frequency of singular first persons (12.9), also show some preference for constructing themselves as part of a wider group (17.1), which contributes to the desubjectivization of personal stances. This can be illustrated with example (9). The reference of *nosotros* morphemes shifts from the political party of the speaker to a different, wider social group he also includes himself in, namely *los jóvenes de Salamanca* 'young people in Salamanca'. This preverbal NP fills the slot of the subject-topic and evidences the referential shift. In the last clauses, discourse is further intersubjectivized through speaker-inclusive second-person forms. Throughout the whole stretch, the singular first person only appears in the metadiscursive construction *como comentaba antes* 'as (I) remarked earlier'.

(9) ahora mismo *estamos* trabajando: / sobre todo: / e:n: la cuestión como *comentaba* antes de la vivienda y el trabajo / en estos momentos *nos* parece m:uy preocupante / la subida: / de los precios de la vivienda / los:- / los jóvenes de Salamanca no *tenemos* capacidad / prime- / no *tenemos* capacidad ni siquiera / prácticamente para alquilar un piso solos / no *tenemo::s:* / m / con los SUELdos que hay en Salamanca / si *tienes* la suerte de conseguir un trabajo / es im:posible alquilar un piso / e independizarte / por lo tanto *te tienes* que quedar en casa de tus padres / o emigrar <Var-Pu-281204-13:00>
'Right now (*we*)'re mainly working, as (*I*) remarked earlier, on issues related to housing and employment. The current rise in housing prices seems (*to us*) rather alarming. Young people in Salamanca (*we*) don't practically have even the capacity to rent an apartment on our own. With such average salaries as there are in Salamanca, if (*you*)'re lucky enough to find a job at all, it's just impossible to rent an apartment and achieve independence. Thus (*you*) need to either stay at your parents' or emigrate.'

At the opposite end, anonymous individuals have the highest frequency of singular first-person morphemes (22.2). These participants tend to speak for themselves and discuss their own experiences and stances (example 10) rather than appear as representatives of any human groups, which explains the lower rate of plurals (12.7). However, the latter situation is frequent in letters to the editor, which can be signed by a certain group or association and thus use plural forms, as in (11). In such contexts, anonymous individuals actually approach the identity features of public figures.

(10) *yo* es que ya *soy* jubilada / y ya: / *me fijo* en esas cositas ¿*sabe*? / y durante: mi ju- / e desde que *me he jubilado* en el noventa y siete el Ipe Ce / automáticamente en el mes de noviembre bajaba / siempre <Var-SE-211204-14:00>
'The fact is *I*'m in retirement and (*I*) do pay attention to those little details, (*you+*) know? And ever since (*I*) retired in '97, the CPI had always automatically decreased in the month of November.'

(11) Para ellos y para nosotros, cada día es el Día del Donante, pero *elegimos* una fecha concreta para intentar dar a conocer nuestro problema a los demás. Para poder llevar a cabo los actos previstos este día, *hemos necesitado* el apoyo y la colaboración de muchas personas y a todos ellos les *queremos* dar las gracias. <Car-Ga-130604-6>
'For them and for us, every day is Donor Day, but (*we*) chose a specific date to make our problem better known to the rest of the people. In order to carry out the celebrations planned for this day, (*we*) have needed the support and cooperation of many people, and (*we*) now want to thank them all.'

Interestingly, a group of people can also choose to construct themselves as an individual through the singular first person, as in this letter collectively signed by the nurses at a public hospital (see a similar case, this time written from a plural viewpoint, in 7 above). They intend to exemplify the excuses any of them would have to give to their patients, as a result of the current policy of spending cuts.

(12) *Tendré* tres minutos para tomarle la tensión, pero si necesita *hablarme* de sus preocupaciones y sus ganas de mejorarse, sepa que habrá perdido sus tres minutos "programados" para su tensión, lo *siento*, perdió su oportunidad, mañana será otro día. <Car-Ga-090604-8>
'(*I*)'ll have just three minutes to take your blood pressure; if you+ need to tell (*me*) about your+ worries and your+ desire to get better, you+ need to know you+'ll be wasting the three minutes "scheduled" for your+ pressure taking. (*I*)'m sorry, you+ lost your chance; tomorrow will be a new day.'

Finally, the respective frequencies of the singular and plural first persons are quite balanced in the discourse produced by public figures (16.6 against 15.1). The former choice is the usual one in profile interviews, both in the written press and the radio, unless the interviewee constructs him/herself into a specific group. In turn, these participants often resort to audience-inclusive plurals as an intersubjectivizing resource in opinion pieces (example 13). The use of exclusive *nosotros* in advertising discourse was already commented on in the preceding section.

(13) ¿Por qué *huimos* de la realidad de la muerte, tabú insoportable de esta crasa y materialista sociedad, si es el final inevitable de todos nosotros, el que iguala a pobres y ricos y descubre si *queremos* verlo el último sentido de nuestra existencia? <Art-Ga-051104-5c>
'Why do (*we*) try to escape the reality of death – that unbearable taboo for this gross and materialistic society – if it is the inevitable ending of us all, makes the poor and the rich equal and reveals, if (*we*) just dare to see it, the ultimate meaning of our existence?'

The choice among the prototypical and displaced second persons is also significant, since it involves the choice of treatment with different addressees and audiences. This is strongly related to relationship management and can be used to highlight shared group membership vs. outwardness (Weyers 2011; Jang 2012; Raymond 2016). Our survey will focus mainly on radio programs and press interviews, given the generally scarce interactivity of the rest of written genres. The patterns of treatment choice and negotiation are probably quite different from those in spontaneous conversation. It is journalists that usually initiate spoken interactions, thus need to choose a certain treatment for their addressees, which the latter can in turn replicate or not. As pointed out in previous chapters, music programs are the only contexts where *tú* – more rarely, *vosotros* – appears to be the default choice for broadcasters with most kinds of addressees and audiences. In the remaining genres, the choice is subject to a more complex array of factors. *Tú* is frequent in more-or-less casual conversation with the usual participants of a program, especially if they are fellow media professionals, as in (14), where the anchor of a magazine talks to a reporter on the phone (see also Chapter 8, example 10, on the choice of *tú* in an interview with a journalist-author).

(14) a mí me gustaría / Elena: <. . .> que nos- que nos: e: / e: *relataras* un poco es decir / e: los pre:cios qué cua:dros son- e: / son paisa:jes son <sic>abstrastos</sic> / *háblanos* un poco de la: / de- de- de este: / mercado de arte que tenemos ahí <Var-SE-230903-12:55>
'I'd appreciate it, Elena, if (*you*) could tell us a little about the prices, and which kinds of paintings there are, I mean, are they landscapes or abstract paintings. . . (*You*) tell us a little about this art market that we have over there.'

Tú is also occasionally chosen with public figures. When it appears, it suggests personal closeness between the journalist and the addressee, be it due to previous knowledge – as noted, some of them are regular collaborators in specific programs or sections – or to some kind of shared affiliation (see also Chapter 7, example 14). In (15), a sports broadcaster who usually addresses soccer coaches and other interviewees with *usted* opts for *tú* when talking to the coach of the local team.

(15) <A> esos tres jugadores que *has citado:* ¿tienen: problemas para el domingo / o no? /
<B> no creo hoy: / g- David ya entrenó: / Lupi / también: / aunque q- e:l:- los dos úl:timos partidos no estuvieron y:- / y Raúl sí que hoy estaba bastante mal <Dep-On-080104-15:15>
'A: Those three players (*you*) mentioned, will they have any problems to play on Sunday? – B: I don't think so. D. already trained today, and so did L., even if neither played the last games. It was R. who was still feeling rather sick today.'

The age of the addressee is known to be one of the most powerful predictors of treatment choice in Spanish-speaking communities (Blas Arroyo 2005, 303–304). Some examples of *tú* in journalists' discourse are probably motivated by the fact that the addressee is a young person. This would be the case in (16), from a journal interview with a high-school student that is taking part in a mathematical competition. Still, the public nature of the interactions, as well as the intention to develop particular interviewer and interviewee identities, often plays in favor of *usted*. The choice of this person with a woman under 30 in (17) is coherent with the fact that she is presented as a teacher and discusses educational and social issues.

(16) – ¿Qué es lo que más *te* gusta de las matemáticas?
– Yo practico en casa y todo me gusta por igual. <Ent-Ga-040604-20>
'A: What do (*you*) like (lit. What pleases [*you*]) most about mathematics? – B: I practice at home and I like everything equally.'

(17) ¿A quién *pondría* un suspenso? ¿Y un sobresaliente? <. . .> ¿Cuál ha sido el mote más gracioso que *le* han puesto? <Ent-Ga-200804-15>
'What person would (*you+*) give an F? And an A? [. . .] What is the funniest nickname someone has given (*you+*)?'

Journalists rarely address politicians with *tú*. This choice might be viewed as contradicting the ideological neutrality and personal detachment they are expected to display towards this group. The only exception in the corpus is a debate already discussed in other sections, where three young political leaders are involved. The use of *tú* on the part of the moderator – a relatively young journalist herself – as well as of all the participants with one another seems to highlight their shared ascription to the same age group above other possible contextual considerations (18).

(18) <A> bien ha sido un año: un- / [complicado en cuanto:-]
<B> [*acércate* un poquito más al] micro / eso es / <Var-Pu-281204-12:30>
'A: Well, it's been a difficult year with respect to... – B: (*You*) get a little closer to the mike. That's it.'

Public figures clearly take the lead as to the overall frequency of both *tú* (8.5) and, with a lower score, *usted* (3.5), just as they also had comparably high figures of the singular and plural first persons. The results are indexical of an orientation to the viewpoints of both the speaker and the addressee, derived from their usual participation in conversational and argumentative interactions. Leaving aside speaker-inclusive uses of *tú* – which also appear in the rest of groups – it is frequent for guests and collaborators to use this treatment with specific interlocutors, usually broadcasters, even when they get *usted* in exchange. In the conversation in (19), while the program anchor systematically indexes a regular collaborator – a lawyer and author – with *usted* forms, the latter returns the prototypical second-person treatment to him. This asymmetry suggests that the public figure is accorded a higher psychosocial status, even if not a superordinate communicative role, since in this excerpt both participants explicitly agree that it is the broadcaster who can decide when the other is allowed to take the floor.

(19) <A> *usté intervendrá* / cuando *le* parezca ¿no? / pero claro que hoy el protago[ni:smo y la- y la in]
<B> [yo cuando me *dejes* / vamos]
<A> -tención que tenemos es de escuchar a nuestro: invitado / (o) sea que: /
<B> m: / yo: cuando me *digas* <Var-Co-230503-12:35>
'A: *You+* can step in whenever it seems OK (*to you+*), right? But of course today the starring role and... – B: I'll come in when (*you*) allow me to, no problem. – A: It is our intention to listen to our guest, so... – B: Just when (*you*) tell me to.'

Interestingly, later in the same conversation this collaborator will choose *usted* to address the guest alluded to above, namely the town mayor, as can be observed in (20). This third participant, displaying a politician identity, will systematically address both of his interlocutors with *usted* and receive the same treatment from them. There is thus no suggestion of personal closeness or of any coincidence in social affiliation.

(20) para ser realistas / e m: / esperemos que / si *usté sigue* siendo alcalde / la concejalía esté dotada con un: / presupuesto: digamos decoroso <Var-Co-230503-12:50>
'In order to be realistic, let's hope that, if *you+* remain mayor, this department will be endowed with a, say, decent budget.'

This particular conversation is especially interesting insofar as treatment choice helps define three partly different statuses within it. The politician is an outsider and guest who always addresses the others and is addressed with *usted*; the public figure is a partial insider whose previous knowledge of the host allows him to address the latter with *tú*, but whose characterization as a prestigious professional makes him receive *usted*; finally, the broadcaster is the real media insider who, in order to preserve his socioprofessional identity, needs to address the others with *usted*, even if they may choose not to do the same with him.

Politicians are the only speakers whose frequency of *usted* (1.3) exceeds that of *tú* (0.8) even if neither person is a usual choice for them, which indicates scarce orientation to the audience's viewpoint in spite of their likely persuasive goals. Political representatives in the texts analyzed often seem to be more concerned with exposing their own stances and those of the groups they belong to rather than explicitly attacking political rivals (see also 9 above). Example (21) again illustrates the construction of rivals as third persons, which downplays interactivity and avoids involving the addressee. The choice is however more pragmatically significant when the referents are present in the interaction, as noted with regard to example (5).

(21) *yo creo* que es el mensaje último que *nos* quieren dar / *debemos* an- / entender / que ellos cambien de chaqueta tan habitualmente / pues no lo *entenderemos* nunca / y no solamente / n:o lo *entenderemos* nunca / sino que *vamos* a seguirlo denunciando <Inf-Pu-171204-13:50>
'In the end *I* think this is the message they want to give (*us*) – that (*we*) need to accept that they should always be changing sides. Well, (*we*) will never accept it. And not only will (*we*) never accept it, but (*we*)'ll keep on denouncing it.'

While most studies dealing with the choice between *tú* and *usted* have focused on their use with specific addressees, contexts of nonspecific reference such as advertising (see 8 above) also offer relevant insights. In Aijón Oliva (2012), the 245 commercials included in the radio subcorpus were analyzed in order to elucidate the main factors associated with the choice between both persons – or, more rarely, their plural counterparts – to address target audiences. It was found that the age range and socio-economic status of the ideal customer have a significant influence on person choice, with *usted* being dominant in clips directed at older and better-to-do audiences, e.g. those offering luxury detached houses as against terraced ones or apartments.

However, reducing the motivations of person choice to sociodemographic features of the target would be oversimplifying. The image a corporation intends to construct of itself, as well as the type of relationship it aspires to entertain with customers, are no less relevant. The following examples, both of them from clips advertising local restaurants, make it possible to compare some of the contextual meanings related to the choice between the second persons. The text in (22), using *usted*, alludes to the celebration of social events, such as weddings and corporate meetings, by way of lexical items suggesting elegance and prestige (*comer es un arte* 'eating is an art form'; *deguste* '(you+) savor') as well as traditional customs (*horno de leña* 'wood-fired oven'). In turn, the commercial in (23), using *tú*, deals with a more relaxed kind of event, namely Christmas meals with friends or workmates. It also highlights the availability of different menus aimed at matching the tastes and financial possibilities of customers. Actually, the aforementioned investigation shows that allusions to low prizes correlate almost systematically with the prototypical second person.[2]

(22) donde comer: / es un arte: / amplios salones: / para celebraciones de bodas: / banquetes: / comuniones: / y: celebraciones de empresa: / *deguste* en Restaurante Carolina N:UEStros asados en hor:no de leña: <Anu-To-080803-12:40>
'Where eating is an art form. Spacious lounges for wedding celebrations, banquets, first communions and corporate meetings. At R. C. (*you*+) can savor our wood-fired oven roasts.'

2 In a study of Mexican advertising, Weyers (2011) finds that *tú* is clearly dominant in "commercial" advertising, while the choices are much more balanced in "institutional" ads providing public information, instructions or warnings. It is difficult to reliably replicate this finding in our corpus, since the great majority of clips belong to the first type.

(23) no lo *pienses* más / Mesón Restaurante Imbis / es el sitio ideal para celebrar en estas fiestas / tus comidas de grupo y empresa: / Mesón Restaurante Imbis / ha elaborado una amplia carta de menús y precios / para que se adapten a tus gustos / y: presupuesto: <Anu-Ci-151204-13:35>
'(*You*) stop thinking – M. R. I. is the ideal place to celebrate your group and corporate meals during these holidays. M. R. I. has elaborated a wide range of menus and prices that will suit your tastes and budget.'

Cases like these confirm that the choice between *tú* and *usted* concerns not just the discursive-cognitive construction of the addressee, but that of the speaker as well. If someone indexes an addressee or audience through a certain grammatical person, it is because he/she feels entitled to do so in the particular interactional context. This is why forms of address can be analyzed as a feature of speaker identity. As pointed out, in the corpus analyzed only politicians are more inclined to *usted*, while the other three types of identity correlate with higher frequencies of *tú*.

As also noted, both of the plural second persons, and especially *vosotros*, are altogether rare in the corpus. Anonymous individuals take the lead in the use of the prototypical plural – but still with a very low frequency – which reflects their occasional participation in music programs and talk magazines where they choose this person to address the team responsible for the program. The choice may be seen as mirroring the usual tendency of radio broadcasters to adopt a plural first-person viewpoint for self-construction (see Chapter 7, examples 17–18). The phone caller in (24) makes an interesting person shift in correlation with a referential one: first she sends a political message with *ustedes* to the whole audience of the program, then she uses *vosotros* to make a request to the team of the station. Even if this could suggest the attribution of a lower psychosocial status to media professionals – as also remarked in the discussion of some previous examples – in other cases anonymous individuals do use *ustedes* to construct those semispecific radio teams (25).

(24) señores / no *se dejen* engañar / porque a Caldera / y compañía / ni me los imagino gobernando la nación / • del trabajo / más vale trabajo en mano / que cientos volando // quisiera // que mañana que es el Día de las Águedas / *tuvierais* un recuerdo para las que: / se llaman Águedas / y cumplen años <Var-Co-050204-13:10>
'Ladies and gentlemen, don't (*you guys+*) let yourselves be fooled, since I just can't imagine C. and his bunch ruling this nation. As for jobs – a job

in hand is worth two in the bush. And since tomorrow is Saint Águeda's Day, I'd appreciate it if (*you guys*) could pay tribute to those whose name is Águeda and also celebrate their birthday.'

(25) hay un: bache grandísimo / que la verdad / tenemos que tener mucho cuidao los peatones / porque si no nos caemos / y lleva muchísimo tiempo MEses así / entonces por favor si *quieren* dar la queja a ver si es posible / que le echen el asfalto <Var-Co-050204-13:00>
'There's a huge hole there, and we pedestrians need to be very careful or we'll just fall into it. And it's been there for a very long time – months. So please, if (*you guys+*) could pass on this complaint, so they can fill it with tarmac.'

It is understandably journalists that achieve the highest score of *ustedes* (1.4), since most tokens of this person occur when these participants address the nonspecific audiences of radio programs in transitional sequences and discourse-organizing comments. With public figures and politicians, both *vosotros* and *ustedes* are rare, given that these participants do not usually need to address plural audiences in media interactions. The only significant exception would be commercials, but, as pointed out, these texts strongly prefer the singular persons for the construction of their target audiences.

In previous chapters, aside from the choice between *tú* and *usted* – or their respective plurals – we discussed that between the singular and plural second persons in the construction of specific addressees across interviews and other kinds of discourse (see especially §7.2.2; §8.2.2). This phenomenon is most often parallel to the very choice between the singular and plural first persons for self-construction. Broadcasters will often shift from the view of their interlocutors as individuals to that as representatives of wider, generally semispecific groups. In some cases, this appears to be related to the topics under discussion, with the plurals helping avoid a specific-addressee viewpoint whenever the content is perceived as excessively personal or potentially troublesome. Example (26) is taken from a journal interview with a local politician. The interviewer, after requesting his opinion on presidencial policies towards the region using the singular, switches to the plural in his next turn just as he raises a potential reproach – that the interviewee and his party are actually dissatisfied because it is not they who are in office. It is also interesting to note that the politician invariably chooses the plural first person, in line with the usual strategy of participants displaying this type of identity.

(26) – ¿Qué *le* parece la política de Zapatero respecto a Castilla y León?
– *Nos* preocupa muchísimo la sensación de abandono y de agravio con la que se está comportando respecto a otras comunidades autónomas <distintas de Cataluña>. <. . .>
– Pero *ustedes* también *se han vuelto* más reivindicativos que cuando gobernaba Aznar.
– *Estamos* pidiendo lo mismo ahora que cuando gobernaba el PP. <Ent-Ad-131104-17>
'A: What do Z.'s policies towards the Castilla y León region seem (*to you+*)? – B: It really disturbs (*us*) to see the careless, offensive attitudes he displays towards regions [other than Catalonia]. – [. . .] A: But *you guys+* are also more exigent now than when A. was in office. – B: (*We*) are requesting just the same as when the PP was in office.'

The discussion has shown that the choice among grammatical persons across media interactions helps participants manage their own socioprofessional identities just as those of their addressees and audiences. Figure 10.2 is intended to synthesize the dominant viewpoint orientation of each identity type, even if the patterns of choice are obviously quite complex and highly dependent on particular contexts. Journalists, when constructing the direct participants – which they do less often than any other group – tend to prefer plural first persons and singular second ones – often with a speaker-inclusive reference – which is indexical of a joint-oriented or intersubjective style. The rest of the groups have higher rates of both first persons, with anonymous individuals leading in the use of the singular one. Politicians are farther from the speaker-oriented vertex, given their preference for *nosotros* – which places them closer to journalists – if usually with an audience-exclusive reference. Their position within the triangle can be somewhat surprising, given the usual view of this type of speakers as strongly oriented to the persuasion of the audience. The analysis of examples has shown that politicians in the corpus actually tend to avoid indexing themselves and the audience, rather alluding to absent groups they are part of, as well as to third persons in order to construct their rivals. Finally, public figures stand out for their frequencies of both the prototypical and displaced singular second persons, which place them halfway between the vertices of speaker and audience orientation. The fact that none of the groups turns out to be primarily audience-oriented may suggest the relative lack of interactivity in media discourse altogether (see also the preceding section).

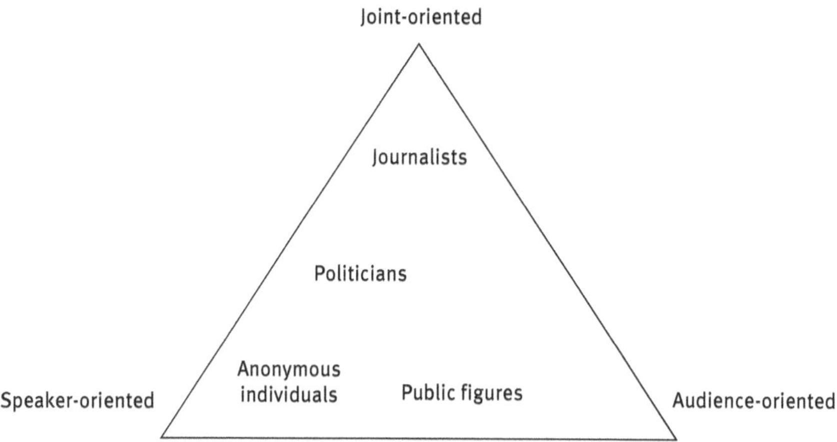

Figure 10.2: Participant identities and orientation towards speaker, audience or joint viewpoints (based on the respective frequencies of grammatical persons).

10.5 Variable expression and placement of pronouns

In Section 9.5 we associated the choices related to the formal configuration of first- and second-person pronouns in the clause with the stylistic dimension of involvement. When it comes to identity, this dimension should be understood as the degree to which each kind of participant is allowed – or expected – to orient discourse to the contrast of their own personal situations and stances with those of others. We will again pay special attention to the choices that proved to be more frequent and stylistically differentiated, namely preverbal placement and omission, even if the different variants of postverbal placement will also cast some eye-catching results. Table 10.3 shows the percentages of each variant with each type of socioprofessional identity.

In contrast with the more-or-less evident patterning of pronoun formulation and placement across genres, it appears that participant identities are not quite differentiated as regards this feature, with only a couple of details worth discussing. Politicians show an unparalleled preference for preverbal expression (25.5%) at the expense of omission, with a result about 15 points below those it has with the remaining groups. This would seem to be more in line with the stereotypical style of political representatives – i.e. explicitly argumentative and straightforwardly focused on the participants – than the figures obtained in the preceding sections, which clearly indicate a tendency to downplay subjectivity. It is again confirmed that a sociocommunicative category can behave in different ways according to different stylistic dimensions. The pronouns formulated by politicians

Table 10.3: Variable expression and placement of pronouns according to participant identity.

Genre	Preverbal		Clause-final postverbal		Clause-intermediate p.		Omitted	
	#	%	#	%	#	%	#	%
Journalists	335	10	42	1.2	97	2.9	2,888	85.9
Public figures	326	10.5	38	1.2	22	0.7	2,723	87.6
Politicians	197	25.5	12	1.6	14	1.8	551	71.2
Anonymous indivs.	135	11.4	13	1.1	23	1.9	1,010	85.5
Total	993	11.8	105	1.2	156	1.9	7,172	85.1

are usually first-person ones, either singular (example 27) or more often – and expectably – plural (28). These speakers, at least in the kinds of interactions analyzed, tend to avoid second-person explicit formulation and thus the enhancement of addressee or audience involvement, which in their case would most likely suggest confrontation.

(27) *yo creo* que esto es una / cosa evidente y clara y que: no- nadie lo discute es decir que el museo funciona bie:n y que / es un- e: / un activo importante para la ciudá / (en)tonces / e: / *yo vuelvo* a reiterar / otra vez / e: mi voluntad de diálogo / como la de todo el patronato / para buscar una solución <Inf-On-080104-13:50>
'*I* think this is an evident and clear notion that no one will challenge – that the museum is doing fine and that it is an important asset for the town. So *I* hereby reiterate my willingness to engage in dialogue, just as that of the whole board of trustees, in order to find a solution.'

(28) *nosotros creemos* / que: el año no ha sido malo / porque: de todas maneras ha cambil- / ha cambiado el signo político / y *creemos* que *hemos* contribua:- / *contribuido* a ello <Var-Pu-281204-12:30>
'*We* believe it's not been a bad year, since there's been a change of government anyway, and (*we*) think (*we*)'ve played a part in it.'

Still, we can find examples like (29), from a recorded clip where a politician formulates preverbal *usted* when reacting to the objections posed by an opponent. The construction *como usted bien sabe* 'as you+ are well aware' is clearly controversial in the sense that the speaker attributes the addressee the obligation to be already aware of what he is exposing. This obligation is enhanced by the overt preverbal pronoun (see also Chapter 3, example 5, on the formulation of preverbal *usted* amidst negatively-regarded contents). Subsequently, there is again formulation of *usted* when establishing a viewpoint contrast with first-person *yo*. However, and in line with the usual strategy of politicians in the corpus, the viewpoint of the speaker is subsequently transferred to that of a wider, audience-exclusive group whose reference is delimitated through a topicalized prepositional phrase (*para el equipo de gobierno municipal* 'to the Town Council cabinet').

(29) la utilización del punto l:- del: día:- / del orden del día de: información de la alcaldía / como *usté* bien *sabe* es discrecional / por parte / de la alcaldía / y por lo tanto lo utiliza si lo estima conveniente o no / en este caso / en el caso: / al que *usté se está* refiriendo / *yo le tengo* que señala:r que para el: equipo de gobierno municipal / *nos* parece absolutamente justificada la lectura de la Sala de lo Social- / de la sentencia de la Sala de lo Social del Tribunal Superior de Justicia <Inf-Pu-021204-13:55>
'Subjection to the informative points of the meeting agenda, as *you+* are well aware, is at the discretion of the Town Council, who will follow the agenda if it is considered appropriate to do so. In this case, in the particular case *you+* are alluding to, *I* must point it out (*to you+*) that, to the Town Council cabinet, the ruling made by the Social Division of the Supreme Justice Court seems (*to us*) totally justified.'

The remaining identity groups are not largely differentiated in quantitative terms. As regards anonymous individuals, their percentages always closely approach the general ones in the corpus, which makes it difficult to highlight significant preferences for any of the variants. This contrasts, for example, with their leading status regarding frequencies of singular first-person indexation. The fact that they do not usually enter direct confrontation with other speakers, but rather are allowed to freely express their views on a given issue – even if most often with a very limited amount of time or space – often results in pronoun omission in argumentative contexts such as (30), uttered by a phone caller to a talk magazine, and (31), from a journal letter. However, the latter participant displays identity features approaching those of public figures.

(30) *llamo* por el incidente que hubo ayer por la tarde: en la calle de Don Benito que se prendió un coche / y lo que *quiero* destacar es la actuación de los bomberos <Var-Co-050204-13:05>
'(*I*) am calling in connection with yesterday evening's incident on D. B. Street, in which a car caught fire. And what (*I*)'d like to underscore is the intervention of the firefighters.'

(31) ¿Por qué se prohíbe vacunar a los animales contra la brucela? *Puedo* demostrar que las vacas que en su día se vacunaron contra la brucela dan negativo y las hijas y nietas dan positivo; algunas han parido normalmente. <Car-Ad-121203-6>
'Why is it prohibited to vaccinate animals against brucella? (*I*) can demonstrate that the cows that were vaccinated in time against brucella test negative, whereas their children and grandchildren test positive; some have had normal deliveries.'

It is perhaps more surprising to find that public figures surpass journalists in pronoun omission by nearly two points, while most other features of choice characterize their sociocommunicative style as more subjective than that of media professionals. Taking into account the relationship between pronoun expression and involvement, it must be acknowledged that public figures often participate in formats such as opinion pieces or interviews, where there is no need for the negotiation of turns and little real contrast between personal stances (see also Section 9.5 on the relative scarcity of expression in argumentative written genres). Seen from this angle, their situation is not very different from that of anonymous individuals. In contexts where they are expected to constrast their stances with those of others, e.g. radio debates, expressed pronouns do appear, as in (32), with some topicalized instances of *yo*.

(32) *yo* / si soy sincero no / *temo:* / m: / pues por el hecho de que:- / *yo* mismo / cuando *era:* niño / pues también había violencia en televisión no había s:in duda / en los estremos en los que ha:- / lo hay ahora <...> yo creo que:- / m: / conFÍo al menos / en que- / e:n que: los seres humanos / pues tienen las ca- / las suficientes capacidades de resistencia para ser de alguna manera escépticos / ante aquello que se les ofrece ¿no? <Var-Pu-211204-12:40>
'*I*, honestly speaking, am not afraid of the fact that – *I* myself, when (*I*) was a kid, there was also violence on TV, even if of course not to the point that there is now. [...] *I* think, or at least (*I*) trust, that human beings, well, they have enough endurance capacity to be somehow skeptical towards what they're offered, right?'

Finally, with respect to journalists, they have the lowest percentage of preverbal expression (10%) and the second-highest one of omission (85.9%), which, as with the rest of the features analyzed so far, places their typical style away from the pole of subjectivity. They are also the group producing most instances of clause-intermediate postverbal pronouns, which account for 2.9% of their total participant indexations, one point above the general figure. We have described this formal variant as helping diminish the informational focalization of the referent naturally entailed by explicit formulation; the pronoun is placed at a scarcely prominent position where it can even resemble inflectional subject morphemes (see especially Sections 8.3 and 9.5). While many of the tokens are instances of *usted* and *ustedes* whose peculiarities have been sufficiently discussed, in others like (33) we can observe the strategy of placing the first-person subject pronoun in a scarcely salient position when exposing a personal assumption (*pensaba yo* 'I thought'). Through such a configuration, the broadcaster implicitly excuses herself, having previously formulated a question that was beyond her guest's competence; also note the intersubjectivizing value of inclusive *nosotros*.

(33) <A> esa ubicación del archivo de la Guerra Civi:l / e: / ¿cómo están las cosas en estos momentos? /
<B> m: bien / b- e: en cuanto al archivo de la Guerra Civil:: / poco puedo decir o- / o NADA / debo / decir / porque: es un archivo estatal y por lo tanto: depende: / del Estado <. . .>
<A> no *sabemos* por tanto todavía NA:da / *pensaba yo* que: a estas alturas del año ya *conocíamos* e: / q- lo q- lo que estaba: / e: / bueno pues larva: do <Var-On-080104-12:55>
'A: Regarding the location chosen for the Civil War archive, what is the situation right now? – B: Well, as for the Civil War archive, there is little I can say – and nothing I ought to say, since it is a state archive and therefore it is the responsibility of the Government. [. . .] – A: So (*we*) still don't know anything. *I* [postv.] thought that at this time of the year (*we*) already knew what was, well, under way.'

Figure 10.3 represents the stylistic characterization of each type of socio-professional identity according to preverbal placement and omission, which we have interpreted as respectively associated with the highest and lowest degrees of participant involvement. It becomes clear that only politicians diverge significantly from the rest of the groups, constructing a more involved style that is in accordance with their usual roles and goals in media communication – their participation is scarcely motivated unless aimed at expressing ideological stances and, crucially for the feature at issue, contrasting them with those of other people. At the other end, journalists are the participants least inclined to involvement if we just pay attention to preverbal pronoun formulation; however, public figures achieve a higher rate of pronoun omission, for the reasons discussed. As also pointed out, journalists show a comparably high frequency of clause-intermediate postverbal expression; the discursive-cognitive meanings of this variant are connected with desubjectivization, as is omission itself.

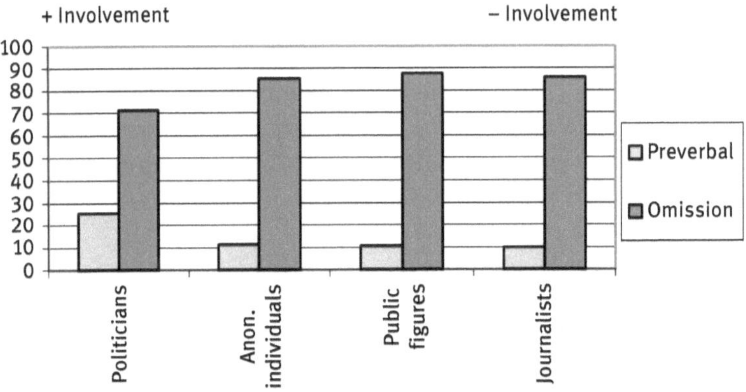

Figure 10.3: Participant identities and involvement (based on preverbal placement vs. omission of first- and second-person pronouns).

10.6 Functional encoding

The last feature to be analyzed is the choice between the subject vs. object encoding of the direct participants, which we have associated with the degree of responsibility attributed to them. Higher responsibility correlates with subject encoding and agentive semantic roles, these being features of cognitive autonomy (see §1.3.1b). The general results for either syntactic function with each identity group are displayed in Table 10.4.

In this case, and bearing in mind that subject encoding is always strongly dominant, the four types of participant identity clearly cluster into two different groups according to their relative preferences. Taking object encoding as related to stylistic desubjectivization, it is once again media professionals that stand out in their preference for it. Less expectably, the scores for anonymous individuals are identical to theirs. Public figures and politicians, being divergent as for some of the features analyzed in the previous sections, have very similar percentages with respect to this one, clearly preferring the encoding of the participants as clause subjects.

Table 10.4: Subject vs. object encoding according to participant identity.

Genre	Subject		Object	
	#	%	#	%
Journalists	2,585	76.9	777	23.1
Public figures	2,592	83.4	517	16.6
Politicians	650	84	124	16
Anonymous individuals	908	76.9	273	23.1
Total	6,735	79.9	1,691	20.1

In Section 9.6 we explained the high percentages of first- and second-person subject encoding in talk magazines and sports programs, as well as the considerable overall frequencies of participant indexation in these genres, as connected with the interactional and contentious orientation of many of their sequences. It must now be added that these are the genres where the participation of public figures and anonymous individuals is more usual. People displaying such kinds of socioprofessional identity are attributed the right – or imposed the duty – to speak for themselves in radio interactions, assuming responsibility for their words. In (34) and (35), different kinds of public figures – respectively a physician and professor, and a soccer coach – elaborate their views on certain issues after being asked to do so by the program anchors. In spite of the repeated use of *yo creo* 'I think', a typical expressed-subject modalizer (see Section 4.4) with a strong subjective orientation, it is also possible to detect intersubjectivization through audience-inclusive plural first persons in the first example (*nos tenemos que tomar, hemos tenido*) and speaker-inclusive second persons in the second one (*te contagias, tienes*, etc.). Besides, epistemic modalizers such as *en principio* 'in principle' make assertions more tentative than repeated subject self-encoding might suggest.

(34) *yo creo:* / que no: que *nos tenemos* que tomar las cosas con tranquilidaz / porque si no solo: / que de sustos ya: / nos:- / *nos podemos* morir <...> vamos *yo creo* que en principio: / no: hay por qué alarmarse / e: / lo que: m:: / tenemos: / previsto: / es: / las vacuna:s / pues a una gripe muy similar a la que *hemos tenido:* / en los últimos años <Var-SE-230903-13:20>
'No, *I* think that (*we*) need to take things easy, because otherwise, with these constant shocks, (*we*) might as well die. That is, *I* think there is in principle no cause for alarm. The kinds of vaccines that have been forecasted are intended, well, for a very similar kind of influenza as (*we*)'ve been having in recent years.'

(35) el primer tiempo resultó: / *yo creo* que de lo más bonito que hemos visto aquí: / y: por eso *digo* que- / que el domingo: con un buen: campo como: es el Helmántico y::- / y: ante un buen equipo / *yo* siempre *digo* lo mismo que: siempre *te contagias* / de lo que *tienes* enfrente y si enfrente *tienes* un equipo / que juega al fútbol / pue:s / *tú:* también: / *hace:s* un buen partido seguro <Dep-Co-080104-15:00>
'The first half was, *I* think, among the most beautiful games we've seen around here. That's why (*I*)'m saying that, on Sunday, on such a good pitch as the Helmántico, and against a good team... *I* always say the same – that (*you*)'re always inspired by what (*you*) have in front of you. And if what (*you*) have is a team that plays real soccer, *you*'ll surely make a great game too.'

By contrast, anonymous individuals, given the incidental nature of their participation in media interactions and their frequent lack of a recognized professional status in the context, can still feel some need to blur their own presence by encoding themselves as objects, which might explain their close alignment with journalists in this respect. Also, they are often not expected to offer anything on their part, but rather to ask things from others (e.g. the radio station, the authorities). The choice of object self-encoding in these cases can help avoid the risk of sounding too impositive. In other cases like (36), speakers can exploit the patienthood prototypically associated with (accusative) object encoding. The caller in (36) presents the whole citizenship as the victim of politicians' lies. She also uses nonspecific *uno* 'one', this being another choice associated with desubjectivization.

(36) uno se pone nervioso viendo cómo las cosas que están ocurriendo / y diciendo los políticos / que *nos* están / es que / p- p- e / irriTAN:do / de las mentiras / que la mayoría y las demagogias dicen <Var-Co-230503-13:45>
'One gets stressed out watching the things that are happening and what politicians say. Because they are just irritating (*us*) with the lies and demagoguery of most of them.'

As we know, journalists are usually the group most inclined to desubjectivizing linguistic choices. Their dedication to the transmission of informational contents, together with the public exposure entailed by their job, is likely to result in some tendency to avoid the responsibility for themselves or others associated with subject encoding (cf. also Patrona 2011, 159). This is patent in singular first-person contexts. As already discussed in Chapter 4, constructions like (*a mí*) *me parece* 'it seems to me', most often with pronoun omission, help these speakers modalize a personal stance in both clearly argumentative contexts (37) and basically epistemic ones (38). In the second example, *me parece* coappears with subject-encoding *creo*, which underlines the pragmatic similarity between both constructions. Besides, here they resemble discourse markers, having been formulated in non-canonical syntactic positions.[3]

(37) *me* parece que: si juega como lo viene haciendo es decir tan atrás / ni falta que le hace a la Unión Deportiva Salamanca <Dep-Co-221104-14:35>
'It seems (*to me*) that, if he keeps playing as he's been doing lately, that is, at such a backward position, the U. D. S. team can do without him.'

(38) y entonces para no: / cargar más: e: / la condición física del jugador / s:e retiró antes como también se retiró antes / Lupidio <...> este *me* parece que por una contratuta- / contracTU:ra / *creo* <Dep-Co-080104-14:40>
'And then, in order not to further exhaust his physical condition, the player stepped out before the end of the game. Just as L. did. This one, it seems (*to me*), did it because of a contracture, (*I*) think.'

Journalists also produce frequent object indexations in largely pragmaticalized constructions used to yield the turn, such as *dime* and *dígame* 'tell me'. In (39) we can compare object self-encoding on the part of the broadcaster – who in addition constructs himself as a plural first person (*díganos* 'tell us') – with subject self-encoding on that of the anonymous individual calling (see also the discussion in Chapter 4, examples 44 and 45). The latter, however, also encodes her addressee as a subject in the introductory marker *mira* 'look' (§6.2.4), which in passing suggests an asymmetry in treatment with the program host, who had opted for the displaced second person.

3 However, the construction *este me parece que por una contractura* 'this one, it seems (to me), did it because of a contracture' could also be explained as a topicalization of the subject pronoun *este*, extracted from a subordinate clause governed by *me parece*. The pragmaticalization of the latter would be clearer if it was not accompanied by the subordinating particle *que: este, me parece, por una contractura*, as has actually been interpreted in the English translation.

(39) <A> ho:la buenas tardes / *díganos* /
<B> *mira* Santiago *yo:* / casi: / m: va: en relación con lo que han hablado anteriormente /
<A> <asentimiento> /
<B> pero: / *quería:* hacerle una llamada de atención a nuestro alcalde: <Var-SE-211204-13:55>
'A: Hello, good afternoon. (*You*+) tell (*us*). – B: Look, S., *I* – well, this is kind of related to what someone said before. – A: [*Nods.*] – B: But (*I*) would like to give a warning call to our mayor.'

Politicians coincide with public figures – the identity group they are in principle closest to – in a strong tendency to subject encoding, which makes their style approach the pole of highest responsibility, as also happened with pronoun expression and placement in the preceding section. However, in some cases they seem to take advantage of the meanings associated with their dispreferred choice, i.e. object encoding, particularly in analogous singular first-person contexts as have just been surveyed with journalists. The participant in (40) comments on the achievements of the regional administration he belongs to, repeatedly using *yo creo* while showing his awareness that his words might be interpreted as self-flattering. In (41), another politician sarcastically recounts the criticisms he often gets from his opponents, encoding himself as a dative object that, in this context, approaches the semantic features of a patient.

(40) *yo creo* que hoy sin:- / sin que esto se entienda: / como una manifestación: / de- de prepotencia de soberbia / que no lo es evidentemente / *yo creo* que la:- / que el: esfuerzo qu(e) ha hecho la Junta de Castilla y León / en materia de protección civil / empieza a verse y empieza a dar sus frutos <Inf-SE-301104-14:15>
'*I* think that today – and this should not be understood as an expression of arrogance or pride, which it is obviously not – *I* think that the effort made by the Castilla y León Government with regard to public safety is starting to show and is starting to pay off.'

(41) "cómo se mete donde nadie le llama / dónde se mete dónde va este hombre / que lo quiere dominar todo" / esas cosas / esas lindezas que insisto / *me* dedican / habitualmente mis a(d)versarios políticos <Var-Co-230503-13:10>
' "Always sticking his nose into others' business! Now, what's this fellow doing? He wants to control everything!" You know, all that stuff, all those beautiful words my political opponents usually dedicate (*to me*).'

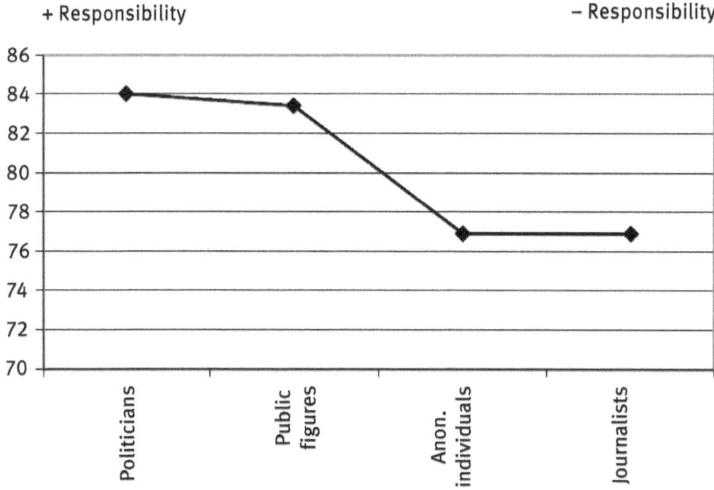

Figure 10.4: Participant identities and responsibility accorded to the direct participants (based on percentages of subject encoding).

Variation between subject and object self-encoding is also significant in contexts with psychological verbs. Whereas *yo creo* could be taken to suggest self-flattering in (40) above, the politician in (42) uses *me gustaría* 'I would like', lit. 'it would please (me)' when expressing the wish that she would have a larger budget at their disposal, in order to render a better service to the people (see also Chapter 3, example 28). In this construction, object encoding again suggests the avoidance of responsibility, while the conditional tense is a co-occurring feature helping modalize the content as hypothetical (RAE 2009, §23.15).

(42) Cuanto más se tiene, más se puede invertir. *Me* gustaría tener otros 96 millones para hacer más carreteras, más abastecimientos, llevar mejor calidad de vida a los ciudadanos del mundo rural. <Ent-Ad-070404-9>
'The more you have, the more you can invest. (*I*)'d like (lit. It would please [*me*]) to have another 96 millions to make more highways, produce more supplies, improve the quality of life of rural residents.'

In sum, the quantitative data indicate that the identity types distinguished form two different groups regarding the functional encoding of the direct participants, as represented in Figure 10.4. While subject encoding is always dominant, it is public figures and politicians that most clearly tend to highlight their own responsibility or that of other participants through this choice, while journalists and anonymous individuals are comparably more inclined to stylistic desubjectivization by way of object encoding. However, we have observed that, in interactions between two speakers respectively pertaining to either of the latter groups, it is usually the journalist that more clearly avoids self-responsibility, encoding him/herself as the object and the addressee as the subject, suggesting that it is anonymous callers that are expected to take the turn and expose their views. As in all cases, statistical calculations only show the general patterning of choices across sociocommunicative categories; it is qualitative observation that helps elucidate their meaningful potential in actual contexts.

10.7 Summary

A central tenet of studies in sociocommunicative style is that speakers develop their social identities, which in turn make them qualify for certain roles in interactional contexts, by making formal choices that can belong to any semiotic code, most significantly verbal language. The investigation of grammatical choice and participant identity carried out across this chapter has shown that, in the domain of media communication, identities and roles are to a large extent predefined by the conventions of textual genres. However, the participants can still take advantage of the discursive-cognitive meanings of linguistic forms in order to nuance their sociocommunicative styles, placing them at different points along the different stylistic dimensions considered, thus further elaborating the kinds of identities they display and achieving particular contextual goals by doing so.

Drawing on extensive observation of local media interactions and on previous proposals, we have distinguished four basic and recurrent types of socio-professional identity in this domain. They are not unrelated to the sociodemographic features of speakers – including their professional qualification and psychosocial status within the community – but are mainly based on the ways of self-presentation and the sets of communicative rights and obligations associated with the kinds of interactions they take part in. Even if other possible taxonomical criteria might also prove to be valid, the analysis has repeatedly shown interesting quantitative and qualitative differences among the groups. Journalists and broadcasters, producing some 60% of the total text in the corpus, show a marked preference for most of the choices we have described as desubjectivizing, namely a low overall frequency of participant indexation, a preference for plural first persons and second ones as against the singular first one, the omission of personal pronouns, and the encoding of participants – most significantly themselves – as syntactic objects. All this reflects the development of a sociocommunicative style that is perceived as adequate to what audiences usually expect from media professionals.

The remaining groups tend to construct more subjective styles, although with differences among them regarding particular dimensions. The usefulness of detaching political representatives from the wider category of public figures is confirmed by the divergence between both groups regarding most of the variables considered, with the only exception of functional encoding. Most politicians in the corpus avoid the assiduous indexation of participants; they also prefer *nosotros* over *yo* and especially *usted* over *tú*. However, at the same time they take the lead as for pronoun expression and preverbal placement, which correlate with higher participant involvement. The explanation is that public figures, unless in debates or particularly contentious interviews, are allowed to construct discourse from their own viewpoint, with little competition from other participants; their discourse thus tends to have a high degree of interactivity, but not of involvement as such. In turn, politicians, while they often perceive it as advantageous to include themselves within a wider group, and even to avoid participant indexation altogether – often constructing their rivals as third persons – are expected to develop a more involved style, given that their stances can and will expectably be challenged by others. Finally, as regards anonymous individuals, the incidental nature of their participation in media interactions and the fact that they are usually not acknowledged any prominent social or professional status seems to manifest itself in their tendency to avoid responsibility. They closely align with journalists in their relative preference for object self-encoding, whereas with the remaining features they approach the behavior of public figures.

As is the case with textual genres, the development of participant identities through sociocommunicative style can only be accurately described by taking into account many different semiotic choices, as well as their contextual motivations and repercussions. Investigations such as the one developed here can serve as a starting point for future research.

11 Conclusions

The shift of the scientific focus from the notion of *linguistic variation* to that of *communicative choice* is parallel to the development of a view of language as essentially motivated by the human need to construct and communicate meaning. Aside from the complex dynamics of first- and second-person usage in Spanish media discourse, the present book should have exposed and illustrated a certain theoretical and analytical approach to the construction of meaning through language. The specific characteristics of this approach are inspired by the purpose of capturing some of the complexity of meaningful choice in communicative contexts.

The investigation started from a set of functional and cognitive principles whereby linguistic configuration is understood as undetachable from the construction of entities (referents) and events (clauses) in the cognitive domain. The notions of *salience* and *informativeness* have been used to formalize the discursive-cognitive status of referents across discourse. They help explain all the choices made for their linguistic encoding, including grammatical person, syntactic function, morphematic indexation vs. explicit formulation, and placement within the clause. In turn, this has made it possible to unveil the most significant meanings constructed by the different grammatical persons under study in oral and written mass-media discourse. The fact that each of these persons is endowed with an inherent meaning – the singular first person being *the speaker*, the singular second one *the addressee*, and so on – results in a wide range of possibilities for meaning construction in context, which are further multiplied thanks to the nuances – often quite subtle ones – provided by the different syntactic features analyzed.

In turn, the sociolinguistic side of the study has been based on the concept of *sociocommunicative style*, understood as the projection of discursive-cognitive meanings onto the social domain. Patterns of choice across textual genres and participant groups have been put in connection with a general stylistic continuum from *subjectivity* to *objectivity*, of which each feature of choice reveals a partially different dimension. This way, the overall frequency of first- and second-person indexations appears to correlate with the stylistic dimension of *interactivity*; variable pronoun formulation and placement are associated with different degrees of *participant involvement* in the content of discourse; the dominance of subject vs. object encoding is parallel to the *responsibility* accorded to the speaker or other participants. Most significantly, the formalization of a bidimensional space for the distribution of the data for person choice – delimited by the vertices of speaker, addressee and joint *viewpoint orientation* – can be taken as a preliminary proposal

https://doi.org/10.1515/9783110643442-012

towards more complex, multifaceted models of variation and choice. It also shows that *intersubjectivity*, rather than a mere intermediate zone between the poles, can be seen as a different dimension of meaning itself. Further research is still needed in order to elucidate the specific contribution of each grammatical person and its formal configuration to the intersubjectivization of discourse. Besides, the addition of different features of communicative choice to the analysis would obviously help refine the dimensions involved in style construction.

It should have become evident that the first and second persons constitute a challenging field of research, being sets of grammatical elements whose basic function is to construct the direct participants in discourse and cognition. The division of the analysis into different grammatical persons, each of them incorporating various features of choice, has shown that participant construction is itself composed of a multiplicity of dimensions. Besides, as repeatedly pointed out, the elements and phenomena investigated in this book are only a small subset of the broad range of semiotic – not just linguistic – resources that speakers have at their disposal in order to cognitively construct the entities and events of the world. The most obvious field of expansion for the investigation developed is that of third persons and the different kinds of impersonal constructions available in Spanish grammar. These choices help set up viewpoints other than those of the speaker, the group the speaker constructs him/herself into, or the different kinds of addressees and audiences. They are all closer to the pole of stylistic objectivity than the persons studied here. Therefore, their study would make it possible to complete the picture of person usage in Spanish, encompassing its various dimensions of meaning. Preliminary observation of the corpus suggests that in some communicative situations – e.g. written informational discourse – and with some types of participant identity – e.g. journalists and broadcasters – the frequencies of first- and second-person indexations are often negligible in comparison with the ones achieved by those other choices. Further research will thus need to combine a wider array of syntactic and discursive contexts in order to enhance both the descriptive adequacy and the explanatory power of the model outlined.

As regards the methodology, the goal has been to combine quantitative and qualitative data as systematically as possible, in order to provide deeper insight into the dynamics of participant construction. The quantitative side of the analysis has avoided the use of a sophisticated statistical apparatus, rather relying on the observation of percentages and normalized frequencies. These were aimed at unveiling general usage tendencies that could subsequently be interpreted through the analysis of particular contexts. Such a technique has made it possible to elucidate the main motivations of the results obtained – even if it is impossible to provide each single linguistic token with an empirical, undisputable explanation, insofar as speaker freedom and creativity cannot be reduced to mathematical rules. In fact, contextual observation has shown that less expectable choices in a given context can be used to construct also less expectable meanings. All this marks a significant departure from the continuous statistical refinement of mainstream variationist analyses. The goal of an investigation of communicative choice and cognitive construction as has been developed here is not to demonstrate the statistical significance and relative weight of a set of supposedly independent variables. Rather, it is to discover how the co-occurrence between inherently meaningful linguistic elements and other, also meaningful, semiotic features results in the astounding richness and complexity of human communication.

12 References

Abbott, Barbara, *Definiteness and Indefiniteness*, in: Horn, Larry R./Ward, Gregory (edd.), *Handbook of Pragmatics*, Oxford, Basil Blackwell, 2005, 122–149.

Aijón Oliva, Miguel A., *Variación morfosintáctica e interacción social: análisis del paradigma de los clíticos verbales españoles en los medios de comunicación*, Salamanca, Ediciones Universidad de Salamanca, 2006 (= 2006a).

Aijón Oliva, Miguel A., *La variación morfosintáctica como recurso de cortesía verbal: acerca del paradigma de los clíticos españoles*, Lingüística Española Actual 28 (2006), 221–246 (= 2006b).

Aijón Oliva, Miguel A., *La posición de* se *en las estructuras pluriverbales: variación y significado*, Boletín de Filología 45 (2010), 11–31.

Aijón Oliva, Miguel A., *Los pronombres de tratamiento en la publicidad radiofónica*, in: Bartol Hernández, José A./García Santos, Juan F. (edd.), *Estudios de filología española*, Salamanca, Luso-Española de Ediciones, 2012, 13–21.

Aijón Oliva, Miguel A., *On the Meanings and Functions of Grammatical Choice: The Spanish First-Person Plural in Written-Press Discourse*, Pragmatics 23 (2013), 573–603 (= 2013a).

Aijón Oliva, Miguel A., *Grammatical Choice and Meaning in Media Discourse: The Spanish Periphrastic Passive*, Studies in Media and Communication 1 (2013), 47–59 (= 2013b).

Aijón Oliva, Miguel A., *La marcación variable de los objetos en español: prominencia cognitiva y elección gramatical*, Estudios de Lingüística 29 (2015), 9–33.

Aijón Oliva, Miguel A., *Elección gramatical y construcción del discurso: la evolución formal y funcional de los referentes textuales*, Onomázein 35 (2017), 82–107.

Aijón Oliva, Miguel A., *The Participants as Objects: Variation and Meaning of First- and Second-Person Object Encoding in Spanish*, Studia Linguistica 72 (2018), 571–607 (= 2018a).

Aijón Oliva, Miguel A., *Not Just You: The Construction of Radio Audiences through Second-Person Choice in Peninsular Spanish*, Language & Communication 60 (2018), 80–93 (= 2018b).

Aijón Oliva, Miguel A./Borrego Nieto, Julio, *La variación gramatical como forma y significado: el uso de los clíticos verbales en el español peninsular*, Lingüística 29 (2013), 91–124.

Aijón Oliva, Miguel A./Serrano, María J., *The Cognitive Bases of Linguistic Style*, Sociolinguistic Studies 4 (2010), 115–144 (= 2010a).

Aijón Oliva, Miguel A./Serrano, María J., *El hablante en su discurso: expresión y omisión del sujeto de "creo"*, Oralia 13 (2010), 7–38 (= 2010b).

Aijón Oliva, Miguel A./Serrano, María J., *Style in Syntax: Investigating Variation in Spanish Pronoun Subjects*, Bern, Peter Lang, 2013.

Aijón Oliva, Miguel A./Serrano, María J., *Moving towards the Realm of the Other: Second-Person Objectivization in Spanish Media Discourse*, Language Sciences 35 (2014), 173–188.

Aijón Oliva, Miguel A./Serrano, María J., *A Matter of Style: Gender and Subject Variation in Spanish*, Gender and Language 10 (2016), 240–269.

Aissen, Judith, *Differential Object Marking: Iconicity vs. Economy*, Natural Language and Linguistic Theory 21 (2003), 435–483.

Alarcos Llorach, Emilio, *Gramática de la lengua española*, Madrid, Espasa Calpe, 1994.

Albentosa Hernández, José I./Moya Guijarro, Arsenio J., *La reducción del grado de transitividad en la oración del discurso científico en lengua inglesa*, Revista Española de Lingüística 30 (2000), 445–468.

https://doi.org/10.1515/9783110643442-013

Alcaide Lara, Esperanza, *Yo me parece que habíamos cinco personas: la concordancia en el discurso*, Español Actual 68 (1997), 5–20.

Álvarez Muro, Alexandra/New, Juana, *Variación en el pronombre de segunda persona en el habla de Mérida*, Boletín Antropológico (Universidad de los Andes) 57 (2003), 47–64.

Anagnostopoulou, Elena, *Clitic Doubling*, in: Everaert, Martin/Van Riemsdijk, Henk (edd.), *The Blackwell Companion to Syntax*, Oxford, Blackwell, 2006, 519–581.

Ariel, Mira, *Referring and Accessibility*, Journal of Linguistics 24 (1988), 65–87.

Ariel, Mira, *Accessing Noun-Phrase Antecedents*, London/New York, Routledge, 1990.

Ariel, Mira, *Accessibility Theory: An Overview*, in: Sanders, Ted/Schilperoord, Joost/Spooren, Wilbert (edd.), *Text Representation: Linguistic and Psycholinguistic Aspects*, Amsterdam/Philadelphia, John Benjamins, 2001, 29–87.

Ariel, Mira, *Pragmatics and Grammar*, Cambridge, Cambridge University Press, 2008.

Ariel, Mira, *Discourse, Grammar, Discourse*, Discourse Studies 11 (2009), 5–36.

Arnold, Jennifer E./Griffin, Zenzi M., *The Effect of Additional Characters on Choice of Referring Expression: Everyone Counts*, Journal of Memory and Language 56 (2007), 521–536.

Auer, Peter, *Introduction*, in: Auer, Peter (ed.), *Style and Social Identities: Alternative Approaches to Linguistic Heterogeneity*, Berlin/New York, Mouton de Gruyter, 2007, 1–21.

Azofra Sierra, María E., *Morfosintaxis histórica del español: de la teoría a la práctica*, Madrid, Universidad Nacional de Educación a Distancia, 2010.

Bachman, Lyle F./Palmer, Adrian S., *The Construct Validation of Self-Ratings of Communicative Language Ability*, Language Testing 6 (1989), 14–29.

Barcia López, Ramiro J., *Los pronombres personales átonos de 3ª persona en gallego-asturiano*, in: Álvarez, Alfredo I., et al. (edd.), *Studium grammaticae: homenaje al profesor José A. Martínez*, Oviedo, Universidad de Oviedo, 2015, 135–148.

Barra Jover, Mario, *Dativo de interés, dativo aspectual y las marcas de aspecto perfectivo en español*, Verba 23 (1996), 121–146.

Barrenechea, Ana M./Orecchia, Teresa, *La duplicación de objetos directos e indirectos en el español hablado en Buenos Aires*, Romance Philology 24 (1970), 58–83.

Beaugrande, Robert de/Dressler, Wolfgang U., *Introduction to Text Linguistics*, London, Longman, 1981.

Bell, Allan, *Language Style as Audience Design*, Language in Society 13 (1984), 145–204.

Bell, Allan, *Audience Accomodation in the Mass Media*, in: Giles, Howard/Coupland, Nikolas/Coupland, Justine (edd.), *Contexts of Accomodation: Developments in Applied Sociolinguistics*, Cambridge, Cambridge University Press, 1991, 69–102.

Bell, Allan, *Hit and Miss: Referee Design in the Dialects of New Zealand Television Advertisements*, Language & Communication 12 (1992), 327–340.

Bell, Allan, *Back in Style: Reworking Audience Design*, in: Eckert, Penelope/Rickford, John R. (edd.), *Style and Sociolinguistic Variation*, Cambridge, Cambridge University Press, 2001, 139–169.

Belloro, Valeria A., *Spanish Clitic Doubling: A Study of the Syntax-Pragmatics Interface*, Ph.D. dissertation, University of New York, 2007.

Belloro, Valeria A., *Pronombres clíticos, dislocaciones y doblados en tres dialectos del español*, Nueva Revista de Filología Hispánica 60 (2012), 391–424.

Belloro, Valeria A., *To the Right of the Verb: An Investigation of Clitic Doubling and Right Dislocation in three Spanish Dialects*, Newcastle, Cambridge Scholars Publishing, 2015.

Benavides, Carlos, *La distribución del voseo en Hispanoamérica*, Hispania 86 (2003), 612–623.

Bentivoglio, Paola, *Los sujetos pronominales de primera persona en el habla de Caracas*, Caracas, Universidad Central de Venezuela, 1987.

Benveniste, Émile, *Problèmes de linguistique générale*, vol. 1, Paris, Gallimard, 1966.

Bernstein, Basil, *Class, Codes and Control*, vol. 1: *Theoretical Studies towards a Sociology of Language*, London, Routledge and Kegan Paul, 1971.

Bertolotti, Virginia, *A mí de vos no me trata ni usted ni nadie. Sistemas e historia de las formas de tratamiento en la lengua española en América*, México, UNAM, 2015.

Bhat, Darbhe N. S., *Pronouns*, Oxford, Oxford University Press, 2004.

Biber, Douglas, *Dimensions of Register Variation: A Cross-Linguistic Comparison*, Cambridge, Cambridge University Press, 1995.

Biber, Douglas/Conrad, Susan, *Register, Genre, and Style*, Cambridge, Cambridge University Press, 2009.

Biber, Douglas/Conrad, Susan/Reppen, Randi, *Corpus Linguistics: Investigating Language Structure and Use*, Cambridge, Cambridge University Press, 1998.

Biber, Douglas/Davies, Mark/Jones, James K./Tracy-Ventura, Nicole, *Spoken and Written Register Variation in Spanish: A Multi-Dimensional Analysis*, Corpora 1 (2006), 1–37.

Bickel, Balthasar, *Grammatical Relations Typology*, in: Song, Jae J. (ed.), *The Oxford Handbook of Linguistic Typology*, Oxford, Oxford University Press, 2010, 399–444.

Bickel, Balthasar/Nichols, Johanna, *Inclusive-Exclusive as Person vs. Number Categories Worldwide*, in: Filimonova, Elena (ed.), *Clusivity: Typology and Case Studies of Inclusive-Exclusive Distinction*, Amsterdam/Philadelphia, John Benjamins, 2005, 49–72.

Bidot Martínez, Irina, *La desfocalización del centro deíctico personal a través de la segunda persona del singular*, Boletín de Lingüística 20 (2008), 62–87.

Billows, Richard A., *Julius Caesar: The Colossus of Rome*, London/New York, Routledge, 2009.

Blake, Renée, *Toward Heterogeneity: A Sociolinguistic Perspective on the Classification of Black People in the Twenty-First Century*, in: Alim, H. Samy/Rickford, John R./Ball, Arnetha F. (edd.), *Raciolinguistics: How Language Shapes our Ideas about Race*, Oxford, Oxford University Press, 2016, 153–170.

Blas Arroyo, José L., *"Mire usted Sr. González..." Personal Deixis in Spanish Political-Electoral Debate*, Journal of Pragmatics 32 (2000), 1–27.

Blas Arroyo, José L., *Sociolingüística del español. Desarrollos y perspectivas en el estudio de la lengua española en contexto social*, Madrid, Cátedra, 2005.

Bolinger, Dwight, *Meaning and Form*, London, Longman, 1977.

Booth, Trudie M., *A Complete French Grammar for Reference and Practice*, Lanham, University Press of America, 2009.

Borthen, Kaja, *On How We Interpret Plural Pronouns*, Journal of Pragmatics 42 (2010), 1799–1815.

Bosque, Ignacio, *Sexismo lingüístico y visibilidad de la mujer*, Real Academia Española, 2012 [http://www.rae.es/sites/default/files/Sexismo_linguistico_y_visibilidad_de_la_mujer_0.pdf; last access: 10/20/2018].

Bosque, Ignacio/Gutiérrez-Rexach, Javier, *Fundamentos de sintaxis formal*, Madrid, Akal, 2009.

Bosque, Ignacio/Moreno Cabrera, Juan C., *Las construcciones con* lo *y la denotación del neutro*, Lingüística 2 (1990), 5–50.

Branigan, Holly P./Pickering, Martin J./Tanaka, Mikihiro, *Contributions of Animacy to Grammatical Function Assignment and Word Order during Production*, Lingua 118 (2008), 172–189.

Brennan, Susan E., *Centering Attention in Discourse*, Language and Cognitive Processes 10 (1995), 137–167.

Brown, Esther/Rivas, Javier, *Subject-Verb Word Order in Spanish Interrogatives: A Quantitative Analysis of Puerto Rican Spanish*, Spanish in Context 8 (2011), 23–49.

Brown, Penelope/Levinson, Stephen C., *Politeness. Some Universals in Language Use*, Cambridge, Cambridge University Press, 1987.

Bucholtz, Mary, *Styles and Stereotypes: The Linguistic Negotiation of Identity among Laotian American Youth*, Pragmatics 14 (2004), 127–147.

Bucholtz, Mary, *White Kids: Language, Race, and Styles of Youth Identity*, Cambridge, Cambridge University Press, 2011.

Bull, Peter/Fetzer, Anita, *Who Are "We" and Who Are "You"? The Strategic Use of Forms of Address in Political Interviews*, Text & Talk 26 (2006), 3–37.

Butt, John/Benjamin, Carmen, *A New Reference Grammar of Modern Spanish*, London, Edward Arnold, 1988.

Bybee, Joan L., *Language, Usage and Cognition*, Cambridge, Cambridge University Press, 2010.

Cameron, Richard, *Ambiguous Agreement, Functional Compensation and Nonspecific "Tú" in the Spanish of San Juan, Puerto Rico, and Madrid, Spain*, Language Variation and Change 5 (1993), 305–334.

Cameron, Richard, *The Scope and Limit of Switch Reference as a Constraint on Pronominal Subject Expression*, Hispanic Linguistics 6/7 (1995), 1–27.

Campos, Héctor, *Construcciones transitivas e intransitivas*, in: Bosque, Ignacio/Demonte, Violeta (edd.), *Gramática descriptiva de la lengua española*, vol. 2, Madrid, Espasa Calpe, 1999, 1519–1573.

Campos, Simone N./Rodrigues-Moura, Enrique, *¿Formal o informal? He ahí la cuestión... Las formas de tratamiento en la clase de E/LE para alumnos brasileños*, in: Losada Aldrey, María C., et al. (edd.), *Español como lengua extranjera, enfoque comunicativo y gramática*, Santiago de Compostela, ASELE, 1998, 175–182.

Chafe, Wallace L., *Cognitive Constraints on Information Flow*, in: Tomlin, Russell S. (ed.), *Coherence and Grounding in Discourse*, Amsterdam/Philadelphia, John Benjamins, 1987, 21–51.

Chafe, Wallace L., *Discourse, Conciousness and Time. The Flow and Displacement of Experience in Speaking and Writing*, Chicago, The University of Chicago Press, 1994.

Chambers, Jack K., *Sociolinguistic Theory*, Oxford, Basil Blackwell, 2003.

Cheshire, Jenny, *Syntactic Variation, the Linguistic Variable, and Sociolinguistic Theory*, Linguistics 25 (1987), 257–282.

Cifuentes Honrubia, José L./Llopis Ganga, Jesús, *Complemento indirecto y complemento de lugar: estructuras locales de base personal en español*, Alicante, Universidad de Alicante, 1996.

Claes, Jerome, *Cognitive, Social, and Individual Constraints on Linguistic Variation. A Case Study of Presentational "Haber" Pluralization in Caribbean Spanish*, Berlin/Boston, De Gruyter, 2016.

Company Company, Concepción, *Multiple Dative-Marking Grammaticalization: Spanish as a Special Kind of Primary Object Language*, Studies in Language 25 (2001), 1–47.

Comrie, Bernard, *Language Universals and Linguistic Typology: Syntax and Morphology*, Chicago, The University of Chicago Press, 1989.

Comrie, Bernard, *Some Argument-Structure Properties of "Give" in the Languages of Europe and Northern and Central Asia*, in: Suihkonen, Pirkko/Comrie, Bernard/Solovyev, Valery (edd.), *Argument Structure and Grammatical Relations: A Crosslinguistic Typology*, Amsterdam/Philadelphia, John Benjamins, 2012, 17–35.

Corbett, Greville C., *Number*, Cambridge, Cambridge University Press, 2000.

Cornillie, Bert, *Epistemic Modality and Evidentiality in Spanish (Semi-)Auxiliaries. A Cognitive-Functional Approach*, Berlin/New York, Mouton de Gruyter, 2007.
Cornish, Francis, *Anaphora, Discourse, and Understanding. Evidence from English and French*, Oxford, Oxford University Press, 1999.
Correa, Maite, *Sobre la "no opcionalidad" del doblado de clíticos en español*, Master dissertation, University of Arizona, 2003.
Cortés Conde, Florencia, *Los angloargentinos en Buenos Aires: lengua, identidad y nación antes y después de Malvinas*, Buenos Aires, Biblos, 2007.
Coupland, Nikolas, *Dialect Stylization in Radio Talk*, Language in Society 30 (2001), 345–375.
Coupland, Nikolas, *Style: Language Variation and Identity*, Cambridge, Cambridge University Press, 2007.
Coveney, Aidan, *Anything "You" Can Do, "Tu" Can Do Better: "Tu" and "Vous" as Substitutes for Indefinite "On" in French*, Journal of Sociolinguistics 7 (2003), 164–191.
Croft, William, *Agreement vs. Case Marking and Direct Objects*, in: Barlow, Michael/Ferguson, Charles A. (edd.), *Agreement in Natural Language*, Stanford, CSLI, 1988, 159–180.
Croft, William, *Syntactic Categories and Grammatical Relations: The Cognitive Organization of Information*, Chicago, The University of Chicago Press, 1991.
Croft, William, *Toward a Social Cognitive Linguistics*, in: Evans, Vyvyan/Pourcel, Stéphanie (edd.), *New Directions in Cognitive Linguistics*, Amsterdam/Philadelphia, John Benjamins, 2009, 395–420.
Croft, William, *Ten Unwarranted Assumptions in Syntactic Argumentation*, in: Boye, Kasper/Engberg-Pedersen, Elisabeth (edd.), *Language Usage and Language Structure*, Berlin/New York, Mouton de Gruyter, 2010, 313–350.
Croft, William/D. Alan Cruse, *Cognitive Linguistics*, Cambridge, Cambridge University Press, 2004.
Cutillas Espinosa, Juan A., *Variación estilística en los medios de comunicación: una aproximación contrastiva a la teoría del diseño de la audiencia*, Tonos Digital 5 (2003) [www.um.es/tonosdigital/znum5/estudios/E-AUDIENCIACutillas.htm; last access: 10/02/2018].
Dahl, Östen, *Egophoricity in Discourse and Syntax*, Functions of Language 7 (2000), 37–77.
Davidson, Brad, *"Pragmatic Weight" and Spanish Subject Pronouns: The Pragmatic and Discourse Uses of "Tú" and "Yo" in Spoken Madrid Spanish*, Journal of Pragmatics 26 (1996), 543–566.
Davies, Matt, *Oppositions and Ideology in News Discourse*, London/New York, Bloomsbury, 2013.
De Cock, Barbara, *La funcionalidad discursiva del esquema construccional "Los españoles hemos hecho historia en Europa"*, Lingüística Española Actual 32 (2010), 173–195.
De Cock, Barbara, *Why "We" Can Be "You": The Use of 1st Person Plural Forms with Hearer Reference in English and Spanish*, Journal of Pragmatics 43 (2011), 2762–2775.
De Cock, Barbara, *Profiling Discourse Participants: Forms and Functions in Spanish Conversation and Debates*, Amsterdam/Philadelphia, John Benjamins, 2014.
De Cock, Barbara, *Register, Genre and Referential Ambiguity of Pronouns*, Pragmatics 26 (2016), 361–378.
De Cock, Barbara/Nogué Serrano, Neus, *The Pragmatics of Person Reference: A Comparative Study of Catalan and Spanish Parliamentary Discourse*, Languages in Contrast 17 (2017), 96–127.
De Fina, Anna/Schiffrin, Deborah/Bamberg, Michael, *Introduction*, in: De Fina, Anna/Schiffrin, Deborah/Bamberg, Michael (edd.), *Discourse and Identity*, Cambridge, Cambridge University Press, 2006, 1–29.

De Jonge, Bob, *El desarrollo de las variantes de "vuestra merced" a "usted"*, Estudios de Lingüística del Español 22:7 (2005) [elies.rediris.es/elies22/cap7.htm; last access: 10/12/2018].

De Kock, Josse, *Norma, libertad y probabilidad. Ocho soluciones del español*, Salamanca, Ediciones Universidad de Salamanca, 1998.

Delbecque, Nicole, *A Construction Grammar Approach to Transitivity in Spanish*, in: Davidse, Kristin/Lamiroy, Béatrice (edd.), *The Nominative and Accusative and their Counterparts*, Amsterdam/Philadelphia, John Benjamins, 2002, 81–130.

Delbecque, Nicole, *El análisis de corpus al servicio de la gramática cognoscitiva: hacia una interpretación de la alternancia lineal SV/VS*, in: Knauer, Gabriele/Bellosta von Colbe, Valeriano (edd.), *Variación sintáctica en español: un reto para las teorías de la sintaxis*, Tübingen, Niemeyer, 2005, 51–74.

DeMello, George, *Objeto directo* vs. *objeto indirecto con verbos de influencia: "A María no la/le dejan salir de noche"*, in: De Kock, Josse (ed.), *Lingüística con corpus. Catorce aplicaciones sobre el español*, Salamanca, Ediciones Universidad de Salamanca, 2001, 139–154.

DeMello, George, *"Leísmo" in Contemporary Spanish American Educated Speech*, Linguistics 40 (2002), 261–283.

Dirven, René, *Major Strands in Cognitive Linguistics*, in: Ruiz de Mendoza Ibáñez, Francisco/ Peña Cervel, Sandra (edd.), *Cognitive Linguistics: Internal Dynamics and Disciplinary Interaction*, Berlin/New York, Mouton de Gruyter, 2005, 17–68.

Dixon, Robert M. W., *Ergativity*, Language 55 (1979), 59–138.

Dixon, Robert M. W., *Demonstratives: A Cross-Linguistic Typology*, Studies in Language 27 (2003), 61–112.

Dumitrescu, Domnita, *"A" personal, duplicación clítica y marcadez: español porteño vs. español madrileño*, in: Ward, Aengus M. (ed.), *Actas del XII Congreso de la Asociación Internacional de Hispanistas*, Birmingham, The University of Birmingham, 1998, 140–152.

Dumont, Jenny, *Third Person References: Forms and Functions in two Spoken Genres of Spanish*, Amsterdam/Philadelphia, John Benjamins, 2016.

Eckert, Penelope, *Linguistic Variation as Social Practice*, Oxford, Basil Blackwell, 2000.

Eckert, Penelope, *Variation and the Indexical Field*, Journal of Sociolinguistics 12 (2008), 453–476.

Edwards, John, *Language and Identity*, Cambridge, Cambridge University Press, 2009.

Elleström, Lars, *The Modalities of Media: A Model for Understanding Intermedial Relations*, in: Elleström, Lars (ed.), *Media Borders, Multimodality and Intermediality*, Basingstoke, Palgrave Macmillan, 2010, 11–48.

Enghels, Renata, *Acusativo y dativo en la construcción factitiva: hacia un replanteamiento en términos multifactoriales*, Revue Romane 47 (2012), 1–24.

Enrique-Arias, Andrés, *La distribución de los pronombres de objeto en español: consideraciones históricas, tipológicas y psicolingüísticas*, Lingüística 5 (1993), 41–75.

Enrique-Arias, Andrés, *The Grammaticalization of Object Agreement in Spanish*, Ph.D. dissertation, University of Southern California, 1997.

Enríquez, Emilia, *El pronombre personal sujeto en la lengua española hablada en Madrid*, Madrid, CSIC, 1984.

Erickson, Frederick, *From Speech as "Situated" to Speech as "Situating": Insights from John Gumperz on the Practical Conduct of Talk as Social Action*, Text & Talk 31 (2011), 395–406.

Fábregas, Antonio, *Differential Object Marking in Spanish: State of the Art*, Borealis: An International Journal of Hispanic Linguistics 2 (2013), 1–80.

Fábregas, Antonio, *El argumento espacio-temporal de ciertos verbos meteorológicos*, Ianua 14 (2014), 1–25.
Farrar, Kimberley/Jones, Mari C., *Introduction*, in: Jones, Mari C./Esch, Edith (edd.), *Contact-Induced Language Change. An Examination of Internal, External and Non-Linguistic Factors*, Berlin/New York, Mouton de Gruyter, 2002, 1–16.
Fauconnier, Gilles, *Espaces mentaux. Aspects de la construction du sens dans les langues naturelles*, Paris, Minuit, 1984.
Fernández, Mauro/Gerhalter, Katharina, *Pronombres de segunda persona y fórmulas de tratamiento en español: una nueva bibliografía (1867–2016)*, Lingüística en la Red (2017) [www.linred.es/informacion_pdf/LR_informacion20_20170219.pdf; last access: 10/ 20/2018].
Fernández Ramírez, Salvador, *Gramática española*, vol. 4: *El verbo y la oración* [[1]1951], ed. Bosque, Ignacio, Madrid, Arco Libros, 1986.
Fernández Ramírez, Salvador, *Gramática española*, vol. 3.2: *El pronombre* [[1]1951], ed. Polo, José, Madrid, Arco Libros, 1987.
Fernández Soriano, Olga, *El pronombre personal. Formas y distribuciones. Pronombres átonos y tónicos*, in: Bosque, Ignacio/Demonte, Violeta (edd.), *Gramática descriptiva de la lengua española*, vol. 1, Madrid, Espasa Calpe, 1999, 1209–1273 (= 1999a).
Fernández Soriano, Olga, *Two Types of Impersonal Sentences in Spanish: Locative and Dative Subjects*, Syntax 2 (1999), 101–140 (= 1999b).
Fernández Soriano, Olga/Táboas Baylín, Susana, *Construcciones impersonales no reflejas*, in: Bosque, Ignacio/Demonte, Violeta (edd.), *Gramática descriptiva de la lengua española*, vol. 2, Madrid, Espasa Calpe, 1999, 1723–1778.
Fernández-Ordóñez, Inés, *Leísmo, laísmo y loísmo*, in: Bosque, Ignacio/Demonte, Violeta (edd.), *Gramática descriptiva de la lengua española*, vol. 1, Madrid, Espasa Calpe, 1999, 1317–1397.
Finegan, Edward/Biber, Douglas, *Register Variation and Social Dialects: Toward an Integrated View*, in: Biber, Douglas/Finegan, Edward (edd.), *Sociolinguistic Perspectives on Register*, New York, Oxford University Press, 1994, 315–347.
Finegan, Edward/Biber, Douglas, *Register Variation and Social Dialect Variation: The Register Axiom*, in: Eckert, Penelope/Rickford, John R. (edd.), *Style and Sociolinguistic Variation*, Cambridge, Cambridge University Press, 2001, 235–267.
Fischer, John L., *Social Influences on the Choice of a Linguistic Variant*, Word 14 (1958), 47–56.
Flores Cervantes, Marcela, *Leísmo, laísmo y loísmo*, in: Company Company, Concepción (ed.), *Sintaxis histórica de la lengua española*, vol. 1: *La frase verbal*, México, Fondo de Cultura Económica/UNAM, 2006, 671–749.
Fontanella de Weinberg, María B., *Los sistemas pronominales de segunda persona en el mundo hispánico*, Boletín de Filología 35 (1995–1996), 151–162.
Fossard, Marion/Garnham, Alan/Cowles, H. Wind, *Between Anaphora and Deixis... The Resolution of the Demonstrative Noun Phrase "That N"*, Language and Cognitive Processes 27 (2012), 1385–1404.
Frago Gracia, Juan A., *El español de América en la Independencia: Adiciones gramaticales I*, Boletín de Filología 46 (2011), 47–74.
Franco, Jon A., *On Object Agreement in Spanish*, PhD dissertation, University of Southern California, 1993.
Franco, Jon A., *Agreement as a Continuum: The Case of Spanish Pronominal Clitics*, in: Beukema, Frits/Den Dikken, Marcel (edd.), *Clitic Phenomena in European Languages*, Amsterdam/Philadelphia, John Benjamins, 2000, 147–190.

Fried, Mirjam, *Word Order*, in: Brisard, Frank/Östman, Jan-Ola/Verschueren, Jef (edd.), *Grammar, Meaning and Pragmatics*, Amsterdam/Philadelphia, John Benjamins, 2009, 289–300.

Fuentes Rodríguez, Catalina, *Diccionario de conectores y operadores del español*, Madrid, Arco Libros, 2009.

Fuller, Janet M., *The Influence of Speaker Roles on Discourse Marker Use*, Journal of Pragmatics 35 (2003), 25–45.

Gal, Susan, *Language Shift: Social Determinants of Linguistic Change in Bilingual Austria*, New York, Academic Press, 1979.

García, Erica C., *The Role of Theory in Linguistic Analysis: The Spanish Pronoun System*, Amsterdam, North-Holland, 1975.

García, Erica C., *Context Dependence of Language and of Linguistic Analysis*, in: Klein-Andreu, Flora (ed.), *Discourse Perspectives on Syntax*, New York, Academic Press, 1983, 181–207.

García, Erica C., *Shifting Variation*, Lingua 67 (1985), 189–224.

García, Erica C., *The Motivated Syntax of Arbitrary Signs: Cognitive Constraints on Spanish Clitic Clustering*, Amsterdam/Philadelphia, John Benjamins, 2009.

García Mouton, Pilar/Molina Martos, Isabel, *La -/d/ en el "Atlas Dialectal de Madrid (ADiM)": un cambio en marcha*, Lapurdum 19 (2015), 277–290.

García Salido, Marcos, *La expresión pronominal de sujeto y objetos en español. Estudio con datos conversacionales*, Annex 70 of Verba, Santiago de Compostela, Universidade de Santiago de Compostela, 2013.

García-Miguel, José M., *La duplicación de objeto directo e indirecto como concordancia*, Verba 18 (1991), 375–410.

García-Miguel, José M., *Las relaciones gramaticales entre predicado y participantes*, Santiago de Compostela, Universidade de Santiago de Compostela, 1995.

García-Miguel, José M., *La expresión de actantes centrales en español (romance) y bribri (chibcha): tipología, discurso y cognición*, in: Vilela, Mário/Silva, Fátima (edd.), *Actas do 1º Encontro de Lingüística Cognitiva*, Porto, Faculdade de Letras do Porto, 1999, 101–121.

García-Miguel, José M., *Integración semántica en las construcciones causativas reflexivas del español*, in: Delbecque, Nicole (ed.), *Aproximaciones cognoscitivo-funcionales al español*, Amsterdam, Rodopi, 2003, 65–82.

García-Miguel, José M., *Variable Coding and Object Alignment in Spanish: A Corpus-Based Approach*, Folia Linguistica 49 (2015), 205–256.

Gardelle, Laure/Sorlin, Sandrine, *Personal Pronouns: An Exposition*, in: Gardelle, Laure/Sorlin, Sandrine (edd.), *The Pragmatics of Personal Pronouns*, Amsterdam/Philadelphia, John Benjamins, 2015, 1–23.

Gast, Volker/Deringer, Lisa/Haas, Florian/Rudolf, Olga, *Impersonal Uses of the Second Person Singular: A Pragmatic Analysis of Generalization and Empathy Effects*, Journal of Pragmatics 88 (2015), 148–162.

Gee, James P., *Language as Saying, Doing and Being*, in: Angermuller, Johannes/Maingueneau, Dominique/Wodak, Ruth (edd.), *The Discourse Studies Reader. Main Currents in Theory and Analysis*, Amsterdam/Philadelphia, John Benjamins, 2014, 234–243.

Geeraerts, Dirk, *Schmidt Redux: How Systematic is the Linguistic System if Variation Is Rampant?*, in: Boye, Kasper/Engberg-Pedersen, Elisabeth (edd.), *Language Usage and Language Structure*, Berlin/New York, Mouton de Gruyter, 2010, 237–262.

Giles, Howard/Coupland, Nikolas/Coupland, Justine, *Accomodation Theory: Communication, Context, and Consequence*, in: Giles, Howard/Coupland, Nikolas/Coupland, Justine (edd.),

Contexts of Accomodation: Developments in Applied Sociolinguistics, Cambridge, Cambridge University Press, 1991, 1–68.
Gili Gaya, Samuel, *Nos-otros, vos-otros*, Revista de Filología Española 30 (1946), 108–117.
Gili Gaya, Samuel, *Curso superior de sintaxis española*, Barcelona, Biblograf, 2000.
Givón, Talmy, *Topic, Pronoun and Grammatical Agreement*, in: Li, Charles N. (ed.), *Subject and Topic*, New York, Academic Press, 1976, 149–188.
Givón, Talmy, *Topic Continuity in Discourse: An Introduction*, in: Givón, Talmy (ed.), *Topic Continuity in Discourse. A Quantitative Cross-Language Study*, Amsterdam/Philadelphia, John Benjamins, 1983, 5–41.
Givón, Talmy, *Syntax: An Introduction*, Amsterdam/Philadelphia, John Benjamins, 2001.
Givón, Talmy, *Where Do Simple Clauses Come from?*, in: Boye, Kasper/Engberg-Pedersen, Elisabeth (edd.), *Language Usage and Language Structure*, Berlin/New York, Mouton de Gruyter, 2010, 167–202.
Goldberg, Adele E., *Constructions. A Construction-Grammar Approach to Argument Structure*, Chicago, The University of Chicago Press, 1995.
Goldberg, Adele E., *Constructions: A New Theoretical Approach to Language*, Trends in Cognitive Sciences 7 (2003), 219–224.
Goldberg, Adele E., *Constructions at Work: The Nature of Generalization in Language*, Oxford/New York, Oxford University Press, 2006.
Gómez Molina, José R., *Pluralización de "haber" impersonal en el español de Valencia (España)*, Verba 40 (2013), 253–284.
Gómez Torrego, Leonardo, *Nuevo manual de español correcto*, Madrid, Arco Libros, 2004.
Grosz, Barbara J./Joshi, Aravind K./Weinstein, Scott, *Centering: A Framework for Modeling the Local Coherence of Discourse*, Computational Linguistics 21 (1995), 203–225.
Guerra Bernal, Nuria, *Funciones pragmalingüísticas del pronombre personal sujeto* tú *en el discurso conflictivo del español coloquial*, Revista Internacional de Lingüística Iberoamericana 9 (2007), 183–199.
Guirado, Kristel, *La alternancia "tú" – "uno" impersonal en el habla de Caracas*, Lingüística 26 (2011), 24–54.
Gundel, Jeanette K./Fretheim, Thorstein, *Information Structure*, in: Brisard, Frank/Östman, Jan-Ola/Verschueren, Jef (edd.), *Grammar, Meaning and Pragmatics*, Amsterdam/Philadelphia, John Benjamins, 2009, 146–160.
Gutiérrez Bravo, Rodrigo, *La identificación de los tópicos y los focos*, Nueva Revista de Filología Hispánica 56 (2008), 363–401.
Gutiérrez Ordóñez, Salvador, *Los dativos*, in: Bosque, Ignacio/Demonte, Violeta (edd.), *Gramática descriptiva de la lengua española*, vol. 2, Madrid, Espasa Calpe, 1999, 1855–1930.
Gutiérrez Ordóñez, Salvador, *Forma y sentido en sintaxis*, Madrid, Arco Libros, 2002.
Haiman, John, *Natural Syntax: Iconicity and Erosion*, Cambridge, Cambridge University Press, 1985.
Halliday, Michael A. K., *An Introduction to Functional Grammar*, London, Edward Arnold, 2004.
Halpern, Aaron L., *Clitics*, in: Spencer, Andrew/Zwicky, Arnold M. (edd.), *The Handbook of Morphology*, Oxford, Basil Blackwell, 1998, 101–122.
Harder, Peter, *Meaning in Mind and Society: A Functional Contribution to the Social Turn in Cognitive Linguistics*, Berlin/New York, Mouton de Gruyter, 2010.
Hasan, Ruqaiya, *Semantic Variation: Meaning in Society and Sociolinguistics*, London, Equinox, 2009.

Haverkate, Henk, *Speech Acts, Speakers, and Hearers: Reference and Referential Strategies in Spanish*, Amsterdam/Philadelphia, John Benjamins, 1984.

Haverkate, Henk, *La cortesía verbal*, Madrid, Gredos, 1994.

Helasvuo, Marja-Liisa/Huumo, Tuomas, *Canonical and Non-Canonical Subjects in Constructions: Perspectives from Cognition and Discourse*, in: Helasvuo, Marja-Liisa/Huumo, Tuomas (edd.), *Subjects in Constructions – Canonical and Non-Canonical*, Amsterdam/Philadelphia, John Benjamins, 2015, 1–9.

Helmbrecht, Johannes, *Grammar and Function of "We"*, in: Duszak, Anna (ed.), *Us and Others*, Amsterdam/Philadelphia, John Benjamins, 2002, 31–49.

Hentschel, Barbara, *La duplicación pronominal del objeto indirecto en español*, Romanische Forschungen 125 (2013), 313–330.

Hernández-Campoy, Juan M., *Sociolinguistic Styles*, Oxford, Wiley-Blackwell, 2016.

Hernanz Carbó, María L., *Personas generales y tiempo verbal*, in: Wotjak, Gerd/Veiga, Alexandre (edd.), *La descripción del verbo español*, Annex 32 of Verba, Santiago de Compostela, Universidade de Santiago de Compostela, 1990, 153–162.

Hidalgo Navarro, Antonio, *Sobre los mecanismos de impersonalización en el español coloquial: el "tú" impersonal*, Estudios de Lingüística 11 (1996–1997), 163–176.

Hinterhölzl, Roland/Petrova, Svetlana, *Rethorical Relations and Verb Placement in Old High German*, in: Chiarcos, Christian/Claus, Berry/Grabsky, Michael (edd.), *Salience: Multidisciplinary Perspectives on its Function in Discourse*, Berlin/New York, Mouton de Gruyter, 2011, 173–202.

Hochberg, Judith G., *Functional Compensation for /s/ Deletion in Puerto Rican Spanish*, Language 62 (1986), 609–621.

Hollmann, Willem B., *Constructions in Cognitive Sociolinguistics*, in: Hoffmann, Thomas/Trousdale, Graeme (edd.), *The Oxford Handbook of Construction Grammar*, Oxford, Oxford University Press, 2013, 491–509.

Holmes, David, *Communication Theory: Media, Technology and Society*, London, SAGE, 2005.

Hopper, Paul J./Thompson, Sandra A., *Transitivity in Grammar and Discourse*, Language 56 (1980), 251–299.

Hopper, Paul J./Traugott, Elizabeth C., *Grammaticalization*, Cambridge, Cambridge University Press, 2003.

Huang, Yan, *Types of Inference: Entailment, Presupposition and Implicature*, in: Bublitz, Wolfram/Norrick, Neal R. (edd.), *Foundations of Pragmatics*, Berlin/New York, Mouton de Gruyter, 2011, 397–422.

Huerta Flores, Norohella, *Gramaticalización y concordancia objetiva en el español. Despronominalización del clítico dativo plural*, Verba 32 (2005), 165–190.

Hymes, Dell H., *On Communicative Competence*, in: Pride, John B./Holmes, Janet (edd.), *Sociolinguistics: Selected Readings*, Harmondsworth, Penguin, 1972, 269–293.

Jang, Ji S., *La dinámica de la alternancia entre* tú/vos y usted *en Medellín (Colombia) desde la teoría de la acomodación comunicativa*, Forma y Función 25 (2012), 40–60.

Jauncey, Dorothy G., *Tamambo, the Language of West Malo, Vanuatu*, Canberra, Pacific Linguistics, 2011.

Kampf, Zohar/Daskal, Efrat, *When the Watchdog Bites: Insulting Politicians on Air*, in: Ekström, Mats/Patrona, Marianna (edd.), *Talking Politics in Broadcast Media*, Amsterdam/Philadelphia, John Benjamins, 2011, 177–197.

Kany, Charles E., *American-Spanish Syntax*, Chicago, The University of Chicago Press, 1951.

Keenan, Edward L., *Towards a Universal Definition of "Subject of"*, in: Li, Charles N. (ed.), *Subject and Topic*, New York, Academic Press, 1976, 303–333.
Kelley, Larry D./Jugenheimer, Donald W., *Advertising Media Planning: A Brand Management Approach*, Armonk (NY), M. E. Sharpe, 2008.
Keniston, Hayward, *The Syntax of Castilian Prose*, Chicago, The University of Chicago Press, 1937.
Kerbrat-Orecchioni, Catherine, *Le discours en interaction*, Paris, Armand Colin, 2005.
King, Ruth/Nadasdi, Terry/Butler, Gary R., *First-Person Plural in Prince Edward Island Acadian French: The Fate of the Vernacular Variant "Je... ons"*, Language Variation and Change 16 (2004), 237–255.
Klein-Andreu, Flora, *Variación actual y evolución histórica: los clíticos "le/s", "la/s", "lo/s"*, München, Lincom Europa, 2000.
Kluge, Bettina, *El uso de formas de tratamiento en las estrategias de generalización*, in: Hummel, Martin/Kluge, Bettina/Vázquez Laslop, María E. (edd.), *Formas y fórmulas de tratamiento en el mundo hispánico*, México/Graz, El Colegio de México/Karl-Franzens-Universität, 2010, 1107–1136.
Kress, Gunther, *Multimodality. A Social Semiotic Approach to Contemporary Communication*, London/New York, Routledge, 2010.
Kristiansen, Gitte/Dirven, René, *Cognitive Sociolinguistics: Rationale, Methods and Scope*, in: Kristiansen, Gitte/Dirven, René (edd.), *Cognitive Sociolinguistics: Language Variation, Cultural Models, Social Systems*, Berlin/New York, Mouton de Gruyter, 2008, 1–17.
Kuznetsova, Julia, *Linguistic Profiles: Going from Form to Meaning via Statistics*, Berlin/New York, Mouton de Gruyter, 2015.
Labov, William, *The Social Motivation of a Sound Change*, Word 19 (1963), 273–309.
Labov, William, *Contraction, Deletion, and Inherent Variability of the English Copula*, Language 45 (1969), 715–762.
Labov, William, *Sociolinguistic Patterns*, Philadelphia, University of Pennsylvania Press, 1972.
Labov, William, *Where Does the Linguistic Variable Stop? A Response to Beatriz Lavandera*, Sociolinguistic Working Papers 44, 1978.
Labov, William, *What Is to Be Learned: The Community as the Focus of Social Cognition*, in: Pütz, Martin/Robinson, Justyna A./Reif, Monika (edd.), *Cognitive Sociolinguistics: Social and Cultural Variation in Cognition and Language Use*, Amsterdam/Philadelphia, John Benjamins, 2014, 23–51.
Laca, Brenda, *El objeto directo. La marcación preposicional*, in: Company Company, Concepción (ed.), *Sintaxis histórica de la lengua española*, vol. 1: *La frase verbal*, México, Fondo de Cultura Económica/UNAM, 2006, 423–475.
Lambrecht, Knud, *Information Structure and Sentence Form: A Theory of Topic, Focus, and the Mental Representations of Discourse Referents*, Cambridge, Cambridge University Press, 1994.
Langacker, Ronald W., *Foundations of Cognitive Grammar*, vol. 1: *Theoretical Prerequisites*, Stanford, Stanford University Press, 1987.
Langacker, Ronald W., *Foundations of Cognitive Grammar*, vol. 2: *Descriptive Application*, Stanford, Stanford University Press, 1991.
Langacker, Ronald W., *Estructura de la cláusula en la gramática cognoscitiva*, in: Maldonado, Ricardo (ed.), *Estudios cognoscitivos del español*, special issue of Revista Española de Lingüística Aplicada, 2000, 19–65.

Langacker, Ronald W., *Cognitive Grammar: A Basic Introduction*, Oxford, Oxford University Press, 2008.
Lapesa, Rafael, *Historia de la lengua española*, Madrid, Gredos, 1981.
Lapesa, Rafael, *Estudios de morfosintaxis histórica del español*, edd. Cano Aguilar, Rafael/ Echenique Elizondo, María T., Madrid, Gredos, 2000.
Lavandera, Beatriz R., *Where Does the Sociolinguistic Variable Stop?*, Language in Society 7 (1978), 171–182.
Lavandera, Beatriz R., *Variación y significado*, Buenos Aires, Hachette, 1984.
Leech, Geoffrey/Svartvik, Jan, *A Communicative Grammar of English*, London/New York, Routledge, 2013.
León-Castro Gómez, Marta, *Sobre el empleo de la segunda persona del singular como mecanismo de indefinición referencial en el habla culta: diferencias entre las formas "tú/vos" y "usted"*, Lingüística y Literatura 65 (2014), 37–63.
Levinson, Stephen C., *Pragmatics*, Cambridge, Cambridge University Press, 1983.
Llorente, Antonio/Mondéjar, José, *La conjugación objetiva en español*, Revista Española de Lingüística 4 (1974), 1–60.
López García, Ángel, *Gramática del español*, vol. 3: *Las partes de la oración*, Madrid, Arco Libros, 1998.
López García, Ángel, *La lengua común en la España plurilingüe*, Madrid/Frankfurt, Iberoamericana/Vervuert, 2009.
Lorenzo Ramos, Antonio, *Algunos datos sobre el leísmo en el español de Canarias*, in: Alvar, Manuel (ed.), *I Simposio Internacional de Lengua Española*, Las Palmas, Excmo. Cabildo Insular de Gran Canaria, 1981, 253–263.
Luján, Marta, *Expresión y omisión del pronombre personal*, in: Bosque, Ignacio/Demonte, Violeta (edd.), *Gramática descriptiva de la lengua española*, vol. 1, Madrid, Espasa Calpe, 1999, 1275–1315.
Lyons, Christopher, *Definiteness*, Cambridge, Cambridge University Press, 1999.
Macaulay, Ronald K. S., *Quantitative Methods in Sociolinguistics*, Basingstoke, Palgrave Macmillan, 2009.
Malchukov, Andrej L., *Animacy and Asymmetries in Differential Case Marking*, Lingua 118 (2008), 203–221.
Marrón, Gabriela A., *¿Cuándo tutear al emperador? Pronombres "tu" (T) / "vos" (V) en las cartas de Quinto Aurelio Símaco*, Revista Española de Lingüística 41 (2011), 59–72.
Martín Zorraquino, María A./Portolés Lázaro, José, *Los marcadores del discurso*, in: Bosque, Ignacio/Demonte, Violeta (edd.), *Gramática descriptiva de la lengua española*, vol. 3, Madrid, Espasa Calpe, 1999, 4051–4213.
Martínez, José A., *La concordancia*, in: Bosque, Ignacio/Demonte, Violeta (edd.), *Gramática descriptiva de la lengua española*, vol. 2, Madrid, Espasa Calpe, 1999, 2695–2786.
Matos Amaral, Patricia/Schwenter, Scott A., *Contrast and the (Non-)ocurrence of Subject Pronouns*, in: Eddington, David (ed.), *Selected Proceedings of the 7th Hispanic Linguistics Symposium*, Somerville (MA), Cascadilla Proceedings Project, 2005 [http://www.lingref.com/cpp/hls/7/paper1092.pdf; last access: 10/ 12/2018].
Melis, Chantal/Flores, Marcela, *Acercamiento diacrónico a la duplicación del objeto indirecto*, in: Vigueras Ávila, Alejandra (ed.), *Homenaje a Rubén Bonifaz Nuño. 30 años del Instituto de Investigaciones Filológicas*, México, UNAM, 2005, 481–503.

Mendikoetxea, Amaya, *Construcciones con "se": medias, pasivas e impersonales*, in: Bosque, Ignacio/Demonte, Violeta (edd.), *Gramática descriptiva de la lengua española*, vol. 2, Madrid, Espasa Calpe, 1999, 1575–1630.

Miyajima, Atsuko, *Aparición del pronombre sujeto en español y semántica del verbo*, Sophia Linguistica 46/47 (2000), 73–88.

Moreno Fernández, Francisco, *El corpus ACUAH: Análisis de los clíticos pleonásticos*, in: De Kock, Josse (ed.), *Lingüística con corpus. Catorce aplicaciones sobre el español*, Salamanca, Ediciones Universidad de Salamanca, 2001, 353–369.

Moure, Teresa, *Sobre el controvertido perfil del complemento directo*, Moenia 1 (1996), 47–110.

Mühlhäusler, Peter/Harré, Rom, *Pronouns and People*, Oxford, Basil Blackwell, 1990.

Myhill, John, *Variation in Spanish Clitic Climbing*, in: Walsh, Thomas J. (ed.), *Synchronic and Diachronic Approaches to Linguistic Variation and Change (GURT '88)*, Washington DC, Georgetown University Press, 1989, 227–250.

Næss, Åshild, *Prototypical Transitivity*, Amsterdam/Philadelphia, John Benjamins, 2007.

Nikiforidou, Kiki, *Constructional Analysis*, in: Brisard, Frank/Östman, Jan-Ola/Verschueren, Jef (edd.), *Grammar, Meaning and Pragmatics*, Amsterdam/Philadelphia, John Benjamins, 2009, 16–32.

Nowikow, Wiaczeslaw, *Sobre la pluralización de personas gramaticales en las lenguas románicas: "nos", "vos" – "nos alteros", "vos alteros"*, Anuario de Lingüística Hispánica 10 (1994), 283–300.

Nuyts, Jan, *Modality: Overview and Linguistic Issues*, in: Frawley, William (ed.), *The Expression of Modality*, Berlin/New York, Mouton de Gruyter, 2006, 1–26.

O'Sullivan, Joan, *Advanced Dublin English in Irish Radio Advertising*, World Englishes 32 (2013), 358–376.

Ormazabal, Javier/Romero, Juan, *The Object Agreement Constraint*, Natural Language & Linguistic Theory 25 (2007), 315–347.

Ortiz López, Luis A., *Pronombres de sujeto en el español (L2 vs L1) del Caribe*, in: Leeman, Jennifer/Lacorte, Manel (edd.), *El español en Estados Unidos y otros contextos de contacto*, Frankfurt am Main/Madrid, Vervuert/Iberoamericana, 2009, 85–110.

Ortmann, Albert, *Anti-Agreement with Subjects and Possessors from a Typological Perspective: A Case for Null Pronouns or for Economy?*, in: Wratil, Melani/Gallmann, Peter (edd.), *Null Pronouns*, Berlin/Boston, De Gruyter, 2011, 223–264.

Padilla García, Xosé A., *El orden de palabras en español coloquial*, Ph.D. dissertation, Universidad de Valencia, 2001.

Paredes García, Florentino, *Nuevos datos sobre el uso y las funciones de los pronombres átonos de tercera persona en Madrid*, in: Cestero Mancera, Ana M./Molina Martos, Isabel/Paredes García, Florentino (edd.), *Patrones sociolingüísticos de Madrid*, Bern, Peter Lang, 2015, 177–250.

Patrick, Peter L., *The Speech Community*, in: Chambers, Jack K./Schilling-Estes, Natalie/Trudgill, Peter (edd.), *The Handbook of Language Variation and Change*, Oxford, Basil Blackwell, 2006, 573–597.

Patrona, Marianna, *Neutralism Revisited: When Journalists Set New Rules in Political News Discourse*, in: Ekström, Mats/Patrona, Marianna (edd.), *Talking Politics in Broadcast Media*, Amsterdam/Philadelphia, John Benjamins, 2011, 157–176.

Pavlidou, Theodossia-Soula, *Constructing Collectivity with "We"*, in: Pavlidou, Theodossia-Soula (ed.), *Constructing Collectivity. "We" across Languages and Contexts*, Amsterdam/Philadelphia, John Benjamins, 2014, 1–22.

Pedersen, Johan, *The Spanish Impersonal "Se"-Construction: Constructional Variation and Change*, Constructions 1 (2005), DOI: 10.1075/slcs.136.07ped.
Pena Seijas, Jesús, *Las unidades del análisis morfológico*, in: Bosque, Ignacio/Demonte, Violeta (edd.), *Gramática descriptiva de la lengua española*, vol. 3, Madrid, Espasa Calpe, 1999, 4305–4366.
Penny, Ralph, *Gramática histórica del español*, Barcelona, Ariel, 1993.
Perlmutter, David, *Deep and Surface Structure Constraints in Syntax*, New York, Holt, Rinehart and Winston, 1971.
Polanco Martínez, Fernando, *Redes polisémicas y niveles de interpretación. Representación semántica de unidades lingüísticas complejas: el caso de "vamos"*, Estudios de Lingüística 27 (2013), 199–249.
Poplack, Shana/Tagliamonte, Sali A., *African American English in the Diaspora*, Oxford, Basil Blackwell, 2001.
Porto Dapena, José A., *Complementos argumentales del verbo: directo, indirecto, suplemento y agente*, Madrid, Arco Libros, 1997.
Portolés Lázaro, José, *Marcadores del discurso*, Barcelona, Ariel, 2001.
Posio, Pekka, *Spanish Subject Pronoun Usage and Verb Semantics Revisited: First and Second Person Singular Subject Pronouns and Focusing of Attention in Spoken Peninsular Spanish*, Journal of Pragmatics 43 (2011), 777–798.
Posio, Pekka, *Who Are "We" in Spoken Peninsular Spanish and European Portuguese? Expression and Reference of First Person Plural Subject Pronouns*, Language Sciences 34 (2012), 339–360.
Posio, Pekka, *Subject Expression in Grammaticalizing Constructions: The Case of "Creo" and "Acho" 'I Think' in Spanish and Portuguese*, Journal of Pragmatics 63 (2013), 5–18.
Posio, Pekka, *You and We: Impersonal Second Person Singular and other Referential Devices in Spanish Sociolinguistic Interviews*, Journal of Pragmatics 99 (2016), 1–16.
Potowski, Kim, *IntraLatino Language and Identity: MexiRican Spanish*, Amsterdam/Philadelphia, John Benjamins, 2016.
Prince, Ellen, *Toward a Taxonomy of Given-New Information*, in: Cole, Peter (ed.), *Radical Pragmatics*, New York, Academic Press, 1981, 223–255.
Pruñonosa Tomás, Manuel/Serra Alegre, Enric, *Las formas del lenguaje*, in: López García, Ángel/Gallardo Paúls, Beatriz (edd.), *Conocimiento y lenguaje*, Valencia, Universitat de València, 2011, 155–216.
Pütz, Martin/Robinson, Justyna A./Reif, Monika, *The Emergence of Cognitive Sociolinguistics: An Introduction*, in: Pütz, Martin/Robinson, Justyna A./Reif, Monika (edd.), *Cognitive Sociolinguistics: Social and Cultural Variation in Cognition and Language Use*, Amsterdam/Philadelphia, John Benjamins, 2014, 1–22.
Radatz, Hans-Ingo, *Non-Lexical Core-Arguments in Basque, Romance and German: How (and why) Spanish Syntax is Shifting Towards Sentential Head-Marking and Morphological Cross-Reference*, in: Detges, Ulrich/Waltereit, Richard (edd.), *The Paradox of Grammatical Change: Perspectives from Romance*, Amsterdam/Philadelphia, John Benjamins, 2008, 181–215.
RAE 2009 = Real Academia Española/Asociación de Academias de la Lengua, *Nueva gramática de la lengua española*, 2 vol., Madrid, Espasa Calpe, 2009.
RAE 2018 = Real Academia Española/Asociación de Academias de la Lengua, *Diccionario de la lengua española*, Madrid, Espasa Calpe, 2018 [dle.rae.es; last access: 10/04/2018].

Raymond, Chase W., *Reconceptualizing Identity and Context in the Deployment of Forms of Address*, in: Moyna, María I./Rivera-Mills, Susana (edd.), *Forms of Address in the Spanish of the Americas*, Amsterdam/Philadelphia, John Benjamins, 2016, 267–288.
Renwick Campos, Ricardo, *Norma, variación y enseñanza de la lengua. Una aproximación al tema desde la lingüística de la variación*, Lexis 31 (2007), 305–329.
Reyes, Graciela, *Polifonía textual: la citación en el relato literario*, Madrid, Gredos, 1984.
Richards, Keith, *Language and Professional Identity: Aspects of Collaborative Interaction*, Houndmills, Palgrave Macmillan, 2006.
Rickford, John R., *Style and Stylizing from the Perspective of a Non-Autonomous Sociolinguistics*, in: Eckert, Penelope/Rickford, John R. (edd.), *Style and Sociolinguistic Variation*, Cambridge, Cambridge University Press, 2001, 220–231.
Rivas, Javier, *Verb-Object Compounds with Spanish "Dar" 'Give': An Emergent "Gustar" 'Like'-type Construction*, Word 62 (2016), 1–21.
Rivero, María L., *La tipología de los pronombres átonos en el español medieval y el español actual*, Anuario de Lingüística Hispánica 2 (1986), 197–220.
Robinson, Justyna A., *Awesome Insights into Semantic Variation*, in: Geeraerts, Dirk/Kristiansen, Gitte/Peirsman, Yves (edd.), *Advances in Cognitive Sociolinguistics*, Berlin/New York, Mouton de Gruyter, 2010, 85–109.
Roegiest, Eugeen, *Variación pronominal en español: el pronombre dativo entre sintaxis y semántica*, in: Knauer, Gabriele/Bellosta von Colbe, Valeriano (edd.), *Variación sintáctica en español: un reto para las teorías de la sintaxis*, Tübingen, Niemeyer, 2005, 171–189.
Romaine, Suzanne, *On the Problem of Syntactic Variation: A Reply to Beatriz Lavandera and William Labov*, Sociolinguistic Working Papers 82, Austin, Texas, 1981.
Romaine, Suzanne, *On the Problem of Syntactic Variation and Pragmatic Meaning in Sociolinguistic Theory*, Folia Linguistica 18 (1984), 409–437.
Romero Morales, Juan, *Los dativos en el español*, Madrid, Arco Libros, 2008.
Rosengren, Per, *Presencia y ausencia de los pronombres personales sujetos en el español moderno*, Stockholm, Almqvist & Wiksell, 1974.
Sanford, Alison J.S./Sanford, Anthony J./Molle, Jo/Emmott, Catherine, *Shallow Processing and Attention Capture in Written and Spoken Discourse*, Discourse Processes 42 (2006), 109–130.
Sankoff, David, *Sociolinguistics and Syntactic Variation*, in: Newmeyer, Frederick J. (ed.), *Linguistics: The Cambridge Survey*, vol. 4, Cambridge, Cambridge University Press, 1988, 140–161.
Sankoff, Gillian, *Above and Beyond Phonology in Variable Rules*, in: Bailey, Charles J. N./Shuy, Roger W. (edd.), *New Ways of Analyzing Variation in English*, Washington DC, Georgetown University Press, 1973, 44–61.
Sankoff, Gillian/Thibault, Pierrette, *The Alternation between the Auxiliaries "Avoir" and "Être" in Montreal French*, in: Sankoff, Gillian (ed.), *The Social Life of Language*, Philadelphia, University of Pennsylvania Press, 1980, 311–345.
Santiago, Ramón, *"Impersonal" "se le(s)", "se lo(s)", "se la(s)"*, Boletín de la Real Academia Española 55 (1975), 83–107.
Santos Río, Luis, *Diccionario de partículas*, Salamanca, Luso-Española de Ediciones, 2003.
Satorre Grau, Francisco J., *Revisión del sistema pronominal español*, Revista de Filología Española 82 (2002), 345–380.
Schilling-Estes, Natalie, *Investigating Stylistic Variation*, in: Chambers, Jack K./Schilling-Estes, Natalie/Trudgill, Peter (edd.), *The Handbook of Language Variation and Change*, Oxford, Basil Blackwell, 2006, 375–401.

Seco, Manuel, *Gramática esencial del español*, Madrid, Espasa Calpe, 1996.

Serrano, María J., *Sociolingüística*, Barcelona, Ediciones del Serbal, 2011 (= 2011a).

Serrano, María J., *"Otras personas y yo": variación socioestilística de la expresión/omisión del sujeto pronominal "nosotros" en las conversaciones espontáneas*, in: Serrano, María J. (ed.), *Variación variable*, Almería, Círculo Rojo/Ministerio de Ciencia e Innovación, 2011, 93–126 (= 2011b).

Serrano, María J., *El sujeto pronominal "usted/ustedes" y su posición. Variación y creación de estilos comunicativos*, Spanish in Context 9 (2012), 109–131.

Serrano, María J., *De la cognición al texto: el efecto de la prominencia cognitiva y la informatividad discursiva en el estudio de la variación de los sujetos pronominales*, Estudios de Lingüística 27 (2013), 275–299 (= 2013a).

Serrano, María J., *El pronombre "tú" como recurso objetivador en español: variación textual y discursiva*, Borealis: An International Journal of Hispanic Linguistics 2, 179–197 (= 2013b).

Serrano, María J., *Cognición y estilo comunicativo: el sujeto posverbal y el objeto sintáctico*, Estudios Filológicos 54 (2014), 139–156.

Serrano, María J., *A Variable Cognitive and Communicative Resource in Spanish: The First-Person Plural Subject and Object*, Journal of Pragmatics 108 (2017), 131–147 (= 2017a).

Serrano, María J., *Going beyond Address Forms: Variation and Style in the Use of the Second-Person Pronouns "Tú" and "Usted"*, Pragmatics 27 (2017), 87–115 (= 2017b).

Serrano, María J., *Los objetos verbales de persona como variantes de tratamiento interpersonal canario en la red social Facebook*, Revista Española de Lingüística Aplicada, in press a (= in press a).

Serrano, María J., *The Variable Functions of Addressing Hearer-Participants with Spanish Second-Person Object Forms in Media Discourse*, in: Moyna, María I./Kluge, Bettina/ Simon, Horst (edd.), *Trends in Address Research*, Amsterdam/Philadelphia, John Benjamins, in press b (= in press b).

Serrano, María J./Aijón Oliva, Miguel A., *Syntactic Variation and Communicative Style*, Language Sciences 32 (2011), 138–153.

Serrano, María J./Aijón Oliva, Miguel A., *Cuando tú eres yo: la inespecificidad referencial de "tú" como objetivación del discurso*, Nueva Revista de Filología Hispánica 60 (2012), 541–563.

Serrano, María J./Aijón Oliva, Miguel A., *"Seguimos con la actualidad..." The First-Person Plural "Nosotros" 'We' across Spanish Media Genres*, Discourse & Communication 7 (2013), 406–430.

Serrano, María J./Aijón Oliva, Miguel A., *Discourse Objectivization, Social Variation and Style in the Use of Spanish "Tú"*, Folia Linguistica 48 (2014), 225–254.

Sidnell, Jack, *Conversation Analysis: An Introduction*, Oxford, Wiley-Blackwell, 2010.

Siewierska, Anna, *Person*, Cambridge, Cambridge University Press, 2004.

Siewierska, Anna, *Person Forms*, in: Song, Jae J. (ed.), *The Oxford Handbook of Linguistic Typology*, Oxford, Oxford University Press, 2010, 322–343.

Silva Menon, Odette P. da, *Pronome de segunda pessoa no sul do Brasil: "tu" / "você" / "o senhor" em "Vinhas da ira"*, Letras de Hoje 35 (2000), 121–164.

Silva-Corvalán, Carmen, *Topicalización y pragmática en español*, Revista Española de Lingüística 14 (1984), 1–19.

Silva-Corvalán, Carmen, *Language Contact and Change: Spanish in Los Angeles*, Oxford, Oxford University Press, 1994.

Silva-Corvalán, Carmen, *Otra mirada a la expresión del sujeto como variable sintáctica*, in: Moreno Fernández, Francisco, et al. (edd.), *Lengua, variación y contexto. Estudios dedicados a Humberto López Morales*, Madrid, Arco Libros, 2003, 849–860.

Silva-Corvalán, Carmen/Enrique-Arias, Andrés, *Sociolingüística y pragmática del español*, Washington DC, Georgetown University Press, 2017.

Silverstein, Michael, *Hierarchy of Features and Ergativity*, in: Dixon, Robert M. W. (ed.), *Grammatical Categories in Australian Languages*, Canberra, Australian Institute of Aboriginal Studies, 1976, 112–171.

Stewart, Miranda, *Hedging your Bets – The Use of "Yo" in Face-to-Face Interaction*, Web Journal of Modern Language Linguistics 5 (2000) [http://wjmll.ncl.ac.uk/issue04-05/stewart.htm; last access: 10/20/2018].

Stewart, Miranda, *"Pragmatic Weight" and Face: Pronominal Presence and the Case of the Spanish Second-Person Singular Subject Pronoun "Tú"*, Journal of Pragmatics 35 (2003), 191–206.

Suñer, Margarita, *The Role of Agreement in Clitic-Doubled Constructions*, Natural Language & Linguistic Theory 6 (1988), 391–434.

Swales, John M., *Genre Analysis: English in Academic and Research Settings*, Cambridge, Cambridge University Press, 1990.

Tagliamonte, Sali A., *Analysing Sociolinguistic Variation*, Cambridge, Cambridge University Press, 2006.

Tagliamonte, Sali A., *Variationist Sociolinguistics: Change, Observation, Interpretation*, Chichester, Wiley-Blackwell, 2012.

Tanghe, Sanne, *El cómo y el porqué de las interjecciones derivadas de los verbos de movimiento*, Zeitschrift für Romanische Philologie 129 (2013), 383–412.

Taylor, John R., *Linguistic Categorization: Prototypes in Linguistic Theory*, Oxford, Oxford University Press, 1995.

Terkourafi, Marina, *The Pragmatic Variable: Toward a Procedural Interpretation*, Language in Society 40 (2011), 343–372.

Theodoropoulou, Irene, *Sociolinguistics of Style and Social Class in Contemporary Athens*, Amsterdam/Philadelphia, John Benjamins, 2014.

Thompson, Sandra A./Hopper, Paul J., *Transitivity, Clause Structure, and Argument Structure: Evidence from Conversation*, in: Bybee, Joan/Hopper, Paul J. (edd.), *Frequency and the Emergence of Linguistic Structure*, Amsterdam/Philadelphia, John Benjamins, 2001, 27–61.

Tomasello, Michael, *Constructing a Language: A Usage-Based Theory of Language Acquisition*, Cambridge (MA), Harvard University Press, 2003.

Torres Cacoullos, Rena/Schwenter, Scott A., *Constructions and Pragmatics: Variable Middle Marking in Spanish "Subir(se)" 'Go up' and "Bajar(se)" 'Go down'*, Journal of Pragmatics 40 (2008), 1455–1477.

Traugott, Elizabeth C., *(Inter)subjectivity and (Inter)subjectification: A Reassessment*, in: Davidse, Kristin/Vandelanotte, Lieven/Cuyckens, Hubert (edd.), *Subjectification, Intersubjectification and Grammaticalization*, Berlin/New York, Mouton de Gruyter, 2010, 29–71.

Travis, Catherine E., *Genre Effects on Subject Expression in Spanish: Priming in Narrative and Conversation*, Language Variation and Change 19 (2007), 101–135.

Travis, Catherine E./Torres Cacoullos, Rena, *What Do Subjects Do in Discourse? Cognitive, Mechanical and Constructional Factors in Variation*, Cognitive Linguistics 23 (2012), 711–748.

Urrutia Cárdenas, Hernán/Fernández Ulloa, Teresa, *Duplicación de clíticos en el español: Chile y País Vasco*, Lingüística Española Actual 17 (1995), 77–106.

Uruburu Bidaurrazaga, Agustín, *Estudios sobre leísmo, laísmo y loísmo*, Córdoba, Universidad de Córdoba, 1993.

Van Knippenberg, Daan/Ellemers, Naomi, *Social Identity and Group Performance: Identification as the Key to Group-Oriented Effort*, in: Haslam, S. Alexander, et al. (edd.), *Social Identity at Work: Developing Theory for Organizational Practice*, New York/Hove, Psychology Press, 2003, 29–42.

Vázquez Rozas, Victoria, *El complemento indirecto en español*, Santiago de Compostela, Universidade de Santiago de Compostela, 1995.

Vázquez Rozas, Victoria, *"Gustar"-Type Verbs*, in: Clements, J. Clancy/Yoon, Jiyoung (edd.), *Functional Approaches to Spanish Syntax. Lexical Semantics, Discourse and Transitivity*, Basingstoke, Palgrave Macmillan, 2006, 80–114.

Vázquez Rozas, Victoria/García-Miguel, José M., *Transitividad, subjetividad y frecuencia de uso*, in: *VII Congrés de Lingüística General* [CD-ROM], Barcelona, Universitat de Barcelona, 2006.

Villars, Rina R., *Alternancia entre el sincrético "nosotros" y el femenino "nosotras" en el español hispanoamericano*, Bulletin of Spanish Studies 85 (2008), 477–505.

Virtanen, Tuija, *Point of Departure: Cognitive Aspects of Sentence-Initial Adverbials*, in: Virtanen, Tuija (ed.), *Approaches to Cognition through Text and Discourse*, Berlin/New York, Mouton de Gruyter, 2004, 79–98.

Vitale, Anthony J., *Swahili Syntax*, Dordrecht, Foris, 1981.

Wales, Katie, *Personal Pronouns in Present-Day English*, Cambridge, Cambridge University Press, 1996.

Weiner, E. Judith/Labov, William, *Constraints on the Agentless Passive*, Journal of Linguistics 19 (1983), 29–58.

Weissenrieder, Maureen, *Indirect Object Doubling: Saying Things Twice in Spanish*, Hispania 78 (1995), 169–177.

Weyers, Joseph R., *"Tú" and "Usted" in Mexican Advertising: The Politeness Systems of Written Public Discourse*, Southwest Journal of Linguistics 30 (2011), 117–133.

Whitley, Melvin S., *Psych Verbs: Transitivity Adrift*, Hispanic Linguistics 10 (1998), 115–153.

Wolf, Hans-Georg/Polzenhagen, Frank, *Cognitive Sociolinguistics in L2-Variety Dictionaries of English*, in: Pütz, Martin/Robinson, Justyna A./Reif, Monika (edd.), *Cognitive Sociolinguistics: Social and Cultural Variation in Cognition and Language Use*, Amsterdam/Philadelphia, John Benjamins, 2014, 133–160.

Xiang, Xuehua, *Multiplicity of Self in Public Discourse: The Use of Personal References in two Radio Sports Shows*, Language Sciences 25 (2003), 489–514.

Zenner, Eline/Kristiansen, Gitte/Geeraerts, Dirk, *Individual Differences and "In Situ" Identity Marking: Colloquial Belgian Dutch in the Reality TV Show "Expeditie Robinson"*, in: Romano, Manuela/Porto, María D. (edd.), *Exploring Discourse Strategies in Social and Cognitive Interaction*, Amsterdam/Philadelphia, John Benjamins, 2016, 39–77.

Zobel, Sarah, *A Pragmatic Analysis of German Impersonally Used First Person Singular "Ich"*, Pragmatics 26 (2016), 379–416.

Appendices

Appendix I: Codes used for the identification of examples

Each excerpt from the corpus is identified by a sequence between angle brackets that is composed of four parts: <genre-medium-date-page/time>. These are the identifying codes for the textual genres and media:

Genres

Written		Oral	
Art	Opinion pieces	Anu	Commercials
Car	Letters to the editor	Dep	Sports programs
Ent	Interviews	Inf	News reports
Not	News items	Mus	Music programs
Rep	Stories	Var	Talk magazines

Media

Newspapers		Radio stations	
Ad	El Adelanto	40	Cadena 40
Ga	La Gaceta	Ci	Cadena Cien
Tr	Tribuna de Salamanca	Co	Cadena Cope
		Di	Cadena Dial
		On	Onda Cero
		Pu	Punto Radio
		SE	Cadena SER
		To	Radio Tormes

https://doi.org/10.1515/9783110643442-014

Appendix II: Conventions used in the transcription of radio texts

/	pause (shorter than one second)
//	pause (longer than one second)
a:	lengthened sound (shorter than one second)
a::	lengthened sound (longer than one second)
AA	emphatic pronunciation
•	change of clause or utterance with no pause
a-	restart or self-correction
[aa]	superposed speech
(aa)	elided phonemes or sequences
<. . .>	omitted excerpt
<risas>	paraverbal features
<A>, <B>	participants in dialogic sequences

www.ingramcontent.com/pod-product-compliance
Lightning Source LLC
Chambersburg PA
CBHW031415230426
43668CB00007B/321